D1554094

# THE JESUS TRADITION IN Q

# THE

# JESUS

# TRADITION IN

# Q

DALE C. ALLISON, JR.

TRINITY PRESS INTERNATIONAL
Harrisburg, Pennsylvania

Trinity Press International, P.O. Box 1321, Harrisburg, PA 17105
Trinity Press International is a division of the Morehouse Group

**Library of Congress Cataloging-in-Publication Data**
Allison, Dale C.
    The Jesus tradition in Q / by Dale C. Allison, Jr.
        p.   cm.
    Includes bibliographical references and index.
    ISBN 1-56338-207-5 (ha)
    1. Jesus Christ – Words.  2. Q hypothesis (Synoptics criticism)
    I. Title.
    BS2555.2.A46   1997
    226'.066 – dc21                                           97-12416
                                                              CIP

Printed in the United States of America

97   98   99   00   01   02      10   9   8   7   6   5   4   3   2   1

*For*
*Emily Melissa*
ἡ καρδία μου

# CONTENTS

# PREFACE

The task of writing a commentary on Matthew has given me the opportunity to investigate in detail all the Matthean passages with parallels in Luke but not Mark, that is, the passages commonly assigned to Q. Such investigation required in turn that I familiarize myself with the recent secondary literature on Q. It was unease with much of this literature that first led me to think I had something to say about Q, or at least about recent scholarship on Q, and that it should go into a book. Originally I envisaged my studies as a collective critique of the various compositional theories of Q, for all of those theories had seemed to me problematic. Indeed, for many years I thought it incredible that modern scholars could reconstruct the stages through which a lost — or rather hypothetical — document had passed. But along the way certain observations began, against all expectation, to subdue my incredulity, and when a sufficient number of observations began to point me in the same direction, I soon found myself, for better or worse, the author of my own compositional history of Q. I ended up doing what I once thought should not be done.

The heart of *The Jesus Tradition in Q* is the long opening chapter, "A Compositional History of Q." Although all the other chapters can be understood in isolation, and while they all attempt to make contributions that do not stand or fall with my compositional history, each one is referred to in chapter 1 because each offers support for a point or points made therein.

Chapters 1, 3, and 5 appear here for the first time. Chapter 2 incorporates portions of "A New Approach to the Sermon on the Mount," *Ephemerides Theologicae Lovanienses* 64 (1988), pp. 405–14, but is mostly new material. Half of chapter 4 is a revised version of "Paul and the Missionary Discourse," *Ephemerides Theologicae Lovanienses* 61 (1985), pp. 369–75. Chapter 6 is a thoroughly revised and very much expanded edition of "The Eye Is the Lamp of the Body," *New Testament Studies* 33 (1987), pp. 61–83. Chapter 7 is a new edition of " 'The Hairs of Your Head Are All Numbered,' " *Expository Times* 101 (1990), pp. 334–36. Chapter 8 is a much expanded version of "Who Will Come from East and West? Observations on Matt 8:11–12 = Luke 13:28–29," *Irish Biblical Studies* 11 (1989), pp. 158–70. Chapter 9 is a corrected and enlarged version of "Matt. 23:39 = Luke 13:35b as a Conditional Prophecy," *Journal for the Study of the New Testament* 18 (1983), pp. 75–84. My conclusions on this text are a bit different from those I made earlier. Permission to reprint these items has been obtained from the editors of the preceding publications and is here gratefully acknowledged. Abbreviations throughout are those of the Society of Biblical Literature.

Thanks go to Raymond A. Martin for his comments on chapter 1, especially regarding the question of Semitic sources behind Q. I wish also to thank those who attended postgraduate seminars in the spring of 1996 at the Universities of Aberdeen, Durham, Glasgow, and St. Andrews, at which I presented a shortened version of the first chapter. The discussions at those sessions proved very helpful. W. D. Davies read every chapter, and as always his astute comments led to very fruitful areas of research. During my happy and all-too-brief residence at the University of Glasgow, Joel Marcus graciously read the entire manuscript. His good eye has saved me much embarrassment, and his good sense moved me to change my mind about a number of things, not all of them negligible. I am much indebted to him. I refrain from trying to thank my wife and children for their continued patient support of a vocation whose rewards lie in something other than monetary gain. Lastly, perhaps I should apologize to my disappointed eight-year-old son, Andrew. He was quite excited to find out that daddy was writing a book on Q — until he learned it had nothing to do with the character by that name on "Star Trek: The Next Generation."

DALE C. ALLISON, JR.
*December 11, 1996*

# ABBREVIATIONS

| | |
|---|---|
| AB | Anchor Bible |
| ABRL | Anchor Bible Reference Library |
| *AJT* | *American Journal of Theology* |
| AnBib | Analecta Biblica |
| ANF | A. Roberts and J. Donaldson, eds., *The Ante-Nicene Fathers*. Reprint. Grand Rapids: Eerdmans, 1978 |
| Arm. | Armenian version |
| ASNU | Acta seminarii neotestamentici upsaliensis |
| *BAR* | *Biblical Archaeology Review* |
| BBB | Bonner biblische Beiträge |
| BETL | Bibliotheca ephemeridum theologicarum lovaniensium |
| BEvT | Beiträge zur evangelischen Theologie |
| *Bib* | *Biblica* |
| *BJRL* | *Bulletin of the John Rylands Library* |
| *BTB* | *Biblical Theological Bulletin* |
| BWANT | Beiträge zur Wissenschaft vom Alten und Neuen Testament |
| *BZ* | *Biblische Zeitschrift* |
| CB | Coniectanea biblica |
| *CBQ* | *Catholic Biblical Quarterly* |
| CBQMS | Catholic Biblical Quarterly Monograph Series |
| CSCO | Corpus scriptorum christianorum orientalium |
| CTM | Calwer Theologische Monographien |
| DJD | Discoveries in the Judaean Desert |
| ÉB | Études bibliques |
| EKKNT | Evangelisch-katholischer Kommentar zum Neuen Testament |
| *ETL* | *Ephemerides theologicae lovanienses* |
| ETS | Erfurter theologische Studien |
| *EvT* | *Evangelische Theologie* |
| *ExpT* | *Expository Times* |
| FRLANT | Forschungen zur Religion und Literatur des Alten und Neuen Testaments |
| *HBT* | *Horizons in Biblical Theology* |
| *HR* | *History of Religions* |
| HTKNT | Herders Theologischer Kommentar zum Neuen Testament |
| *HTR* | *Harvard Theological Review* |
| IBS | Irish Biblical Studies |
| ICC | International Critical Commentary |
| *Int* | *Interpretation* |
| Jastrow | Marcus Jastrow, *A Dictionary of the Targumim, the Talmud Babli and Yerushalmi, and the Midrashic Literature*. Brooklyn: Traditional Press, n.d. |
| *JBL* | *Journal of Biblical Literature* |
| *JETS* | *Journal of the Evangelical Theological Society* |

| | |
|---|---|
| *JJS* | *Journal of Jewish Studies* |
| *JSJ* | *Journal for the Study of Judaism* |
| *JSNT* | *Journal for the Study of the New Testament* |
| JSNTSS | Journal for the Study of the New Testament Supplement Series |
| *JSOT* | *Journal for the Study of the Old Testament* |
| L | Material occurring only in Luke |
| LD | Lectio divina |
| Levy | J. Levy, *Wörterbuch über die Talmudim und Midraschim*. Darmstadt: Wissenschaftliche Buchgesellschaft, 1963 |
| LXX | The Septuagint |
| M | Material occurring only in Matthew |
| MeyerK | H. A. W. Meyer, Kritisch-exegetischer Kommentar über das Neue Testament |
| MT | Masoretic text |
| *NovT* | *Novum Testamentum* |
| NovTSup | Novum Testamentum, Supplements |
| NTAbh | Neutestamentliche Abhandlungen |
| *NTS* | *New Testament Studies* |
| *PG* | J. Migne, *Patrologia graeca* |
| *RB* | *Revue Biblique* |
| *RevQ* | *Revue de Qumran* |
| *RHPR* | *Revue d'Histoire et de Philosophie Religieuses* |
| RNT | Regensburger Neues Testament |
| SB | H. Strack and P. Billerbeck, *Kommentar zum Neuen Testament aus Talmud und Midrash*. Munich: C. H. Beck, 1926–63 |
| SBS | Stuttgarter Bibelstudien |
| SBT | Studies in Biblical Theology |
| SM | Sermon on the Mount |
| SNTSMS | Society for New Testament Studies Monograph Series |
| SNTU | Studien zum Neuen Testament und seiner Umwelt |
| SP | Sermon on the Plain |
| *ST* | *Studia theologica* |
| SUNT | Studien zur Umwelt des Neuen Testament |
| *TDNT* | G. Kittel and G. Friedrich, eds., *Theological Dictionary of the New Testament*. Grand Rapids: Eerdmans, 1964–74 |
| *TDOT* | G. J. Botterwick and H. Ringgren, eds., *Theological Dictionary of the Old Testament*. Grand Rapids: Eerdmans, 1974ff. |
| Theod. | Theodotian |
| *ThQ* | *Theologische Quartalschrift* |
| TU | Texte und Untersuchungen |
| *TynBull* | *Tyndale Bulletin* |
| WBC | Word Biblical Commentary |
| WMANT | Wissenschaftliche Monographien zum Alten und Neuen Testament |
| WUNT | Wissenschaftliche Untersuchungen zum Neuen Testament |
| *ZNW* | *Zeitschrift für die neutestamentliche Wissenschaft* |
| *ZTK* | *Zeitschrift für Theologie und Kirche* |

# THE COMPOSITIONAL HISTORY OF Q

Once scholars rightly concluded that both Matthew and Luke knew and used Mark, it remained to account for the large amount of non-Markan material — mostly sayings — common to the First and Third Gospels. Did Luke draw upon Matthew?[1] Did Matthew draw upon Luke?[2] Or did the two evangelists use not only Mark but some other source as well? For reasons which need not be rehearsed here, the conventional wisdom now holds that Matthew and Luke employed a second written source, a document now lost.[3] It is today known as Q (from the German *Quelle*, "source").[4]

---

1. See esp. M. D. Goulder, *Luke — A New Paradigm* (Sheffield: JSOT, 1989). For criticism see Christopher M. Tuckett, "The Existence of Q," in *The Gospel Behind the Gospels*, ed. Ronald A. Piper, NovTSup, vol. 75 (Leiden: E. J. Brill, 1995), pp. 19–47. Robert H. Gundry, "Matthean Foreign Bodies in Agreements of Luke with Matthew against Mark: Evidence That Luke Used Matthew," in *The Four Gospels 1992: Festschrift Frans Neirynck*, ed. F. Van Sebroeck et al., BETL, vol. 100 (Leuven: Leuven University Press, 1992), pp. 1467–95, accepts both the existence of Q and Luke's use of Matthew. See further Frans Neirynck, "Luke 10:25–28: A Foreign Body in Luke?" in *Crossing the Boundaries: Essays in Biblical Interpretation in Honour of Michael D. Goulder*, ed. S. E. Porter, P. Joyce, and D. E. Orton (Leiden: E. J. Brill, 1994), pp. 149–65; R. H. Gundry, "A Rejoinder on Matthean Foreign Bodies in Luke 10,25–28," *ETL* 71 (1995): 139–50; and Frans Neirynck, "The Minor Agreements and Lk 10,25–28," *ETL* 71 (1995): 151–60.

2. This is a rare judgment; but see R. V. Huggins, "Matthean Posteriority: A Preliminary Proposal," *NovT* 34 (1992): 1–22.

3. See further Charles E. Carlston and D. Norlin, "Once More — Statistics and Q," *HTR* 64 (1971): 59–78; Joseph A. Fitzmyer, "The Priority of Mark and the 'Q' Source in Luke," in *To Advance the Gospel: New Testament Studies* (New York: Crossroad, 1981), pp. 3–40; David R. Catchpole, *The Quest for Q* (Edinburgh: T. & T. Clark, 1993), pp. 1–59; Tuckett, "The Existence of Q." A revised version of this last appears in Tuckett's valuable new book, *Q and the History of Early Christianity: Studies on Q* (Edinburgh: T. & T. Clark, 1996), pp. 1–39.

4. Surveys of research include Ulrich Luz, "Die wiederentdeckte Logienquelle," *EvT* 33 (1973): 527–33; Ronald D. Worder, "Redaction Criticism of Q: A Survey," *JBL* 94 (1975): 532–46; Frans Neirynck, "Recent Developments in the Study of Q," in *Logia: Les Paroles de Jésus — The Sayings of Jesus*, ed. Joël Delobel, BETL, vol. 59 (Leuven: Leuven University Press, 1982), pp. 29–75; John S. Kloppenborg, *The Formation of Q: Trajectories in Ancient Christian Wisdom Collections*, Studies in Antiquity and Christianity (Philadelphia: Fortress, 1987), pp. 8–101; Arland D. Jacobson, *The First Gospel: An Introduction to Q* (Sonoma, Calif.: Polebridge, 1992), pp. 19–60; Kloppenborg, "Introduction," in *The Shape of Q: Signal Essays on the Sayings Gospel*, ed. John S. Kloppenborg (Minneapolis: Fortress, 1995), pp. 1–21; Tuckett, *Q*, pp. 41–82.

Q has been more than just part of the solution to the synoptic problem. It has also been thought to be testimony to the circumstances and theological outlook of a particular author or community.[5] B. H. Streeter already urged that Q was a "prophetic book like Jeremiah" with "apologetical value" which was written "at a time and place where the prestige of John [the Baptist] was very considerable."[6] Much more recently Burton L. Mack has discovered behind Q a group which undoes our usual assumptions about Christian origins: it did not recognize Jesus as the Messiah, or interpret his death as a saving event, or imagine that he had been raised from the dead.[7] Mack even goes so far as to affirm provocatively that "the people of Q were Jesus people, not Christians."[8] While this is assuredly not the scholarly consensus, many are now convinced that, in the words of John Kloppenborg, Q "represents a distinct theological vision and social configuration within early Christianity."[9]

Both redaction criticism and the desire to see behind Q, to envisage what sort of group or community produced it, have fostered investigation into its compositional history. Siegfried Schulz, for example, sought to demonstrate that the first stage of Q presented the apocalyptic kerygma of a Transjordanian Palestinian Jewish-Christian community,[10] that the second stage was a Hellenistic Jewish-Christian expansion,[11] and that there was a final Hellenistic redaction.[12] According to Athana-

---

5. Earlier researchers sometimes thought of Q as a collection of authentic sayings of Jesus without "discernable editorial bias"; so Adolf Harnack, *The Sayings of Jesus* (London: Williams and Norgate, 1908), p. 171.

6. *The Four Gospels* (London: Macmillan, 1936), pp. 291–92. His conclusion, on pp. 290–91, that "the passages of Luke that we can identify as Q represent that document, not only approximately in its original order, but very nearly in its original extent," is a presupposition for the present investigation. Cf. Tuckett, *Q*, p. 94: "It seems that Luke quite often omits a Markan pericope precisely in order to retain a parallel version of the same pericope from Q. This suggests that Luke may have had a higher regard for Q than for Mark, and this in turn makes it less likely that Luke has made wholesale omissions from Q."

7. *The Lost Gospel: The Book of Q and Christian Origins* (San Francisco: Harper, 1993), p. 4.

8. Ibid., p. 5. Cf. Jacobson, *First Gospel*, p. 32: "To call Q a gospel, even if only provisionally, is not, however, to imply that it is Christian."

9. "The Sayings Gospel Q: Recent Opinion on the People behind the Document," *Currents in Research: Biblical Studies* 1 (1993): 9. For a survey of the Q community in recent discussion see Edward P. Meadors, *Jesus the Messianic Herald of Salvation*, WUNT, ser. 2, vol. 72 (Tübingen: J. C. B. Mohr [Paul Siebeck], 1995), pp. 18–35.

10. Q 6:20–21, 27–30, 31, 32–36, 37–38, 41–42; 11:1–4, 9–13, 39, 42–44, 46–48, 52; 12:4–7, 8–9, 22–31, 33–34; 16:17, 18. Throughout this investigation Q passages will be introduced with their Lukan numbering; that is, Q 6:20–21 refers to the Q text in Lk 6:20–21.

11. This was characterized by a Son of God Christology (Q 4:1–13; 10:21–22), use of the LXX (4:1–13; 7:22; 10:13–15; 12:53; 13:18–19, 26–27, 28–29, 34–35; 17:26–27), wisdom interests (7:31–35; 10:12, 13–15; 11:31–32, 49–51; 13:28–29, 34–35; 17:26–27), and awareness of the delay of the *parousia* (e.g., 12:39–40, 42–46; 13:18–19; 19:12–19). Schulz conjectures a location in the Transjordanian Decapolis.

12. *Q: Spruchquelle der Evangelisten* (Zürich: Theologischer Verlag, 1972). For

sius Polag portions of the Sermon on the Plain (6:27–38), sayings about John the Baptist (7:18–26), instructions on mission (10:4–11, 16), and the Beelzebul controversy (11:14–23) constituted an early collection. This was later expanded through at least two editorial stages.[13] Yet another proposal has come from Migaku Sato. Although the burden of his work is to argue that Q should be classified as a prophetic book, he also outlines a compositional history. His contention is that the materials now in Q 3:7–7:28 (with the exception of the temptation narrative and a few lines here and there) constituted the original collection ("Redaction A"). Another hand then gathered most of Q 9–10 ("Redaction B"). At the final stage Q 3:7–7:28 and 9–10 were combined and additional material added ("Redaction C"). Sato envisages Q as a parchment notebook bound with leather thongs. Until its incorporation into Matthew and Luke it continued to grow, and Sato thinks that the two evangelists used different versions of the source (Q$^{mt}$ and Q$^{lk}$).[14]

## An Early Sapiential Recension of Q?

Although students of Q seem generally to agree with Vincent Taylor that the document "changed, as it had to change, because it was responsive to the life it fed,"[15] no one's reconstruction of Q's history has won the day. Of the various proposals, however, that of John Kloppenborg has proven to be the most significant, at least for students in North America. Several are convinced he is close to the truth.[16]

---

criticism see the review by Paul Hoffmann in *BZ* 19 (1975): 104–15; also John S. Kloppenborg, "Tradition and Redaction in the Synoptic Sayings Source," *CBQ* 46 (1984): 36–45.

13. *Die Christologie der Logienquelle,* WMANT, vol. 45 (Neukirchen-Vluyn: Neukirchener, 1977). For critical discussion see Migaku Sato, *Q und Prophetie: Studien zur Gattungs- und Traditionsgeschichte der Quelle Q,* WUNT, ser. 2, vol. 29 (Tübingen: J. C. B. Mohr [Paul Siebeck], 1988), pp. 30–33.

14. *Q und Prophetie,* passim. See the critique of James M. Robinson, "Die Logienquelle: Weisheit oder Prophetie? Anfragen an Migaku Sato, *Q und Prophetie,*" *EvT* 53 (1993): 367–89. Sato responds on pp. 389–404. For additional discussion of Sato see Jacobson, *First Gospel,* pp. 53–60. Jacobson himself offers a rather complex compositional theory; for discussion of it see Paul Hoffmann, "The Redaction of Q and the Son of Man," in R. A. Piper, *Behind the Gospels,* pp. 173–86.

15. Vincent Taylor, *The Formation of the Gospel Tradition* (London: Macmillan, 1968), p. 182.

16. Kloppenborg, *Formation;* "The Formation of Q and Antique Instructional Genres," *JBL* 105 (1986): 443–62. Mack's analysis of Q$^1$ and Q$^2$ draws heavily upon Kloppenborg; he reports that by 1988 Kloppenborg's "identification of three layers of textual tradition of Q had already become an acceptable working hypothesis" for the Q Seminar of the Society of Biblical Literature (*Lost Gospel,* p. 44). Wendy Cotter, "Prestige, Protection, and Promise: A Proposal for the Apologetics of Q$^2$," in R. A. Piper, *Behind the Gospels,* pp. 117–38, speaks of "a general and growing support for the position of John Kloppenborg...." Cotter includes herself. Cf. Ron Cameron, "'What Have You Come Out to See?' Characterizations of John and Jesus in the Gospels," in *The Apoc-*

   Kloppenborg contends that Q contained two major types of sayings — "prophetic sayings (often framed as chreiai) which announce the
impending judgment of this generation and which evince the Deuteronomistic understanding of history"[17] as well as "community-directed exhortations concerning self-definition and general comportment toward
the world, discipleship, and mission, and the prospect of persecution
and death."[18] The latter were the formative component of Q and can be
classified as "instruction." To this were later added the prophetic sayings
and additional interpolated sayings[19] which turned Q into a collection
of chreiai. These more than doubled the original document. Finally, the
temptation story (Q 4:1–13) was added at the third and final stage.
   Kloppenborg's work, although full of useful review, helpful discussion, and new insights, has its share of difficulties. The first is that the
distinction between sapiential and prophetic layers is worrisome. Is it
perhaps an ahistorical construct? That the figure of Wisdom appears not
in Kloppenborg's sapiential stratum but in his prophetic layer[20] moves
one to ask whether the dichotomy between wisdom and prophecy is not
artificial. The same doubt arises from the circumstance that we have ancient Jewish literature — the *Testaments of the Twelve Patriarchs* and
*4 Ezra* being obvious examples — which freely mix apocalyptic and wisdom materials.[21] That Kloppenborg must argue that the sayings in his

---

ryphal Jesus and Christian Origins, ed. Ron Cameron (Atlanta: Scholars Press; *Semeia*
49 [1990]), pp. 61–62; also P. J. Hartin, "The Wisdom and Apocalyptic Layers of the
Sayings Gospel Q," *Hervormde Teologiese Studies* 50 (1994): 556–82, and Stephen J.
Patterson, "Wisdom in Q and Thomas," in *In Search of Wisdom: Essays in Memory of
John G. Gammie*, ed. Leo Perdue, Bernard Brandon Scott, and William Johnston Wiseman
(Louisville: Westminster, 1993), pp. 187–222. According to James M. Robinson, "The Q
Trajectory: Between John and Matthew via Jesus," in *The Future of Early Christianity:
Essays in Honor of Helmut Koester*, ed. B. A. Pearson et al. (Minneapolis: Fortress, 1991),
p. 173, the discovery of an early sapiential layer "is the most important discovery of the
current phase of Q research." But he adds that the basic position was originally forwarded
by Helmut Koester; see, e.g., Koester's book, *Ancient Christian Gospels: Their History and
Development* (Philadelphia: Trinity Press International, 1990), pp. 133–62, and below,
n. 19.
   17. Q 3:7–9, 16–17; 7:1–10, 18–28; (16:16?), 31–35; 11:14–26, 29–36, 39–52;
12:39–40, 42–46, 49, 51–53, 54–59; 17:23–37; 19:12–13, 15–26; 22:28–30.
   18. "Formation of Q," p. 454. See Q 6:20–49; 9:57–60 (61–62?); 10:2–16; 11:2–4,
9–13; 12:2–12, 22b–34; 13:24; 14:26–27, 34–35; 17:33.
   19. Q 6:23c; 10:12, 13–15, 21–24; 12:8–9, 10; 13:25–30, 34–35; 14:16–24. Cf. already the surmise of Helmut Koester, "Apocryphal and Canonical Gospels," *HTR* 73
(1980): 113: "If the genre of the wisdom book was the catalyst for the composition of
sayings of Jesus into a 'gospel,' and if the christological concept of Jesus as the teacher of
wisdom and as the presence of heavenly Wisdom dominated its creation, the apocalyptic
orientation of the *Synoptic Sayings Source* with its christology of the coming Son of man
is due to a secondary redaction of an older wisdom book." Koester has more recently spoken favorably of Kloppenborg's reconstruction: "Q and Its Relatives," in *Gospel Origins
and Christian Beginnings*, ed. J. E. Goehring et al. (Sonoma, Calif.: Polebridge, 1990),
pp. 49–63.
   20. See Q 7:35 and 11:49.
   21. Also relevant are Tobit, the Wisdom of Solomon, Matthew, and the *Didache*.

sapiential sections that reflect a Deuteronomistic outlook (and so characterize the prophetic layer) are all interpolations[22] gives one further cause for concern, as does the fact that the beatitudes in the inaugural sermon (Q 6:20–49), a sermon which Kloppenborg labels "sapiential," have "little of the sapiential content or formulation."[23] Kloppenborg himself writes that "the first three [beatitudes] depend upon a logic of eschatological reversal, while the last uses the motif of eschatological reward."[24] Can one really then so neatly distinguish sapiential complexes from prophetic complexes? Or is this a distinction more at home in the world of modern scholars than in ancient Judaism?[25] Q 11:31–32 compares Jesus with both Solomon, a wise man, and Jonah, a prophet.

The question is the more urgent given Sato's demonstration, in response to Kloppenborg, that if one examines the wisdom statements in Q, over half "are employed to manifest either the future-eschatological coming of the eschaton or the present-eschatological commencement

---

For discussion see J. J. Collins, "The Court Tales of Daniel and the Development of Apocalyptic," *JBL* 95 (1975): 218–34; J. Z. Smith, "Wisdom and Apocalyptic," in *Religious Syncretism in Antiquity*, ed. B. A. Pearson (Missoula, Mont.: Scholars Press, 1975), pp. 131–70; Michael Stone, "Lists of Revealed Things in the Apocalyptic Literature," in *Magnalia Dei: The Mighty Acts of God*, ed. Frank Moore Cross, Werner E. Lemke, and Patrick D. Miller, Jr. (Garden City, N.Y.: Doubleday, 1976), pp. 414–52; J. J. Collins, "Cosmos and Salvation: Jewish Wisdom and Apocalyptic in the Hellenistic Age," *HR* 17 (1977): 121–42; idem, "Wisdom, Apocalypticism, and Generic Compatibility," in Perdue et al., *In Search of Wisdom*, pp. 165–86; E. Elizabeth Johnson, *The Function of Apocalyptic and Wisdom Traditions in Romans 9–11*, SBLDS, vol. 109 (Atlanta: Scholars Press, 1989), pp. 55–109; George W. E. Nickelsburg, "Wisdom and Apocalypticism in Early Judaism: Some Points for Discussion," in *Society of Biblical Literature 1994 Seminar Papers*, ed. Eugene H. Lovering, Jr. (Atlanta: Scholars Press, 1994), pp. 715–32. According to Koester, *Gospels,* p. 135, in Q "the apocalyptic announcement of judgment and of the coming of the Son of man . . . conflicts with the emphasis upon the presence of the kingdom in wisdom sayings and prophetic announcements." This inevitably subjective judgment is troubling. If the final editor of Q as well as Matthew and Luke simply incorporated this conflict whole, and if similar supposed conflict can be found in the writings of a single early Christian author — Paul's epistles for instance (contrast 1 Thess 4:13–5:11 with Rom 14:17) — then is the conflict anywhere but in the modern mind?

22. 6:23c; 10:12–15, 21–24; 12:8–9, 10; 13:25–30, 34–35; 14:16–24.

23. Joseph A. Fitzmyer, "A Palestinian Collection of Beatitudes," in Van Segbroeck, *Four Gospels*, vol. 1, p. 513. Cf. Koester, *Gospels*, pp. 156–57: the Q beatitudes "introduce Jesus as a prophet, not as a teacher of wisdom."

24. *Formation*, p. 173. Cf. Catchpole, *Quest*, p. 86.

25. See further Charles E. Carlston, "Wisdom and Eschatology in Q," in Delobel, *Logia*, pp. 101–19; Richard Horsley, "Questions about Redactional Strata and the Social Relations Reflected in Q," in *Society of Biblical Literature 1989 Seminar Papers*, ed. David J. Lull (Atlanta: Scholars Press, 1989), pp. 186–203; idem, "Wisdom Justified by All Her Children: Examining Allegedly Disparate Traditions in Q," in Lovering, *1994 Seminar Papers*, pp. 733–51. Horsley, in "The Q People: Renovation, Not Radicalism," *Continuum* 1, no. 3 (1991): 54, writes: "Sociologically it is clear that in a society in which any literature was written primarily by professional scribes and sages, it was the sapiential teachers such as *maskilim* who actually wrote apocalyptic literature. Would there be any reason to expect a separation between sapiential and prophetic/apocalyptic elements at a more popular level such as the transmission of Jesus-sayings?"

of the new age."[26] Q 6:47–49 (the two builders), for instance, takes up imagery with "an affinity to the language used in the prophetic books of the Old Testament"[27] and reminds us of the prophetic oracles in which obedience brings salvation, disobedience doom. Sato also rightly observes that other wisdom statements, "which are not particularly eschatological in their wording, are so construed that they are highly compatible with the notion that the new era of salvation has already begun."[28] Thus Q 11:10 ("Everyone who asks receives, and everyone who seeks finds, and everyone who knocks, the door will be opened") is "hardly sanctioned by experience"; rather, this exaggerated optimism about prayer likely has its explanation in the conviction that eschatological salvation is already entering the present.[29] Sato's point then is that "if we were to presuppose...that Q is basically sapiential, it would become extremely difficult to explain why and how such a strong prophetic vein could come into the source...."[30] The argument has force.[31]

Yet another difficulty for Kloppenborg is that there are literary patterns and editorial techniques that cut across his proposed layers. He assigns Q 6:20–23b to Q[1]; 3:16–17, 7:18–23, and 13:34–35 to Q[2]. It is true that 3:16–17; 7:18–23; and 13:34 belong together. Whereas in 3:16–17 the Baptist prophesies a coming one, in 7:18–23 Jesus himself, by referring to the elements of his own ministry, indirectly claims (in answer to the Baptist's question) that he is this coming one.[32] He supports this christological claim by alluding to texts from Isaiah — 35:5 (the blind see); 35:6 (the lame walk); 35:5 (the deaf hear); 26:19 (the dead are raised); and 61:1 (the poor have good news preached to them). Finally, in 13:34–35 Jesus explicitly says that he is the eschatological figure who will come and be blessed in the name of the Lord.

What needs to be noticed is that Q 7:18–23 is not the first time Q alludes to Isaiah 61. Q 6:20–23 alludes to this same text. "Blessed are the poor, for yours is the kingdom of God" draws upon Isa 61:1; "Blessed

---

26. Migaku Sato, "Wisdom Statements in the Sphere of Prophecy," in R. A. Piper, *Behind the Gospels*, pp. 139–58 (quotation from p. 157). See also Carlston, "Wisdom and Eschatology in Q."

27. Here Sato refers to Ulrich Luz, *Das Evangelium nach Matthäus*, vol. 1 (Zürich and Neukirchen-Vluyn: Benziger and Neukirchener, 1985), p. 414 n. 13. Luz cites Isa 28:17, 30:30; Ezek 13:11–14, 38:22; Hos 8:7; and Nah 1:3. To this one may add eschatological parallels from extracanonical texts, such as 1QH 3:14; *Sib. Or.* 3:689–92, 5:377–80; *2 Bar.* 53:7–12. Q itself uses the imagery of Noah's flood to anticipate the eschatological tempest (Q 17:27).

28. "Wisdom Statements," p. 157.

29. Ibid., p. 150. Cf. Tuckett, *Q*, pp. 152–55.

30. Ibid., p. 157.

31. See further Tuckett, *Q*, pp. 139–63, 325–54.

32. Because there is no evidence that "the coming one" was a recognized title, the article in Q 7:19 ("*the* coming one") is probably anaphoric: it refers back to 3:16.

are those who mourn, for you will be comforted" takes up the language of Isa 61:2;[33] and "Rejoice and be glad" recalls Isa 61:10. So the development in Q regarding the subject of Jesus as the coming one evolves in stages:

- John prophesies one who is to come (3:16–17).

- Jesus implicitly associates himself with Isaiah 61 (6:20–23).

- Jesus, in answer to a question about the coming one, associates himself with Isaiah 61 and other texts (7:18–23).

- Jesus calls himself "the one who comes" (13:35).

Surely this christological sequence is due to deliberate design, and it is natural to assign the four texts to the same redactional stage.[34]

A final problem with Kloppenborg's view is that the assigning of the Deuteronomistic theology to the second stage seems artificial when the first stage is so full of the theme of rejection. The Deuteronomistic scheme, as outlined by Odil H. Steck, is a way of coming to terms with Israel's disobedience;[35] but in Q this disobedience as well as the theme of the martyrdom of God's messengers is already manifest in 6:22–23b (rejection on account of the Son of man); 9:58 (the Son of man's homelessness); 10:3 (lambs in the midst of wolves); 10:10–11 (rejection of missionaries); 10:16 (rejection of missionaries); 12:4–5 (killing the body); and 12:11–12 (appearance before synagogues) — all passages Kloppenborg assigns to the sapiential layer.

Despite the advances brought to the study of Q by Kloppenborg's useful contributions, his reconstruction of an early wisdom document is not persuasive.[36] A more promising direction for further investigation

---

33. Matthew's form is here original; see Catchpole, *Quest*, pp. 84–86; Tuckett, *Q*, pp. 223–26.

34. See further James M. Robinson, "The Sayings Gospel Q," in Van Segbroeck, *Four Gospels*, vol. 1, pp. 361–88. The argument would be all the stronger if, with some, one were to assign Lk 4:16–21 to Q; see, e.g., C. M. Tuckett, "Luke 4:16–30 and Q," in Delobel, *Logia*, pp. 343–54. But one hesitates to do this; see J. Delobel, "La rédaction de Lc. IV.14–16a et le 'Bericht vom Anfang,' " in *L'Évangile de Luc*, ed. Frans Neirynck, 2d ed., BETL, vol. 32 (Leuven: Leuven University Press, 1989), pp. 113–33, 306–12, and David R. Catchpole, "The Anointed One in Nazareth," in *From Jesus to John: Essays on Jesus and New Testament Christology in Honour of Marinus de Jonge*, ed. Martinus C. de Boer, JSNTSS, vol. 84 (Sheffield: JSOT, 1993), pp. 230–51.

35. *Israel und das gewaltsame Geschick der Propheten*, WMANT, vol. 23 (Neukirchen-Vluyn: Neukirchener, 1967).

36. See further Tuckett, *Q*, pp. 69–75, and Dieter Zeller, "Eine Weisheitliche Grundschrift in der Logienquelle?" in Van Segbroeck, *Four Gospels*, vol. 1, pp. 389–401. Zeller observes, among other things, that the instructions for missionaries do not have a proverbial character and are stamped by belief in the appearance of the end time.

The recent attempts to dissociate Jesus himself from apocalyptic and to make him out to be a sort of Jewish Cynic cannot lend support to Kloppenborg's reconstruction because those attempts are unlikely to be correct; see Dale C. Allison, Jr., "A Plea for Thorough-

comes from the work of Dieter Zeller. He has argued that "the kernel
of many of the sayings groups was composed and transmitted by wandering and wonder-working *missionaries*."[37] Later "the tradition of the
itinerant preachers found a new *Sitz im Leben* in the *communities* that
were founded by them. In this setting, it was used partly for paraenetic
purposes."[38] I should like to take this suggestion seriously and make it
the starting point for offering a new thesis regarding the compositional
history of Q. I begin with a brief section-by-section analysis of Q.

## THE FIRST SECTION, Q 3:7–7:35

According to the common opinion, Q opened with five sections which,
from T. W. Manson on, have often been reckoned to constitute a larger
literary unit:[39]

1. The Proclamation of John the Baptist (Q 3:7–9, 16–17)[40]

2. The Temptations of Jesus (Q 4:1–13)[41]

3. The Sermon on the Plain (Q 6:20–49)

4. The Centurion's Servant (Q 7:1–10)

5. John and Jesus (Q 7:18–35)

---

going Eschatology," *JBL* 113 (1994): 651–68; also James G. Williams, "Neither Here Nor
There: Between Wisdom and Apocalyptic in Jesus' Kingdom Sayings," *Forum* 5, no. 2
(1989): 7–30. Moreover, the *Gospel of Thomas* does not supply evidence for a primitive
wisdom gospel behind Q; see C. M. Tuckett, "Q and Thomas: Evidence of a Primitive
'Wisdom Gospel'? A Response to H. Koester," *ETL* 67 (1991): 346–60.

37. "Redaktionsprozesse und wechselnder 'Sitz im Leben' beim Q-Material," in Delobel, *Logia*, p. 407. Italics his. I quote from the English translation, "Redactional Processes
and Changing Settings in the Q-Material," in *The Shape of Q: Signal Essays on the Sayings
Gospel*, ed. John S. Kloppenborg (Minneapolis: Fortress, 1994), p. 129.

38. Ibid.

39. *The Sayings of Jesus* (London: SCM, 1949), p. 5. Q 3:7–7:35 has regularly been
viewed as a literary unit, albeit made up of various materials; so, e.g., Sato, *Q und
Prophetie*, pp. 33–36; Jacobson, *First Gospel*, p. 77; Elisabeth Sevenich-Bax, *Israels Kon-
frontation mit den letzten Boten der Weisheit: Form, Funktion und Interdependenz der
Weisheitselemente in der Logienquelle*, Münsteraner Theologische Abhandlungen, vol. 21
(Altenberge: Oros, 1993).

40. On the inclusion of v. 17 in Q see Tuckett, *Q*, p. 109, n. 5. Although I used to
believe that Q probably had an account of Jesus' baptism, I now think my reasons inad-
equate. Robinson, "The Sayings Gospel Q," makes the case for inclusion. For the other
side see F. Neirynck, "The Minor Agreements and Q," in R. A. Piper, *Behind the Gospels*,
pp. 65–72. If Q had a title or general opening sentence it has been lost; for discussion see
J. M. Robinson, "The *Incipit* of the Sayings Gospel Q," *RHPR* 75 (1995): 9–33.

41. Kloppenborg, *Formation*, pp. 246–62, is not alone in thinking of the temptation
narrative as a foreign body and late addition. But C. M. Tuckett, "The Temptation Narrative in Q," in Van Segbroeck, *Four Gospels*, vol. 1, pp. 479–507, disposes of most
of the usual arguments for this position (although his nonchristological interpretation of
"Son of God" seems dubious). See also Hugh M. Humphrey, "Temptation and Authority:
Sapiential Narratives in Q," *BTB* 21 (1991): 43–50.

One of the more obvious features of this section is that the opening and closing units concern John the Baptist and have much in common. In unit 1 John speaks about an eschatological figure who is coming (3:16, ἐρχόμενος). In unit 5 Jesus, who in response to a question reveals that he is this coming one (ὁ ἐρχόμενος, 7:19), speaks about John the Baptist. Both units, unlike those between them, have speeches which address the "crowds" as "you." Thus in 3:7 John the Baptist speaks to the crowds (ὄχλοις)[42] that come out to be baptized by him whereas in 7:24 Jesus speaks to the crowds (ὄχλοις) that went "out into the wilderness." The two are addressing the very same group of people. One may also observe that if in 3:8, at the very beginning of the section, John speaks of God raising up children (τέκνα) to Abraham, in 7:35, at the very end of the section, Jesus speaks of wisdom being justified by her children (τέκνων).[43] Clearly much in unit 5 was designed to recall and extend unit 1. The two should be read together.

Although the fact is less evident, units 2 and 4 likewise belong together.[44] Q 4:1–13 and 7:1–10 offer the only two extended narratives in Q[45] and its only real dialogues.[46] Everywhere else we find only sayings, although occasionally these do have a narrative setting. So the two units correspond formally.

Their contents are also similar in that, in both, Jesus is asked to make use of his supernatural powers. While in unit 2 Satan wants him to multiply bread, in unit 4 the centurion wants him to heal his son or servant. The difference is that whereas in the former the miracle would be illegitimate, in the latter it is not, and so Jesus consents. Juxtaposing the two texts invites reflection on what is and what is not an appropriate miracle.

One is further encouraged to read units 2 and 4 in the light of one another because the devil and the centurion have more in common than a desire to have Jesus work miracles. In 4:1–13 the request for wonders comes from one who says he can give to Jesus "all the kingdoms of the world and their splendor" (4:5). Clearly he is a figure of great authority — as the ἐξουσίαν of Lk 4:6 makes explicit (although we do not

---

42. So Luke. Matthew's "Pharisees and Sadducees" (3:7) is surely redactional, as it is in 16:1, 6, 11–12.

43. Matthew has "deeds," but this is usually reckoned secondary (cf. the *inclusio* created between Mt 11:2 and 11:19); see the commentaries and D. A. Carson, "Matthew 11:19b/Luke 7:35: A Test Case for the Bearing of Q Christology on the Synoptic Problem," in *Jesus of Nazareth: Lord and Christ*, ed. Joel B. Green and Max Turner (Grand Rapids: Eerdmans, 1994), pp. 128–46.

44. Cf. Sevenich-Bax, *Konfrontation*, pp. 265–67.

45. The only other narrative is the very brief 11:14.

46. Whether or not the International Q Project is correct to print Q 7:2 after 7:3–4, and whether or not the delegations in Luke but not Matthew belonged to Q, Q 7:1–10 must have included at least (1) an original petition, (2) initial response of Jesus, (3) centurion's statement of unworthiness, and (4) final response of Jesus.

know whether the word stood in Q).[47] The situation is similar in 7:1–10. In asking Jesus to perform a miracle the centurion lays claim to his own authority, albeit in words that are difficult to understand: "I also am a man set under authority (ἐξουσίαν), with soldiers under me; and I say to one, 'Go,' and he goes, and to another, 'Come,' and he comes...." Once again, then, unit 2 can be related to unit 4.

Turning from units 1–2 and 4–5 to unit 3, there is no consensus regarding the outline of Q's Sermon on the Plain. But it does appear that the beginning and end correspond.[48] The sermon opens with blessings: "Blessed are you poor," and so forth (6:20–23). It ends with a warning, with the parable about the person who hears and does not act and so is likened to a house which the storm destroys (6:47–49). One is led, then, to the possibility that Q's first five units are arranged in a chiasmus in which each correlation is a pair of opposites:

1. John speaks to the crowds about the coming one.

  2. A figure of authority asks for a miracle that Jesus refuses.

    3. Blessings

      3. Main body of sermon

    3. Warnings

  4. A figure in authority asks for a miracle that Jesus grants.

5. The coming one speaks to the crowds about John.

It is always wise to hesitate about such literary patterns, and we can have no certainty that a contributor to Q consciously arranged his material in this fashion. But whatever one makes of the chiastic proposal, it remains indisputable that Q 3–7 is thematically united and contains intratextual references and allusions. Unit 5 does plainly hark back to unit 1. Further, if in unit 1 John illustrates his demand by referring to trees that bear good fruit (3:9: δένδρον...ποιοῦν καρπὸν καλόν), Jesus does the same in unit 3 (6:43–45: δένδρον...ποιοῦν καρπὸν καλόν). And if in unit 3 Jesus says, "Blessed are the poor" (6:20: πτωχοί), in unit 5 he says, "and the poor (πτωχοί) have good news preached to them" (7:22).

Before proceeding to the second section of Q, two additional observations need to be recorded. First, units 1–5 are further linked by the way in which the theme of the coming one (a figure referred to in 3:16 and 7:19) is developed with reference to Isaiah 61 (which is alluded to

---

47. Matthew does not have it. For inclusion in Q: Robert H. Gundry, *Matthew: A Commentary on His Literary and Theological Art* (Grand Rapids: Eerdmans, 1982), p. 58. Against inclusion: Schulz, *Q*, pp. 180–81.
48. Cf. Sevenich-Bax, *Konfrontation*, pp. 373–74.

in 6:20–22 and quoted in 7:22). For this the reader is referred to the discussion on pp. 6–7 above. Second, units 1–5 show a great interest in Jesus' miracles. In 4:1–13 the devil asks Jesus to turn bread into stones and throw himself down from a great height. In 7:1–10 the centurion asks Jesus to heal his son or servant. And in 7:18–23 Jesus, in answer to John the Baptist, composes a list of the miracles he has performed.

## THE SECOND SECTION, Q 9:57–11:13

Manson gave this section the title, "Jesus and his Disciples,"[49] which seems accurate enough. It, like the opening section, has five large units:

6. Call Stories (Q 9:57–62)[50]

7. Instructions for Missionaries (Q 10:1–16)[51]

8. Teaching about Eschatological Revelation (Q 10:21–24)

9. The Lord's Prayer (Q 11:2–4)

10. On Seeking and Finding (Q 11:9–13)

There is in all this a striking absence of the features that characterize Q's first five units. Here nothing takes us back to Isaiah 61. There is no reference to Jesus as the coming one. Nothing is said about Jesus' miracles or John the Baptist. And the crowds have disappeared.

Q 9:57–11:13 also distinguishes itself from 3:7–7:35 in that it contains materials that were initially addressed to missionaries, not believers in general. The detailed directions in 10:1–16, for example, must have first been composed as guidance for a select group.[52] The demands to carry no purse, to go without shoes, and to salute no one were not originally addressed to a community at large. Rather were they specialized

---

49. *Sayings*, p. 5.

50. Lk 9:61–62 has no Matthean parallel, but it more likely than not belonged to Q; so Martin Hengel, *The Charismatic Leader and His Followers* (New York: Crossroad, 1981), p. 4 n. 5; John Dominic Crossan, *In Fragments: The Aphorisms of Jesus* (San Francisco: Harper & Row, 1983), pp. 237–44; Kloppenborg, *Formation*, p. 190 n. 80; Karl Löning, "Die Füchse, die Vögel und der Menschensohn (Mt 8,19f par Lk 9,57f)," in *Vom Urchristentum zu Jesus: Für Joachim Gnilka*, ed. Hubert Frankemölle and Karl Kertelge (Freiburg: Herder, 1989), pp. 83–84. Contrast Sato, *Q und Prophetie*, p. 55.

51. The woes in 10:13–15 are with good reason often regarded as secondary. See below, p. 35.

52. My own judgment is that Q's missionary discourse may have consisted of Lk 10:2 + Mt 10:5–6 + Lk 10:3–12 + Mt 10:23 + Lk 10:16 + Lk 10:13–15. See W. D. Davies and Dale C. Allison, Jr., *A Critical and Exegetical Commentary on the Gospel according to St. Matthew*, vol. 2, ICC (Edinburgh: T. & T. Clark, 1991), pp. 163–64. But this conviction does not affect my main argument.

instruction for itinerant preachers.[53] Those preachers depended upon
and identified themselves with communities made up of nonitinerants,[54]
but these last are nowhere clearly addressed in 10:1–16.[55] The missionary discourse presupposes a distinction between two sorts of people and
addresses only one.[56]

---

53. Cf. Rudolf Laufen, *Die Doppelüberlieferungen der Logienquelle und des Markusevangeliums*, BBB, vol. 54 (Königstein: Peter Hanstein, 1980), pp. 278–80; Kloppenborg,
*Formation*, p. 239; Sato, *Q und Prophetie*, pp. 379–80, 389.

54. See Gerd Theissen, *Sociology of Early Palestinian Christianity* (Philadelphia: Fortress, 1978), pp. 17–23. But Ernst Käsemann, *New Testament Questions of Today*
(Philadelphia: Fortress, 1969), p. 119, could be read to mean that all members of what
he calls "the primitive Jewish Christian community" were in some sense missionaries. I
rather envisage itinerant missionaries involved with settled communities which gave them
support. Here Paul is typical. Cf. Dieter Lührmann, "The Gospel of Mark and the Sayings
Collection Q," *JBL* 108 (1989): 70–71. On the other hand, given the presumed Palestinian setting, "Itinerancy is more likely to have looked like brief excursions than like the
extended journeys of Paul"; so John S. Kloppenborg, "Literary Convention, Self-Evidence,
and the Social History of the Q People," in *Early Christianity, Q, and Jesus*, ed. John S.
Kloppenborg and Leif E. Vaage (Atlanta: Scholars Press; *Semeia* 55 [1992]), p. 89. See
further on the whole question, Richard A. Horsley, *Sociology and the Jesus Movement*,
2d ed. (New York: Continuum, 1994); also Thomas Schmeller, *Brechungen: Urchristliche Wandercharismatiker im Prisma soziologisch orientierter Exegese*, SBS, vol. 136
(Stuttgart: Katholisches Bibelwerk, 1989). These two works contain much useful criticism
of Theissen's influential studies.

55. In 2 John 10–11 and *Didache* 11–13 by contrast we find instruction to nonitinerants on how to treat itinerants. Q 10:2–16 is different. Contrast the way in which
the missionary discourse is reworked in Matthew 10. Although 10:5–25 is concrete advice
that would not have been of much relevance to many of Matthew's readers, 10:32–42 is
different: its demands could be heeded equally by all. A concern to broaden the scope of
the discourse appears also in the concluding 10:42, which is a word not to missionaries
but to those who can share in their mission.
   Kloppenborg, "'Easter Faith' and the Sayings Gospel Q," in *The Apocryphal Jesus and
Christian Origins*, ed. Ron Cameron (Atlanta: Scholars Press; *Semeia* 49 [1990]), pp. 73–
76, contends that "Q's mission speech shows signs of redactional reformulation from an
ecclesial perspective" and finds this perspective in Q 10:2 and 10:7b. One may doubt this.
Q 10:7 seems to be an integral part of the discourse (cf. David R. Catchpole, "The Mission
Charge in Q," in Kloppenborg and Vaage, *Early Christianity, Q, and Jesus*, pp. 169–
70); the ecclesiastical orientation of Q 10:2 is far from obvious. But even if Q 10:2 and
10:7 were thought to have been added at a secondary stage of Q (so Kloppenborg; see
A. D. Jacobson, "The Literary Unity of Q: Lc 10,2–16 and Parallels as a Test Case," in
Delobel, *Logia*, pp. 419–23) that would entail that the original composition was addressed
to itinerants.

56. Leif E. Vaage, "Q and Cynicism: On Comparison and Social Identity," in R. A.
Piper, *Behind the Gospels*, pp. 198–229, urges that the "formative stratum of Q [includ-
ing the missionary discourse] was for all intents and purposes a 'Cynic Document.'" Such
a conclusion might vitiate the distinction I here draw between an itinerant and settled
populace. But Vaage is unconvincing. A specifically Jewish background is more plausible.
Among other things, the instructions to do without silver (Mt 10:9; Lk 9:3), sandals (Mt
10:10; Lk 10:4), and staff (Mt 10:10; Lk 9:3) do not require a Cynic background. Judaism was well acquainted with provocative prophetic deeds and dress (recall only Ezekiel
and John the Baptist) as well as with asceticism and religious poverty (cf. the Qumran Essenes and Josephus, *Vita* 5:11, on Bannus). In the present instance we have the congruence
with Jesus' teaching about poverty and self-defense. (The staff, which was also associated
with rabbinic teachers — cf. *m. Ber.* 9:5, which also mentions sandal and wallet — could
be used as a defensive weapon.) Moreover, if we take Josephus, *Bell.* 2:125 ("they carry

This differentiation between missionary and nonmissionary presumably goes back to Jesus himself. Jesus did not call all to be his disciples, that is, to "follow" him.[57] Discipleship in that sense was quite restricted. He summoned only certain individuals to leave family and work that they might be able to enter fully into service with him. The canonical gospels accurately preserve the memory of a distinction between what they call apostles — those selected to share in Jesus' task of proclaiming the kingdom of God — and others. Jesus demanded of people in general that they repent and accept his proclamation, not that they leave all and follow him or leave the dead to bury their own dead. In Hengel's words, "Only once the 'proclaimer' had become the 'proclaimed' were 'following after' and 'faith' identified, the 'disciples' becoming the believing community."[58]

Returning now to Q, it seems that 10:1–16 is hardly the only section that was initially drawn up with missionaries or disciples in the narrow sense in view. Q 9:57–62, which contains two or three stories of Jesus' radical call to discipleship that together introduce the missionary discourse, was also probably aimed at such persons. For it makes concrete the homeless way of life of those who are called to follow him and proclaim his cause.[59] In the words of Christopher Tuckett, the homeless Son of man in 9:58 "acts as a paradigm for the Christian disciple whose task is about to be outlined in the missionary charge which follows."[60]

If units 6–7 can be associated because of their common origin as instruction for itinerants, units 8–10 belong together because they are thematically united. In unit 8 (10:21–24) Jesus prays. In unit 9 (Q 11:2–

---

nothing whatever with them on their journeys except arms as a protection against brigands") literally, Jesus' disciples would have very much resembled the Essenes. Finally, it remains possible, despite Vaage's demurral, that Jesus' prohibition of staff and traveler's bag were intended to differentiate followers of Jesus from Cynic philosophers. For further critical discussion of the Cynic hypothesis with regard to Jesus, earliest Christianity, and Q, see Paul Rhodes Eddy, "Jesus as Diogenes? Reflections on the Cynic Jesus Thesis," *JBL* 115 (1996): 449–69; Richard Horsley, "Jesus, Itinerant Cynic or Israelite Prophet?" in *Images of Jesus Today*, ed. James H. Charlesworth and Walter P. Weaver (Valley Forge, Pa.: Trinity Press International, 1994), pp. 68–97; idem, *Sociology*, pp. 108–11; James M. Robinson, "The History-of-Religions Taxonomy of Q: The Cynic Hypothesis," in *Gnosisforschung und Religionsgeschichte*, ed. Holger Preissler and Hubert Seiwert (Marburg: Diagonal, 1994), pp. 247–65 (this is primarily a critique of Mack); C. M. Tuckett, "A Cynic Q?" *Biblica* 70 (1989): 349–76; idem, *Q*, pp. 368–92; Ben Witherington III, *Jesus the Sage: The Pilgrimage of Wisdom* (Minneapolis: Fortress, 1994), pp. 117–45.

57. For this and what follows see Hengel, *Charismatic Leader*, pp. 61–80; also Rudolf Schnackenburg, *The Moral Teaching of the New Testament* (New York: Seabury, 1979), pp. 42–53.

58. Hengel, *Charismatic Leader*, p. 62.

59. Kloppenborg, *Formation*, pp. 200–201, affirms that 9:57–62 "broadens the original mission instruction by setting them [sic] within the more comprehensive framework of a speech on discipleship." But it seems much more likely that the stories in 9:57–62 were originally paradigmatic only for itinerant missionaries.

60. Tuckett, *Q*, p. 288.

4) he gives the Lord's Prayer. And in unit 10 (11:9–13) he tells his disciples that they will be given what they ask for.

Units 8–10 are linked not only by the theme of prayer but also by their focus upon the heavenly Father. In unit 8 Jesus' prayer opens with "Father," and he goes on to speak of "Father" and "Son." In unit 9 Jesus tells his disciples to address God as "Father." And in unit 10 they are told that "the heavenly Father" will give to them good things (so Matthew) or the Holy Spirit (so Luke).

Q 10:21–24, 11:2–4, and 11:9–13 do not just concern similar subjects: they are also related in more formal ways. For example, if in 10:21–24 the Father is "the Lord of heaven (οὐρανοῦ) and earth," in 11:13 he is "your heavenly Father" (ἐξ οὐρανοῦ). And if in 11:3 God gives (δός) "bread (ἄρτον) for the morrow," in 11:11 no earthly father will give (ἐπιδώσει) a stone when asked for "bread" (ἄρτον).[61]

If units 6–7 (9:57–62 and 10:1–16) are united by their original function as direction for itinerant missionaries, and if units 8–10 (10:21–24, 11:2–4, and 11:9–13) are united by theme, the latter in their entirety bind themselves to the former. Units 8–10 open with "at that hour/ time,"[62] which, if it has any function at all, must refer to the giving of instruction to missionaries, to the time when Jesus spoke of the great harvest. Further, in unit 8 Jesus speaks of "these things," the things hidden from the wise (10:21). One cannot be sure exactly what the antecedent is, but it almost certainly lies in the missionary discourse. Finally, units 8–10 have to do with prayer, and the missionary discourse itself is introduced by a call to prayer: "Pray the Lord of the harvest to send out laborers into his harvest" (10:2). So Kloppenborg is right that "despite the apparently new beginning signaled by the prayer formula, 10:21–22 belongs with the preceding material."[63]

Why were units 8–10 linked to units 6–7? The former addresses those who have been called to the hard way of life outlined in the latter and proffers encouragement. Q's instructions for the itinerant are almost life-threatening. Missionaries can take no purse, no bag, no sandals (10:4); and some people will not welcome them (10:6, 10–12). They are like lambs in the midst of wolves (10:3). They are at the mercy of others; they will eat and have shelter only if they find sympathizers (10:7).

Against this background, unit 8 appears to be reassuring. Jesus thanks God that "these things" have been revealed to "infants" (that is, to the missionaries and those who have embraced their message) but hidden

---

61. In Mt 7:9–10 the contrasts are between bread and stone and fish and serpent; in Lk 11:11–12 they are between fish and serpent and egg and scorpion. While we cannot be certain, Luke's version may be under the influence of Lk 10:19. Cf. Catchpole, *Quest*, pp. 211–12.

62. Mt 11:25: ἐν ἐκείνῳ τῷ καιρῷ; Lk 10:21: ἐν αὐτῇ τῇ ὥρᾳ.

63. *Formation*, p. 197.

from "the wise and understanding" (who are among those who have not embraced the mission).[64] All this underlines the unsurpassed privilege the missionaries have — their eyes and ears are witnesses to unprecedented eschatological realities (10:24). Implicit is the overriding value of what they do: their work is the most important thing in the world.

Unit 9 next hands down the Lord's Prayer. The missionaries are not only to proclaim the coming of the kingdom (10:9) but also to pray for its coming (11:2). The burden of their itinerant existence, which puts them at the mercy of the hospitality of others — "eat what is set before you" (10:8)[65] — is lightened by the faith that just as God long ago, in the days of the Exodus, supplied bread for his people for the coming day, so God now will give to eschatological missionaries the bread they need for the coming day.

After the Lord's Prayer comes unit 10, which enjoins asking, seeking, and knocking. The teaching enlarges on the theme of prayer, or rather encourages those who pray the Lord's Prayer to have faith that God will hear and answer them. Those who ask and seek and knock will be given what they need.

If the three sections are at one in offering reassurance for a difficult way of life, they also agree in that each concerns the activity of God the Father on behalf of his children. In unit 8 the Father reveals himself to "infants," delivers "all things" to "the Son," and brings eschatological realities into the present ("many prophets and kings desired to see the things which you see and saw them not"). In unit 9 the Father in heaven brings his kingdom, gives bread, forgives sins, and delivers his own from trial. In unit 10 God is compared with earthly fathers and said to be better, so that he will certainly give to those who ask of him.

To sum up, then, it appears that the original *Sitz im Leben* of the materials now collected in 9:57–11:13 was the missionary work of itinerants. Q 9:57–62 offered them examples of what Jesus' demanding call to follow him could mean. Q 10:1–16 then contained directions on how to carry on their mission. And 10:21–11:13 followed with encouraging words which focused on prayer, which is to be addressed to the generous Father in heaven who provides for his children.

---

64. Jacobson, *First Gospel*, p. 149, urges that in Q 10:21–22 "most of Israel is said to have no knowledge of God" and we "have the view that God in fact intended this failure." One can concur on neither point. The first reads far too much into the text, and as for the second, Chrysostom, *Hom. on Mt.* 38:1, was right: "And while his being revealed to these [the babes] was fit matter of joy, his concealment from those [the wise and understanding] was not for joy but tears. Thus at any rate he acts, where he weeps for the city. Not therefore because of this does he rejoice, but because what wise men knew not, was known to these; as when Paul says, 'I thank God, that you were servants of sin, but you obeyed from the heart the form of doctrine which was delivered to you.' "

65. This line, without parallel in Matthew, is not Lukan redaction, nor does it reflect the Gentile mission. See below, p. 109.

## THE THIRD SECTION, Q 11:14–52

Kloppenborg rightly reckons Q 11:14–26, 29–52 as a literary unit and
gives it the title, "controversies with Israel."[66] So similarly Polag, who
categorizes the section as an *Auseinandersetzung*.[67] There are six units:

11.  Beelzebul (Q 11:14–23)

12.  Unclean Spirit (Q 11:24–26)

13.  Sign of Jonah (Q 11:29–32)

14.  Light (Q 11:33–36)

15.  Woes against Pharisees (Q 11:39–44)[68]

16.  Woes against Lawyers (Q 11:45–51 + 13:34–35 + 11:52)[69]

These units are filled with polemic. People accuse Jesus of casting out
demons by Beelzebul (11:15). Jesus refutes their position in unit 11 and

---

66. *Formation*, p. 101.

67. Athanasius Polag, *Fragmenta Q: Textheft zur Logienquelle* (Neukirchen-Vluyn:
Neukirchener, 1979), p. 24. Cf. Witherington, *Sage*, p. 220. Manson, *Sayings*, p. 5, put
the rubric "Jesus and his opponents" over Q 11:14–12:34. But this is accurate only for
the first part; 12:2ff. introduces new concerns.

68. The parallels between Mt 23:13–36 and Lk 11:37–54 may be set forth thus:

| Matthew 23 | Luke 11 |
|---|---|
| 4, burdens | 39–41, cup |
| 6–7a, seats and greetings | 42, tithes (woe 1) |
| 13, key (woe 1) | 43, seats and greetings (woe 2) |
| 15, proselytes (woe 2) | 44, tombs (woe 3) |
| 16–22, oaths (woe 3) | 46, burdens (woe 4) |
| 23–24, tithes (woe 4) | 47–48, murder (woe 5) |
| 25–26, cup (woe 5) | 49–51, lament over Jerusalem |
| 27–28, tombs (woe 6) | 52, key (woe 6) |
| 29–33, murder (woe 7) | |
| 34–36, lament over Jerusalem | |

Two of Matthew's woes (2, 3) do not appear in Luke, and Luke's parallel to Mt 23:25–
6 (woe 5) is not a woe. Moreover, two of Luke's woes (2, 4) have parallels of content
but not form in Matthew; that is, they are woes in the former but not the latter. Another
major difference is that whereas all but the third of Matthew's seven woes are addressed
to "scribes and Pharisees, hypocrites," in Luke there are two triads: woes 1–3 are directed
to the Pharisees, woes 4–6 to the lawyers. The International Q Project has reconstructed
this seven-woe sequence: Q 11:42, 39ab + 40 + 41 (in woe form, as in Matthew but
not Luke), 43, 44, 46, 47 + 48, 52; see J. M. Robinson, "The International Q Project:
Work Sessions 12–14 July, 22 November 1991," *JBL* 111 (1992): 504–5. But Luke is
probably even closer to Q than this reconstruction indicates. Luke's redactional introduction, 11:37–38, which has a Pharisee complain about Jesus not washing before eating,
shows us that 11:39–41 introduced Q's series of woes (cf. Leif E. Vaage, *Galilean Upstarts: Jesus' First Followers according to Q* [Valley Forge, Pa.: Trinity Press International,
1994], pp. 133–34). Further, Luke's triadic arrangement reminds one of other triads in Q
(see below, p. 18). Matthew's series is best explained as a conflation of M and Q material
(cf. the Sermon on the Mount); so already Streeter, *Four Gospels*, pp. 254–55.

69. On the original position of 13:34–35 see below, pp. 201–2.

in unit 12 turns the argument around to claim that the exorcisms of his rivals are ineffectual.[70] In unit 13 he rebukes "this generation," which will stand condemned at the last judgment. In unit 14 Jesus appears to explain why his opponents do not accept the light of his ministry: their evil eye causes them to dwell in the realm of darkness.[71] In units 15 and 16 Jesus utters woes against the Pharisees and lawyers.

The connection between all this polemic and Q's second section, 9:57–11:13, is less than obvious. One might argue that 11:14–52 explores the theme of the rejection of the missionaries' proclamation (cf. Q 10:13–15). But the transition from Q 11:13 to 11:14 remains rough, and it is telling that topical groupings of Q consistently draw a line between Q 11:13 and 11:14.[72] It is also noteworthy that nothing in units 11–16 need ever have been directed to itinerant missionaries in particular.

The polemic of 11:14–52 reminds one not of 9:57–11:13 but of Q's opening section, 3:7–7:35. In 3:7–9, 16–17 John the Baptist rails against those who come out to him, and in 7:18–35 Jesus mourns "this generation," which has rejected both the Baptist and himself. Moreover, the interest in Jesus' miracles, so prominent in 3:7–7:35, but not mentioned in 9:57–11:13, also resurfaces here. Q's third section opens with a controversy about Jesus' exorcisms, and the request for a miraculous sign, which Jesus refuses to grant, takes one back to 4:1–13, where the devil makes an improper request for a miracle.

There are other interesting links between 3:7–7:35 and 11:14–52. Taken together these two sections contain

- all of Q's references to Jesus' miracles (4:1–13; 7:1–10, 22; 11:14–22, 29–30)

- all of Q's sayings on "this generation" (7:31; 11:29, 30, 31, 32, 50, 51)[73]

---

70. See below, pp. 120–32.

71. See below, pp. 165–67.

72. See the survey of the schemes of T. W. Manson, John Dominic Crossan, Athanasius Polag, and Wolfgang Schenk in Kloppenborg, *Formation,* pp. 90–92. R. Uro, *Sheep among the Wolves: A Study of the Missionary Instructions of Q* (Helsinki: Suomalainen tiedeakatemia, 1987), p. 95, writes that Q 11:14ff. introduces "a totally new subject."

73. D. Lührmann, *Die Redaktion der Logienquelle,* WMANT, vol. 33 (Neukirchen-Vluyn: Neukirchener, 1969), argued that Q's sayings about "this generation" reflect a single redactional level. (The "this generation" saying in Lk 17:25, although it appears in the middle of Q material, is usually thought to be Lukan; cf. Rudolf Schnackenburg, "Der eschatologische Abschnitt Lk 17,20–37," in *Mélanges Bibliques en hommage au R. P. Béda Rigaux,* ed. A. Descamps and R. P. André de Halleux [Gembloux: Duculot, 1970], pp. 222–23.) For the argument that in Q ἡ γενεὰ αὕτη means "this type" and refers primarily to the Pharisees see R. A. Horsley, "Q and Jesus: Assumptions, Approaches, and Analyses," in Kloppenborg and Vaage, *Early Christianity, Q, and Jesus,* pp. 186–87, 191. For criticism see John S. Kloppenborg, "Recent Opinion," in *Conflict and Invention: Lit-*

- all of Q's statements about *sophia* (7:35; 11:31, 49)

- all of Q's material on demonology (4:1–13; 11:14–23, 24–26)

- all of Q's uses of πατήρ to mean "ancestor" (3:8; 6:23; 11:47, 48)

- eight of nine of Q's uses of πονηρός (6:22, 35, 45 [three times]; 11:13, 26, 29, 34).

Further, if one were to hold that, in Q, 16:16 appeared between 7:28 and 31 (an uncertain matter), then these sections would also contain all of Q's traditions about the Baptist.[74]

Another striking circumstance is that of the ten places in Q where a phrase or formula is repeated three times in near succession, nine of them belong to the first and third sections:[75]

| | |
|---|---|
| 4:3 | καὶ εἶπεν αὐτῷ ὁ διάβολος· εἰ |
| 4:5–6 | ὁ διάβολος    καὶ εἶπεν αὐτῷ . . . . . . . . . ἐάν |
| 4:9 | ὁ διάβολος . . . καὶ εἶπεν αὐτῷ·              εἰ |
| | |
| 4:4 | καὶ ἀπεκρίθη    ὁ Ἰησοῦς· γέγραπται |
| 4:8 | καὶ ἀποκριθεὶς ὁ Ἰησοῦς εἶπεν αὐτῷ· γέγραπται |
| 4:12 | καὶ εἶπεν αὐτῷ ὁ Ἰησοῦς·            γέγραπται |
| | |
| 6:20 | μακάριοι οἱ . . . ὅτι |
| 6:21a | μακάριοι οἱ . . . ὅτι |
| 6:21b | μακάριοι οἱ . . . ὅτι[76] |
| | |
| 6:32 | ποία ὑμῖν χάρις ἐστίν |
| 6:33 | ποία ὑμῖν χάρις ἐστίν |
| 6:34 | ποία ὑμῖν χάρις ἐστίν[77] |

---

*erary, Rhetorical, and Social Studies on the Sayings Gospel Q*, ed. John S. Kloppenborg (Valley Forge, Pa.: Trinity Press International, 1995), pp. 23–24, and for further discussion C. M. Tuckett, "Les Logia et le Judaïsme," *Foi et Vie* 92, no. 5 (1993): 80–83, and idem, *Q*, pp. 196–201. The latter is probably correct to conclude that "this generation" is "simply the non-responsive part of the Jewish people."

74. See the review of opinion in Kloppenborg, *Formation*, pp. 113–14.

75. The exception is in the missionary discourse:

    10:5    εἰς ἣν δ' ἂν          εἰσέλθητε οἰκίαν
    10:8    εἰς ἣν    ἂν πόλιν εἰσέρχησθε
    10:10   εἰς ἣν δ' ἂν πόλιν εἰσέλθητε

Although I am not among their number, many do not assign Lk 10:8 to Q, so for them Q's missionary discourse did not have a thrice-repeated formula (see p. 109).

76. The fourth beatitude deliberately breaks the pattern; see chap. 3 herein.

77. The parallels in Mt 5:46 (τίνα μισθὸν ἔχετε) and 5:47 (τί περισσὸν ποιεῖτε) are editorial. μισθός (Mt: 10 times; Mk: 1; Lk: 3) is Matthean, μισθός + ἔχετε is redactional in Mt 6:1, and τί περισσὸν ποιεῖτε recalls the redactional 5:20 and forms an editorial *inclusio*. Luke's phrase, on the other hand, is not clearly redactional (Joachim Jeremias, *Die Sprache des Lukasevangeliums*, MeyerK [Göttingen: Vandenhoeck & Ruprecht, 1980], p. 144). Further, the Lukan expression has a parallel in *Did.* 1:3 (cf. 1 Pet 2:20), which does not

| 6:41 | τὸ κάρφος τὸ ἐν τῷ ὀφθαλμῷ τοῦ ἀδελφοῦ σου |
|------|-------------------------------------------|
| 6:42 | τὸ κάρφος      ἐκ τοῦ ὀφθαλμοῦ        σου |
| 6:42 | τὸ κάρφος τὸ ἐν τῷ ὀφθαλμῷ τοῦ ἀδελφοῦ σου |

| 7:24 | τί ἐξήλθατε ... θεάσασθαι |
|------|---------------------------|
| 7:25 | ἀλλὰ τί ἐξήλθατε   ἰδεῖν |
| 7:26 | ἀλλὰ τί ἐξήλθατε   ἰδεῖν |

| 11:18 | ἐν Βεελζεβοὺλ   ἐκβάλλειν με τὰ δαιμόνια |
|-------|------------------------------------------|
| 11:19 | ἐγὼ ἐν Βεελζεβοὺλ   ἐκβάλλω     τὰ δαιμόνια |
| 11:20 | ἐν δακτύλῳ θεοῦ ἐκβάλλω     τὰ δαιμόνια |

| 11:42 | οὐαὶ ὑμῖν τοῖς Φαρισαίοις ὅτι + verb ending in -τε |
|-------|--------------------------------------------------|
| 11:43 | οὐαὶ ὑμῖν τοῖς Φαρισαίοις ὅτι + verb ending in -τε |
| 11:44 | οὐαὶ ὑμῖν                ὅτι + verb ending in -τε |

| 11:46 | ὑμῖν τοῖς νομικοῖς οὐαί ὅτι + verb ending in -τε |
|-------|------------------------------------------------|
| 11:47 | οὐαὶ ὑμῖν                ὅτι + verb ending in -τε |
| 11:52 | οὐαὶ ὑμῖν τοῖς νομικοῖς   ὅτι + verb ending in -τε[78] |

Before making further observations it is necessary to consider the location of Q 13:34–35, the lament over Jerusalem. There is no consensus as to where this stood in Q. It appears in Mt 23:37–39, at the end of Matthew's woes. Did Luke position the piece after Jesus' remark that a prophet should not perish away from Jerusalem (Lk 13:33)?[79] Or did Matthew arrange things so as to make the lament end chapter 23 and prepare for chapter 24?[80] Luke is, as a general rule, closer to Q's order. But in this particular case it would seem that Luke moved the unit in order to bring together texts about Jerusalem. Lk 13:22–30 (with its redactional introduction naming Jerusalem) is followed by 13:31–33 ("it is impossible for a prophet to be killed outside of Jerusalem") which is in turn followed by 13:34–35 ("Jerusalem, Jerusalem, the city that kills the prophets"). Moreover, Lk 13:34–35 belongs better with the cluster of polemical sayings in Q 11:14–52 than with the hortatory material in Q = Lk 13:33ff.

If this is the right conclusion,[81] if the lament over Jerusalem did, as in Matthew, conclude the series of woes, then Q's first and third sec-

---

depend upon Luke but an oral tradition related to the pre-Q tradition behind Q 6:27–38 (see p. 89 below).

78. One wonders whether Q had woes directed first against Pharisees and then against scribes. In this case Matthew's "scribes and Pharisees" would be redactional (as in 5:20), and Luke would have substituted "lawyers" (νομικός: Mt: 1; Mk: 1; Lk: 6) for "scribes" (γραμματεύς) as he did in 10:25–28 = Mk 12:28–34.

79. So Lührmann, *Redaktion*, p. 45; Koester, *Gospels*, pp. 143–44; Wolfgang Schenk, *Synopse zur Redenquelle der Evangelien* (Düsseldorf: Patmos, 1981), p. 81.

80. So Jacobson, *First Gospel*, pp. 209–10; Schulz, *Q*, p. 349.

81. See further below, pp. 201–3.

tions would give us, in addition to the common items listed above, also all of Q's

- citations of Scripture[82]

- addresses to outsiders as "you"[83]

- references to Jesus as the coming one[84]

- plainly deuteronomistic declarations.[85]

There is one final way in which 11:14–52 takes one back to 3:7–7:35. Units 12, 13, 14, and 15 are all linked by a key word, πονηρός. Q 11:24–26 refers to seven spirits more evil (πονηρότερα) than the first. Q 11:29–32 refers to an evil (πονηρά) generation. Q 11:33–36 speaks of an evil (πονηρός) eye. 11:39–44 says that the Pharisees are full of evil (πονηρίας).[86] This is not coincidence but a literary strategy. Moreover, if 11:24–26 concerns an unclean (ἀκάθαρτον) spirit, 11:39–44 talks about cleansing (καθαρίζετε) the outside of cup and dish and says that giving alms will make all "clean (καθαρά) for you."[87] And if in 11:14–23 the climactic saying is Jesus' declaration that he casts out demons by the finger (δακτύλῳ) of God, 11:45–52 opens by asserting that the lawyers do not move a finger (ἑνὶ τῶν δακτύλων) to lift the burden of others. So one can find in Q's third section a chiastic structure:

---

82. See Q 4:4 (Deut 8:3, introduced with γέγραπται), 4:8 (Deut 6:13, introduced with γέγραπται), 4:10–11 (Ps 91:11–12, introduced with γέγραπται), 4:12 (Deut 6:16); 7:27 (Exod 23:20; Mal 3:1, introduced with γέγραπται); 13:35 (Ps 118:26). In the other parts of Q, Scripture is only alluded to, and in no instance is an allusion to a biblical text clearly editorial. Cf. 10:15 (Isa 14:12–15); 12:52–53 (Mic 7:6); 13:19 (Ps 104:12; Dan 4:21 Theod.), 13:27 (Ps 6:9), 13:29 (see pp. 194–95 herein); 17:27 (Gen 7:7, 13).

83. 3:7–17; 7:9, 24–28; 10:13–15; 11:33–52.

84. See above, pp. 6–7.

85. 6:23; 10:13–15; 11:47–51; 13:34–35. I exclude 14:16–24, the parable of the great banquet, because although this has often been interpreted in terms of salvation history (cf. Matthew's clear interpretation), the immediate Q context suggests rather that the unit functions, as do the parables in 12:35ff., as paraenesis for insiders.

86. Instead of πονηρίας, Mt 23:25 uses ἀκρασίας (="excess," "intemperance"). This is a Matthean hapax legomenon, but Luke's πονηρίας is also a hapax. The decisive factor in favor of Luke's originality is Q's fondness for the related πονηρός (see p. 33).

87. The differences here between Matthew (23:26: "First cleanse the inside of the cup so that the outside also may become clean") and Luke (11:41: "But give for alms those things which are within; and behold, everything is clean for you") are notorious. An explanation in terms of either Matthean or Lukan redaction seems farfetched. One suspects that Wellhausen was correct: the phrase "give for alms those things which are within" goes back to the Aramaic zakkau, "cleanse the inside" to the Aramaic dakkau. See his Einleitung in die drei ersten Evangelien (Berlin: G. Reimer, 1905), pp. 36–37; and cf. M. Black, "The Aramaic Dimension in Q with Notes on Luke 17:22 and Matthew 24:26 (Luke 17:23)," JSNT 40 (1990): 37. The likelihood that Matthew and Luke here preserve translation variants is possible if Matthew knew not only the woes of Q but a related tradition in M; see n. 68.

a. Jesus casts out demons by God's δακτύλῳ $\left.\vphantom{\begin{array}{c}a\\b\end{array}}\right\}$ *demonology*

   b. ἀκάθαρτον spirit and seven πονηρότερα spirits

      c. the πονηρά generation

      c. the πονηρός eye

   b. how those full of πονηρίας can become καθαρά $\left.\vphantom{\begin{array}{c}a\\b\end{array}}\right\}$ *woes*

a. lawyers do not lift one of their δακτύλων to help others

As in the chiastic structure proposed for Q's first section, here too we find pairs of opposites (a-a, b-b).

## Q'S FOURTH SECTION, 12:2–32

Q's fourth section, I should like to suggest, contains just two large units:

17. Do not Fear (Q 12:2–12)

18. Do not be Anxious (Q 12:22–32)

The latter, whose key word is μεριμνάω (12:22, 25, 26),[88] calls for contemplation of the ravens and the lilies in order to put earthly anxiety to rest. The former, whose key word is φοβέομαι (12:4, 5, 7), is about being unafraid — unafraid to proclaim the gospel (12:2–3), unafraid of those who can kill the body (12:4–7), unafraid of those before whom one stands when put on trial (12:8–12).

Surely Q 12:2–12, as others have observed, had its original *Sitz im Leben* "in the consoling and admonishing paraenesis for the wandering missionaries."[89] The passage is primarily a call to faithful martyrdom. It is addressed to people who must worry about the death of the body (12:4), about confession before the authorities (12:8–9), about defense before synagogues and rulers (12:11). Now while we have sufficient evidence that some early Christians were indeed persecuted and (on very rare occasions) even killed, these were in every instance leaders or missionaries. That missionaries are indeed in view throughout Q 12:2–12 is strongly suggested by its introduction (Q 12:2–3), which appears to be about proclamation: "What I say to you in the dark, tell in the light; and what you hear whispered, proclaim from the housetops" (Q 12:3).[90]

An original *Sitz im Leben* in the Christian mission must also be reck-

---

88. Cf. Mt 6:25, 27, 28, 31, 34.

89. Sato, *Q und Prophetie*, p. 389. Cf. Kloppenborg, *Formation*, p. 239 (for 12:4–7); Uro, *Sheep*, pp. 195–97.

90. Here Luke's form is secondary, Mt 10:27 original; see Davies and Allison, *Matthew*, vol. 2, pp. 204–205; Kloppenborg, *Formation*, p. 207 n. 148.

oned highly likely for 12:22–32, which poetically depicts the ravens and lilies, which neither sow nor reap and yet are fed and dressed in splendor.[91] This famous passage opens with διά τοῦτο, which presumably harks back to 12:11–12, where the missionaries brought before authorities are told they need not be anxious.[92] One doubts that 12:22–32 was originally addressed either to the Jewish public at large or to a Christian community in general (although it is addressed to such in Matthew and Luke).[93] According to David Catchpole, the passage does not contain prescriptions for normal existence but rather implies "abandonment of life-sustaining work."[94] In the words of Ulrich Luz, "Why does Jesus say that birds do not do the work of men, and that lilies do not do the work of women? This makes sense only if it is applied to men and women who have left their ordinary work for the sake of the kingdom of God."[95] Luz infers, as have others, that "in the *Sayings Source* [Q] the text probably was related primarily to itinerant radicals."[96] While it would make sense to tell missionaries to lay aside anxiety about food and drink and clothing as they go about wholly occupied with serving the kingdom of God, as general religious instruction the relevance or even meaning of most of the sayings in Q 12:22–32 remains difficult to fathom. The section — as the history of its interpretation reveals[97] —

---

91. Lk 12:32, which contains no Lukan redactional traits (Jeremias, *Sprache*, p. 218), may be tentatively assigned to Q. Although it has no Matthean parallel, it is in the middle of Q material, and its inclusion in Mt 6:33 would be anomalous given the Sermon on the Mount's general audience (cf. Mt 7:28–29). Further, "do not fear" in Q 12:32 harks back to Q 12:4, "your father" links up with Q 12:30, and "kingdom" appears in 12:31.

92. Cf. Odar Wischmeyer, "Matthäus 6,25–34 par. Die Spruchreihe vom Sorgen," *ZNW* 85 (1994): 5.

93. Paul Hoffmann, "Die Sprüche vom Sorgen in der vorsynoptischen Überlieferung," in *Tradition und Situation: Studien zur Jesusüberlieferung in der Logienquelle und den synoptischen Evangelien* (Münster: Aschendorff, 1995), pp. 88–106, argues that Jesus himself — he accepts the authenticity of Q 12:22c, d, 24, 27–28, 29, 30b — was concerned with the overcoming of anxiety in the conditions of daily life. However that may be (I am not persuaded), he does rightly contend that in Q the words were for missionaries.

94. David R. Catchpole, "The Question of Q," *Sewanee Theological Review* 36 (1992): 40. Catchpole goes on to speak, surely justly, of "this frankly unrealistic teaching."

95. Ulrich Luz, *Matthew in History: Interpretation, Influence, and Effects* (Minneapolis: Fortress, 1994), p. 29.

96. *Matthew 1–7: A Commentary* (Minneapolis: Augsburg, 1989), p. 408. Cf. Heinz Schürmann, "Das Zeugnis der Redenquelle für die Basileia-Verkündigung Jesu," in Delobel, *Logia*, p. 158; Dieter Zeller, *Die weisheitlichen Mahnsprüche bei den Synoptikern*, FB, vol. 17 (Würzburg: Echter, 1977), p. 92. Kloppenborg, *Formation*, p. 239, acknowledges that 12:22b–28 is among those texts (including 10:4–11) which "may have had their *Sitz im Leben* in the instructions given to and carried by wandering charismatic preachers." Sato, *Q und Prophetie*, pp. 218–19, 389–90, believes that although the unit originally addressed disciples in the narrow sense, it came in Q to be instruction for the entire community. Wischmeyer, "Matthäus 6,25–34 par.," pp. 14–15, unpersuasively counters Luz by offering that the text is not exclusively oriented toward a particular social stratum and that the disciples of Jesus were in principle an open group.

97. See Luz, *Matthew 1–7*, pp. 409–11.

does not "address ordinary people's realistic anxieties about the basic necessities of life, food and clothing."[98] Gerd Theissen is correct:

> It is wrong to read words like this [Q 12:22–32] in the mood of a family walk on a Sunday afternoon. There is nothing here about delight in birds and flowers and green fields. On the contrary, these words express the harshness of the free existence of the wandering charismatics, without homes and without protection, travelling through the country with no possessions and no occupation. The final words, "Therefore do not be anxious about tomorrow, for tomorrow will be anxious for itself. Let the day's own trouble be sufficient for the day" (Matt. 6.34), may well be born of bitter experience.[99]

One can readily imagine Paul, given his way of life as a missionary, taking Q 12:22–32 to heart (even though there is no evidence that he did); but can we so easily envisage him who warned the Thessalonians to stay at their jobs (2 Thess 3:6–13) telling his congregations to live according to Q 12:22–32? Certainly both Matthew and Luke, by putting the verses where they did, sought to make the instruction somehow germane to all. But this application involved a shift in meaning (just as did the later adoption of the missionary discourse by the synoptic evangelists). In the beginning, "Seek his kingdom and these things will be given to you as well" (Q 12:31) was an expression to itinerants of "the confidence that the problem of finding enough to live on would be solved."[100]

Units 17 (12:2–12) and 18 (12:22–32), originally composed for the same setting in life, also exhibit a common structure in their central parts, in 12:4–7 and 12:22–31:[101]

Identification of speaker and audience:
"I say to you" (λέγω ὑμῖν) (Q 12:4)
"I say to you" (λέγω ὑμῖν) (Q 12:22)

Opening imperative:
"Do not fear" (Q 12:4)
"Do not be anxious" (Q 12:22)

---

98. With due respect to Richard A. Horsley, "Q and Jesus," p. 203. One must in any case avoid easy generalizations about the economic deprivation of Galilean peasants or Jesus' first followers; see Thomas E. Schmidt, *Hostility to Wealth in the Synoptic Gospels*, JSNTSS, vol. 15 (Sheffield: JSOT, 1987), pp. 17–30.

99. Theissen, *Sociology*, p. 13.

100. Ibid., p. 14.

101. Although I have modified his analysis, for what follows I am greatly indebted to Ronald A. Piper's original work, *Wisdom in the Q Tradition: The Aphoristic Teaching of Jesus*, SNTSMS, vol. 61 (Cambridge: Cambridge University Press, 1989).

Supporting statement (introduced with preposition):
"But (δέ) I will warn you whom to fear" (Q 12:5)
"For (γάρ) life is more than food" (Q 12:23)[102]

First illustration:
"Are not five sparrows sold?" (Q 12:6)
"Consider the ravens" (Q 12:24)

Second illustration:
"Even the hairs of your head" (Q 12:7a)
"Consider the lilies" (Q 12:27–28)

Conclusion:
"Fear not; you are of more value" (Q 12:7b)
"Do not be anxious
    ...these will be yours" (Q 12:29–31)[103]

Both units are also related in that both concern the Father's care for his own and argue from the lesser to the greater (Q 12:7, 24, 28).

We can be fairly confident that the common structure is due to deliberate editorial activity. For both Q 12:4–7 and 12:22–31 only fit the pattern because someone expanded originally smaller units. At the very least, Q 12:7a and 12:29–31, which are essential to the scheme, must be regarded as secondary.[104] It seems, then, that units 17 (12:2–12) and 18 (12:22–31) reflect the same editorial hand, one concerned with encouraging itinerant missionaries.[105]

We have already met this concern before, in Q's second section, 9:57–11:13. And this is not the only strong link between sections 2 (= units 6–10, Q 9:57–11:13) and 4 (= units 17–18, Q 12:2–32). Q 12:2–3 refers to things covered and uncovered, that is, hidden and revealed. This reminds one of 10:21–24, which also pertains to hidden things be-

---

102. Although the International Q Project prints the Matthean form of Q 12:23 (see Mt 6:25), this is probably secondary; see Davies and Allison, *Matthew*, vol. 1, p. 648.

103. The analysis omits Lk 12:25 (cf. Mt 6:27); this, however, does not belong to the original composition but is a secondary insertion; so already T. W. Manson, *The Teaching of Jesus* (Cambridge: Cambridge University Press, 1935), p. 56. Cf. R. A. Piper, *Wisdom*, p. 28. But note R. J. Dillon, "Ravens, Lilies, and the Kingdom of God (Matthew 6:25–33/Luke 12:22–31)," *CBQ* 53 (1991): 605–27.

104. On Q 12:7a see herein, p. 173, and Jacques Schlosser, "Le Logion de Mt 10,28 par. Lc 12,4–5," in Van Segbroeck, *Four Gospels*, vol. 1, p. 622. For the secondary character of Q 12:29–31 see Kloppenborg, *Formation*, p. 218. Tuckett, *Q*, pp. 149–50, argues for the secondary character of 12:23.

105. Tuckett, *Q*, pp. 315–19, argues that in both 12:4ff. and 12:22ff. "an earlier tradition expressing confidence in God's care for His creation" has been "overlaid by a secondary layer of tradition placing concern for the material needs of life very low on any agenda of priorities and placing all weight on the eschatological future kingdom of God." If so this is additional reason for finding the same editorial hand in these two units.

ing revealed. Much more important, the structure common to 12:4–7 and 12:22–31 also appears in 11:9–13:

Identification of speaker and audience:
"And I say to you" (λέγω ὑμῖν) (Q 11:9)

Opening imperative:
"Ask ... seek ... knock" (Q 11:9)

Supporting statement (introduced with preposition):
"For (γάρ) everyone who asks" (Q 11:10)

First illustration:
Loaf and stone (Q 11:11)[106]

Second illustration:
Fish and serpent (Q 11:12)

Conclusion:
"How much more will your heavenly Father" (Q 11:13)[107]

Not only is the arrangement identical but the theme is once again God's care, and the argument, just like the arguments in 12:7, 12:14, and 12:28, moves from the lesser (evil human fathers) to the greater (God the Father, cf. 12:30). Indeed, 11:13, 12:7, 12:24, and 12:28 contain closely related expressions:

| | | |
|---|---|---|
| 11:13 | ὅσῳ μᾶλλον | |
| 12:7 | | πολλῶν ... διαφέρετε |
| 12:24 | (πόσῳ) μᾶλλον | διαφέρετε |
| 12:28 | πόσῳ μᾶλλον | |

Once more then we see evidence of the same hand; that is, the same editor probably put together at least 11:9–13, 12:4–7, and 12:22–31.[108]

---

106. The τίς/τίνα ἐξ ὑμῶν of 11:11 recalls the τίς ἐξ ὑμῶν of 12:25.

107. R. A. Piper, *Wisdom*, argues that, on the basis of structure, 6:37–42 and 6:43–45 belong with Q 11:9–13, 12:4–7, and 12:22–31. But 6:37–42 and 6:43–45 are different. The latter lacks an imperative opening and makes no reference to God's care; and "the composition of Luke 6:43–45 is more likely a three-part chiastic form with the sayings about the good and bad trees (vv. 43–44a) balancing the sayings about good and bad people (v. 45) on either side of the saying about gathering figs from thorns (v. 44b)" (so Harry T. Fleddermann, review of *Wisdom in the Q Tradition*, by R. A. Piper, *CBQ* 53 [1991]: 716). Q 6:37–42 also makes no reference to God's care, and it fails to argue from the lesser to the greater. There is also the problem that many regard 6:37–38 as thematically separate from 6:39ff; see chap. 2 herein, pp. 92–93.

108. Because Jesus himself probably composed Q 11:9–13, which cannot be decomposed (see Allison and Davies, *Matthew*, vol. 1, p. 682; Luz, *Matthew 1–7*, p. 421), one presumes that it was the model for 12:4–7 and 12:22–31. (The closest parallel outside the Jesus tradition known to me is Prov 6:25–29.)

## THE FIFTH SECTION, Q 12:33–22:30

Following the central portion of Q and its missionary material is Q 12:33–22:30, Q's fifth and final section. It consists of the following units, many of them very brief:

19. Treasure in Heaven (Q 12:33–34)[109]

20. Watching for the *Parousia* (Q 12:35–40)[110]

21. Parable of Servants (Q 12:42–46[+ 47–48?])

22. Fire and Division (Q 12:49–53)[111]

23. Interpreting Signs (Q 12:54–56)[112]

24. Parable of Reconciliation (Q 12:58–59)

25. Parable of the Mustard Seed (Q 13:18–19)

26. Parable of the Leaven (Q 13:20–21)

27. The Narrow Door (Q 13:23–24)

28. The Shut Door (Q 13:25–27)

29. Sayings about Eschatological Reversal (Q 13:28–30 + 14:11)

30. The Great Supper (Q 14:16–24)

31. Hating Family (Q 14:26)

32. Taking Up the Cross (Q 14:27)

33. Parable of Salt (Q 14:34–35)

---

109. For the good possibility that Q 12:33–34 was prefaced by Mt 6:19 see W. Pesch, "Zur Exegese von Mt 6,19–21 und Lk 12,33–34," *Bib* 40 (1960): 356–78.

110. Only vv. 39–40 are paralleled in Matthew; but vv. 35(36)-38 should be assigned to Q; see B. Kollmann, "Lk 12.35–38 — ein Gleichnis der Logienquelle," *ZNW* 81 (1990): 254–61, and Claus-Peter März, "… *lasst eure Lampen brennen!" Studien zur Q-Vorlage von Lk 12,35–14,24*, ETS, vol. 20 (Leipzig: St. Benno, 1991), pp. 58–71.

111. There is disagreement about whether or not vv. 49–50 stood in Q. Against inclusion is their omission from Matthew. But in favor of inclusion are (1) the close thematic connection with v. 51 (which "dwells further on the point made in v. 49" — so Manson, *Sayings*, p. 120); (2) the pre-Lukan character of Lk 12:49–50 (see Jeremias, *Sprache*, p. 223); (3) the use of βάλλω in both Lk 12:49–50 and Matthew's parallel to 12:51 (Mt 10:34 = Q); and (4) the catchword connection that would exist if one were to accept the International Q Project's text for Q 12:54–56 (πῦρ in Q 12:49, πυρράζει in Q 12:54; but see next note). See further März, *Lampen*, pp. 9–20; also P. Sellew, "Reconstruction of Q 12:33–59," in *Society of Biblical Literature 1987 Seminar Papers*, ed. Kent Harold Richards (Atlanta: Scholars Press, 1987), pp. 645–46. März assigns v. 49 but not v. 50 to Q and sees Matthew's πυρράζει (Mt 16:2–3), not as part of a catchword connection that existed in Q, but as a Matthean reminiscence of Lk 12:49.

112. Is the Q text to be found in the obscure Mt 16:2–3 (so the International Q Project) or in the easier-to-understand Lk 12:54–56 (which reflects Palestinian conditions)? Full discussion in März, *Lampen*, pp. 32–43.

34. The Lost Sheep (Q 15:4–7)

35. God and Mammon (Q 16:13)

36. Law and Prophets (Q 16:16–17)

37. Divorce (Q 16:18)

38. Offending and Forgiving (Q 17:1–4)

39. Faith (Q 17:6)

40. Day of the Son of Man (Q 17:22–37)

41. Parable of the Pounds (Q 19:12–26)

42. Thrones and the Twelve Tribes (Q 22:28–30)

Examination of this concluding portion of Q reveals several things not seen previously in Q — long narrative parables which have to do explicitly with eschatological judgment (Q 12:42–48; 14:16–24; 19:12–26), detailed teaching on the latter days (17:22–37; 22:28–30), counsel to be prepared for the day of the Son of man (12:35–40, 42–48; 17:22–37; 19:12–26), and short units seemingly unconnected to surrounding material (14:34–35; 16:13, 16–18; 17:6). Q 12:33ff. also distinguishes itself by its concern with reconciliation (Q 12:58–59; 17:1–4), the delay of the *parousia* (Q 12:38, 45; 19:13), and the possible dangers of conventional family ties (Q 12:49–53; 14:20, 26).

Just as noticeable are the things that are not present. There is nothing here particularly directed to itinerant missionaries. Nor is there much attempt to console. Nor is the polemic so characteristic of Q's first and third sections present. The material, rather, is hortatory from beginning to end. Hearers are not told that God the Father will care for them, or how their opponents have gone wrong, but how they must act in the eschatological crisis, how they should prepare themselves for the day of the Son of man. The nearness of the end is not assumed (as it is in the earlier sections) but rather taught and expanded upon at length, and its suddenness becomes a motive for preparation. Here, especially in the parables with unfaithful servants, we are again and again faced with the possibility that the followers of Jesus may themselves not be ready for the eschatological judgment.

T. W. Manson set the rubric, "The future," over Q 12:35–17:37.[113] But much here has little to do with eschatology. The section contains, for instance, the saying about taking up one's cross (Q 14:27), the parable about salt (Q 14:34–35), the illustration of the lost sheep (Q 15:4–7), the logion about God and mammon (Q 16:13), and the prohibition of divorce (Q 16:18). The truth is that, although eschatology

---

113. *Sayings,* p. 5.

seems to be the main interest in some portions, one can hardly find a consistent theme within Q 12:33ff. — another fact which separates it from Q's earlier sections. Kloppenborg is reduced to collecting Q 15:3– 7, 16:13, 16:17–18, and 17:1–6 under the title "various parables and sayings."[114] Jacobson has been honest enough to confess, "I have not yet been able to discern... unity in this... 'section' of Q."[115] I have had the same experience.

But if there is no thematic unity, there is a *functional* unity. From beginning to end the material presents practical advice and exhortation. We here meet counsels that were relatively commonplace in the early church.[116] Many early Christian sources enjoin believers to discern the time and prepare for the end (even though the Lord may delay),[117] to beware of drunkenness and intemperance,[118] to forgive and to be reconciled with others,[119] to strive to enter the kingdom of God because not all will,[120] to serve God instead of mammon,[121] to fulfil the commandments,[122] to avoid causing others to stumble,[123] and to have faith.[124] There are also texts which teach that those who have suffered will be rewarded.[125]

While Q 12:33ff. may not be catechetical in the proper sense of the word,[126] the section remains transparently practical wisdom with a strong eschatological component. Even if the precise setting is unclear, the unit must nonetheless have been composed to shape the behavior of ordinary Christians. It is paraenesis.

---

114. *Formation*, p. 92.

115. Arland D. Jacobson, "The History of the Composition of the Synoptic Sayings Source, Q," in Richards, *1987 Seminar Papers*, p. 288. Cf. his comments in *First Gospel*, p. 184, and Horsley, "Q and Jesus," p. 195 ("it is difficult to discern how Q materials are 'clustered' once we move into Luke 13–16").

116. Contrast the counsels in 12:2–12 and 22–32: it is harder to find parallels to these outside the Jesus tradition.

117. Q 12:35–48, 54–56; 14:16–24; cf. Rom 13:11–14; 1 Cor 7:26; Col 4:5; 1 Thess 5:1–11; Jas 5:7–8; 1 Pet 1:13; 4:7; 2 Pet 3:1–13; *Didache* 16; Ignatius, *Smyr.* 9; *2 Clem.* 16.

118. Q 12:45; cf. Rom 13:13; 1 Cor 5:11; 6:9–11; Gal 5:20–21; Eph 5:18; 1 Thess 5:6–7; 1 Pet 4:3.

119. Q 12:58–59, 17:1–4; cf. Rom 12:16; 14:13 (this may depend upon the Jesus tradition), 14:19; 15:5; 2 Cor 13:11; Gal 5:26–6:1; Eph 4:32; 1 Thess 5:13, 15; Jas 4:11–12; 5:9, 19–20; 1 Pet 2:1; 3:8–9; *Did.* 2:7; 14; 15:3–4.

120. Q 13:23–30, 14:34–35 (cf. the interpretation of Kloppenborg, *Formation*, p. 234: "The saying warns that those who do not take seriously the demands of discipleship outlined in 14:26, 27 and 17:33 will be cast forth like insipid salt"); cf. 1 Cor 6:9; Gal 5:21; Eph 5:5; Jas 1:22–2:25; Ignatius, *Ephesians* 16.

121. Q 12:33–34; 16:13; cf. 1 Tim 6:10; Jas 1:9–11; 2:1–7; 5:1–6; Polycarp, *Ep.* 4.

122. Q 16:16–17; cf. Rom 13:8–10; Gal 5:13–15; Jas 2:8–13; *Did.* 4:13.

123. Q 17:1–2; cf. Rom 14:13; 1 Cor 8:9, 13.

124. Q 17:6; cf. Romans 3–4; Galatians 3; Jas 1:6; 5:15.

125. Q 22:28–30; cf. Acts 14:22; 1 Pet 1:6–9; 3:14; 4:12–13; Rev 2:9–11.

126. See W. D. Davies, *The Setting of the Sermon on the Mount* (Cambridge: Cambridge University Press, 1963), pp. 366–86.

Many of the units in Q 12:33ff. were probably at one time connected by catchword, as one can see at a glance:

12:33–34  κλέπτης διορύσσουσιν
12:35–40  κλέπτης διορυχθῆναι
          κύριον οἰκοδεσπότης/οἶκον ὥρᾳ δοῦλοι
12:42–48  κύριος οἰκονόμος      ὥρᾳ δοῦλος
          διχοτομήσει
12:49–53  διχάσαι
          τὴν γῆν πῦρ
12:54–56  τῆς γῆς πυρράζει[127]
          διακρίνειν
12:58–59      κρίνετε/κριτῇ/κριτής    βληθήσῃ[128] εἰς
13:18–19                              ἔβαλεν    εἰς
          βασιλεία τοῦ θεοῦ
13:20–21  βασιλείαν τοῦ θεοῦ

13:23–24  θύρας
13:25–26  θύραν[129]

14:26     μου μαθητής
14:27     μου μαθητής

16:16     νόμος
16:17     νόμου

17:1–4    θάλασσαν    σου ἀκούσῃ
17:6      θαλάσσῃ     ὑπήκουσεν... ὑμῖν

Given that many of the units, but not all, are apparently ordered according to a catchword scheme,[130] one must wonder whether the person who first put together Q 12:33–22:30 expanded an already-existing col-

---

127. On this possible link see n. 111; also Claus-Peter März, "Zur Q-Rezeption in Lk 12,35–13,35 (14,1–24)," in *The Synoptic Gospels: Source Criticism and the New Literary Criticism*, ed. Camille Focant, BETL, vol. 110 (Leuven: Leuven University Press, 1993), pp. 191–92.

128. So Matthew. Luke has βαλεῖ.

129. πολλοί appears in Q 13:23–24 and 13:28–29 as well as in the Matthean versions of Q 13:25 (Mt 7:22) and 13:30 (Mt 20:16). This makes it possible that in Q there was a string of four sayings about "the many," about those excluded from the kingdom. Further, the subsequent parable of the great supper in its Lukan version has invitations being sent to "many" (Lk 14:16), and Mt 22:1–14 ends with yet another saying about "many."

130. There are some catchword links in Q's first four sections, but the difference is that there is always also a thematic connection; see, e.g., 10:21–24; 11:2–4, 9–13 (see pp. 14–15) and 24–26, 29–32, 33–36, 39–44 (see pp. 16–17). Note also 12:6ff.:

    12:6    ἐνώπιον         τοῦ θεοῦ
    12:9    ἐνώπιον τῶν ἀγγέλων τοῦ θεοῦ
    12:8    ὁ υἱὸς τοῦ ἀνθρώπων

lection whose compositional procedure of abutting units with common words he or she abandoned. However that may be, the artificial nature of the links helps explain why scholars have struggled to generalize about the content of 12:33ff. At the same time, the absence of a uniting theme — as opposed to a uniting function, exhortation — means that many of the units can function in splendid isolation, so that their meaning is not dictated by immediate context; they remain open to broad and even multiple interpretations.

## A THEORY OF Q's COMPOSITIONAL HISTORY

As already observed, Dieter Zeller associated Q with missionaries. He is hardly the only one to have done so. Ernst Käsemann thought that "the original *Sitz im Leben*" was in the early Jewish Christian mission: Q supplied "injunctions for its discipleship and provision for its mission."[131] H. Kasting proposed that Q was a memory aid for the missionaries of the early community.[132] Steck similarly claimed that Q was instruction for "Israelprediger," preachers to Israel.[133] So too Horst Robert Balz,[134] Paul Hoffmann,[135] and Joachim Gnilka.[136] Luise Schottroff and Wolfgang Stegemann have written that "the people behind the Sayings-source" were "wandering preachers."[137]

To these assertions it has been objected that parts of Q "are directed at a much broader group than simply missionaries."[138] This complaint is valid if one is thinking about all of Q. But if, with Zeller, we are instead thinking about an early stage of Q to which much material was later added, the objection loses its force.[139] There is much to be said for the view that at least Q 9:57–11:13 (our second section) plus 12:2–32

| | |
|---|---|
| 12:10 | τὸν υἱὸν τοῦ ἀνθρώπου |
| 12:10 | τὸ ἅγιον πνεῦμα |
| 12:12 | τὸ ἅγιον πνεῦμα |
| 12:11 | μὴ μεριμνήσητε |
| 12:22 | μὴ μεριμνᾶτε |

131. *New Testament Questions*, pp. 119–20. Cf. Werner Georg Kümmel, *Introduction to the New Testament*, rev. ed. (Nashville: Abingdon, 1975), p. 73.

132. *Die Anfänge der urchristlichen Mission*, BEvT, vol. 55 (Munich: Kaiser, 1969), p. 97.

133. *Israel*, p. 288.

134. *Methodische Probleme der neutestamentlichen Christologie*, WMANT, vol. 25 (Neukirchen-Vluyn: Neukirchener, 1967), pp. 167–71.

135. *Studien zur Theologie der Logienquelle*, 3d ed., NTAbh, vol. 8 (Münster: Aschendorff, 1982), pp. 333–34.

136. *Theologie des Neuen Testaments* (Freiburg: Herder, 1994), p. 134.

137. *Jesus and the Hope of the Poor* (Maryknoll, N.Y.: Orbis, 1986), p. 38.

138. Kloppenborg, *Formation*, p. 25. Cf. R. A. Piper, *Wisdom*, pp. 184–85.

139. Cf. Uro, *Sheep*, on the missionary discourse.

(our fourth section) preserves a source which originally functioned as guidance for itinerant missionaries.

Both Q 9:57–11:13 and 12:2–32 were, as we have seen, originally put together with missionaries in mind, and they are separated by Q 11:14–52, which exhibits altogether different interests. When one adds that the transitions from 11:13 to 11:14 and from 11:52 to 12:2 are anything but smooth, the thought arises that maybe 11:14–52, our third section, is an interpolation of the sort met with so frequently in the biblical literature, especially the prophets. If one removes 11:14–52 from Q, the result is the juxtaposition of three concurrent units (11:9–13; 12:2–12, 22–32) which (1) exhibit the very same structure (see pp. 23–25), and (2) in similar ways encourage itinerants to trust to the care of the heavenly Father (see pp. 14–15).

There is, then, reason to postulate that 11:14–52 is a large insertion which separates two sections that were once united in a single document. That is, one may tentatively reconstruct behind Q an old document of instruction and encouragement for missionaries which included at least the following:

- Call Stories (9:57–62)

- Instructions for Missionaries (10:2–16)

- Teaching on Eschatological Revelation (10:21–24)

- The Lord's Prayer (11:2–4)

- On Seeking and Finding (11:9–13)

- Counsel against Fear (12:2–12)

- Counsel against Anxiety (12:22–32)

Regarding the *Sitz im Leben* of this material, which I shall label $Q^1$, we should probably not envisage individual missionaries wandering about with copies to consult. For most early Christians, and so presumably most Christian missionaries, were probably illiterate.[140] So one conjectures that among the early missionaries there was a literate teacher who drew up for his or her own use a document — a looseleaf notebook such as Sato envisions? — to help instruct and encourage other missionaries.[141]

---

140. Cf. Harry Y. Gamble, *Books and Readers in the Early Church: A History of Early Christian Texts* (New Haven: Yale University Press, 1995), pp. 1–10.

141. William G. Doty once wondered whether Paul intended his letters to be summaries that would be expounded upon by their commissioned carriers: *Letters in Primitive Christianity* (Philadelphia: Fortress, 1972), pp. 46–47. One wonders whether, in like fashion, $Q^1$ was a sort of outline of instruction, a foundation for further teaching.

What then of the remainder of Q? First of all, the phenomenon of "updating" a document for a new audience is quite common in the biblical tradition. Hosea, for instance, reworks northern prophecies and applies them to Judah.[142] It seems a good guess that, in an analogous fashion, someone took up the missionary source behind Q 9:57–11:13 and 12:2–32 and, in order to make it pertinent to a new situation, added the various traditions in Q 12:33ff. Units 19–42 do not have itinerant missionaries in particular in view but rather disciples in the broader sense. So at this stage, which I shall call $Q^2$, the audience addressed by Jesus' words was enlarged. The earlier collection, with its narrow focus upon itinerants, was, through supplementation with common paraenetical materials, turned into a tract of general Christian exhortation. This creative reapplication of the Jesus tradition can be viewed as a large step toward the synoptics, wherein all sorts of sayings that must have been first addressed to disciples in the narrow sense, that is, missionary companions of Jesus, were made relevant to all church members.[143]

The hypothesis so far is that a document addressed to missionaries (Q 9:57–11:13 + 12:2–32, my sections 2 and 4) was expanded by the addition at the end of the general counsels in 12:33–22:30 (my section 5). This leaves the following units unaccounted for:

- 1. The Proclamation of John the Baptist (3:7–9, 16–17)

- 2. The Temptations of Jesus (4:1–13)

- 3. The Sermon on the Plain (6:20–49)

- 4. The Centurion's Servant (7:1–10)

- 5. John and Jesus (7:18–35)

- 11. Beelzebul (11:14–23)

- 12. Unclean Spirit (11:24–26)

- 13. Sign of Jonah (11:29–32)

- 14. Light (11:33–36)

- 15. Woes against Pharisees (11:39–44)

- 16. Woes against Lawyers (11:45–51 + 13:34–35 + 11:52)

---

142. E.g., 1:7; 2:2; 4:15; 5:5; 6:4, 11; 8:14; see Brevard S. Childs, *Introduction to the Old Testament as Scripture* (Philadelphia: Fortress, 1979), pp. 378–79.

143. Although his conclusions are very different from mine, Kloppenborg, "'Easter Faith' and Q," p. 75, still recognizes that "missionary instructions have in the course of redaction been enveloped and bracketed literarily by sayings which reflect a broader ecclesial *Sitz*."

My working hypothesis is that all of this material, which comprises my sections 1 and 3, was added at the third stage of Q's formation ($Q^3$). In other words, someone prefaced most of it to $Q^1$ + $Q^2$ (= 9:57–11:13 + 12:2–32 + 12:33–22:30) and then inserted Q 11:14–52 (section 3) between Q 11:13 and 12:2. Pictorially —

$$Q^1$$
$$9:57–11:13$$
$$12:2–32$$

| $Q^1$ | + | $Q^2$ |
|---|---|---|
| 9:57–11:13 | | 12:33–22:30 |
| 12:2–32 | | |

| $Q^3$ | + | $Q^1$ | + | $Q^3$ | + | $Q^1$ | + | $Q^2$ |
|---|---|---|---|---|---|---|---|---|
| 3:7–7:35 | | 9:57–11:13 | | 11:14–52 | | 12:2–32 | | 12:33–22:30 |

It says much for the postulated compositional history that the units left, after the missionary and paraenetic materials in the middle and end of Q have been set aside, are united by common themes, interests, and key expressions, and that these differentiate the units from the rest of Q. As already observed, Q 3:7–7:35 (section 1) and 11:14–51, 13:34–35, and 11:52 (section 3) are both filled with polemic against outsiders[144] and when taken together account for

- all of Q's references to Jesus' miracles[145]
- all of Q's sayings about "this generation"
- all of Q's statements about *sophia*
- all of Q's material on demonology
- all of Q's uses of πάτηρ to mean "ancestor"
- all of Q's citations of Scripture
- all of Q's addresses to outsiders as "you"
- all of Q's references to Jesus as the coming one
- Q's plainly Deuteronomistic declarations
- nine of Q's ten texts where a phrase or formula is repeated three times in near succession
- eight of nine of Q's uses of πονηρός.

144. Q's polemic has been clarified by Tuckett, *Q*, pp. 283–323: it is the response not to persecution but apathy.

145. Note also that in both 4:1–13 and 11:29 Jesus refuses to perform a miracle at another's behest.

$Q^3$ is characterized by a very rich Christology. $Q^1$ does record the saying about revelation being made through the Son (10:21–24), and throughout $Q^2$ Jesus is the coming Son of man. But there is no elaboration of christological topics in either $Q^1$ or $Q^2$. It is otherwise in $Q^3$. Q 3:16–17 prophesies the coming one who will baptize with fire. Q 4:1–13 presents Jesus as the embodiment of the new Israel who overcomes the temptations to which the old Israel succumbed. Q 6:20–23 and 7:18–23 make Jesus the anointed one of Isa 61:1. Q 7:1–10 shows him to be a miracle worker. So too 11:14–26, where Jesus' exorcisms in particular mark the presence of the kingdom of God. And 13:34–35 makes Jesus the eschatological figure whom the people will someday bless in the name of the Lord.

The interest in Christology naturally goes hand in hand with $Q^3$'s focus on John the Baptist.[146] If Jesus is the coming one (3:16–17), the Son of God (4:1–13), the Son of man (6:22), and the anointed one of Isaiah 61 (6:20–23; 7:18–23; cf. 13:34–35), then who is John the Baptist? The answer is that he is the eschatological prophet foretold in Mal 3:1, which Jewish and Christian tradition identified with Elijah (cf. Mal 4:5). Although the interest in John is congruent with the interest shown by $Q^3$ in outsiders, there does not seem to be any polemic against John.[147] Some indeed have found such in 7:28. In this view the phrase "but the least in the kingdom of God is greater than he" qualifies "among those born of women there has not arisen one greater than John" and puts John in his place. But 7:28 is not the product of the joining of two originally independent statements. Nor is the second half a correction of the first half. The two halves go together. John's greatness (the subject of Q 7:24–28a) is the foil for the surpassing greatness of the kingdom, which is the whole point. Those who are alive now and who submit themselves to the rule of God are the most fortunate of all, even more fortunate than the great John himself.

Yet another feature of $Q^3$ that distinguishes it from $Q^1$ and $Q^2$ is its apologetical interest in the Scriptures. It is precisely in $Q^3$, that is, in

---

146. Cf. Sato, *Q und Prophetie*, p. 389; he recognizes the unity of most of Q 3:7–7:28 and thinks that the section reflects an *Auseinandersetzung* with sympathizers of the Baptist. Jacobson, *First Gospel*, pp. 111–25, is unconvincing when he finds different and contradictory evaluations of John in this section. With Kloppenborg, we can assign Q 7:18–23, 24–28, and 31–35 to the same stage. See also Tuckett, *Q*, pp. 107–37, on the general coherence of Q's traditions about John.

147. Cf. Streeter, *Four Gospels*, pp. 291–92: Q "was composed at a time and place where the prestige of John was very considerable." He observes a contrast between Q, where John's testimony is valued because "all held John to be a prophet," and Mark, where "it is not John's personal prestige which is appealed to, but the fact that his coming at all was part of that 'programme,' so to speak, of events, anciently foretold and in the career of our Lord recently fulfilled, which was the main plank of early Christian apologetic." See further now Tuckett, *Q*, pp. 107–37. On p. 119 Tuckett writes that "there is little evidence to suggest that Q in its present form has any concern to downgrade John."

3:7–7:35 (section 1) plus 11:14–52 (section 3), that one finds the Scriptures which Q explicitly quotes. In every case the OT text agrees with the LXX. This strongly implies that at least $Q^3$ was originally composed in Greek. $Q^3$ is also distinctive in that it uses the Scriptures in every case to interpret Jesus in eschatological categories. In 4:1–13 the quotations from Deuteronomy, which Jesus himself cites, advance an Israel typology that teaches, among other things, that the last things are like the first. In 6:20–23 and 7:18–23, as already observed, Jesus is the anointed one of Isaiah 61. In 7:27 John the Baptist fulfills the eschatological oracle in Mal 3:1. And in Q 13:35, Ps 118:26 is applied to Jesus in his future coming. There is thus in $Q^3$ not only a developed concern to root the story of Jesus in Scripture but also a concern to use Scripture to give that story an eschatological interpretation.

Before proceeding any further two Q texts require comment. First, 10:13–15, in which Jesus utters woes against cities in Galilee, has struck almost everyone as being out of place.[148] It is indeed a rude interruption into $Q^1$'s missionary discourse. It does, however, cohere perfectly with the interests of $Q^3$. It has to do with outsiders, refers to miracles, uses the positive response of Gentiles as a foil for unbelief in Israel,[149] and furthers the theme of rejection — all otherwise features of $Q^3$. Moreover, οὐαί plus ὅτι, which introduces 10:13–15, appears otherwise in Q only in $Q^3$.[150] So it may well be that Q 10:13–15 is an interpolation from $Q^3$ and did not originally belong to $Q^1$'s missionary discourse. (If this analysis is correct it means that whereas $Q^1$ and $Q^2$ each has only one place name,[151] $Q^3$ shows a very strong geographical interest, for it refers to Jerusalem [4:9; 13:34], Capernaum [7:1; 10:15], Bethsaida [10:13], Chorazin [10:13], Tyre [10:13–14], Sidon [10:13–14], and Nineveh [11:30, 32]).

Q 22:28–30 also invites comment. Q, after the parable of the talents (Mt 25:14–30 = Lk 19:12–27), presumably had something close to this: "You are those who have followed me. I appoint you as my Father appointed me to reign in my kingdom; and you will sit on thrones, judging the twelve tribes of Israel" (Q 22:28–30; cf. Mt 19:28).[152] This is often

---

148. Cf. Kloppenborg, *Formation*, p. 194; Tuckett, *Q*, p. 184. For the reasons see Catchpole, "Mission Charge in Q," pp. 162–63; also *Quest*, pp. 171–76.

149. See Q 7:1–10 and 11:31–32. (I do not cite Q 13:28–29 because it is about Diaspora Jews; see pp. 176–91 herein.)

150. 11:42, 43, 44, 46, 47, 52.

151. Sodom is named in 10:12 and 17:29.

152. Matthew probably (1) affixed "in the παλιγγενεσίᾳ" (which has no Aramaic equivalent), (2) dropped "I appoint you," etc. (the clause is assumed by the free variant in Rev 3:21), (3) added "whenever the Son of man sits on the throne of his glory" (the clause enhances the parallelism between Jesus and his disciples and anticipates 25:31), (4) inserted καὶ αὐτοί (to adjust to the previous insertion), and (5) perhaps qualified "thrones" with "twelve" (again making for increased parallelism).

thought to have concluded Q, and there is no need to reject this judgment. This would mean, on the theory of Q's history put forward in this chapter, that Q 22:28–30 terminated $Q^1 + Q^2$ as well as $Q^1 + Q^2 + Q^3$. But one also wonders whether it earlier ended $Q^1$, that is, whether it originally followed Q 12:32 ("Fear not, little flock, for it is your Father's good pleasure to give you the kingdom")[153] as the appropriate climax of the encouragement to missionaries. In favor of this conjecture — it is nothing more — are (1) the close thematic link between Q 12:32 and 22:28–30, (2) the catchword connection between the two verses ("kingdom," "father"), (3) the rough transition from the parable of the pounds to Q 22:28–30, (4) the ease of explaining the displacement — the author of $Q^2$ simply wished to retain the happy ending of $Q^1$ — and (5) the creation of an appropriate and very satisfying *inclusio:* "those who have followed me" harks back to the very beginning of $Q^1$, to Q 9:57–62, where Jesus calls people to follow him (ἀκολουθέω appears three times in Q 9:57–62[154]).

The chart on the following page summarizes the results of this section by assigning each Q unit to its compositional stage.

## Parallels to the Proposed Compositional Theory

One might urge against a three-stage theory of Q's compositional history the simpler proposal that a single author was responsible for the entirety. That author began by making certain christological points with the aid of Scripture. Then his or her mind moved to the needs of itinerant missionaries. Finally he or she decided to round off the collection with paraenetical materials.

One cannot disprove this hypothesis. There are, however, reasons to suspect that it is not true. First, Q 11:14–52 (section 3) disrupts the thematic connection between Q 11:9–13 (section 2) and 12:2–32 (section 4) and separates three paragraphs which formally belong together. This seems the work of a later hand. Second, although it is of course possible that an author worked with one set of interests for a while and then passed on to others, one is struck by the large number of stylistic and thematic interests which differentiate Q's first and third sections (3:7–7:35 + 11:14–52) from Q's second and fourth sections (9:57–11:13 + 12:2–32) and which distinguish section five (12:33–22:30) from the other four. The differences are sufficiently significant and numerous to invite explanation in terms of multiple authors.

---

153. On this verse as part of Q see n. 91.

154. And elsewhere in Q only in Q 22:28–30 and 7:9; but this last does not bear the technical sense of discipleship.

|          Q¹          |          Q²          |          Q³          |
|----------------------|----------------------|----------------------|
|                      |                      | 3:7–9, 16–17         |
|                      |                      | 4:1–13               |
|                      |                      | 6:20–49              |
|                      |                      | 7:1–10               |
|                      |                      | 7:18–35              |
| 9:57–62              |                      |                      |
| 10:2–12              |                      |                      |
| (10:13–15) - - - - - - - - - - - - - - - - - - - - - ->?? |  |      |
| 10:16                |                      |                      |
| 10:21–24             |                      |                      |
| 11:2–4               |                      |                      |
| 11:9–13              |                      |                      |
|                      |                      | 11:14–23             |
|                      |                      | 11:24–26             |
|                      |                      | 11:29–32             |
|                      |                      | 11:33–36             |
|                      |                      | 11:39–44             |
|                      |                      | 11:45–51             |
|                      |                      | 13:34–35             |
|                      |                      | 11:52                |
| 12:2–12              |                      |                      |
| 12:22–32             |                      |                      |
|                      | 12:33–34             |                      |
|                      | 12:35–40             |                      |
|                      | 12:42–46 (+47–48?)   |                      |
|                      | 12:49–53             |                      |
|                      | 12:54–56             |                      |
|                      | 12:58–59             |                      |
|                      | 13:18–19             |                      |
|                      | 13:20–21             |                      |
|                      | 13:23–24             |                      |
|                      | 13:25–27             |                      |
|                      | 13:28–30             |                      |
|                      | 14:11                |                      |
|                      | 14:16–24             |                      |
|                      | 14:26                |                      |
|                      | 14:27                |                      |
|                      | 14:34–35             |                      |
|                      | 15:4–7               |                      |
|                      | 16:13                |                      |
|                      | 16:16–17             |                      |
|                      | 16:18                |                      |
|                      | 17:1–4               |                      |
|                      | 17:6                 |                      |
|                      | 17:22–37             |                      |
|                      | 19:12–26             |                      |
| ??<- - - - - - - - - - - - - - (22:28–30) | |           |

But there is also a third reason. My proposal concerning the formation of Q postulates that one finds the original Q document in the middle, and the major expansions at the beginning and end. Such a postulated history has parallels in other old Jewish documents.

There are numerous ancient texts that were enlarged by someone simply adding material at the end. Although the method seems rather mechanical to us, it was evidently common enough. Eccl 12:9–14; Jeremiah 52; Hos 13:16–14:8, 9; Amos 9:11–15; Mic 7:8–20; Mal 4:4, 5–6; *LAE* 51; and Mk 16:9–20 are all, according to many modern scholars, brief terminal addenda. Closer to what I envisage for Q is the book of Isaiah, which the experts tell us grew from front to back. Chapters 1–39 contain mostly pre-exilic material. Isaiah 40–55 was then added during the exile. Finally postexilic authors added chapters 56–66.[155] Again, it is a good assumption that someone took the court stories in the first half of Daniel and to them added the visions of the last half.[156] And Bel and the Dragon was added to the end still later. Zechariah seems to have gone through a similar evolution: to the oracles already gathered in 1–8 someone subsequently added chapters 9–14.[157] The second half of the *Ascension of Isaiah,* chapters 6–11, probably once circulated independently and were joined by someone to chapters 1–5.[158] *First Enoch* 106–108 contains late additions.[159] John 21, which follows the obvious conclusion in Jn 20:30–31, is roundly reckoned a secondary ending. The *History of the Rechabites* ends with five chapters (19–23) which, like John 21, appear to be late because they also follow an obvious conclusion (18:1–4). Proverbs may supply us with an example from the wisdom tradition: the latter chapters are often thought to contain a series of successive appendices.[160] Some collections of the Psalms likewise grew in this way, as is apparent from Psalms 150A–155, which do not appear in the MT but are known from the Dead Sea Scrolls and ancient versions.

Just as books were enlarged through additions placed at the end, they were also enlarged through additions placed at the beginning. Genesis 1

---

155. For a review of recent work on Isaiah see H. G. M. Williamson, *The Book Called Isaiah: Deutero-Isaiah's Role in Composition and Redaction* (Oxford: Clarendon, 1994), pp. 1–29.

156. André LaCocque, *Daniel in His Time* (Columbia: University of South Carolina Press, 1988), pp. 59–81.

157. Otto Eissfeldt, *The Old Testament: An Introduction* (New York: Harper & Row, 1965), pp. 434–40.

158. See J. M. T. Barton, in *The Apocryphal Old Testament*, ed. H. F. D. Sparks (Oxford: Clarendon, 1984), pp. 779–80.

159. See R. H. Charles, "The Martyrdom of Isaiah," in *Pseudeprigrapha*, vol. 2 of *The Apocrypha and Pseudepigrapha of the Old Testament in English*, ed. R. H. Charles (Oxford: Clarendon, 1913), pp. 168–70.

160. This is the standard view; but see Claus Westermann, *The Roots of Wisdom: The Oldest Proverbs of Israel and Other Peoples* (Louisville: Westminster/John Knox, 1994).

is generally reckoned a late preface from the P source.[161] Judg 1:1–2:5, the introduction to the entire book, is a secondary introduction.[162] Susanna is placed before Daniel in Theodotian as well as in the Old Latin, Coptic, and Arabic versions. Whoever put together Baruch introduced the already existing sources with Bar 1:1(3)-14.[163] To judge both by content and the Qumran manuscripts, 1QS 1–4 circulated apart from the rest of 1QS; that is, it is not the original introduction but was affixed only later.[164] Someone prefaced an epitome of Jason of Cyrene to the Maccabeans with two epistles to give us the work now known as 2 Maccabees.[165] Those who believe there was an extensive pre-Markan passion narrative may think of Mark as having supplied a long introduction to that. The *Apocalypse of Sedrach* commences with a sermon composed by a Christian, which was made the introduction to the entire book.[166] The situation may be similar in the *Apocalypse of Elijah*, although there the sermon in chapter 1 may have been Jewish (to which Christian insertions were later added).[167]

Given the frequency with which literature was expanded either by adding materials to the beginning or to the end, it is no surprise that some books were enlarged by both techniques — exactly what I postulate for Q. There is wide agreement, for instance, that Deut 4:44–28:68 was expanded through additions at the beginning and end.[168] And although the compositional history of Judges is highly complex and disputed, it does at least seem that a form of the book circulated without 1:1–2:5 and chapters 16 or 17–21.[169] 1QS appears to have grown out from the original core in columns 8 and 9.[170] The Greek Daniel has secondary stories at both beginning and end (Susanna, Bel and the Dragon). Second Peter is an updating of Jude: the pseudonymous writer surrounded Jude 4–16 (= 2 Peter 2) with words on holiness (2 Peter 1) and teaching on eschatology (2 Peter 3). Fourth Ezra was expanded first by the addition of 2 Esdr 1:1–2:48 at the beginning and then later

---

161. Gordon J. Wenham, *Genesis 1–15*, WBC, vol. 1 (Waco, Tex.: Word, 1987), p. xxxi.

162. See Childs, *Introduction*, pp. 256–59.

163. Eissfeldt, *Old Testament*, p. 594.

164. Jerome Murphy-O'Connor, "La Genèse littéraire de la règle de la communauté," *RB* 76 (1969): 528–49.

165. The original opening of the abridger appears in 2 Macc 2:19. Cf. Jonathan A. Goldstein, *II Maccabees*, AB, vol. 41A (Garden City, N.Y.: Doubleday, 1983), pp. 24–27.

166. Cf. S. Agourides, in *Apocalyptic Literature and Testaments*, vol. 1 of *The Old Testament Pseudepigrapha*, ed. James H. Charlesworth (Garden City, N.Y.: Doubleday, 1983), p. 606.

167. See O. S. Wintermute, in Charlesworth, *Apocalyptic Literature*, pp. 721–22.

168. Cf. Moshe Weinfeld, *Deuteronomy 1–11*, AB, vol. 5 (New York: Doubleday, 1991), pp. 9–13.

169. See Robert G. Boling, *Judges*, AB, vol. 6A (Garden City, N.Y.: Doubleday, 1975), pp. 29–38.

170. See Murphy-O'Connor, as in n. 164.

by the addition of 2 Esdr 15:1–16:78 at the end (both appear in the Latin but not in the Oriental versions). *Barnabas* surrounds the preexisting doctrine of the two ways (chapters 18–20) with chapters 1–17 and 21.[171] The *Didache* seems to have been put together by someone who interpolated into a Jewish text on the two ways[172] materials from the Jesus tradition near the beginning (1:3–6) and then, after reproducing that traditional text, added a church order and an apocalypse (chapters 7–16).[173] And the *Sophia of Jesus Christ* appears to have rewritten Nag Hammadi's *Eugnostos the Blessed*, or the source upon which this latter is based, and in so doing supplied new matter at the beginning and end.[174]

The three-stage compositional history of Q postulated herein holds that the Sayings Source was expanded not only by placing material at its beginning and end but also by the secondary intrusion of Q 11:14–52 into the old missionary section of $Q^1$. I need only remind readers that the phenomenon of large interpolations in the middle of documents is as well attested as expansions placed in front or after a book. Suffice it to mention, as relatively uncontroversial examples, the additions to Esther, Isaiah's apocalypse (24–27), the Song of the Three Young Men, the parables of Enoch, Jn 7:53–8:11, and *Apoc. Abr.* 19:3–13.[175]

It should be emphasized that while a relatively simple three-stage history is envisaged, I do not exclude the possibility that some verses or phrases I have assigned to $Q^1$ may be later additions, from the author of $Q^2$ or $Q^3$, or that some of the verses or phrases I have assigned to $Q^2$ might be from $Q^3$. In other words, I am not insisting that those responsible for $Q^2$ and $Q^3$ did nothing other than add large blocks. They are indeed likely to have retouched the text in smaller ways. For example, Q 10:2 and 10:7b just might, as Kloppenborg has urged, be addressed not to itinerants but to their supporters and so be secondary additions (from $Q^2$ or $Q^3$). I have myself urged that Q 10:13–15, which coheres so well with the judgment materials in $Q^3$, should probably be attributed not to $Q^1$ but to $Q^3$. In other cases, however, one can hardly be confident.

---

171. For a review of the discussion see Klaus Wengst, *Tradition und Theologie des Barnabasbriefes* (Berlin: de Gruyter, 1971), pp. 5–70.

172. Cf. 1QS 3:13–4:14 and *Barnabas* 18–20.

173. See Kurt Niederwimmer, *Die Didache* (Göttingen: Vandenhoeck & Ruprecht, 1989), pp. 64–78.

174. See Douglas M. Parrott, in *The Nag Hammadi Library*, ed. James M. Robinson (New York: Harper & Row, 1977), pp. 206–28.

175. 2 Cor 6:14–7:1 is more controversial, but it too appears to be an intrusion. On the whole subject of interpolations it is still profitable to read James Moffatt, *The Historical New Testament* (Edinburgh: T. & T. Clark, 1901), pp. 615–708.

## THE IMPLICATIONS FOR Q'S GENRE

There has been much recent discussion regarding Q's genre. The primary alternatives have been set forth by Kloppenborg and Sato. The former, following James Robinson, classifies Q as a sapiential sayings collection. The latter, on the other hand, thinks of it as prophetic. There is, of course, something to be said for each position. That both Kloppenborg and Sato can make good cases should foster reflection. Certainly no one would dream of including Proverbs among the latter prophets, or of classifying Jeremiah among Jewish wisdom literature. How can it be that Q looks like two things at once?

The first observation is that many ancient writings mix genres. What exactly is the book of Job? It seems to be several things at the same time.[176] The Qumran Pesharim are in some respects like rabbinic midrash and in other respects like apocalyptic literature.[177] The *Damascus Document* contains general exhortations and interpretations of the Bible in the context of a retrospective on Israel's history, but then ends with a list of statutes. Is anything else quite like it? Both Revelation and *2 Baruch* are apocalypses with long epistolary sections. The *Testaments of the Twelve Patriarchs* can be classified as apocalyptic literature or as a collection of testaments, but the sapiential features are strong. The Gospel of Matthew has been thought to be a sort of omnibus of genres: apocalypse (chapters 24–25), community rule (chapter 18), catechism (perhaps the Sermon on the Mount), cult aetiology (the institution of the Lord's Supper), and so forth.[178] Philostratus's *Vita Apolloni* supplies yet one more example of a book that is rather hard to classify because it seems to be more than one thing.[179] Might Q not be something similar?

The question is the more forceful when one takes into account Q's compositional history. Q[1], directed towards missionaries, was neither a collection of proverbs nor a collection of prophetic oracles. It was rather a book of directions and encouragement for itinerants. But, as readers of the works of Kloppenborg and Sato know, there are both sapiential and prophetic features in the sayings themselves. There is further resemblance with the rules of Qumran insofar as one finds concrete instruction for a special way of life.

---

176. Cf. Roland E. Murphy, *Wisdom Literature: Job, Proverbs, Ruth, Lamentations, Ecclesiastes, and Esther* (Grand Rapids: Eerdmans, 1981), pp. 16–20.

177. See Maurya P. Horgan, *Pesharim: Qumran Interpretations of Biblical Books*, CBQMS, vol. 8 (Washington: Catholic Biblical Association of America, 1979), pp. 249–59.

178. Davies and Allison, *Matthew*, vol. 1, pp. 2–3.

179. Cf. G. Petzke, *Die Traditionen über Apollonius von Tyana und das Neue Testament* (Leiden: E. J. Brill, 1970), p. 60.

Q² adds to this last resemblance because it contains a community rule (16:18, on divorce). But Q² even more contributes sapiential material (e.g., 12:58–59; 14:34–35; 16:13), and its focus upon paraenesis reminds us of the wisdom tradition. So Q² enhances Q's resemblance to wisdom literature. Q²'s paraenesis, however, is typically wedded to the prospect of eschatological judgment: one must watch, enter in by the narrow door, and take up a cross or risk being cast out of the kingdom. There is accordingly much in Q² to which Sato can appeal in his case for Q as a prophetic document.

Q²'s expansion of Q also reminds one of the testament genre.[180] Q² has parables in which Jesus speaks of his coming.[181] But Jesus cannot come without first going away. So the paraenesis of Q² is for the time during which the Lord is absent (cf. 12:45: "my master delays"). In other words, Jesus is telling his disciples what to do after he is gone — which is exactly what one finds in Jewish testaments, in which, as in Q, there is so often a mixture of sapiential and eschatological materials.

Sapiential and eschatological elements also typify Q³. But Q³ takes us a step towards what we may call biography. Not only are there lengthier stories about Jesus (Q 4:1–13; 7:1–10), but there is also a sense of chronology. Material is less connected by catchword or ordered by topic than it is put in a chronological sequence. John, who looks forward to the coming one, speaks first. Then the temptation narrative, which shows Jesus overcoming temptation and acting as he himself will demand that others act, legitimizes him. After overcoming trial he then delivers a sermon, after which he heals someone, after which he addresses the disciples of John the Baptist, after which he speaks to the crowds.

Hans Dieter Betz has called Q "a kind of collection of collections."[182] He is right, and it is Q's composite nature which makes it so difficult to categorize the work.[183] The authors of Q¹ and Q² and Q³ did not have exactly the same audience in view or the same goals in mind, so it is hardly surprising that Q cannot be easily categorized. One should be content to say that it, like other old Jewish books, mixes genres.

---

180. Ernst Bammel, "Das Ende von Q," in *Verborum Veritas: Festschrift für Gustav Stählin zum 70. Geburtstag*, ed. O. Böcher and K. Haacker (Wuppertal: Rolf Brockhaus, 1970), pp. 39–50, suggested that Q in its entirety might reflect the form of a testament. This goes too far, and Bammel has not won support for his position. But I confine my suggestion to Q², that is, the last portion of Q.

181. 12:36, 37, 38, 39, 43, 45, 46.

182. Hans Dieter Betz, "The Sermon on the Mount and Q," in Goehring et al., *Gospel Origins and Christian Beginnings*, p. 34.

183. Cf. John P. Meier, *Mentor, Message, and Miracles*, vol. 2 of *A Marginal Jew: Rethinking the Historical Jesus*, ABRL (New York: Doubleday, 1994), pp. 179–81. Walter Schmithals, *Einleitung in die drei ersten Evangelien* (Berlin: Walter de Gruyter, 1985), p. 229, speaks of Q's *Mischform*.

## THE IMPLICATIONS FOR Q'S PLACE
## WITHIN EARLY CHRISTIANITY

Much recent discussion of Q has focused on what it does not say or contain. Q does not have a passion narrative. It does not view Jesus' death as salvific. It does not tell us that Jesus rose from the dead. While all this could be explained by the simple proposition that Q contained mostly words of Jesus, who did not much speak, if at all, about his death and resurrection,[184] there are other possibilities. One is that Q reveals a community with "another 'kerygma' — one which had no special place for the death of Jesus and which, unlike Paul, did not view the vindication of Jesus through the apocalyptic metaphor of resurrection."[185]

The most vigorous statement of this position has come from Burton Mack. His tendency is to argue that if a particular belief did not appear in Q, that belief did not appear in the Q community, or, if known, was unimportant to its members. This allows him to propose that the people behind Q "did not think of Jesus as a messiah or the Christ.[186] They did not take his teachings as an indictment of Judaism. They did not regard his death as a divine, tragic, or saving event. And they did not imagine that he had been raised from the dead to rule over a transformed world."[187]

This is hazardous reasoning. At best these are possibilities, not established facts. What independent evidence is there for the existence of such people in the earliest church? Where are the Q people in Paul or Acts?[188] One could just as well contend, without fear of direct refutation, that the author of Pseudo-Philo thought all history after David theologically inconsequential because the *Liber Antiquitatum Biblicarum* ends with the death of Saul, or that those Dead Sea Scrolls which fail to name the

---

184. So Martin Hengel, "Kerygma oder Geschichte? Zur Problematik einer falschen Alternative in der Synoptikerforschung aufgezeigt an Hand einiger neuer Monographien," *ThQ* 101 (1971): 334.

185. Leif E. Vaage and John S. Kloppenborg, "Early Christianity, Q, and Jesus: The Sayings Gospel and Method in the Study of Christian Origins," in Kloppenborg and Vaage, *Early Christianity, Q, and Jesus*, p. 6.

186. But even in Mark, Jesus explicitly calls himself "Christ" only once, in 9:41. In Matthew he does this only in 23:10, in Luke not at all. (At Caesarea Philippi and at the trial before the Sanhedrin others bring up the title, and Jesus himself does not speak it.) Surely the failure of Jesus in Q to call himself "Christ" is a feature of the Jesus tradition in general, not some telling fact about the Q people in particular.

187. *Lost Gospel*, p. 4.

188. According to Koester, *Gospels*, p. 165, "it is evident now" that the opponents of 1 Corinthians 1–4, the opponents of the Gospel of John, the *Gospel of Thomas*, and the *Dialogue of the Savior* all had a theology "that had no relationship to the kerygma of the cross and resurrection." But the identity and theology of Paul's opponents in 1 Corinthians 1–4 is surely not "evident" (or else there would not be so much debate on the subject); and the other sources Koester cites are all on the way to Gnosticism and probably have nothing to tell us about the very earliest Christians.

Teacher of Righteousness were composed by sectarians who disputed his prominence, or — to carry things to absurdity — that the group responsible for producing the infancy traditions behind Matthew 1–2 was uninterested in the adult Jesus. Why treat Q as a sort of systematic theology, or as an exhaustive statement of someone's christological beliefs? According to Ben Witherington, "Arguing there was a Q community is rather like arguing there was a Proverbs community, or an Aboth community."[189] If by this he means that Q cannot be taken as the full expression of what a particular community was all about one must concur.[190] Certainly the people who used Q had important rituals and a community organization; but about them Q tells us nothing.[191] Leander Keck has wisely written, "Given the occasional character of the NT texts, as well as their several genres and functions, a text's christology is but a partial expression of what a writer thought about Jesus' identity and significance."[192]

The argument from silence can also be countered by examination of Q's compositional history, which gives no reason to think that any contributor to Q intended to state a full range of important theological convictions. A passion narrative would have no place at all in $Q^1$, a set of instructions to missionaries. Nor would it belong with the paraenetic material of $Q^2$.[193] The paraenetical sections of Paul's epistles do not ground themselves in the passion and resurrection of Jesus, nor do the synoptic passion narratives as we have them contain much paraenetical material. The interests of $Q^3$ — including John the Baptist (Q 3:7–9, 16–17), Jesus as miracle worker (Q 4:1–13; 7:1–10), paraenesis (Q 6:20–49), and polemic against Jewish exorcists, scribes, and Pharisees (Q 11:14–52) — also did not lend themselves to including sayings or narratives about Jesus' death or resurrection. This also explains the absence of the Lord's Supper.

There are other things to keep in mind. The arguments of Mack and like-minded others are indeed arguments from silence. There is in Q no explicit denial of the atoning value of Jesus' death, no explicit rejection of his resurrection from the dead, no explicit rejection of Jesus' status

---

189. *Sage*, p. 211.

190. Martin Hengel, "Aufgaben der neutestamentlich Wissenschaft," *NTS* 40 (1994): 336, seemingly doubts that we should speak of a Q community at all. Cf. J. Meier, *Mentor, Message, and Miracles*, p. 179: "I do not see any historical proof that one and only one community either created, gathered, or carried the Q tradition through early Christianity until it wound up in the Gospels of Matthew and Luke. On the contrary, the very fact that Q apparently existed and functioned for some time in each of these evangelists' churches before it was absorbed into their Gospels tells against this idea of one Q community."

191. Cf. Harold W. Attridge, "Reflections on Research into Q," in Kloppenborg and Vaage, *Early Christianity, Q, and Jesus*, pp. 228–29.

192. "Toward the Renewal of New Testament Christology," *NTS* 32 (1986): 371.

193. $Q^2$ does, however, contain the saying on bearing one's own cross, and this might presuppose the image of Jesus carrying his cross: Q 14:27.

as the Messiah. Moreover, Q was taken up by both Matthew and Luke, who held the beliefs that Mack denies to the Q community.[194] Paul also used Q, or at least traditions taken up into it.[195] But if Q was produced by a community with beliefs so opposed to those of Matthew and Luke, how did they come to embrace it as an authoritative source? One suspects that they accepted it because they thought it congruent with their own convictions. In any case we know that Q circulated among some people who treasured passion narratives.[196]

The truth is that while Q may omit some things, it does not include anything really at odds with what Matthew or Luke held dear. Almost everything in Q — John's testimony to Jesus, Jesus' victory over the devil and temptation, the imperative to love instead of taking revenge, the radical call to discipleship, the mission charge, the belief in Jesus as Son of God and revealer of the Father, Jesus' success as exorcist, polemic against Jewish leaders, and so forth — is found elsewhere in early Christian literature.[197] This makes the argument from silence hard to accept. If in the past we have tended to find too much unity in the early church, perhaps now, as citizens of a pluralistic and fragmented society, we are going too far the other way.[198] One may even wonder whether for its first decade or two early Christianity was not the complex thing modern scholars imagine but instead a very small movement with a few recognizable leaders who, as Paul tells us, agreed on quite a bit.

Has anyone noticed that the traditions unique to Matthew, the so-called M materials, have nothing to say about Jesus' death and resurrection? Should we then reconstruct another community which had no place for a kerygma like Paul's? But then this material is universally thought of as coming from Matthew's own community, which evidently used the Markan passion narrative. The same point can be made with regard to most of Luke's special traditions. And Mark, despite its focus on the death and vindication of Jesus, has very little to say about the atoning value of Jesus' death and resurrection. Even the Markan passion narrative contains only a single text (14:24) interpreting Jesus' death as salvific.[199] "When Matthew, Mark and Luke rarely present di-

---

194. Luz, *Matthew 1–7*, p. 83, has argued that the Q community became the Matthean community, or that the Matthean community was founded by "the wandering messengers and prophets of the Son of man of the Sayings Source."

195. See below, pp. 54–60.

196. And who also treasured miracle stories, another area in which Q comes up a bit short.

197. See further Meadors, *Jesus*, passim.

198. See Arland J. Hultgren, *The Rise of Normative Christianity* (Philadelphia: Fortress, 1994).

199. Cf. Philipp Vielhauer, *Geschichte der urchristlichen Literatur: Einleitung in das Neue Testament, die Apokryphen und die Apostolischen Väter* (Berlin: de Gruyter, 1975), pp. 326–28.

rect references to the atoning benefits of Jesus' death, should we find it remarkable that Q is silent on the same issue?"[200]

We know for a fact that Q's authors believed in much that Q does not tell us about. Q quotes from and alludes to the First Testament. It would be strange to suppose that the contributors to Q regarded as authoritative only those books which their work refers to. Does Q not presuppose the authority of the entire Tanak and quote only what furthers its immediate agenda? Q also fails to tell us that God created the world, or that God gave the commandments to Moses, or that God made a covenant with David — and yet we should still think that these were things the authors no doubt believed, indeed things that were for them foundational.

Also instructive is Q 7:18–23. Here Jesus says that through his ministry the blind see, the lame walk, lepers are cleansed, the deaf hear, and the dead are raised. Yet Q (unlike Mark) contains no account of such things. Surely we should imagine that Q presupposes knowledge of miracle stories that it does not recount. Otherwise Q 7:18–23 would do nothing but raise questions.

At all three of Q's stages, the contributors were no more interested in telling us everything they knew about Jesus, or everything they thought important about him, than they were in telling us everything they knew and thought important about God or the Bible. They took up traditions which furthered their immediate agendas, and nothing more. They had no intention of passing on every Christian tradition they had received, no intention of saying everything they believed about God or Jesus. One recalls that even Romans, which is as close to a systematic presentation as Paul ever got, fails to discuss the Lord's Supper or the foundational tradition of 1 Cor 15:3ff. No less instructive is the peculiar circumstance that the person who wrote the so-called Gospel of Luke also wrote another book, Acts, in which the teaching of Jesus plays a very small role.[201] Obviously even a very long book need not reflect the full range of an author's interests or address every matter of import to that author's community.

---

200. Edward P. Meadors, "The Orthodoxy of the 'Q' Sayings of Jesus," *TynBull* 43 (1992): 239. The entire article is quite instructive. He effectively demonstrates that there is little cause to suppose that Q interpreted Jesus' death solely in Deuteronomic terms. According to Jacobson, *First Gospel*, p. 74, "Jesus' death would be understood not as a salvific act but as evidence of Israel's continuing impenitence." But the two things could certainly have gone together.

201. See esp. C. K. Barrett, "Sayings of Jesus in the Acts of the Apostles," in *A cause de l'Évangile. Études sur les Synoptiques et les Actes offertes au P. Jacques Dupont*, LD, vol. 123 (Paris: Cerf, 1985), pp. 681–708.

## THE QUESTION OF ORIGINAL LANGUAGE

Kloppenborg, following and building upon Nigel Turner's work, has argued that "the balance of the linguistic evidence does not favor a translation hypothesis."[202] Q, that is, was not an Aramaic but a Greek document. Both Kloppenborg and Turner, however, examine Q in its entirety. What happens when one instead looks at the three stages Q appears to have gone through, at $Q^1$ and at $Q^1 + Q^2$ and at $Q^1 + Q^2 + Q^3$?

$Q^1 + Q^2 + Q^3$, which came to Matthew and Luke in Greek, was probably put together in Greek. The quotations from Deut 8:3; Ps 91:11; and Deut 6:16 in the temptation narrative are all derived from the LXX;[203] and the citation in 13:35 agrees exactly with Ps 117:26 (LXX). Moreover, as we shall see in chapter 2, although the Sermon on the Plain (hereafter SP) incorporates an old source (6:27–38) that gives every appearance of being translation Greek, it is surrounded by materials which do not give that appearance. This only reinforces the inference drawn from $Q^3$'s use of the LXX: the compiler of $Q^1 + Q^2 + Q^3$ was working in Greek.

We also have reason to believe that $Q^1 + Q^2$ was composed as a Greek text. For one thing, Q 17:27 (ἄχρι ἧς ἡμέρας εἰσῆλθεν Νῶε εἰς τὴν κιβωτόν) borrows the language of Gen 7:7 in the LXX (εἰσῆλθεν δὲ Νῶε...εἰς τὴν κιβωτόν).[204] For another, the strings of Greek catchwords strongly point to composition in Greek (although it remains theoretically possible that a translator sought to reproduce the catchword links in a Semitic document).

But what of $Q^1$? Here artificial Greek catchwords are not the key to the order of the pericopae, and there seems to be no trace of the LXX. It is true that $Q^1$ never explicitly cites the OT. But 9:58 probably alludes to Psalm 8,[205] and Q 12:8–9 probably depends upon Daniel 7,[206] and in neither case is the LXX as opposed to the MT clearly presupposed. Further, the allusions to 1 Kgs 19:19–21 in Q 9:57–62 and to Isa 14:13–15 in Q 10:15 show no significant contact with the LXX, and the same is true of the general references to "prophets and kings" in Q 10:23–24 and to Solomon in glory in 12:27.[207]

---

202. Kloppenborg, *Formation*, pp. 59–64; Nigel Turner, "Q in Recent Thought," *ExpT* 80 (1969): 324–28.

203. Q 4:4 = Deut 8:3 (LXX); Q 4:10–11 = Ps 90:11–12 (LXX); Q 4:12 = Deut 6:16 (LXX; here against the MT). Cf. also Q 6:21 with Isa 61:2 (LXX) and Q 7:27 with Exod 23:20 (LXX).

204. But this is suggestive, not demonstrative; for the translator of a Semitic text might naturally assimilate scriptural citations or allusions to the LXX.

205. See M. H. Smith, "No Place for a Son of Man," *Forum* 4, no. 4 (1988): 83–107.

206. See Davies and Allison, *Matthew*, vol. 2, pp. 214–15.

207. For the possibility that 11:3 alludes to Exod 16:4 (MT), see ibid., vol. 1, pp. 608–9.

Perhaps the most objective means of determining the original language of $Q^1$ is the work of Raymond A. Martin. In his book, *Syntax Criticism of the Synoptic Gospels*,[208] Martin has established that several syntactical features tend to occur at certain rates in both original Greek and translation Greek.[209] While his grid of seventeen criteria is hardly an infallible means for detecting whether or not a Semitic original lies behind a particular Greek document or portion of that document, it is at the least suggestive. Now Martin has examined most of the Q materials in their Matthean and Lukan wording, with this result for our purposes:

- 70 percent of the units assigned to $Q^1$ herein qualify as translation Greek in either Matthew or Luke[210]

- 58 percent of the units assigned to $Q^2$ herein qualify as translation Greek in either Matthew or Luke[211]

- 60 percent of the units assigned to $Q^3$ herein qualify as translation Greek in either Matthew or Luke[212]

Clearly Q in its entirety was strongly Semitic and must in part, and at all three stages, have drawn upon materials that were originally composed in Aramaic.[213] But it is precisely $Q^1$ that seems to have the strongest Semitic flavor. Moreover, only two passages in $Q^1$ do not, according to Martin's statistics, qualify as translation Greek, and both of these nonetheless contain Semitic features.[214] So although one can hardly

---

208. Lewiston, N.Y.: Edwin Mellen Press, 1987.

209. For full explanation see his earlier work, *Syntactical Evidence of Semitic Sources in Greek Documents* (Cambridge, Mass.: Society of Biblical Literature, 1974), pp. 1–86. Martin has responded to his critics in *Syntax Criticism of Johannine Literature, the Catholic Epistles, and the Gospel Passion Accounts* (Lewiston, N.Y.: Edwin Mellen Press, 1989), pp. 163–81.

210. From $Q^1$ Martin examines the following (TR = translation Greek): 9:57–60; 10:3–12 (TR); 10:21–24 (TR); 11:2–4 (TR); 11:9–13 (TR); 12:2–9 (TR); and 12:22–32. If Q 22:28–30 were included (see p. 35) the percentage would rise to 75.

211. Martin examines the following from $Q^2$: 12:33–34 (TR), 35–38 (TR), 39–40 (TR), 42–46 (TR), 54–56, 58–59; 14:15–24 (TR), 26–27; 15:4–7 (TR); 17:1–2 (TR); 19:11–27 (TR). He does not review 12:49–53; 13:18–21; 13:23–30; 14:11, 34–35; 16:13 (at least in isolation), 16, 17, 18; 17:3–4, 6, 22–37.

212. Martin examines the following from $Q^3$: 3:7–9; 4:1–13 (TR); 6:20–23, 27–31 (TR), 32–36 (TR), 37–38 + 39–40, 41–42 (TR), 43–45, 47–49; 7:1–10 (TR), 18–23 (TR), 24–35; 10:13–15 (TR); 11:14–23 (TR), 24–26, 29–32 (TR), 33–35 (TR), 39–44 (TR), 45–51 (TR); 13:34–35. He does not review 3:16–17. Note that three of these units come from the old source behind the SP.

213. Martin observes that Matthew and Luke are generally less Semitic than Mark in the triple tradition; that is, Matthew and Luke rewrote Markan material to make it less Semitic. This tendency implies that the Greek text of Q was even more Semitic than the Matthean and Lukan passages from the double tradition that Martin analyzes.

214. On 9:57–60 see the chart on p. 100 of *Syntax Criticism of the Synoptic Gospels*, and on 12:22–32, p. 101. For further reflections on the possible Aramaic background of the latter see Matthew Black, *An Aramaic Approach to the Gospels and Acts*, 3d ed. (Oxford: Clarendon, 1967), pp. 178–79.

prove the point, there is something to be said for the possibility that $Q^1$ was originally a collection of Aramaic traditions. If this possibility is accepted, whether $Q^1$ came to the author of $Q^2$ as a text already translated into Greek, or whether that author himself or herself translated $Q^1$, is a question we cannot answer.

## Q's DATE AND PLACE OF COMPOSITION

The latest possible date for $Q^1 + Q^2 + Q^3$ is dictated by its having been known to the authors of Luke and Matthew, who presumably wrote their Gospels during the 80s or 90s of the first common century.[215] So Q could not have been produced later than the 70s. If one held that Q influenced Mark[216] one could push the date back further, for Mark was known to both Matthew and Luke and was evidently written shortly before or after the Jewish War.[217] But those who have found Mark to be independent of Q probably have the better of the argument.[218]

Paul Hoffmann has recently submitted that Q may have been written as late as ca. 70 C.E.[219] Such a late date would be consistent with the identification of the Zacharias of Q 11:51 with the man in Josephus (*Bell.* 4:334–44) who was active during the Jewish War. But the reference is surely not to this figure but to 1 Chr 24:20–22.[220] The truth is that Q seems to exhibit "a total unawareness of the events of the war against Rome in 66–73 C.E."[221]

A much earlier date for Q would be established if one were able to place James in the 50s and also accept P. J. Hartin's case that the author of James knew Q.[222] But one can hardly be confident about the dating

---

215. For Matthew see Davies and Allison, *Matthew*, vol. 1, pp. 127–38. For Luke see Joseph A. Fitzmyer, *The Gospel according to Luke*, vol. 1 (New York: Doubleday, 1981), pp. 53–57.

216. See now esp. Harry T. Fleddermann, *Mark and Q: A Study of the Overlap Texts*, BETL, vol. 122 (Leuven: Leuven University Press, 1995).

217. Joel Marcus, "The Jewish War and the *Sitz im Leben* of Mark," *JBL* 113 (1992): 441–62.

218. See F. Neirynck's "Assessment" of Fleddermann in *Mark and Q*, pp. 263–303, and the important work of Laufen, *Die Doppelüberlieferungen*; also Joachim Schüling, *Studien zum Verhältnis von Logienquelle und Markusevangelium*, FB, vol. 65 (Würzburg: Echter, 1991); C. M. Tuckett, "Mark and Q," in Focant, *Synoptic Gospels*, pp. 149–75; and Ismo Dunderberg, "Q and the Beginning of Mark," *NTS* 41 (1995): 501–11.

219. "The Redaction of Q." Mack offers a similarly late date for his $Q^3$; cf. *Lost Gospel*, pp. 204–5.

220. Discussion in Davies and Allison, *Matthew*, vol. 3, pp. 318–19.

221. Catchpole, "The Question of Q," p. 36. On Hoffmann see further Tuckett, *Q*, pp. 357, 361–64.

222. *James and the Sayings of Q*, JSNTSS, vol. 47 (Sheffield: JSOT, 1991). Hartin finds parallels in James to texts in all three of Q's stages as postulated herein.

of James.[223] No less important, it is not clear that Hartin has made his case regarding James's relationship to Q.[224]

According to David Catchpole, Q 17:23–24 (from my $Q^2$) suggests "a timing for Q sometime after 45 C.E."[225] This warns against those who say, " 'Look there! or 'Look here!' Do not go, nor follow after them." His assumption appears to be that Q 17:23–24 adverts to the so-called sign prophets known from Josephus. Theudas, a self-proclaimed prophet who promised to divide the Jordan, was active during the procuratorship of Cuspius Fadus (44–48 C.E.; cf. *Ant.* 20:97–99; Acts 5:36). Within the procuratorship of Felix (52–60 C.E.) were the Egyptian prophet, who sought to make the walls of Jerusalem fall down (*Ant.* 20:169–72; *Bell.* 2:261–63; Acts 21:38), and certain unnamed men who enticed people into the desert with the promise of "marvels and signs" (*Ant.* 20:167–68; *Bell.* 2:259). Others with similar expectations were active during the time of Porcius Festus (60–62 C.E.; *Ant.* 20:188) and right before the destruction of the temple (*Bell.* 6:285–86).

Catchpole is probably right in holding that Q 17:23–24 reflects knowledge of certain Jewish sign prophets. At the same time, there is no reason to believe we have a record of all who said "Look here!" or "Look there!"[226] and we know of at least one who was active in 36 C.E. Josephus (*Ant.* 18:85–87) tells of a Samaritan who led a mob to Mount Gerizim, where he declared he would reveal the sacred vessels Moses had deposited. He evidently made himself out to be the prophet like Moses of Deut 18:15, 18.[227] So 17:23–24 hardly proves that Q was written after 45 C.E.

Gerd Theissen has also attempted to date Q.[228] His argument centers around the temptation narrative, in which Jesus is tempted to turn stones into bread, to jump off the temple, and to worship Satan. The first two temptations may be linked with Mark's temptation narrative, where Jesus is served by angels (Q cites Ps 91:11: "He will give his angels charge of you") and where it may be assumed that Jesus fasts (but this is not explicit). The temptation to worship Satan, however, has no parallel in Mk 1:12–13. Where did it come from?

---

223. Kümmel, *Introduction*, pp. 411–14, speaks for many when he dates James "toward the end of the first century."

224. I hope to review the evidence in a forthcoming publication. For additional discussion see Peter H. Davids, "James and Jesus," in *The Jesus Tradition Outside the Gospels*, vol. 5 of *Gospel Perspectives*, ed. David Wenham (Sheffield: JSOT, 1985), pp. 63–84.

225. "The Question of Q," p. 39.

226. Cf. N. H. Taylor, "Palestinian Christianity and the Caligula Crisis," *JSNT* 61 (1996): 111–13; 62 (1996): 25–26.

227. Marilyn F. Collins, "The Hidden Vessels in Samaritan Tradition," *JJS* 3 (1972): 97–116.

228. *The Gospels in Context: Social and Political History in the Synoptic Tradition* (Minneapolis: Fortress, 1991), pp. 203–34.

The third temptation involves three elements: prostration before the ruler of the earth, the claim to universal authority, and the conflict with the worship of God. For Theissen, these three elements have as their background events during the reign of Gaius Caligula. It was Caligula who introduced *proskynesis* into his ceremonies, and it was Caligula, the ruler of the world, who ordered an effigy of himself to be set up in the Jerusalem temple. The third temptation then reflects the tribulations of Caligula's reign, when Jews chose between idolatry and the God of Israel. Q must have been written later.

It is in favor of Theissen's thesis that, in Revelation 13, *proskynesis* before Satan should indeed be associated with emperor worship. Still, it is not at all necessary to refer to Caligula in explaining Q's final temptation. Q 4:1–13 is much indebted to exodus traditions. Deut 8:3 is quoted in Q 4:4, Deut 6:16 in Q 4:10, and Deut 6:13 in Q 4:8. Clearly we are working here with a haggadic tale much informed by Scripture. As Israel entered the desert to suffer a time of testing, so too Jesus, whose forty days is the typological equivalent of Israel's forty years of wandering. Just as Israel was tempted by hunger (Exod 16:2–8), was tempted to put God to the test (Exod 17:1–3; cf. Deut 6:16), and was tempted to idolatry (Exodus 32), so too Jesus. In this interpretation, the temptation to worship the devil is the typological correlate of the making of the golden calf: the people "worshiped" (Exod 32:8) a false god while Moses was on the mountain, and in like manner Jesus, on a mountain, was tempted to worship Satan. The parallel is not exact, but it is close enough. An idol was a god, and gods were demons, so idolatry was demon worship.[229] Further, idolatry was sometimes represented as the worship of Satan. Thus in 2 Kings 21 Manasseh commits idolatry, and *Asc. Isa.* 2:1–7 equates that idolatry with worship of Satan. Note also that, according to *Pirke R. Eliezer* 45, Samma'el was in the golden calf, and that when a temple of idols is destroyed in the *Testament of Job* 2–6, Satan soon appears to avenge himself. Moreover, the notion of Satan's universal rule need not be connected with Roman sovereignty. That Satan was "the ruler of this world" (Jn 12:31) or "the god of this world" (2 Cor 4:4) was a common conviction. In short, then, Theissen's attempt to associate Q's temptation with Caligula's reign is not necessary. His thesis cannot be disproved, but one hesitates to accept it because the haggadic imagination could have produced the third temptation if Caligula had never existed. The literary history does not require being correlated with an external political history. Once again, then, the date of Q has not been determined.

It is in truth impossible to have great confidence regarding the date when and place where $Q^1 + Q^2 + Q^3$ or its forerunners first saw the light

---

229. Cf. Deut 32:17; Ps 106:37–38; *1 Enoch* 99:7.

of day. Still, a few tentative conjectures may be offered. $Q^1$ probably appeared in the 30s, $Q^1 + Q^2 + Q^3$ in the 40s or 50s, and $Q^2$, necessarily, between them. Further, all three were probably produced in Palestine.

$Q^1$ presumably goes back to a very early time indeed. It primarily consists, as shall be observed below, of sayings generally reckoned to go back to Jesus, and it represents a relatively undeveloped stage of Christian reflection. It was plausibly composed not long after there came to be Christian missionaries who had themselves not known or worked with Jesus. It is these especially who would have benefited from the instructions for and encouragement of itinerants in $Q^1$. The early date and the absence of any hint of the Gentile mission are consistent with a Palestinian origin, and such an origin is also consistent with the possibility, already raised, that $Q^1$ was first composed in Aramaic. The only place named is Sodom (10:12).

Regarding the origin of $Q^1 + Q^2$, its concern with the delay of the *parousia* is of some help. Those who first proclaimed Jesus' resurrection did so in the conviction that it was only one act in an ongoing eschatological drama. With Jesus' suffering, death, and resurrection the last things had truly begun to arrive. So believers did not expect the world to keep on its old course for long, and it would only have taken perhaps a few months, at the most a few years, before believers began to wonder why God had not yet wrapped things up.[230] One nonetheless detects behind such passages as Q 12:35–48 not just intellectual questioning but the possibility of a disillusionment serious enough to lead to moral lapse — something altogether absent from $Q^1$. Surely this takes us a few years beyond $Q^1$, in which the near end is not argued for but confidently assumed.

As for the local origin of $Q^1 + Q^2$, three observations are congruent with a Palestinian provenance. First, Q 13:29, as argued in chapter 8, presupposes not only that Israel and its capital are the center of the world but seemingly addresses people who live in that center. Second, in Lk 12:54–56, which may preserve the text of Q,[231] clouds in the west are a sign of rain, and winds from the south herald heat. The perspective is Palestinian: clouds from the west are from the sea and so bring rain, winds from the south are from the desert and so presage heat. Third, the warning of Q 17:23 probably envisages sign prophets of the sort we learn of from Josephus, and they were, to our knowledge, concentrated in Palestine.[232]

---

230. See my work, *The End of the Ages Has Come* (Philadelphia: Fortress, 1985), pp. 142–62.

231. See above, n. 112.

232. See above, p. 50.

Turning finally to $Q^1 + Q^2 + Q^3$, its Palestinian origin seems as likely as the Palestinian origin of its predecessors.

(1) $Q^3$ refers to five places in Palestine: Capernaum (Q 7:2), Chorazin (Q 10:13), Bethsaida (Q 10:13), Capernaum (Q 10:15), and Jerusalem (Q 13:34). Tyre and Sidon are also mentioned, in Q 10:13; but these serve as illustrations from the Bible. $Q^3$ also contains the only two references in Q to the Jerusalem temple (4:1–13; 11:51).

(2) Even if the mission to Gentiles is evidenced (which is doubtful), the text does little or nothing to encourage that mission.[233] Moreover, "disparaging comments on both the self-interest with which they [Gentiles] show love (Q 6:32–33, with the original Q 'tax collectors… gentiles' preserved by Matthew) and also the materialistic preoccupation they have with food and clothing (Q 12:30a), with the common theme of needing to behave better than they do, are scarcely the natural reflex of a community which possesses, and is pleased to possess, mixed membership."[234] In other words, we are looking at a Jewish Christianity.

(3) One might guess, from the mention of Chorazin, Bethsaida, and Capernaum (10:13–15; cf. 7:1), all Galilean cities, that Q was the product of a group in the south with ties to the north, or, alternatively, of a group which had moved from the north to the south (cf. the presentation in Luke-Acts: the earliest followers of Jesus were Galileans who settled in the south). One might also, given that Chorazin, Bethsaida, and Capernaum are very near each other at the north end of the Sea of Galilee, and because those three cities are not otherwise significant in the biblical tradition, guess that Q was put together in that area.[235]

(4) Despite the views of some scholars, the treatment of John the Baptist in Q 3:7–7:35 is consistently positive. Q opens with John warning of the eschatological judgment of the one coming after him (Q 3:16–17). John is said by Jesus to be a prophet (Q 7:26). He is indeed more than a prophet, for he is the messenger of Mal 3:1 (Q 7:27). "Among those born of women no one is greater than John" (Q 7:28).[236] Q 7:33–34 even puts John and Jesus side by side: both were rejected by "this generation." The amount of material having to do with the Baptist shows a special interest in him and his ministry. At the same time, the absence of polemic against John reflects a situation in which Chris-

---

233. Cf. Catchpole, "The Question of Q," pp. 38–39; Paul D. Meyer, "The Gentile Mission in Q," *JBL* 89 (1970): 405–17; Tuckett, *Q*, pp. 393–404. The observation is all the stronger if one can assign Mt 10:5–6 and 10:23 to Q.

234. Catchpole, "The Question of Q," p. 38.

235. See further Jonathan L. Reed, "The Social Map of Q," in Kloppenborg, *Conflict and Invention*, pp. 17–36, and cf. I. Havener, *Q: The Sayings of Jesus* (Wilmington, Del.: Michael Glazier, 1987), pp. 42–45. W. Schenk, "Die Verwünschung der Küstenorte Q 10,13–15: Zur Funktion der Konkreten Ortsangaben und zur Lokalisierung von Q," in Focant, *Synoptic Gospels*, pp. 477–90, argues for an origin in Tiberias.

236. For the interpretation of this see p. 34.

tology did not need to denigrate the forerunner in order to exalt the coming one. One naturally thinks of people who had themselves known the Baptist and remembered him in a positive light.[237] Perhaps indeed the group to which Q[1] + Q[2] + Q[3] was first addressed included converts from the John the Baptist movement.[238]

What of the date of Q[1] + Q[2] + Q[3]? If Q's third stage incorporates a document produced in the 30s (Q[1]) as well as a second document dependent upon that first (Q[2]), and if it further shows no knowledge of the Jewish War, then a date in the 40s or 50s seems feasible.

## PAUL AND Q

The genuine letters of Paul show possible or probable contact with at least the following traditions that found their way into Q:

Appearing in Q[1]:
- a missionary discourse[239]

Appearing in Q[2]:
- something close to Q 12:35–48[240]
- Jesus' prohibition of divorce[241]
- Jesus' word about faith that can move mountains[242]
- the warning about scandalizing others[243]

---

237. Cf. Catchpole, "The Question of Q," p. 38.

238. Cf. Sato, *Q und Prophetie*, p. 189.

239. Cf. 1 Cor 9:4, 7, 13, 14 with Q 10:7; 1 Cor 10:27 with Q 10:8; 1 Thess 4:8 with Q 10:16. See chap. 4 below; also David Wenham, *Paul: Follower of Jesus or Founder of Christianity?* (Grand Rapids: Eerdmans, 1995), pp. 190–200.

240. 1 Thess 5:2-6 alludes not only to Jesus' parable of the thief (Q 12:39) but Paul's use of "night," "watch," and "drunk" in his elaboration of that allusion shows knowledge of the immediate Q context. See further C.-P. März, "Das Gleichnis vom Dieb. Überlegungen zur Verbindung von Lk 12,39 par Mt 24,43 und 1 Thess 5,2.4," in Van Segbroeck, *Four Gospels*, vol. 1, pp. 633–48. Cf. also perhaps 1 Cor 4:1-2 with Q 12:42. Richard Bauckham, "Synoptic Parousia Parables and the Apocalypse," *NTS* 23 (1977): 162–76, and "Synoptic Parousia Parables Again," *NTS* 29 (1983): 129–34, has shown that the parables of the watching servants, the thief, and the servant in authority circulated together and were often alluded to.

241. Cf. 1 Cor 7:10 with Q 16:18 and see David L. Dungan, *The Sayings of Jesus in the Churches of Paul* (Philadelphia: Fortress, 1971), pp. 81–131.

242. Cf. 1 Cor 13:2; but Paul is closer to the Markan version (Mk 11:23) rather than to Q 17:6.

243. Cf. Rom 14:13 and 1 Cor 8:13 with Q 17:1-2; see on this esp. M. Thompson, *Clothed with Christ: The Example and Teaching of Jesus in Romans 12:1–15:13*, JSNTSS, vol. 59 (Sheffield: JSOT, 1991), pp. 174–84. But the warning against scandalizing others was also part of the pre-Markan tradition behind Mk 9:42–50; see my article, "The Pauline Parallels and the Synoptic Gospels: The Pattern of the Parallels," *NTS* 28 (1982): 13–15, and Ernest Best, "Mark's Preservation of the Tradition," in *L'Évangile de Marc: Tradition et redaction*, ed. M. Sabbe, BETL, vol. 34 (Leuven: Leuven University Press, 1974), pp. 28–29. Indeed, it is not clear that Paul's transitive use of σκανδαλίζω

Appearing in $Q^3$:
- the SP's beatitudes[244]
- the central part of the SP[245]
- the saying strangely attributed to "the Wisdom of God"[246]

What, if anything, does all this tell us about Q? Paul seems to have known texts that belonged to all three of Q's major stages of development. But that alone is hardly enough to establish that the apostle, like Matthew and Luke later, already knew Q. For we have no reason to think that any of the materials just cited were known only in Q. Q, rather, adopted them from its tradition. To establish that Paul or his tradition drew upon Q, one needs to show his knowledge, not of traditions taken up into Q, but of something that appeared uniquely in Q. Can this be done?

(1) 1 Cor 4:8 has been thought to allude to Q 6:20–21, and 1 Cor 4:12–13 definitely makes use of traditions closely related to Q 6:27–38 — traditions Paul also uses elsewhere in his correspondence.[247] Now because there are good reasons to believe that the editor of $Q^3$ prefaced the beatitudes to Q 6:27ff.,[248] one might infer that Paul knew both the beatitudes and Jesus' teaching on nonretaliation because he knew Q.

---

had its parallel in Q; see Neirynck, "The Minor Agreements and Q," pp. 57–59; also Fleddermann, *Mark and Q*, pp. 159–63.

244. Cf. Q 6:20–21 ("Blessed are the poor, for yours is the kingdom [βασιλεία] of God. Blessed are the hungry, for you will be satisfied") with 1 Cor 4:8 ("Already your are filled! Already you are rich, and are reigning [ἐβασιλεύσατε]!"). Paul goes on to observe that the apostles, in contrast to the Corinthians, are "hungry" (4:11). Did some of the Corinthians promote a "realized eschatology" on the basis of the Jesus tradition, which Paul then found necessary to counter? Cf. the apparent use of the first beatitude in Jas 2:5: "Has not God chosen the poor in the world to be rich in faith and to be heirs of the kingdom that he has promised to those who love him?"

245. Cf. Rom 2:1 with Q 6:37; Rom 12:14 with Q 6:28; Rom 12:17 with Q 6:27–36; Rom 12:21 with Q 6:27–36; 1 Cor 4:12 with Q 6:28; and 1 Thess 5:15 with Q 6:27–36. For discussion see chap. 2 below, pp. 86–87, and David Wenham, "Paul's Use of the Jesus Tradition: Three Samples," in *The Jesus Tradition Outside the Gospels*, vol. 5 of *Gospel Perspectives*, ed. David Wenham (Sheffield: JSOT Press, 1985), pp. 15–24 — although Wenham's contention that the form of 5:38–48 is more original than the form of Lk 6:27–36 is problematic.

246. Cf. 1 Thess 2:14–16 with Lk 11:47–51 and Mt 23:29–36, and see below, pp. 57–60. There is not sufficient reason to suppose that Paul knew Q's parable of the two builders (cf. 1 Cor 3:10–12 and see Allison, "Pauline Parallels," pp. 6–7) or the Great Thanksgiving (although see James M. Robinson, "Kerygma and History," in *Trajectories through Early Christianity*, ed. James M. Robinson and Helmut Koester [Philadelphia: Fortress, 1971], p. 42, and Peter Richardson, "The Thunderbolt in Q and the Wise Man in Corinth," in *From Jesus to Paul: Studies in Honor of F. W. Beare*, ed. Peter Richardson and J. C. Hurd [Waterloo: Wilfred Laurier, 1984], pp. 91–111) or the logion about the unforgivable sin (cf. 1 Cor 12:3 with Q 12:10). For useful discussion and additional literature see C. M. Tuckett, "1 Corinthians and Q," *JBL* 102 (1983): 607–19; also Frans Neirynck, "Paul and the Sayings of Jesus," in *Evangelica II: 1982–1991*, BETL, vol. 99 (Leuven: Leuven University Press, 1991), pp. 511–67.

247. See nn. 244 and 245.

248. See below, p. 80.

This remains a possibility, especially given the correlation in sequence between Q 6:20ff. and 1 Cor 4:8ff.: in Q the beatitudes preface Jesus' teaching on nonretaliation, whereas in 1 Corinthians 4 the proposed allusion to the former leads into clear allusions to the latter. Nevertheless, one cannot be sure that 1 Cor 4:8 is in fact an allusion to the Jesus tradition; and even if it were thought to be so, why could Paul not have known both the beatitudes and something close to Q 6:27–38 as separate oral traditions? That Q united the two does not entail that they were already united for Paul.

(2) As argued in chapter 4 herein, 1 Corinthians 9 not only cites a line which appeared in Q's missionary discourse (1 Cor 9:14 = Q 10:7b: the worker is worthy of reward) but also alludes to the broader Q context for that line. This implies that Paul knew some version of the missionary discourse. It indeed implies that he knew a form of that discourse that was closer to Q 10:2–16 than to Mk 6:6–13, which has nothing corresponding to Q 10:7. This matters so much because David Catchpole has recently attributed Q 10:16, to which there is a very close parallel in 1 Thess 4:8 (cf. Gal 4:14), to Q redaction.[249] So here one might find evidence that Paul knew not just the tradition behind Q's missionary discourse but Q's missionary discourse itself, with its redactional addition.

Unfortunately, however, Catchpole's case for the redactional character of Q 10:16 is inconclusive. That the saying is "self-sufficient" and "could" have survived apart from a missionary discourse (so Catchpole) hardly proves that it did. Catchpole himself observes that there is "an essential harmony" between Q 10:16 and the rest of Q's missionary discourse. Q 10:16 "overlaps with the explicit 'sending' saying, Q 10:3, at the start of the pre-Q tradition," and "it matches the recurrent pattern of positive and negative elements in Q 10:5–7, 8–12." Further, Q 10:16 "in and of itself demands a Sitz im Leben in mission."[250] These observations tell against Catchpole's claim. A redactional origin for Q 10:16 has not been established.[251]

But even if one were, against the evidence, to attribute 10:16 to Q redaction, and even if one were to go on from there and suspect that Paul knew Q's missionary discourse, we would still encounter the difficulty that Q 10:2–16 appeared already in Q¹. We could conclude with assurance nothing more than that Q¹ had come into existence before Paul wrote 1 Thessalonians and 1 Corinthians, that is, before 50 C.E. — something already known on other grounds. And we would still not know anything more about the date of the later expansions of Q.

---

249. "Mission Charge in Q," pp. 147–74. Cf. his *Quest*, pp. 178–79.
250. "Mission Charge in Q," p. 166.
251. Cf. Frans Neirynck, "Literary Criticism: Old and New," in Focant, *Synoptic Gospels*, pp. 31–32.

(3) 1 Thess 2:14–16 holds more promise of helping us to date Q in its entirety. It reads as follows:

> For you, brothers and sisters, became imitators of the churches of God in Christ Jesus that are in Judea, for you suffered the same things from your own compatriots as they did from the Judeans,[252] [15]who killed both the Lord Jesus and the prophets, and drove us out; they displease God and oppose everyone [16]by hindering us from speaking to the Gentiles so that they may be saved. Thus they have constantly been filling up the measure of their sins; but God's wrath is just about to overtake them at last.[253]

In Luke 11:47–51 we find this:

> [47]Woe to you! For you build the tombs of the prophets whom your fathers killed. [48]So you are witnesses and approve of the deeds of your fathers; for they killed them, and you build their tombs. [49]Therefore also the Wisdom of God said, "I will send them prophets and apostles, some of whom they will kill and persecute," [50]so the blood of all the prophets shed since the foundation of the world may be required of this generation, [51]from the blood of Abel to the blood of Zechariah, who perished between the altar and the sanctuary. Yes, I tell you, it will be charged against this generation.

The parallel in Matthew, 23:29–32, 34–36, has this:

> [29]Woe to you, scribes and Pharisees, hypocrites! For you build the tombs of the prophets and adorn the monuments of the righteous, [30]saying, "If we had lived in the days of our fathers, we would not have taken part with them in shedding the blood of the prophets." [31]Thus you witness against yourselves, that you are sons of those who murdered the prophets. [32]Fill up, then, the measure of your fathers. [33]You serpents, you brood of vipers, how are you to escape being sentenced to hell? [34]Therefore I send you prophets and wise men and scribes, some of whom you will kill and crucify, and some you will scourge in your synagogues and persecute from town to town, that upon you may come all the righteous blood shed on the earth, from the blood of innocent Abel to the blood of Zechariah the son of Barachiah, whom you murdered between the sanctuary and the altar. [36]Truly I say to you, all this will come upon this generation.

---

252. Although τῶν Ἰουδαίων is usually translated "the Jews," the presence of ἐν τῇ Ἰουδαίᾳ just a few words earlier tells us that the meaning is "Judeans." See Jon A. Weatherly, "The Authenticity of 1 Thessalonians 2.13–16: Additional Evidence," *JSNT* 42 (1991): 84–86.

253. For the aorist ἔφθασεν signifying imminent arrival see ibid., pp. 90–91.

The Pauline text and the Q tradition both associate the killing (ἀποκτείνω: Lk 11:49; Mt 23:31, 34; 1 Thess 2:15) of the prophets (προφῆται: Lk 11:49–50; Mt 23:31, 34; 1 Thess 2:15) with the persecution ([ἐκ]διώκω: Lk 11:49; Mt 23:34; 1 Thess 2:15) of the faithful and refer to a fulfilling ([ἀνα]πληρόω; Mt 23:32; 1 Thess 2:16) of a measure of sins which will bring down eschatological judgment upon the present generation (Mt 23:32, 35–36; Lk 11:50; 1 Thess 2:16). Carol Schlueter has further made the intriguing observation that Paul and perhaps Matthew have a "diminishing hierarchy." Paul speaks first of the Lord Jesus, then of prophets, then of "us." Matthew refers first to prophets, then to wise men, then to scribes.[254] At the least both Paul and Matthew mention three individuals or groups upon which persecution has fallen.

These parallels of vocabulary, thought, and even structure, being "concentrated in such a short span of verses," are "too unusual to be coincidental."[255] Moreover, ἐκδιώκω and ἐναντίος (in 1 Thess 2:15) are Pauline *hapax legomena*, and both the harsh view of Israel and the use of ἀποκτείνω in connection with Jesus' death are unusual for Paul. Here, then, we have tradition (cf. also Acts 7:51–52).[256]

How exactly do we explain the relationship between 1 Thess 2:15–16 and Q 11:47–51? Michael Goulder's hypothesis that Matthew knew and used Paul's epistles, in this case 1 Thessalonians, would explain the overlap.[257] But his view is, rightly, not shared by others: it remains idiosyncratic.[258] One could also urge that 1 Thess 2:15–16 is a post-Pauline interpolation dependent upon Matthew. That 1 Thess 2:15–16 is not Pauline is the view of Birger Pearson,[259] and he is not alone in his judgment.[260] Still, the authenticity of 1 Thess 2:15–16 has gained strong support from recent studies,[261] and it shall be assumed in what follows.

---

254. Carol J. Schlueter, *Filling Up the Measure: Polemical Hyperbole and 1 Thessalonians 2.14–16*, JSNTSS, vol. 98 (Sheffield: JSOT, 1994), p. 72.

255. David E. Garland, *The Intention of Matthew 23*, NovTSup, vol. 52 (Leiden: E. J. Brill, 1979), p. 169. Contrast B. Rigaux, *Les Épîtres aux Thessaloniciens*, ÉB (Paris: J. Gabalda, 1956), pp. 445–46, and C. M. Tuckett, "Synoptic Tradition in 1 Thessalonians," in *The Thessalonian Correspondence*, ed. R. F. Collins, BETL, vol. 87 (Leuven: Leuven University Press, 1990), pp. 165–67.

256. See further R. Schippers, "The Pre-synoptic Tradition in 1 Thessalonians 2:13–16," *NovT* 9 (1967): 223–34.

257. *Midrash and Lection in Matthew* (London: SPCK, 1974), p. 165.

258. One wonders, for example, whether Paul's epistles had been collected before Matthew wrote.

259. "1 Thess 2.13–16: A Deutero-Pauline Interpolation," *HTR* 64 (1971): 79–94.

260. See esp. Daryl Schmidt, "1 Thess. 2:13–16: Linguistic Evidence for an Interpolation," *JBL* 102 (1983): 269–79.

261. Karl P. Donfried, "Paul and Judaism. 1 Thess 2:13–16 as a Test Case," *Int* 38 (1984): 242–53; J. W. Simpson, "The Problems Posed by 1 Thessalonians 2:15–16 and a Solution," *HBT* 12 (1990); Weatherly, "1 Thessalonians 2.13–16," pp. 79–98; and Schlueter, *Filling Up the Measure*.

Two choices remain. Either Paul and Q independently adopted a (Jewish?) tradition which was not originally attributed to Jesus, or in 1 Thess 2:15–16 Paul made use of the Jesus tradition.[262] In favor of the former possibility, Lk 11:49 introduces its quotation with a reference to "the Wisdom of God." Bultmann and others have understandably taken the words so introduced as a quotation from some lost text.[263] Maybe they are right. Perhaps then both Paul and Q made use of that lost text.

The problem with this is that while Q's quotation of "the Wisdom of God" cannot extend beyond Q 11:49–51, Paul's overlap with Q does. That is, the links between Paul and Q are not confined to 1 Thess 2:15–16 and Q 11:49–51 but reach beyond the oracle of doom to include material both before and after. Thus Paul's remark that "they have constantly been filling up the measure of their sins" is close to Mt 23:32: "Fill up, then, the measure of your fathers." There is admittedly no precise Lukan parallel. But nothing else points to Matthean redaction,[264] Luke has elsewhere in this section abbreviated,[265] and the logic of Mt 23:32 is implicit in Q: the addressees will finish what their fathers began; that is, they too will murder the righteous (Jesus and his followers). One supposes that Luke substituted "so you are witnesses and consent to the deeds of your fathers" (Lk 11:48) for the more obscure "fill up then the measure of your fathers."[266] If so, then Paul in 1 Thess 2:15–16 alludes not only to the oracle in Q 11:49–51 but to the unit that preceded it in Q.

Beyond this, 1 Thess 2:14 speaks about unbelieving Jews in Judea. The commentators on 1 Thessalonians regularly discuss why Paul, in writing the Thessalonians, should speak in particular about opposition in Judea.[267] But the verses following Q 11:47–51, that is, Q 13:34–35,[268] make it plain that the oracle of doom is addressed specifically to people in Jerusalem.[269]

---

262. So J. B. Orchard, "Thessalonians and the Synoptic Gospels," *Bib* 19 (1938): 20–23, and David Wenham, *The Rediscovery of Jesus' Eschatological Discourse* (Sheffield: JSOT, 1984), pp. 351–52.

263. *History of the Synoptic Tradition* (New York: Harper & Row, 1963), p. 114.

264. πληρόω is usually used of scriptural fulfillment in Matthew; μέτρον (Mt: 2; Mk: 1; Lk: 2); πατήρ (not of God) (Mt: 19; Mk: 13; Lk: 37).

265. E.g., Lk 11:47 ("Woe to you, for you build the memorials of the prophets, but your fathers killed them") as opposed to Mt 23:30 is so compressed as to be unintelligible: memorializing prophets does not constitute consent to their murders.

266. So also D. Wenham, *Paul*, pp. 336–37.

267. See, e.g., Rigaux, *Épîtres aux Thessaloniciens*, pp. 442–43.

268. On the order of Q here see below, pp. 201–2.

269. Note also that Q 13:34–35 refers to judgment upon Jerusalem in particular, and that some commentators on 1 Thess 2:14–16 have found there a reference to some calamity in Jerusalem (e.g., the massacre of C.E. 49; see Josephus, *Bell.* 2:223–27). Cf. Orchard, "Thessalonians," p. 22.

Where does this then leave us? There are good reasons for thinking that it was precisely the editor of Q³ who inserted the oracle of doom into a traditional list of woes and so gave 11:49–51 its Q context. First, that someone interpolated Q 11:49–51 into an already existing series of woes seems highly probable.[270] Q 11:49–51, which is joined to 11:47–48 by catchword,[271] destroys the balance between the first three woes and the last three woes and renders the final woe, 11:52, anticlimactic.[272] Second, the editor of Q³ had a special interest in the themes of rejection and persecution.[273] Third, 11:50 speaks of "this generation." This expression, which enlarges the polemic of a passage that is otherwise confined to Jewish leaders, is important for Q³ but altogether absent from Q¹ and Q². Fourth, 11:49 refers to *sophia*. This word is likewise important for Q³ but altogether absent from Q¹ and Q². Indeed, both of the large chiastic sections of Q³ approach their conclusions with climactic sayings about *sophia*.[274] This seems to be literary design.

The argument comes down to this: *if* 1 Thessalonians shows knowledge not just of Q 11:49–51 but also of its Q context, and *if* Q 11:49–51 was given that context by the editor of Q³, it follows that Q¹ + Q² + Q³ was in circulation before 1 Thessalonians was written (50 C.E.). Neither condition can be established beyond reasonable doubt. But both conditions seem to be very good possibilities. So one is sorely tempted to go beyond the conclusion, drawn above on other grounds, that Q passed through its third stage sometime in the 40s or 50s and to be more specific: Q¹ + Q² + Q³ saw the light of the day in the 40s.

## JESUS AND Q

Q¹ can be reckoned a very good source for the historical Jesus. It is fair to say that most scholars have thought that the hard sayings about discipleship tell us about Jesus,[275] that the missionary discourse rests upon

---

270. Cf. Kloppenborg, *Formation*, pp. 143–47. Contrast Tuckett, *Q*, pp. 166–68.

271. προφητῶν, 11:47/προφήτας, 11:49/ἀπέκτειναν, 11:48/ἀποκτενοῦσιν, 11:49.

272. Some, however, would argue that Q 11:52 was moved to its final place by Luke. Cf. Tuckett, *Q*, pp. 166–67.

273. See 6:22–23 (whose last few words may be Q redaction; see p. 101); 6:27–30; 7:31–35; 10:13–15; 11:14–23, 29–32.

274. 7:35 concludes Q's opening section, and 11:49 introduces the final words of Q's third section. I owe this observation to Ron Piper in personal conversation.

275. Harry T. Fleddermann, "The Demands of Discipleship: Matt 8,19–22 par. Luke 9,57–62," in Van Segbroeck, *Four Gospels*, vol. 1, pp. 541–61, endeavors to show that Q 9:57–62 "probably does not give us access to the historical Jesus." Certainly the scenes are "ideal" — what scene in the synoptics is not? — and based upon biblical models; but these are not good reasons to question that historical encounters or authentic sayings lie behind the text. Hengel, *Charismatic Leader*, remains persuasive.

dominical directions,[276] that Jesus uttered the sayings about revelation in
Q 10:21 and 10:23–24,[277] that the Lord's Prayer comes from the pre-
Easter period,[278] that the passage about asking, seeking, and knocking
is authentic,[279] that the consolation in Q 12:2–12 includes sayings of
Jesus,[280] and that it was he who first asked others to consider the ravens
and the lilies.[281]

Q[1] remains such a good source for the historical Jesus not only because it remembered his words, adding little to them, but because it
preserved something of their original context. Most of the sayings in
Q[1] were no doubt spoken by Jesus not to the public at large but to
the small circle that shared his missionary task. But Q[1] was addressed
to a very similar group, that is, itinerant Christian missionaries. So Q[1]
uses the sayings of Jesus in the same manner in which they were first
used, namely, to instruct and console missionaries. This explains why
the signs of post-Easter alteration are minimal: at this point the pre- and
post-Easter settings were pretty much the same, and manipulation of
the tradition was not much needed. Similar contexts permitted similar
content.

If Q[1] tells us as much or more about Jesus than about anyone else,
this is less clear with Q[2]. Here indeed there are sayings — many sayings — which we should assign to Jesus, for example, the sayings about

---

276. Laufen, *Die Doppelüberlieferungen*, pp. 260–68. It is quite possible in fact that
Q 10:3–12 was originally composed as a unit (cf. Catchpole, "Mission Charge in Q") by
Jesus himself. In any case it was expanded by placing secondary material at the beginning
and end — Q 10:2, (Mt 10:5–6?), (Mt 10:23?), 13–15, 16.

277. On Q 10:23–24 see Bultmann, *History*, p. 126.

278. See J. Meier, *Mentor, Message, and Miracles*, p. 294. Even though he does not
attribute it to Jesus, John Dominic Crossan, *Jesus: The Life of a Mediterranean Jewish
Peasant* (San Francisco: Harper Collins, 1991), p. 294, says that the Lord's Prayer "must
be a very early summary of themes and emphases from Jesus' own lifetime." His skepticism is excessive, as is that of Hal Taussig, "The Lord's Prayer," *Forum* 4, no. 4 (1988):
25–42. Taussig regards the Lord's Prayer as a collection "from prior, unassociated prayer
sentences."

279. See n. 108 and cf. Luz, *Matthew 1–7*, p. 421.

280. See Luz, *Matthäus*, vol. 2, pp. 123–24. On Q 12:4–5 in particular see Schlosser,
"Le Logion," pp. 621–32.

281. See Hoffmann, "Jesu 'Verbot des Sorgens' und seine Nachgeschichte in der synoptischen Überlieferung," in his *Tradition und Situation*, pp. 107–34. Contrast Michael G.
Steinhauser, "The Sayings on Anxieties," *Forum* 6, no. 1 (1990): 67–79. In general one
fails to see complex tradition histories behind any of the units in Q[1]. This is not to say
that none of them is composite. Q 12:2–12 seems obviously to be so. But sometimes
our hypothetical tradition histories which envisage multiple authors and the passage of
time may be off the mark. Should we not more often entertain the possibility of a single author putting together diverse materials at one time? Cf. Leif E. Vaage, "Composite
Texts and Oral Myths: The Case of the 'Sermon' (6:20b–49)," in Lull, *1989 Seminar Papers*, pp. 428–32 (although I do not share his conclusions about the SP). For instance,
the author of Q[1] could very well have started with Q 12:4–5 + 6–7a, which he prefaced
with 12:2–3. He or she could then have gone on to add 12:7b + 8–9, then 12:10 (which
would not be so difficult in an Aramaic text with a nontitular use of "son of man"), then
12:11–12.

divorce, stumbling, and forgiveness. There is nonetheless a significant shift in setting. $Q^2$ often exhibits what Joachim Jeremias, in his work on the parables, famously cataloged as signs of secondary expansion in an ecclesiastical context.[282] Although genuine parables may lie beneath them, 12:35–40 and 12:42–48 are now, for instance, allegories of Christian experience. The master of Q 12:35–38 is the coming Son of man. The servants and stewards of the parables are Christian believers. The delay of the master (Q 12:45) is the delay of the *parousia*. Again, the warnings of Q 13:23–30, which probably originated as polemic, are now hortatory; and the condemnation of adultery in Q 16:18 has become a community regulation. So the new *Sitz im Leben* of $Q^2$, that of a settled Christian community, led to a reworking of the Jesus tradition and gave it new sense. Here then we feel the presence of the church almost or as much as the presence of Jesus.

The same is to be said of $Q^3$. Although it probably preserves authentic words of John — in Q 3:7–17 — and of Jesus — especially in the old source behind the SP — $Q^3$ is equally stamped by Christian interests. It is concerned not only with Christian fraternal relations[283] but also with religious rivals, namely, non-Christian exorcists, Pharisees, and scribes. It reflects an apologetic need to cite Scripture. And it aims to understand and interpret aright Jesus' miracles as well as the significance of John the Baptist. It is no surprise that these and other interests have led not only to a theologically meaningful arrangement and expansion of traditional materials but also to the *creation* of entirely new materials.[284] Here the temptation narrative offers proof enough. It is in no way the record of a historical event but a Christian interpretation of Jesus as the new Israel, the Son obedient to Torah. With $Q^3$ then we see the first long strides toward the uninhibited creativity that later led to, among other things, the canonical infancy stories and, still later, the apocryphal gospels. At the same time, it is $Q^3$ we must thank for the preservation of the SP, which is not only one of Western literature's great religious treasures, but also on the whole a reliable indicator of the sort of uncompromising moral demands Jesus characteristically made.

## Papias Once Again

One last question remains. Eusebius, a fourth-century bishop of Caesarea, attributed to Papias, a first-century bishop of Hierapolis, the

---

282. *The Parables of Jesus*, 2d rev. ed. (New York: Charles Scribner's Sons, 1972), pp. 23–114.

283. Q 6:39–45; see pp. 91–94 herein.

284. This is seemingly not the case in either $Q^1$ or $Q^2$. In those sections secondary additions are either minimal expansions of or commentary upon already existing traditions.

following quotation: "Now Matthew made an ordered arrangement of the oracles (τὰ λόγια) in the Hebrew [or: Aramaic] language, and each one translated [or: interpreted] it as he was able" (*H.E.* 3:39). These words cannot readily be referred to the Gospel of Matthew, which was neither written by an eyewitness nor composed in Hebrew or Aramaic. Because of this some scholars have proposed that Papias's words — which were presumably already tradition for Papias[285] — originally referred not to our canonical Matthew but to an Aramaic sayings source used by Matthew (so Schleiermacher); and the conjecture has therefore been attached to Q.[286] I should like to raise the possibility — it can be no more — that it should be attached to $Q^1$.[287]

Recent scholars have by and large declined to connect Papias's testimony with Q. Their reasons include the following: (1) the Sayings Source used by Matthew and Luke was a Greek document; (2) Papias's remarks are about Matthew, not a source of Matthew;[288] (3) proposed translation variants and translation mistakes are too uncertain to prove that the Greek Q was a translation,[289] and a Semitizing style does not demand a literary formulation in Aramaic.[290]

The first point, however, does not really pertain to the thesis put forward herein, which holds that only a portion of Q ($Q^1$) might be thought of as an Aramaic text. The second and third stages of Q, al-

---

285. T. W. Manson, "The Gospel of Matthew," in *Studies in the Gospels and Epistles*, ed. M. Black (Edinburgh: T. & T. Clark, 1962), p. 70, observes that, according to Eusebius, (1) Papias "set great store by what was handed down from earlier times and took great pains to acquire such traditional material wherever he could," and (2) Papias was "a man of exceedingly small intelligence," and would Eusebius "have troubled to quote the private opinion of a man, whom he rated as low as this, on a point of such importance?"

286. See esp. Manson, *Sayings*, pp. 15–20; idem, "Gospel of Matthew," pp. 68–104. Cf. Streeter, *Four Gospels*, p. 501, and those listed by Kümmel, *Introduction*, p. 120 n. 69; also now Koester, *Gospels*, pp. 166–67.

287. Cf. David Hill, *The Gospel of Matthew*, New Century Bible (London: Oliphants, 1977), pp. 22–27, who follows Manson but thinks of "a Matthean (apostolic) collection of sayings (which formed *part* of Q)" (italics his). André Tuilier, "La Didachè et le problème synoptique," in *The Didache in Context: Essays on Its Text, History, and Transmission*, ed. Clayton N. Jefford, NovTSup, vol. 77 (Leiden: E. J. Brill, 1995), pp. 110–30, similarly argues that Papias's tradition refers to one of Q's sources.

288. J. Kürzinger, *Papias von Hierapolis und die Evangelien des Neuen Testaments* (Regensburg: F. Pustet, 1983), argues that the Greek words I have translated "in the Hebrew [or: Aramaic] language" should instead be rendered "in Jewish style." But this possible if unlikely rendering comes up against the fact that patristic tradition (in likely dependence upon Papias) is unanimous in speaking about a "Hebrew Gospel." Cf. Matthew Black, "The Use of Rhetorical Terminology in Papias on Mark and Matthew," *JSNT* 37 (1989): 33–34. Moreover, surely Ἑβραΐδι διαλέκτῳ + ἑρμηνεύω suggests translation from one language to another.

289. See esp. Kloppenborg, *Formation*, pp. 54–59. But for a response to this see Black, "Aramaic Dimension," pp. 33–41.

290. See further Heinz O. Guenther, "The Sayings Gospel Q and the Quest for Aramaic Sources: Rethinking Christian Origins," in Kloppenborg and Vaage, *Early Christianity, Q, and Jesus*, pp. 41–76. He seemingly believes that the Jesus tradition was at all stages Greek.

though they incorporate many sayings and even some large sections that were first formulated in Aramaic (e.g., Q 6:27–38), were composed as Greek texts.

The second objection is no more challenging. If Papias was, as seems likely, himself passing on tradition, it is easy to imagine that, after the disappearance of Q and the appearance of Matthew, something thought to be true of the former might be thought true of the latter. Jewish tradition often expanded and remade books such as Isaiah and yet kept the original prophet's name for the entire collection. In like manner it seems plausible enough that if a person of apostolic reputation had been the author of $Q^1$ (in this case Matthew), his name might have remained associated with its subsequent expansions, including the Gospel of Matthew.[291]

The third objection against associating Papias and Q is more forceful. One can never *prove* that the Semitisms of a Greek text require that it be translation Greek.[292] But if there can be no proof, there remain cases in which the style is such that it is sensible to postulate a Semitic original. Raymond Martin's statistical tables seem to tell us that this generalization applies to $Q^1$. It could be the Greek rendering of a Semitic document.

If the usual arguments against linking Papias's testimony to Q are not decisive against a link with $Q^1$, what is to be said in favor of such a link? There are several correlations between $Q^1$ and Papias's words:

1. Papias's tradition concerns λόγια, a word whose first meaning is "oracle."[293] $Q^1$ was a collection of sayings of Jesus.

2. Papias's tradition is about a certain Matthew, a man the NT tells us received missionary instructions from Jesus and was sent out as a missionary.[294] $Q^1$ was written for missionaries.

3. The NT also assumes that this Matthew was a Palestinian Jew (see esp. Mt 9:9). $Q^1$ was written in Palestine.

4. Papias said the oracles were written "in the Hebrew [or: Aramaic] language." $Q^1$, as we have seen, could be translation Greek according to the statistical tables of Raymond Martin.

---

291. Cf. Koester, *Gospels*, p. 167: "The Gospel of Matthew may have taken over the name of its author from the source of sayings that was used in its composition."

292. Cf. esp. E. P. Sanders, *The Tendencies of the Synoptic Tradition*, SNTSMS (Cambridge: Cambridge University Press, 1969).

293. Even if Papias used the term with broader meaning, this cannot determine what his tradition might have meant. See the still-useful review of T. W. Manson, "Gospel of Matthew."

294. Mt 10:3; Mk 3:18; Lk 6:15; cf. Acts 1:13.

5. Eusebius understood Papias's words to concern the Gospel of Matthew. $Q^1$ eventually became part of the Gospel we know as Matthew.

6. Anything written by a companion of Jesus might be a good source for Jesus' teaching. $Q^1$ is a good source for the teaching of the historical Jesus.

The correlations between $Q^1$ and Papias's words about Matthew do not, I freely confess, prove anything. What is offered here is only a very tentative hypothesis, the hypothesis that Matthew the missionary gathered the traditions of Jesus which lie behind a document now embedded within one of the First Gospel's sources. Obviously one is here in the realm of speculation. But the conjecture does have the virtue of coming to terms with Papias. For it makes explicable what is otherwise a very baffling tradition. Although it is quite common today to dismiss Papias (as well all patristic tradition about the NT documents), one should wonder whether we can disregard his words without offering some explanation for them. Were they just conjured out of thin air?[295]

One is unhappy at returning an affirmative answer. Not only must Papias's tradition be dated "to the time shortly before or after 100,"[296] that is, perhaps only a decade after the composition of Matthew; but the apostle Matthew seems to have been a figure of little stature in early Christianity. He was not a man about whom stories and legends soon developed, or at least there is no evidence of such. In first-century sources he is not much more than a name on some lists. Later Christian tales about him exhibit nothing but constant flux and delightful variety: there were seemingly no firm traditions about the man.[297] So one hesitates to characterize Papias's tradition as nothing but unfounded legend. Why a legend about this particular apostle? One may well agree with Donald Hagner: "Papias had reasons for saying what he did, and although our knowledge now is partial, we do well to attempt to make sense of his testimony."[298]

---

295. Luz, *Matthew 1–7*, pp. 93–94, supposes that Mt 9:9 and 10:3 were the source of the tradition. The argument is unclear. What is there in 9:9 and 10:3 that could have suggested to somebody that Matthew was the author? There are many named believers in the First Gospel. Why was the First Gospel attributed to Matthew rather than, say, Andrew, or James, or Philip, or Bartholomew? Certainly Peter, James, and John play more significant roles than Matthew.

296. Ibid., p. 94. Papias's dates should perhaps be pushed back to the very beginning of the second century; see Gundry, *Matthew*, pp. 610–11; U. H. J. Körtner, *Papias von Hierapolis: Ein Beitrag zur Geschichte des frühen Christentums*, FRLANT, vol. 133 (Göttingen: Vandenhoeck & Ruprecht, 1983); R. W. Yarbrough, "The Date of Papias: A Reassessment," *JETS* 26 (1983): 181–91.

297. Davies and Allison, *Matthew*, vol. 1, p. 146 n. 125. Strangely enough, Matthew shows up on the list of five disciples of Jesus in *b. Sanh.* 43a.

298. Donald A. Hagner, *Matthew 1–13*, WBC, vol. 33A (Dallas: Word, 1993), p. xlvi.

One final point. Canonical Matthew may itself hint at a connection
with Matthew. Mk 2:14 tells of Jesus passing along and seeing "Levi the
(son) of Alphaeus sitting at the toll booth." In Mt 9:9 Levi has become
"Matthew." This change has puzzled commentators, who have offered
several different explanations for it.[299] But one recurrent suggestion is
that while Levi was of no interest to the author of the First Gospel and
his readers, they did know of a Matthew who was somehow connected
with their traditions.[300] This guess seems as good as any.

---

Koester, *Gospels*, pp. 166–67, speculates that *Gos. Thom.* 13 may reflect belief in
Matthew's authorship of a sayings collection.

299. See Davies and Allison, *Matthew*, vol. 2, pp. 98–99.

300. So, e.g., Alexander Sand, *Das Evangelium nach Matthäus*, RNT (Regensburg:
Friedrich Pustet, 1984), p. 196. Cf. Joachim Gnilka, *Das Matthäusevangelium*, vol. 1.,
HTKNT (Freiburg: Herder, 1986), p. 331.

# – 2 –

# THE SERMON ON THE PLAIN,
# Q 6:20–49

## Its Plan and Its Sources

Most modern commentators and exegetes have believed that Matthew's Sermon on the Mount (hereafter SM) was composed by the author of the rest of the First Gospel. The First Evangelist, drawing upon Q, Mark, and his distinctive tradition, M, forged the discourse in accordance with his own aims and interests. This is the common opinion not only about Matthew 5–7 but also about all the major Matthean discourses, which are usually taken to be five in number: the SM, chapters 5–7; the missionary discourse, chapter 10; the parable discourse, chapter 13; the community discourse, chapter 18; and the eschatological discourse, chapters 24–25.[1] On the other hand, the Lukan counterpart to the SM, namely, Lk 6:20–49, the so-called Sermon on the Plain (hereafter SP), is widely regarded as a speech which Luke only lightly retouched: it brings us very close to Q.

## THE THEORY OF HANS DIETER BETZ

This is not, however, the only view that has been taken of the matter. Hans Dieter Betz has recently outlined six different ways one might explain the relationship between the SM and SP.[2] (1) The majority opinion already introduced holds that the SP is close to Q while the SM is a Matthean expansion. (2) The SM is close to Q, the SP a Lukan abridgement.[3] (3) Both the SM and SP are different redactional elaborations of

---

1. Matthew 23 is also sometimes considered a major discourse, or part of 24–25; but it is better understood as the conclusion of the long narrative section, 19:1–23:39.

2. For what follows see *The Sermon on the Mount: A Commentary on the Sermon on the Mount, Including the Sermon on the Plain (Matthew 5:3–7:27 and Luke 6:20–49)*, Hermeneia (Minneapolis: Fortress, 1995), pp. 42–43.

3. Ibid., p. 43: "No scholar today holds this option, and rightly so." Supporters of the Griesbach hypothesis, however, would presumably regard the SP as to great extent a condensation of the SM.

the same Q sermon. (4) The SM is mostly from $Q^{mt}$, the SP mostly from $Q^{lk}$. That is, the original Q sermon passed through different developments in different recensions of Q before coming to our evangelists.[4] (5) The SM and SP were formulated independently of each other as separate sayings collections and were later joined to Q.[5] (6) The SM and SP were formulated independently of each other as separate sayings collections and were never joined to Q.

In evaluating these options Betz observes that the SM and SP have similar settings and are followed by the story of the centurion's servant or son (Mt 8:5–13 = Lk 7:1–10), so Q must have contained a sermon. This eliminates option six. He also contends that the SM cannot be explained as a redactional expansion of SP, nor can the SP be explained as a redactional reduction of the SM — whether we are thinking of Matthew or Luke or their predecessors. This eliminates options one and two. Betz then goes on to urge as "most likely" the conclusion that "Matthew as well as Luke found the SM and the SP, respectively, in their recensions of Q ($Q^{Matt}$ and $Q^{Luke}$)."[6] But this is not solution four, for "the SM and the SP constitute textual units composed by presynoptic redactors and then included in different versions or recensions of Q."[7] This appears to be solution five. The SM had its genesis in a Jewish-Christian community which was in dialogue with Hellenistic philosophy and can be considered an epitome. The SP is also an epitome, but it was drawn up for minds "formed by Greek ideas."[8]

Betz first put forward his opinion in a series of essays that were gathered and published in both English and German in 1985.[9] But his thesis is now above all both argued and presupposed in his massive and learned Hermeneia commentary on the SM and SP. If he is correct,[10] then those who regard Lk 6:20–49 as a large block of Q material which was thoroughly rewritten and turned by Matthew into the SM are in error.

---

4. Cf. the comments of Ulrich Luz, "Sermon on the Mount/Plain: Reconstruction of $Q^{Mt}$ and $Q^{Lk}$," in *Society of Biblical Literature 1983 Seminar Papers*, ed. Kent Harold Richards (Chico, Calif.: Scholars Press, 1983), p. 473: "The collection Q existed in different versions," and regarding the SM or SP in particular: "This is one of the most-used texts in early Christianity. Here the difference between the versions of Q becomes particularly visible."

5. Betz, *Sermon on the Mount*, p. 43: "The analogy for this option would be the inclusion of smaller collections of sayings into larger ones as we find it in Greek and Latin *gnomologia*."

6. Ibid., p. 44.

7. Ibid., p. 42. At the beginning one must ask how two different but related sermons came to be placed in apparently the same place in two different recensions of Q.

8. Ibid., p. 44.

9. *Essays on the Sermon on the Mount* (Philadelphia: Fortress, 1985); also published as *Studien zur Bergpredigt* (Tübingen: J. C. B. Mohr [Paul Siebeck], 1985).

10. Koester, *Gospels*, pp. 133, 167–68, is favorably inclined. (In a footnote he refers to Betz's intention to "put forward a conclusive presentation of his arguments" in his Hermeneia commentary.)

Further, Betz's hypothesis, if I understand it aright, requires that we re-think our conceptions of Q. One may doubt, however, that Betz has made his case, and it is the purpose of this chapter to argue that a more con-ventional view of things does a much better job of explaining the data.[11]

The first serious difficulty with Betz's rejection of the Matthean origin of the SM is that one of its key compositional techniques, the arrange-ment of materials into triads, must be regarded as typical of Matthew. Betz recognizes that Mt 5:17–7:12 (which follows what he calls the *Ex-ordium*, 5:3–16) concerns three main topics: the interpretation of the Torah (5:17–48), the practice of the cult (6:1–18), and the conduct of daily life (6:19–7:12).[12] He also sees that the central section (6:1–18) offers "specific instruction concerning three most important cultic acts," namely, almsgiving, prayer, and fasting. But this hardly exhausts the SM's triads. There are nine (= 3 x 3) sentences which open with μακάριοι (5:3–12), and the six paragraphs that follow the general state-ment about Torah in 5:17–20[13] obviously divide themselves into two sets of three.[14] One can see this at a glance:

You have heard that it was said to those of old
(full formula)...
  But I say to you (ὅτι πᾶς ὁ)...
You have heard that it was said...
  But I say to you (ὅτι πᾶς ὁ)...
It was said...
  But I say to you (ὅτι πᾶς ὁ)...

Again (πάλιν),

You have heard that it was said to those of old
(full formula)...
  But I say to you + imperative...

---

11. Some of the following arguments were originally made in my "A New Approach to the Sermon on the Mount," *ETL* 54 (1988): 205–14. Although the article is cited in the bibliography to Betz's commentary, he nowhere responds. He unfortunately further fails to reply to most of the criticisms from Charles E. Carlston, "Betz on the Sermon on the Mount: A Critique," *CBQ* 50 (1988): 47–57. He does, on pp. 72–73 of *The Sermon on the Mount*, answer Graham N. Stanton, *A Gospel for a New People: Studies in Matthew* (Edinburgh: T. & T. Clark, 1992), pp. 307–25, who doubts that the SM is an epitome akin to Epicurus's *Kyriai Doxai;* but Stanton's other critical observations about Betz go unanswered.

12. Cf. my own analysis, "The Structure of the Sermon on the Mount," *JBL* 106 (1987): 423–45: Jesus and the Torah (5:17–48), the Christian cult (6:1–18), social issues (6:19–7:12); also Davies, *Setting*, pp. 305–7.

13. 5:21–26, 27–30, 31–32, 33–37, 38–42, 43–48.

14. Cf. William R. Farmer, "The Sermon on the Mount: A Form-Critical and Redac-tional Analysis of Matt 5:1–7:29," in *Society of Biblical Literature 1986 Seminar Papers,* ed. Kent Harold Richards (Atlanta: Scholars Press, 1986), pp. 68–69; Robert A. Guelich, *The Sermon on the Mount: A Foundation for Understanding* (Waco, Tex.: Word, 1982), pp. 177, 211–12. Betz himself recognizes this: *Sermon on the Mount,* p. 263.

You have heard that it was said...
    But I say to you + imperative...
You have heard that it was said...
    But I say to you + imperative...

There are almost certainly additional triads,[15] but these are perhaps less obvious, and the point is in any event made.

What of the rest of Matthew? At the very beginning, following 1:1 (which names three people), we find a genealogy which explicitly divides itself into three series of fourteen: from Abraham to David, from David to the captivity, from the captivity to the Christ (1:2–17). Then, in the infancy narrative, the angel of the Lord appears and speaks to Joseph in a dream three times (1:20; 2:13, 19–20). To move forward, in chapters 8–9 the material is arranged in three sets of three.[16] Visually:

| 8:1–22 | 8:1–4 a healing | |
| | 8:5–13 a healing | + summary report and words of Jesus, 8:16–22 |
| | 8:14–15 a healing | |
| 8:23–9:17 | 8:23–27 a nature miracle | |
| | 8:28–34 two demoniacs cured | + call of Levi and words of Jesus, 9:9–17 |
| | 9:1–8 a healing | |
| 9:18–38 | 9:18–26 two people healed | |
| | 9:27–31 two people healed | + summary report and words of Jesus, 9:35–38 |
| | 9:32–34 a healing | |

Chapter 13 shows us yet again the same technique. The author, after largely following Mark up to 13:23, thereafter goes his own way; as

---

15. See my article, "Structure."
16. Cf. John P. Meier, *Matthew* (Wilmington, Del.: Michael Glazier, 1980), pp. 79–80.

soon as he does, there are three consecutive parables of growth: 13:24–30, 31–32, 33. Each is introduced by this formula:

13:24 ἄλλην παραβολὴν παρέθηκεν αὐτοῖς λέγων +
ὡμοιώθη ἡ βασιλεία τῶν οὐρανῶν + dative
13:31 ἄλλην παραβολὴν παρέθηκεν αὐτοῖς λέγων +
ὁμοία ἐστὶν ἡ βασιλεία τῶν οὐρανῶν + dative
13:33 ἄλλην παραβολὴν ἐλάλησεν αὐτοῖς +
ὁμοία ἐστὶν ἡ βασιλεία τῶν οὐρανῶν + dative

Mt 13:24–33 is then followed by a small, interpretative discourse, 13:34–43, which is in turn succeeded by a second triadic grouping: 13:44, 45–46, 47–50. Once again there are three parables, and once again they all have similar introductions:

13:44 ὁμοία ἐστὶν ἡ βασιλεία τῶν οὐρανῶν + dative
13:45 πάλιν ὁμοία ἐστὶν ἡ βασιλεία τῶν οὐρανῶν + dative
13:47 πάλιν ὁμοία ἐστὶν ἡ βασιλεία τῶν οὐρανῶν + dative.

The link between these three is all the closer as the formula in the second and third parables is prefaced by πάλιν. The author is counting as clearly as possible: ὁμοία ἐστίν, πάλιν ὁμοία ἐστίν, πάλιν ὁμοία ἐστίν: one, two, three.

I shall here cease to enumerate Matthean triads, although not for lack of additional examples. It is evident enough that both the SM and other portions of Matthew employ the triad as a compositional device. Does this not put presumption on the side of those who would assign Matthew 5–7 to the author of the First Gospel? Although there is no need to deny that the triad, probably because it was of great aid in structuring oral tradition, was popular with many in Matthew's world, he seems, when composing on his own, to have made regular recourse to the device. Because the SM is no different in this regard from the rest of the Gospel, one wonders about the wisdom of assigning it to another hand.

There is a second way in which the structure of the SM would seem to betray the same authorial hand as that of the other discourses. The concluding section of Matthew 5–7 consists of three hortatory subsections, each of which draws its life from eschatological expectation: 7:13–14 (the two ways), 7:15–23 (false prophets), and 7:24–27 (the two builders).[17] This is the first instance of a pattern that is to be repeated several times outside the SM. The final three units of the missionary discourse (10:32–33, 34–39, 40–42) also have to do with eschatological rewards and punishments. The same is true of the second group of kingdom parables in chapter 13 (13:44, 45–46, 47–50). The great eschatological discourse, 24:1–25:46, ends up with three lengthy sections

---

17. See Davies and Allison, *Matthew*, vol. 1, pp. 693–94. But Betz separates 7:21–23 from 7:15–20. See *Sermon on the Mount*, p. 520.

about the last day (25:1–13, 14–30, 31–46). And then there is chapter 18, whose final unit is a parable about the sad fate of those who fail to forgive their brothers from the heart (18:23–35). So the eschatological conclusion is the rule for the Matthean discourses. Once again, then, one is led to ask: does not the common feature imply a common origin?

According to Kari Syreeni, "When Dibelius contended that Matthew in his Sermon gave 'the best example' of Jesus' teaching,[18] or when Hoffmann considered this section 'the hidden centre' of the Gospel,[19] or when practically oriented Christians have felt that Christianity means to live according to the Sermon on the Mount, they have recognized that Mt 5–7 is more than one discourse section among others in Mt."[20] The SM is without question Matthew's premier discourse. So would we not expect to find here, if anywhere, the evangelist's hand at work? But we can judge by something more than theoretical expectations. The SM contains many features that are characteristic of the Gospel as a whole. Consider the following list, with the number of occurrences listed after each word or phrase:[21]

- βασιλεία τῶν οὐρανῶν (5:3, 10, etc.); this is Matthew's distinctive phrase (Mt: 32; Mk: 0; Lk: 0)

- δικαιοσύνη (5:6, 10, 20; 6:1, 33); the word, which occurs in the synoptics outside Matthew only in Lk 1:75, is redactional in 3:15 and 21:32

- διώκω (5:10, 11, 12, 44); Mt: 7; Mk: 0; Lk: 3

- πονηρός (5:11, 37, 39, 45; 6:13, 23; 7:11, 17, 18); Mt: 26; Mk: 2; Lk: 13

- μισθός (5:12, 46; 6:1, 2, 5, 15); Mt: 10; Mk: 1; Lk: 3

- κρύπτω (5:14); Mt: 7; Mk: 0; Lk: 3

- κόσμος (5:14); Mt: 9; Mk: 3; Lk: 3

- ἔμπροσθεν τῶν ἀνθρώπων (5:16; 6:1); Mt: 5; Mk: 0; Lk: 1

---

18. Martin Dibelius, *The Sermon on the Mount* (New York: Charles Scribner's Sons, 1940), pp. 16–17.

19. Paul Hoffmann, "Auslegung der Bergpredigt," *Bibel und Leben* 10 (1969): 65.

20. Kari Syreeni, *The Making of the Sermon on the Mount: A Procedural Analysis of Matthew's Redactoral Activity*, pt. 1, *Methodology and Compositional Analysis*, Annales Academiae Scientiarum Fennicae Dissertationes Humanarum Litterarum, vol. 4 (Helsinki: Suomalainen tiedeakatemia, 1987), p. 101. One could enlarge this comment with a hundred quotations. The similarities between the SM and the Hellenistic epitome, so stressed by Betz, are explained by the fact that Matthew composed the SM as a sort of summary of Jesus' moral demands upon Israel.

21. Cf. Stanton, *Gospel*, pp. 315–16. Stanton's comments on the theological continuity between the SM and the rest of Matthew (pp. 318–25) are also helpful.

- πατήρ + personal pronoun (5:16, 45, 48; 6:1, 4, 6, 8, 9, 14, 15, 18, 26, 32; 7:11, 21); Mt: 20; Mk: 1; Lk: 3

- πατὴρ ὁ ἐν (τοῖς) οὐρανοῖς (5:16, 45; 6:1, 9; 7:11); Mt: 13; Mk: 1; Lk: 0

- Jesus came not to abolish the law but to fulfill it (5:17); Matthew is very conservative about the Torah; the differences between Mt 15:1–20 and Mk 7:1–23 are particularly instructive (see the commentaries)

- νόμος καὶ προφῆται (5:17; 7:12); the expression is redactional in 22:40

- ἀμήν + γάρ (5:18); Mt: 4; Mk: 0; Lk: 0

- ἀπό, of material source (5:18; 7:16); Mt: 5; Mk: 0; Lk: 2

- γραμματεῖς + Φαρισαῖοι (5:20); Mt: 9; Mk: 1; Lk: 3

- ἀκούω + ὅτι (5:21, 27, 33, 38, 43); redactional in 4:12 and 22:34

- μωρός (5:22, 7:26); Mt: 6; Mk: 0; Lk: 0

- γέεννα (5:22, 29, 30); Mt: 7; Mk: 3; Lk: 1

- προσφέρω (5:23, 24); Mt: 9; Mk: 1; Lk: 2

- δῶρον (5:23, 24); Mt: 14; Mk: 3; Lk: 4

- θυσιαστήριον (5:23, 24); Mt: 6; Mk: 0; Lk: 2

- βάλλω, of final judgment (5:25, 29); Mt: 9; Mk: 2; Lk: 1

- ἀποδίδωμι (5:26, 33; 6:4, 6, 18); Mt: 18; Mk: 1; Lk: 9

- ἐκεῖθεν (5:26); Mt: 12; Mk: 5; Lk: 3

- πρὸς τό + infinitive (5:28; 6:1); Mt: 5; Mk: 1; Lk: 1

- δεξιός (5:20, 30, 39); Mt: 12; Mk: 6; Lk: 6

- ἀπολύω (=divorce) + γυνή (5:31, 32); Mt: 5; Mk: 1; Lk: 1

- "except for the cause of πορνεία" (5:32); compare the redactional 19:9

- ὁ πονηρός/τὸ πονηρόν (5:37, 39; 6:13); Mt 5; Mk: 0; Lk: 1

- ἐθνικός (5:47; 6:7); Mt: 3; Mk: 0; Lk: 0

- "You, therefore, must be perfect" (5:48); compare Mt 19:21 diff. Mk 10:21

- πατήρ + οὐράνιος (5:48; 6:14, 26, 32); Mt: 7; Mk: 0; Lk: 0

- θεάομαι, in infinitive forms (6:1); Mt: 4; Mk: 0; Lk: 1

- "hypocrite(s)" (6:2, 5, 16; 7:5); Mt: 13; Mk: 1; Lk: 3

- ὥσπερ (6:2, 7); Mt: 10; Mk: 0; Lk 2

- "Thy will be done" (6:10); this is redactional in 26:42

- aorist passive imperative of γίνομαι (6:10); Mt: 5; Mk: 0; Lk: 0

- γίνομαι + ὡς + noun (6:10); Mt: 4; Mk: 1; Lk: 1

- οὐρανός…γῆ (6:10); Mt: 10; Mk: 2; Lk: 4–5

- ὡς καί (6:12); Mt: 3; Mk: 0; Lk: 0

- λέγω δὲ ὑμῶν ὅτι (6:29); Mt: 6; Mk: 0; Lk: 0

- ὀλιγόπιστος (6:30); Mt: 5; Mk: 0; Lk: 1

- προσέξω + ἀπό (7:15); Mt: 5; Mk: 0; Lk: 2

- ἀπό, instrumental (7:16, 20); Mt: 5; Mk: 0; Lk: 0–1

- σαπρός (7:17, 18); Mt: 5; Mk: 0; Lk: 2

- φρόνιμος (7:24); Mt: 7; Mk: 0; Lk: 2

This list, which is hardly exhaustive,[22] and which encompasses several major themes of the SM (for example, righteousness and the inviolate nature of the law), is proof enough that the SM is thoroughly Matthean. The discourse is not "an undigested morsel."[23] One could perhaps retort that the real reason that certain themes and words are common to the SM and the rest of the First Gospel is that the author of the latter was much influenced by the former. But surely, unless there are very strong reasons for thinking otherwise, the simplest explanation is that Matthew 5–7 is so Matthean because it was put together by the author of the rest of Matthew.

Betz could counter that the SM cannot be Matthean because it "contains a consistent Jewish-Christian theology of a period earlier than Matthew, a theology remaining in the context of Judaism."[24] He in fact imagines that the SM conflicts with Matthew in a number of particulars. For instance, Betz affirms that whereas the SM opposes the Gentile mission,[25] Matthew does not; and that whereas in the SM Jesus is neither

---

22. See further n. 29.

23. This is the characterization of Betz's view in Syreeni, *Sermon on the Mount*, p. 67.

24. Betz, *Sermon on the Mount*, p. 44.

25. Ibid., pp. 188–89, even accepts the old idea that 5:19 contains an oblique reference to Paul. This of course remains only a conjecture, and the tension between Paul and the SM can be much overdone. See the lengthy and satisfying discussion of Davies, *Setting*, pp. 316–341; cf. Stanton, *Gospel*, pp. 312–14.

Son of man nor Son of God,[26] in Matthew Jesus is both Son of man and Son of God;[27] and that whereas Jesus' salvific death and his resurrection from the dead play no role in the SM,[28] they are of foundational significance elsewhere in Matthew; and that whereas in the SM Jesus is the eschatological advocate/*paraclete*,[29] elsewhere in Matthew he is the eschatological judge.[30] None of these arguments, however, holds up to examination, as argued in the footnotes. And does not the overwhelming harmony between the SM and the rest of Matthew more than outweigh the few questionable contradictions which Betz (but not others) has espied? Ulrich Luz has rightly spoken of "the impossibility of detecting any manner of difference between the author or redactor of...[Betz's hypothetical] source and that of the Gospel of Matthew."[31]

There is another difficulty with Betz's thesis. Betz finds in 6:1–6, 16–18 an old source which the pre-Matthean compiler of the SM incorporated and combined with 6:7–15.[32] This thesis fails to reckon with

26. Regarding the "my Father" of 7:21, Betz, *Sermon on the Mount*, p. 548, contends that Jesus is here just a faithful Jew: all Jews could address God as "Father" (cf. 6:9). "By speaking of God as 'my Father' Jesus sharply separates himself from the Gentile Christians he rejects." But why then does Jesus not speak of "our Father"? And is it not legitimate to read the SM in the light of what we otherwise know about early Christianity, which throughout its old sources — Q, Mark, Acts, Paul — holds Jesus to be God's Son in a special sense?

27. But there are many portions of the Gospel that fail to contain important christological themes found elsewhere. Jesus is not "Son of man" in Matthew 1–4, nor is there a single christological title in the speech in chapter 18. In chapter 10 Jesus is once "the Son of man" but never "Lord," "Christ," "Son of David," or "Son of God." "Son of David" is missing from every single major discourse, "Son (of God)" from every discourse save 24–25.

28. But 5:38–42 alludes to both Isa 50:4–9 (LXX) and the passion narrative; see my article, "Anticipating the Passion: The Literary Reach of Matthew 26:47–27:56," *CBQ* 56 (1994): 701–14. Mt 5:38–42 along with 10:17–23; 17:1–8; and 20:21 display a recurrent rhetorical strategy: each borrows language from the passion narratives. If so, then once more we find in the SM what we find elsewhere in Matthew.

29. 7:21–23. See *Sermon on the Mount*, pp. 554–56. But this is not the judgment of most commentators and is hardly demanded by the text. Moreover, Betz's attempt to find here a view not shared by Matthew flounders on the likelihood that 7:21–23 is (despite what he writes on p. 545) the product of intense Matthean redaction of Lk 6:46 = Q; cf. Davies and Allison, *Matthew*, vol. 1, pp. 711–14; Luz, *Matthew 1–7*, pp. 440–41 ("Matthew has redacted the section very determinedly and incisively, as is rarely his manner elsewhere"). Characteristically Matthean are οὐ πᾶς (redactional in 19:11; Mk: 0; Lk: 0); εἰσέρχομαι + βασιλεία τῶν οὐρανῶν (Mt: 4; Mk: 0; Lk: 0); βασιλεία τῶν οὐρανῶν (Mt: 32; Mk: 0; Lk: 0); ποιέω + θέλημα + πατρός (Mt: 3; Mk: 0; Lk: 0); πατὴρ ὁ ἐν (τοῖς) οὐρανοῖς (Mt: 13; Mk: 1; Lk: 0); ἐκεῖνος (Mt: 54; Mk: 23; Lk: 33); the triad in v. 22; δυνάμεις = "miracle" (Mt: 7; Mk: 2; Lk: 2); ὁμολογέω (Mt: 4; Mk: 0; Lk: 2); οὐδέποτε (Mt: 5; Mk: 2; LK: 2); γινώσκω + personal pronoun (Mt: 3; Mk: 0; Lk: 0); ἐργάζομαι (Mt: 4; Mk: 1; Lk: 1); ἀνομία (Mt: 4; Mk: 0; Lk: 0). While word statistics must always be used with caution, this list speaks rather loudly.

30. For Betz the christological identification of Jesus as advocate is more primitive than his identification as judge; but see Carlston, "Betz," pp. 54–55.

31. *Matthew 1–7*, p. 213 n. 4.

32. *Sermon on the Mount*, pp. 330–51.

the parallels in 23:1–12. When one subtracts from this last passage the elements from Mark and Q and what is redactional one is left with this:[33] "The scribes sat on Moses' seat; so practice and observe whatever they tell you; but do not do what they do, for they speak but do not practice. They do all their deeds in order to be seen by others; for they make their phylacteries broad and their fringes long, and ... to be called 'Rabbi, rabbi' by others. But you are not to be called rabbi, for you have one teacher, and you are all brethren. And call no one on earth your father, for you have one Father, who is in heaven. Neither be called masters, for you have one master, the Christ." Now the number of formal, thematic, and linguistic parallels between this paragraph — which stands on its own and reads smoothly if a passive ("they are called") be substituted for an infinitive ("to be called") — and the cult didache preserved in 6:1–6, 16–18, is remarkable. In both

1. Jewish religious behavior, cited first, serves as a foil for proper Christian behavior; that is, positive imperatives follow negative descriptions;

2. the synagogue is clearly in view (6:2, 5; 23:2–3);

3. the triad is the structural key (6:1–6, 16–18 concern prayer, almsgiving, and fasting; in 23:2–3, 5, 7b–10 the scribes and Pharisees do three things, and Christians are not to be called three things);

4. the chief sins are hypocrisy and piety for show;

5. ποιεῖν/ποιοῦσιν πρὸς τὸ θεαθῆναι (τοῖς) αὐτοῖς/ἀνθρώποις appears (6:1; 23:5);

6. ἐν τοῖς οὐρανοῖς (6:1) or ὁ οὐράνοις (23:9) qualifies πατρί (6:1)/ πατήρ (23:9);

7. ὑπὸ τῶν ἀνθρώπων is used (6:2, "glorified by people," 23:7, "called by people");

8. "but you" (σὺ δέ, 6:3, 6, 17; ὑμεῖς δέ, 23:8) marks the transition from negative description to positive exhortation;

9. "you" and "your" are catchwords (6:1–6, 16–18: ὑμῶν/ὑμῖν/σου/ σοι/σύ: 24 times; 23:2–3, 5, 7b–10: ὑμῖν/ὑμεῖς/ὑμῶν: 7 times).[34]

---

33. In the two-source theory Matthew supplied an introduction and combined Mark (vv. 6–7a, 11; cf. Mk 9:35; 10:43–44; 12:38–39) with Q (vv. 4, 6–7a, 12; cf. Lk 11:43, 46; 14:11; 18:14; 20:46) and M (vv. 2–3, 5, 7b–10). Verse 1 is redactional; so too perhaps 23:7b (which has no Markan or Lukan parallel). See Stephenson H. Brooks, *Matthew's Community: The Evidence of the Special Sayings Material*, JSNTSS, vol. 16 (Sheffield: JSOT, 1987), pp. 59–64.

34. One may also observe (although the proposition cannot be defended here) that both passages seem to contain not so much sayings of Jesus but Christian admonitions.

There is one very good explanation for these parallels: the two pieces were the work of the same author or compiler. Now we have our choice: that person was either Matthew or a predecessor. If the latter, then Matthew took up a pre-Matthean text on Christian piety, broke it in two, and deposited the first half in chapter 6, the other half in chapter 23. If the former, then we are no longer speaking of units preexisting Matthew. Neither scenario is that of Betz. His view could indeed be accommodated by postulating that a pre-Matthean compiler used the source behind Mt 6:1–6, 6:16–18, and 23:1–12 to construct the SM, and that later Matthew used another part of the very same source to compose chapter 23. But this seems unnecessarily involved and hypothetical.

## THE SERMON ON THE PLAIN IN Q

If Betz's theory does not persuade, what should we then think about the SM, SP, and Q? The proposition that the SM is Matthew's expansion of Q, and that Q contained a section very much like Lk 6:20–49, is reinforced by a number of observations.

First, a general point: Charles Carlston, in his critique of Betz, has called attention to his own 1971 study, with Dennis Norlin, in which an attempt was made to measure the agreement between Matthew and Luke in both the double and triple tradition.[35] While the details of their statistics cannot be reviewed here, it is undeniable that very often Matthew and Luke are even closer to each other in the double tradition materials than in the triple tradition materials. It follows that if, as the consensus has it, in the triple tradition Matthew and Luke used a common written source (Mark), how much more so in the double tradition, to which we give the name Q.[36] Not only this, but the Greek text of Q known to Matthew must have been very close to the Greek text of Q known to Luke. This discourages us from postulating too many major differences between $Q^{mt}$ and $Q^{lk}$.[37] When one adds that Matthew omitted very little of Mark, and that Luke, aside from the major omission

---

35. "Once More," pp. 59–78.

36. Thomas Bergemann, *Q auf dem Prüfstand: Die Zuordnung des Mt/Lk-Stoffes zu Q am Beispiel der Bergpredigt*, FRLANT, vol. 158 (Göttingen: Vandenhoeck & Ruprecht, 1993), on the contrary, observes that the statistical agreement between Matthew and Luke in the double tradition varies widely in different passages traditionally reckoned to Q, and goes on to argue that many of those passages should be excluded from Q. Concerning the SM and SP in particular, Bergemann urges that they go back to an old Aramaic source which was translated into different Greek recensions, and that those two recensions continued to be revised until they came to Matthew and Luke. But his case has not been made, as appears from the persuasive critique of Adelbert Denaux, "Criteria for Identifying Q-Passages: A Critical Review of a Recent Work by T. Bergemann," *NovT* 37 (1995): 105–29.

37. Cf. Carlston, "Betz," pp. 48–49.

of Mk 6:48–8:26, also omitted very little of Mark, we may infer that probably neither omitted very much of Q. That this generalization holds for the SM and SP in particular is confirmed by the circumstance that, apart from the woes (Lk 6:24–26) and two short proverbs (Lk 6:39–40), all of the units in the SP have parallels in the SM; and even the two proverbs appear elsewhere in Matthew (10:24–25; 15:14). Indeed, all of the materials common to the SM and SP, with the sole exception of the golden rule, are in the same order:

| | |
|---|---|
| Lk 6:20a | cf. Mt 5:1–2 |
| Lk 6:20b–23 | cf. Mt 5:3–12 |
| Lk 6:24–26 | ——— |
| Lk 6:27–36 | cf. Mt 5:38–48; 7:12 |
| Lk 6:37–38 | cf. Mt 7:1 |
| Lk 6:39 | (cf. Mt 15:14) |
| Lk 6:40 | (cf. Mt 10:24–25) |
| Lk 6:41–42 | cf. Mt 7:3–5 |
| Lk 6:43–45 | cf. Mt 7:16–18 |
| Lk 6:46 | cf. Mt 7:21 |
| Lk 6:47–49 | cf. Mt 7:24–27 |
| Lk 7:1 | cf. Mt 7:28–8:1 |

These parallels in order are more than consistent with the view that Matthew used something very close to the SP as an outline or skeleton for his SM.

Second, even without having Luke at hand there are parts of the SM that scholars would undoubtedly reckon to be secondary intrusions. For example, the Beatitudes in Mt 5:7–9 are, as is universally recognized, in several important respects different from the other beatitudes,[38] and their later character has been manifest to many.[39] Obviously someone added them to an earlier collection. Again, the cult didache in 6:1–6, 16–18 is a coherent, independent piece which, it is reasonable to suppose, was inserted by the evangelist into its present context. It is also evident that someone interpolated 6:7–15, which includes the Lord's Prayer, into the cult didache. The point is that as we remove more and more of the obviously secondary additions, we get closer and closer to the SP, which shares so much with the SM; so the thought that the SM is an expansion of something like the SP begins to commend itself.

Third, if we can judge from the remainder of the First Gospel, it was not Matthew's wont to take over speeches without modifying them. The discourses in chapters 10, 13, 18, and 24–25 are composites. Mt

---

38. E.g., they do not speak of eschatological reversal.
39. Cf. Syreeni, *Sermon on the Mount*, p. 134.

10:1–42 differs greatly from both Mk 6:6–13 and Lk 10:1–16 = Q. Mt 13:1–52 is much larger than its basic source, Mk 4:1–34. Mt 18:1–9 resembles Mk 9:33–50, but the rest of the community discourse is a collection of scattered materials. And Mt 24:1–25:46 follows Mark only through its first half; thereafter again Matthew melds diverse traditions. So it was Matthew's literary habit to conflate sources, to expand passages in Mark or Q with non-Markan and non-Q materials. It can be no surprise then that the SM differs so much from the SP = Q. In this respect the SM is just like the other discourses, and this too is consistent with the hypothesis of Matthean authorship.

Finally, if Betz dissents from the common opinion regarding the SM, he agrees with the consensus regarding the SP: it is largely a pre-Lukan speech. In this latter judgment there is no reason to think him or the majority opinion wrong. Most of the recent commentaries on the SP see relatively little Lukan redactional activity in Lk 6:20–49; and Joachim Jeremias's examination of the language of Lk 6:20–49 led him to the conclusion that Lukan features are here minimal.[40] One can assuredly find scholars who believe that Luke added and/or composed the woes,[41] or that he inserted 6:34 ("and if you lend to those from whom you expect repayment, what credit is that to you? Even sinners lend to sinners, to receive as much again"),[42] or 6:37c–38 ("forgive, and you will be forgiven; give, and it will be given to you; they will put into your lap a full measure, pressed down, shaking together, overflowing"),[43] or 6:39a ("He also told them a parable").[44] But these are little more than possibilities, for which the evidence is minimal. On the whole Lk 6:20–49 appears to be a pre-Lukan unit which opened with beatitudes (6:20–23), then commanded love of enemies (6:27–36), then discouraged judging others (6:37–42), then spoke of good and evil fruit (6:43–45), and finally warned of judgment (6:46–49). Notwithstanding Betz, we may confidently identify it as a speech in Q and think of it as one of the sources of the SM.

## THE SOURCES OF THE SERMON ON THE PLAIN

If this is the correct judgment about Q 6:20–49, it is possible to go further and inquire into the compositional history of the SP. How much

---

40. *Sprache*, pp. 138–51.
41. 6:24–26; cf. Syreeni, *Sermon on the Mount*, pp. 133–36.
42. See the review of opinion in John S. Kloppenborg, *Q Parallels* (Sonoma, Calif.: Polebridge, 1988), p. 30.
43. See ibid., p. 34.
44. Cf. 5:36 diff. Mk 2:20–21; 21:29 diff. Mk 13:28.

should be attributed to Q? What had already been brought together before Q?

The beginning and end of the discourse correspond: blessings come at the beginning (6:20–23),[45] a warning at the end (6:46–49;[46] note that "hears my words" not only refers to the entire preceding discourse but creates an *inclusio* with 6:27, "I say to you who hear"). This arrangement, which brings the command to "do good to those who hate you" (6:27) into immediate connection with "Blessed are you when people hate you" (6:22),[47] was probably first created in Q (my Q³). For one thing, the four beatitudes,[48] with their allusions to Isaiah 61, their mention of the poor, and their implicit Christology, prepare for Jesus' answer to John the Baptist's query about the coming one in 7:18–23.[49] For another, the balancing of prefatory blessing with a concluding warning reminds one of Deuteronomy, and Q has just offered us a story — one perhaps composed by the editor of this section of Q[50] — that is partly spun out of citations from Deuteronomy (4:1–13). There is also the observation that if Q³ otherwise shows a Deuteronomistic view of things,[51] the same view belongs to the fourth beatitude, whose concluding "for that is what their fathers did to the prophets" (6:23) may very well come from its Q editor.[52]

Following the beatitudes are verses whose theme is loving enemies and doing good.[53] The limits of the section are indicated by an *inclusio*:

Opening (6:27):
    Love your enemies (ἀγαπᾶτε τοὺς ἐχθροὺς ὑμῶν)
    Do good (καλῶς ποιεῖτε) to those who hate you

Conclusion (6:35–36):
    Love your enemies (ἀγαπᾶτε τοὺς ἐχθροὺς ὑμῶν)
    and do good (ἀγαθοποιεῖτε)

---

45. For beatitudes at the beginning of a new section of discourse see Job 5:17; Ps 1:1; 32:1–2; 41:1; 119:1; Prov 8:32; Ecclus 14:20; 26:1; *1 Enoch* 58:1–2; Rev 1:3; *2 Enoch* 42:6–14; 52:1–14.

46. Was 6:46 an isolated logion before Q (cf. P. Eg. 2.2r. lines 52–54; 2 *Clem.* 4:2)?

47. The woes of Lk 6:24–26 were probably added either by Luke or a contributor to Q^lk; cf. Matthew 5. Did the editor of Q add μισέω to either 6:22 or 27?

48. On their original unity see chap. 3.

49. See above, pp. 6–7.

50. See my essay, "Behind the Temptations of Jesus," in *Authenticating the Deeds of Jesus*, ed. B. Chilton and C. A. Evans (Leiden: E. J. Brill, forthcoming).

51. See esp. 11:31–32, 47–51; 13:34–35 and Arland D. Jacobson, "The Literary Unity of Q," *JBL* 101 (1982), esp. pp. 383–88 — although he presupposes another compositional history of Q.

52. See p. 101, n. 26.

53. The following discussion assumes that Lk 6:27–38 preserves Q's sequence; see Kloppenborg, *Formation*, pp. 173–76. For a different view of things see R. A. Piper, *Wisdom*, pp. 78–82. But Piper's arguments have been effectively criticized by Vaage, *Galilean Upstarts*, pp. 121–27.

The unit marked out by this *inclusio* also has a short introduction (6:27: "But I say to you"[54]) and comes to its conclusion with a strong "nevertheless" (6:35: πλήν).

The section as a whole, 6:27–36, has the so-called golden rule at its center (6:31). On one side of this is a series of eight parallel imperatives (6:27–30), and on the other a series of three questions (6:31–34) and a concluding summary (6:35–36). The opening imperatives are neatly arranged into two quatrains, with the first set using the second-person plural, the second set the second-person singular:

> Love your enemies (27a)
> Do good to those who hate you (27b)
> Bless those who curse you (28a)
> Pray for those who revile you (28b)
>
> To the one striking you on the cheek offer also the other (29a)
> And from the one taking your coat do not withhold your
>      shirt (29b)
> To everyone who asks give (30a)
> And from the one borrowing[55] do not ask back (30b)

The first four imperatives are all held together by the same pattern: second-person plural, present imperative + participle (describing opponents) + ὑμῶν/ᾶς. But we also have here two pairs. For both the first and third imperatives have four words, the second and fourth five; and while the first and third commands consist of imperative + τούς + participle + ὑμῶν/ᾶς, the second and third commands exhibit slightly different arrangements. Visually:

> 1. imperative + τούς + object ending in -ους + ὑμῶν (27a)
> 2. imperative (with adverb) + τοῖς + participle + ὑμᾶς (27b)
>
> 1. imperative + τούς + object ending in -ους + ὑμῶν (28a)
> 2. imperative + περί + τῶν + participle + ὑμῶν (28b)

As can be seen at a glance, matters are similar with the second set of imperatives; that is, here too are two pairs created by alternating formulas:

> 1. dative + σε + imperative (29a)
> 2. καὶ ἀπὸ τοῦ + imperative with μή (29b)
>
> 1. dative + σε + imperative (30a)
> 2. καὶ ἀπὸ τοῦ + imperative with μή (30b)

---

54. On the pre-Lukan character of this see Jeremias, *Sprache*, pp. 140–41. An origin in Q is suggested by the similar formulation of contrast in Mt 5:22, 28, 32, 34, 39, 44.

55. Here Matthew seems to preserve the original. This is suggested by the threefold use of δανίζω in Q 6:33–35 — verses which otherwise hark back to 6:27–30. See n. 59.

Clearly 6:27–30 is built out of pairs: the eight imperatives are grouped into two sets which are in turn grouped into two more sets:

So leading up to the golden rule is a string of eight imperatives whose extensive parallelism is clearly the result of conscious design, perhaps at an oral stage.[56]

Following the golden rule are sentences which also feature an extensive parallelism:

32: And if you love those who love you
    what credit is that to you?
        For also toll collectors[57] love those who love them.

33: And if you do good to those who do good to you[58]
    what credit is that to you?
        Also Gentiles do the same.

34: And if you lend to those from whom you hope to receive
    what credit is that to you?
        Also sinners lend to sinners to receive as much again.[59]

---

56. Once one perceives this pattern, the common explanation of the switch from second-person plural in 6:27–28 to second-person singular in 6:29–30 in terms of source criticism (see, e.g., Kloppenborg, *Formation,* p. 176) becomes dubious: we have here rather a literary or mnemonic device. See further Vaage, *Galilean Upstarts,* pp. 122–24.

57. Luke has "sinners" (ἁμαρτωλός: Mt: 5; Mk: 6; Lk: 18) both here and in Q 6:33. The expression is widely reckoned to be Lukan. Matthew's more Jewish "toll collectors" (in Mt 5:46 = Lk 6:32) and "Gentiles" (in Mt 5:47 = Lk 6:33) probably stood in Q.

58. Mt 5:47 has, "And if you salute [cf. the redactional 10:12] only your brothers...." But Luke is here closer to Q; see Jeremias, *Sprache,* p. 145.

59. There is no Matthean parallel to Lk 6:34, and it is just possible the verse is Lukan redaction. For the problem see Kloppenborg, *Formation,* p. 125, who is probably right in

It seems plain enough that these lines never circulated in isolation, for they are commentary on 6:27–30. "If you love those who love you" and "love those who love them" (6:32) take us back to the opening command of 6:27a: it is nothing special to love those who love you; Jesus even demands love of enemy. "If you do good to those who do good to you" (6:33) takes up 6:27b, where Jesus enjoins his listeners to do good to those who do not do good to them. And "if you lend (δανίσητε) to those from whom you hope to receive" links up with the probable text of Q 6:30: "[A]nd from the one borrowing (δανισαμένου — see n. 55) do not ask back." So Q 6:32–34 is either a secondary, parasitic composition[60] or — and this is more likely — from the beginning the verses followed Q 6:27–30; that is, whoever composed 6:27–30 elaborated upon it with 6:32–34. It is only the golden rule, 6:31, that separates the two units. But that rule is the sort of saying that, being part of the common wisdom,[61] must have been known in isolation; and as it interrupts the thematic coherence of its present context we may regard it as a secondary insertion.[62]

The section on love of enemy ends with the lengthy 6:35–36, which consists of (1) three succinct imperatives ("love your enemies and do good and lend") which take one back to 6:27 and at the same time summarize 6:32–34; (2) a general promise of reward ("your reward will be great"); (3) a specific promise that "you will be sons of the Most High" who is kind to the ungrateful and the wicked; and (4) a final imperative which furthers the theme of the *imitatio Dei*: "Be merciful, just as your Father is merciful." As with 6:32–34, this complex conclusion should not be reckoned a one-time isolated logion, or even a collection of originally disparate logia;[63] rather was it composed as the fitting conclusion of 6:27ff. It presumably originated with the same author as the rest.

One portion of it, nonetheless, could very well come from the Q editor. "Your reward (ὁ μισθὸς ὑμῶν) will be great (πολύς)" echoes 6:23, where "your reward (ὁ μισθὸς ὑμῶν) is great (πολύς) in heaven" also belongs to a conclusion. One must wonder whether the person who prefaced 6:27–36 with the beatitudes — to be identified with the Q editor — assimilated the former to the latter by adding to it the promise of great

---

judging "that Q 6:34 originally concerned lending and corresponded to Matt 5:42, and that Luke 6:34 belonged to Q. Because of its position between 6:29 and the generalizing statement in 6:31, Luke changed 6:30 into a summary of 6:29 and an anticipation of 6:31, but thereby obscured its link with 6:34."

60. Cf. Catchpole, *Quest*, pp. 18–19, 106–109.

61. The numerous parallels are well known; see Tob 4:15; Ecclus 31:15; Aristeas, *Ep.* 207; Philo, *Hypothetica* in Eusebius, *Praep. ev.* 8:7; *T. Naph.* 1:6 (Hebrew); 2 *Enoch* 61:1–2; *b. Šabb.* 31a; etc.

62. This is a common judgment.

63. Although 6:36 might have been known by itself.

reward. This is all the more so in that "you will be sons of the Most High" offers sufficient motive for the preceding imperatives.

However that may be, 6:27–36 contains an old unit which preexisted Q's editorial work. But had that unit already, before its adoption into Q, gathered to itself 6:37–38? This last contains four related, parallel imperatives. The first two are structural twins, as are the last two (cf. 6:27–30); but the final member, like the fourth beatitude, breaks the parallelism in order to add emphasis:

37a:　And do not judge (καὶ μή + imperative)
　　　and you will not be judged (καὶ οὐ μή + aorist
　　　　　subjunctive passive);
37b:　And do not condemn (καὶ μή + imperative)
　　　and you will not be condemned (καὶ οὐ μή + aorist
　　　　　subjunctive passive);

37c:　Forgive (imperative)
　　　and you will be forgiven (καί + future passive);
38:　Give (imperative)
　　　and it will be given to you (καί + future passive) —
　　　a good measure, pressed down, shaken together,
　　　running over, will be put into your lap; for the
　　　measure you give will be the measure you get back.

That 6:37–38 was added to 6:27–36 at an early stage[64] and that the combined text circulated apart from Q is made likely by *1 Clem.* 13:2, which opens with, "remembering[65] the words of the Lord Jesus which he spoke,[66] teaching forbearance and long-suffering:"

1. Show mercy, that you may receive mercy (cf. Q 6:36)[67]

2. Forgive, that you may be forgiven (cf. Q 6:37)[68]

3. As you do, it will be done to you (cf. Q 6:30 [?], 37–38)

4. As you give, so will it be given to you (cf. Q 6:38)

5. As you judge, so will you be judged (cf. Q 6:37)

---

64. The connections between 6:36 and 6:37–38 are brought out by Catchpole, *Quest,* pp. 116–25.

65. The author appears to assume that his or her audience already knows the following citation.

66. On this formula as an introduction to oral tradition see Ron Cameron, *Sayings Traditions in the Apocryphon of James* (Philadelphia: Fortress, 1984), pp. 92–116. The same tradition appears in Clement of Alexandria, *Strom.* 2.18.91, but depends upon *1 Clement.*

67. Cf. also Mt 5:7 and Polycarp, *Ep.* 2:3.

68. Cf. also Mt 6:14–15; Q 11:4; Mk 11:25.

6. As you show kindness, so kindness will be shown to you (cf. Q 6:27, 33, 35)

7. With what measure you give, it will be measured to you (cf. Q 6:38)

These seven stylized imperatives are striking for several reasons. Not only does the content overlap with portions of Q 6:27–36, 37–38, but there are formal resemblances. The pairing of the first two commands (both have an imperative + ἵνα) recalls the pairing of imperatives in Q 6:27–30 and 37–38. The string of four similar sentences (3–6, all with ὡς...οὕτως) is analogous to the groups of four in the very same Q texts. That the final unit, with its introductory dative (ᾧ μέτρῳ), breaks the parallelism of the preceding commands puts one in mind of Q 6:38, which similarly breaks the parallelism of its passage—and with the very same saying, that about getting back the measure one gives.

Obviously there is a close relationship between Q 6:27–38 and *1 Clem.* 13:2. We have here partial variants of the same tradition. Given that three times Q and Clement use different words for the same concept,[69] one might guess that the two texts go back to closely related Semitic sources.[70] The point for us, however, is that if Clement's tradition is, as it seems to be, independent of the synoptics and Q,[71] then it offers good reason for supposing that the joining of Q 6:37–38 to 6:27–36 was already tradition for Q.

---

69. γίνομαι/εἰμί + οἰκτίρμων (Q) = ἐλεάω (*1 Clement*); ἀπολύω (Q) = ἀφίημι (*1 Clement*); ἀγαθοποιέω/καλῶς ποιέω (Q) = χρηστεύομαι (*1 Clement*)

70. According to Martin, *Syntax Criticism of the Synoptic Gospels*, pp. 91–100, the entirety of Lk 6:27–38 qualifies as translation Greek, while from the remainder of the SP only 6:41–42 similarly qualifies. That is, Q 6:20–23, 39, 40, 43–45, and 46–49 do not seem to be translation Greek. So that which appears on other grounds to be likely, namely, that Q 6:27–38 rests upon an old pre-Q unit, is confirmed by the circumstance that it is surrounded by less-Semitic units. It may also be worth observing that for Black, *Aramaic Approach*, pp. 179–81, "alliteration, assonance, and wordplay are all prominent features of the Aramaic of" Lk 6:27–36 and its parallel.

71. On the probable independence of *1 Clement* from Matthew and Luke see Donald A. Hagner, *The Use of the Old and New Testaments in Clement of Rome*, NovTSup, vol. 34 (Leiden: E. J. Brill, 1975). Most of his arguments work just as well for independence from Q. Hagner himself concludes that *1 Clem.* 13:2 is an "oral extra-canonical tradition." Although we should not exclude the bare possibility that Clement knew Matthew (cf. *1 Clem.* 16:17 with Mt 11:29–30 — in both, meekness and yoke appear together — and *1 Clem.* 46:8 with Mt 18:6 — note the common καταποντίζομαι), *1 Clem.* 13:2 at least seems to be independent of the synoptics. Even Édouard Massaux, *The Influence of the Gospel of Saint Matthew on Christian Literature before Saint Irenaeus*, bk. 1, *The First Ecclesiastical Writers*, ed. Arthur J. Bellinzoni (Macon, Ga.: Mercer University Press, 1990), pp. 7–12, who is otherwise disposed to see Matthean influence in the Apostolic Fathers, thinks here not of dependence upon Matthew but a "'catechism' summarizing the teaching of Christ" (although he imagines that this catechism drew upon Matthew). Cf. Wolf-Dietrich Köhler, *Die Rezeption des Matthäusevangeliums in der Zeit vor Irenäus*, WUNT, ser. 2, vol. 24 (Tübingen: J. C. B. Mohr [Paul Siebeck], 1987), pp. 67–71.

This judgment is reinforced by examination of the Pauline epistles. For the evidence strongly suggests that even if the apostle may have known Q,[72] he also knew an independent collection closely related to Q 6:27–38. Consider the following parallels:

Rom 2:1: "Thus you have no excuse when you judge others, for in passing judgment on another you judge yourself" (cf. Q 6:37).[73]

Rom 12:14: "Bless those who persecute you; bless and do not curse them" (cf. Q 6:28).[74]

Rom 12:17: "Do not repay anyone evil for evil" (cf. Q 6:27–36).[75]

Rom 12:21: "Do not be overcome by evil but overcome evil with good" (cf. Q 6:27–36).

1 Cor 4:12: "[W]hen reviled, we bless" (cf. Q 6:28).[76]

1 Thess 5:15: "See that none of you repays evil for evil, but always seek to do good to one another and to all" (cf. Q 6:27–36).[77]

These parallels may be explained in more than one way. Perhaps they are insubstantial and largely due to coincidence. Or perhaps Paul and Q 6:27–38 drew upon common Jewish tradition.[78] Or perhaps Paul drew upon isolated sayings of Jesus that were eventually gathered into Q. But given (1) that the parallels between Q and Rom 2:1; 12:14; and 1 Cor 4:12 are close in both wording and content;[79] (2) that Q 6:27–38 is to

---

72. See above, pp. 54–60.

73. See also Rom 14:10 and 14:13 and Thompson, *Clothed with Christ*, pp. 161–73. While the content of Rom 2:1 is parallel to Q 6:37, the introductory dative (ἐν ᾧ γὰρ κρίνεις) resembles Q 6:38 (ᾧ γὰρ μέτρῳ μετρεῖτε) and *1 Clem.* 13:2 (ᾧ μέτρῳ μετρεῖτε). It is pertinent to observe that throughout exegetical history commentators have associated Rom 2:1 and 14:1–13 with Lk 6:37 and its parallel; see, e.g., Photius, *Hom.* 13:3 (found on p. 224 of the Mango translation).

74. Paul has εὐλογεῖτε (twice) and καταρᾶσθε; Q has εὐλογεῖτε and καταρωμένοις. There do not appear to be good Jewish or Greco-Roman parallels; cf. Thompson, *Clothed with Christ*, pp. 97–98, 100–102.

75. In Polycarp, *Ep.* 2:2, "not rendering evil for evil" summarizes and introduces Jesus' teaching on nonretaliation. See also n. 88, on 1 Pet 3:9. The use of this same phrase in 1 Thess 5:15 and *Jos. Asen.* 23:9; 28:4, 14; and 29:3 (see John Piper, *"Love Your Enemies:" Jesus' Love Command*, SNTSMS, vol. 38 [Cambridge: Cambridge University Press, 1979], pp. 37–39) as well as *Apoc. Sed.* 7:9 probably means that early Christians took over the phrase from Jewish tradition and used it to summarize Jesus' demand for nonretaliation.

76. Both Q and Paul use εὐλογέω.

77. Paul uses ἀγαθός, Q ἀγαθοποιέω.

78. Cf. J. Sauer, "Traditionsgeschichtliche Erwägungen zu den synoptischen und paulinischen Aussagen über Feindesliebe und Wiedervergeltungsverzicht," ZNW 76 (1985): 1–28.

79. Regarding Rom 2:1, "The idea of 'measure for measure' was probably already an old one at this time (cf. Mark 4:24 pars. with *m. Soṭa* 1:7), but the particular expression of it in terms of the one who judges being condemned by his own judgment is too similar

be reckoned, on other grounds, an early collection; (3) that Rom 2:1; 12:17; and 1 Thess 5:15 show contact with extracanonical traditions related to Q 6:27–38;[80] (4) that both Romans 12–15 and Q 6:27–38 have a similar structure: both first treat the subject of loving enemies and then go on to discourage judging others;[81] and (5) that Q 6:27–38 contains authentic sayings of Jesus[82] (a circumstance which guarantees the direction of borrowing), the most likely conclusion is that Paul knew the collection behind Q 6:27–38 and that he drew upon and alluded to it in his correspondence.[83]

Also pertinent in this connection is Polycarp, *Ep.* 2:2–3, which contains the following: "He that raised him from the dead will raise us also if we do his will . . . not rendering evil for evil or railing for railing or blow for blow or cursing for cursing; but remembering the words which the Lord spoke when he taught:[84] Judge not that you be not judged, forgive, and you will be forgiven, have mercy that you may receive mercy; with what measure you give, it will be measured to you. And again: Blessed are the poor and they that are persecuted for righteousness' sake, for theirs is the kingdom of God." Because the concluding beatitude depends upon the redactional Mt 5:10, it cannot be related to Q or its sources.[85] But the preceding lines resemble not Matthew but Luke = Q, and even more *1 Clem.* 13:2.[86] Polycarp, *Ep.* 2:2–3, offers two sets of injunctions:

---

to Matt 7:1–2 [= Luke/Q 6:37] to be accidental" (James D. G. Dunn, *Romans 1–8*, WBC, vol. 38 [Dallas: Word, 1988], p. 80). On Rom 12:14 see Thompson, *Clothed with Christ.* A. M. Hunter, *Paul and His Predecessors*, 2d ed. (London: SCM, 1961), p. 47, remarked: "In Rom 12.14 Paul changes his construction from a participle to imperative (the participle appears again in the next sentence) — a fact which suggests that he employs borrowed words and does not trouble to adapt them to their grammatical context."

80. So even if Paul knew Q he knew other traditions as well.

81. Cf. Heinz-Wolfgang Kuhn, "Das Liebesgebot Jesu als Tora und als Evangelium," in Frankemölle and Kertelge, *Vom Urchristentum zu Jesus*, pp. 198–99.

82. See Dieter Lührmann, "Liebet eure Feinde (Lk 6:27–36/Mt 5:39–48)," *ZTK* 69 (1972): 427–36; Norman Perrin, *Rediscovering the Teaching of Jesus* (New York: Harper & Row, 1976), pp. 146–49; J. Piper, *Love*, pp. 49–65; and Kuhn, "Liebesgebot," pp. 222–30. On the setting within Jesus' Galilean ministry see Richard A. Horsley, *Jesus and the Spiral of Violence: Popular Jewish Resistance in Roman Palestine* (San Francisco: Harper & Row, 1987), pp. 259–73.

83. Cf. Heinz Schürmann, *Das Lukasevangelium*, vol. 1, HTKNT (Freiburg: Herder, 1969), pp. 385–86.

84. Cf. *1 Clem.* 13:2 and see n. 66.

85. Cf. Köhler, *Rezeption*, pp. 99–100.

86. The four commands beginning with "judge not" are all paralleled in *1 Clem.* 13:2, but the formulations and order are different. Although J. B. Lightfoot, *The Apostolic Fathers*, rev. ed., vol. 1, pt. 1, *S. Clement of Rome* (London: Macmillan, 1890), pp. 149–52, in his convincing demonstration that Polycarp had read Clement, listed Polycarp, *Ep.* 2:2, as parallel to *1 Clem.* 13:2, the differences between the two texts as well as the parallels between Polycarp and *Did.* 1:3 make literary dependence at this point unlikely; see Hagner, *Clement*, pp. 142–43, and Köhler, *Rezeption*, pp. 105–108. Contrast Koester, *Gospels*, pp. 19–20. According to Otto Knoch, "Kenntnis und Verwendung des Matthäus-Evangeliums bei den Apostolischen Vätern," in *Studien zum Matthäusevangeliums: Festschrift für Wilhelm Pesch*, ed. Ludger Schenke, SBS (Stuttgart:

Not returning:

1. Evil for evil (cf. Q 6:27–30)[87]

2. or railing for railing[88]

3. or blow for blow (cf. Q 6:29)

4. or cursing for cursing (cf. Q 6:28)[89]

Remembering the words which the Lord spoke:

5. Judge not that you not be judged (cf. Q 6:37)

6. Forgive and you will be forgiven (cf. Q 6:37)

7. Show mercy that you receive mercy (cf. Q 6:36)

8. With the measure you measure it will be measured to you (cf. Q 6:38)

As with *1 Clem.* 13:2 there are parallels not only with the content of Q 6:27–38 but also with the latter's formal features. (1) Both units first enjoin nonretaliation and second list correlations between what one gives and what one gets. (2) Polycarp's material is grouped into two sets of four; with this one may compare Q 6:27–30 and 37–38. (3) Sayings 5–8 in Polycarp end with an irregularity, just like Q 6:37–38: three parallel imperatives give way to the saying about measure for measure with its dative plus indicative construction (cf. *1 Clem.* 13:2). (4) Just as the two units of four members in Q 6:27–30 sort themselves into pairs, so too do the two units of four in Polycarp — and by exactly the same method: the first and third lines and the second and fourth lines resemble each other:

1. accusative ending in -ov + ἀντί + genitive ending in -ου
2. accusative ending in -αν + ἀντί + genitive ending in -ιας

---

Katholisches Bibelwerk, 1988), p. 170, Polycarp, *Ep.* 2:3, like *1 Clem.* 13:2, draws upon "catechetical and paraenetical tradition." Cf. Édouard Massaux, *The Influence of the Gospel of Saint Matthew on Christian Literature before Saint Irenaeus*, bk. 2, *The Later Christian Writings*, ed. Arthur J. Bellinzoni (Macon, Ga.: Mercer University Press, 1990), p. 29: Polycarp draws from the same "primitive catechism" as Clement.

87. Cf. Rom 12:17; 1 Thess 5:15; 1 Pet 3:9.

88. λοιδορίαν ἀντὶ λοιδορίας; cf. 1 Pet 3:9: "not returning evil for evil or railing for railing (λοιδορίαν ἀντὶ λοιδορίας) but, on the contrary, (respond with) a blessing." This draws not upon Matthew (as do plausibly 1 Pet 2:1 [cf. Mt 5:16], 3:14 [cf. Mt 5:10], and maybe 4:13–14 [cf. Mt 5:11–12]; see Rainer Metzner, *Die Rezeption des Matthäusevangeliums im 1.Petrusbrief*, WUNT, ser. 2, vol. 74 [Tübingen: J. C. B. Mohr (Paul Siebeck), 1995], pp. 7–68) but oral tradition (cf. Rom 12:14). That 1 Peter contains parallels not only to Q 6:28 (cf. also 1 Pet 3:16) but also to 6:32–33 (see 1 Pet 2:19–20) is consistent with the contention that 6:32–34 circulated not in isolation but only as commentary on 6:27–30. For further discussion see Ernest Best, "1 Peter and the Gospel Tradition," *NTS* 16 (1969), esp. pp. 105–106.

89. κατάραν ἀντὶ κατάριας; Q 6:28 uses καταρωμένους.

1. accusative ending in -ov + ἀντί + genitive ending in -ου
2. accusative ending in -αν + ἀντί + genitive ending in -ιας

1. imperative + ἵνα + verb ending in -ητε
2. imperative + verb ending in -θησεται + ὑμῖν
1. imperative + ἵνα + verb ending in -ητε
2. imperative + verb ending in -θησεται + ὑμῖν

All this indicates once more that the materials in Q 6:27–38 circulated as a collection, and also that, although the content was not always the same, certain patterns were consistently employed as an aid to memory.[90]

These patterns appear in yet another extracanonical text with parallels to the SP. *Did.* 1:3–5[91] contains these words:

Now of these words the doctrine is this:

1. Bless those who curse you (cf. Lk 6:28 = Q)[92]

2. And pray for your enemies (cf. Lk 6:27–28, Mt 5:44)[93]

3. Fast for those who persecute you (cf. Mt 5:44)[94]

4. For what credit is it (cf. Lk 6:32–34 = Q and
   Mt 5:46–47)[95]
   if you love those who love you? (cf. Lk 6:32 = Q
   and Mt 5:46)[96]
   Do not also the Gentiles do the same? (cf. Mt 5:47 = Q)

5. Love those who hate you (cf. Lk 6:27 = Q)[97]
   and you will have no enemy (no parallel)

6. Abstain from fleshly and bodily lusts (no parallel)

---

90. It is noteworthy that even two of the Pauline parallels to Q 6:27–38, namely, Rom 12:14 and 1 Cor 4:12–13, feature parallelism. Cf. also Justin, *1 Apol.* 15:14.

91. *Did.* 1:3b–5 is often considered a Christian interpolation into a preexisting Jewish text on the two ways. But the point is irrelevant for our purposes.

92. There is no Matthean parallel. But cf. Justin, *1 Apol.* 15:9.

93. Cf. Justin, *1 Apol.* 15:9; *Dial.* 96:3, 133:6; *Didascalia* 5:14; *Ps. Clem. Hom.* 12:32. Presumably the natural conflation of "love your enemies" with "do good to those who hate you" to obtain "love those who hate you" led in turn to the conflation of "pray for those who abuse you" (Q 6:28; cf. Mt 5:44) with "love your enemies" (Q 6:27, 35 = Mt 5:44). But it may be that early Christian tradition wished to soften the stark imperative, "Love your enemies"—which appears nowhere outside of Matthew and Luke until Justin; see Kuhn, "Liebesgebot," pp. 196–98.

94. There is nothing about fasting in Mt 5:38–48 or Lk 6:27–38; but Mt 5:44 has "pray for those who persecute you."

95. ποία χάρις appears in the *Didache* and Luke; Matthew has τίνα μισθόν.

96. The P. Oxy. 1782 frag. for *Did.* 1:3 has φιλῆτε...φιλοῦντας, which might be original. The synoptic parallels use ἀγαπάω.

97. This is another conflation of "love your enemies" and "do good to those who hate you." Cf. the parallels in Justin, *1 Apol.* 15:9; *Dial.* 133:6; *Ps. Clem. Hom.* 3:19.

7. If anyone strikes you on the right cheek (cf. Mt 5:39)[98]
   turn to that one also the other (cf. Mt 5:39)[99]
   and you will be perfect (cf. Mt 5:48)[100]

8. If anyone compel you to go one mile (cf. Mt 5:41)[101]
   go two (cf. Mt 5:41)

9. If anyone take from you your outer garment
   (cf. Lk 6:29)[102]
   give to that one also your inner garment (cf. Lk 6:29)[103]

10. If anyone takes from you what is yours (no parallel)
    do not ask it back (cf. Lk 6:30 = Q)[104]

11. To all asking of you give (cf. Lk 6:30, Mt 5:42)
    and do not ask back (cf. Lk 6:30 = Q)[105]

12. For the Father wants gifts to be given from his own bounties
    to all (cf. Lk 6:35–36, Mt 5:45)

Here it is not possible to enter into a detailed analysis of this text and its relationship to the SM and SP. It suffices to remark upon two facts. First, *Did.* 1:3–5 sometimes agrees with Lk 6:27–38 over against a Matthean parallel[106] and sometimes it agrees with a Matthean parallel over against Lk 6:27–38.[107] Second, whereas some of the latter agreements betray the influence of Matthean redaction,[108] none of the latter shows the influence of Lukan redaction.[109] So given that there is otherwise no evidence that the *Didache* knew or used Luke, it is a good bet

---

98. Lk 6:29 lacks "right." The word is probably redactional; cf. Fitzmyer, *Luke*, vol. 1, p. 638: "Luke's fondness for the 'right' hand/ear...makes it difficult to think that he would have suppressed the adjective here, if it were in his source."

99. There is a parallel in Lk 6:29; but the Greek of the *Didache* is here closer to Matthew, which is in turn presumably closer to Q than Luke; see Davies and Allison, *Matthew*, vol. 1, p. 543.

100. There is no parallel in Luke, and Matthew's text is redactional; see the commentaries.

101. There is no Lukan parallel. Was the line an addition of Q^mt?

102. The *Didache* and Luke have ἱμάτιον, Matthew χιτών.

103. The *Didache* and Luke have χιτών, Matthew ἱμάτιον.

104. μὴ ἀπαίτει appears in both the *Didache* and Luke but not Matthew.

105. Again, μὴ ἀπαίτει appears in both the *Didache* and Luke but not Matthew.

106. See sayings 1, 4, 5, 9, 10, 11.

107. See sayings 3, 4, 7, 8.

108. So, e.g., sayings 3, 7.

109. This against C. M. Tuckett, "Synoptic Tradition in the Didache," in *The New Testament in Early Christianity*, ed. J.-M. Servin (Louvain: Louvain University Press, 1989), pp. 197–230. For a response to Tuckett see Willy Rordorf, "Does the Didache Contain Jesus Tradition Independently of the Synoptic Gospels?," in *Jesus and the Oral Gospel Tradition*, ed. Henry Wansbrough, JSNTSS, vol. 64 (Sheffield: JSOT, 1991), pp. 394–423.

that *Did.* 1:3–5 preserves an oral composition which the author of the *Didache* modified under Matthew's influence.[110]

This conclusion unfortunately does not allow us to sort out exactly what the *Didache*'s source looked like before material from Mt 5:39–48 was added.[111] But the main point for us is that the *Didache* shows yet again that the materials now gathered in the central section of the SP were traditionally associated with certain patterns which presumably reflect the handling of tradition in an oral environment. (1) When one perceives that saying 4 is actually the beginning of or introduction to saying 5, then it becomes clear that the unit opens with four imperatives (cf. the groups of four in Q 6:27–28, 29–30, 37–38; 1 *Clem.* 13:2; Polycarp, *Ep.* 2:2–3). Further, sayings 7–10 constitute an obvious quatrain:

> 7. ἐάν + τις + σοι + verb
> 8. ἐάν + verb + σέ + τις
> 9. ἐάν + verb + τις + neuter noun with def. article + σου
> 10. ἐάν + verb + τις + σου + neuter noun with def. article

(2) As appears from the preceding representation, sayings 9 and 10 (both of which concern losing property) seem to be formally related, as do 7 and 8. Imperatives 1 and 2 are linked with καί, whereas imperatives 3 and 4 both have δέ in second position. Here too, as with Q 6:27–38; Rom 12:14; 1 Cor 4:12–13; 1 *Clem.* 13:2; and Polycarp, *Ep.* 2:2–3, lines are formed into pairs.[112] (3) The entire unit ends with a dative construction which breaks the parallelism of the preceding lines.

---

110. Cf. Davies and Allison, *Matthew,* vol. 1, p. 539. Köhler, *Rezeption,* pp. 43–47, argues for independence from Matthew. Contrast Massaux, *Influence,* pp. 148–50, who contends that the *Didache* conflates Matthew and Luke. For further discussion see Clayton N. Jefford, *The Sayings of Jesus in the Teaching of the Twelve Apostles* (Leiden: E. J. Brill, 1989), pp. 38–52. That the *Didache* here used a nonsynoptic source is made the more plausible by Justin, 1 *Apol.* 15:9: "Pray for your enemies and love those who hate you; bless those who curse you and pray for them who despitefully use you." Although Justin knew both Matthew and Luke as well as a harmonized gospel source, he also had access to extracanonical tradition, as in the words just quoted. See further Koester, *Gospels,* pp. 360–402, and Köhler, *Rezeption,* pp. 166–69.

111. One cannot reconstruct a hypothetical source simply by subtracting from the *Didache* elements with parallels in Matthew, for (1) sometimes Matthew rather than Luke preserves the earlier tradition (= Q) and (2) when a parallel to the *Didache* appears in the same form in Matthew and Luke we cannot determine whether it came from Matthew or the *Didache*'s other source. It may, however, be significant that the *Didache* contains parallels to Q 6:27–36 but not 6:37–38. In this particular the *Didache* is more primitive than Q, Clement, or Polycarp.

112. The parallel in Justin, 1 *Apol.* 15:9 (see n. 110) contains a chiastic quatrain:

> εὔχεσθε ὑπὲρ τῶν + -ων + ὑμῶν
> imperative ending in -τε + τούς + participle + ὑμᾶς
>
> imperative ending in -τε + τούς + participle + ὑμῖν
> εὔχεσθε ὑπὲρ τῶν + -ων + ὑμῶν

This recalls Q 6:38; *1 Clem.* 13:2; and Polycarp, *Ep.* 2:2–3. And if say-ing 4 is indeed the introduction to 5, then again we have an irregular final member. (4) *Did.* 1:5 ends the section on loving enemies with an appeal to the goodness of God the Father. One is inevitably reminded of Q 6:36, which once concluded Q 6:27ff. with the very same appeal.

Having argued that 6:27–36, 37–38 was a unit before Q, that this unit or relatives of it are attested outside the synoptics, and that the compiler of Q³ was responsible for putting the beatitudes at the begin-ning of the discourse and the parable of the two builders (6:47–49) at the end, it remains to consider the material in 6:39–46.

There is first 6:39–42, which contains three originally independent units that now function as a whole — the saying about the blind leading the blind (6:39), the saying about the disciple not being above the master (6:40), and the parable about the splinter in the eye (6:41–42).[113] The last consists of two parallel questions followed by a strong exhortation introduced with "hypocrite":

Question 1:
    Why do you see the speck in your brother's eye
    but do not see the log in your own eye?

Question 2:
    How can you say ... let me take out the speck from
        your eye
    and behold! there is a log in your own eye?

Concluding command:
    Imperative: Hypocrite, first take the log out of your
        own eye
    Result: then you will see clearly to remove the speck from
        your brother's eye

The rhetorical questions remind one of the rhetorical questions in 6:32–34, and the parallelism also recalls earlier lines. But the harshness of the concluding address ("hypocrites") is new. New too is the ecclesiastical orientation, signaled by the use of "brother" (6:41, 42). Unlike 6:27–38, in which the issue is how disciples should act towards their enemies, in 6:39–42 the issue is how they should relate to one another. Obviously the materials in 6:39–42 envisage a situation different from those in 6:27–38.

---

113. The transparently independent origin of the materials is consistent with their being separated in the *Gospel of Thomas.* The parallels to Q 6:39 and 6:41–42 appear in *Gos. Thom.* 34 and 26, respectively; Q 6:40 is without parallel in *Thomas.* Catchpole, *Quest,* pp. 79–80, urges that Lk 6:40 owes its placement in the SP to Luke; its Q context cannot be discovered.

This judgment is reinforced by the beginning of 6:39: "He also told them a parable." Although this is Lukan in its present form,[114] it could rewrite an editorial transition that stood in Q, a transition which would presumably reflect the circumstance that at this juncture someone joined two distinct sources. But even were the editorial comment purely Lukan redaction,[115] it would still show that at least Luke felt there to be some sort of transition at this point.

Whoever added 6:39–42 also probably added 6:43–46. For the function of the latter, which features καρπός three times, is the function of the former, which features κάρφος three times: both call those within the community to examine themselves. The continuing focus on fraternal relations in contrast to the focus of 6:27–38 explains the tension between 6:35, where the wicked (πονηρούς) are outside the community, and 6:43–45, where the wicked (ὁ πονηρός) are plainly inside.

Q 6:43–46 also presents us with more parallelism:[116]

Opening generalization in antithetical parallelism (6:43):
    No good  tree makes rotten fruit
    No rotten tree makes good  fruit

Explanatory phrase (6:44a):
    For each tree is known by its fruit

Concrete illustrations of 6:43 in synthetic parallelism (6:44b):
    They do not gather from thorns  figs
    nor                  from bramble grapes

Application to human sphere in antithetical parallelism (6:45a):
    The good person out of the treasure of the heart brings forth good
    The evil      out of          the evil  brings forth evil

Explanatory phrase/conclusion (6:45b):
    For out of the abundance of the heart the mouth speaks

But as with 6:39–42, the other formal features so conspicuous in 6:27–38 and its extracanonical parallels are either absent (strings of imperatives, sets of fours, breaking parallelism with the last entry in a series) or less prominent (resemblance between alternating lines to create pairs). Q 6:43–46 also links itself with 6:39–42, but not with 6:27–38, in that it features parabolic speech[117] and singular subjects and imperatives instead of plural subject and imperatives.[118]

---

114. See Jeremias, *Sprache*, p. 146.

115. See n. 44.

116. On the pre-Q evolution of this unit see Kloppenborg, *Formation*, pp. 182–83. Perhaps the editor of Q³ added 6:45b.

117. Outlines of the SP have often labelled Lk 6:39–49 a parabolic section; see I. H. Marshall, *Commentary on Luke* (Grand Rapids: Eerdmans, 1978), p. 243.

118. The exceptions are 6:29–30 (singular nouns and verbs; but see n. 56) and 6:46 (plural imperative).

That it was a contributor to Q who added not only 6:39–42 but also 6:43–45[119] follows from several considerations.[120] First, 6:43–45 establishes a link with the wider Q context: Jesus' words about trees and fruit echo John the Baptist's words about the same two things (3:8–9).[121] Second, 6:43–45 supplies a good introduction to the redactional conclusion of the discourse. Not only do both units have to do with the two sorts of people who live within the community,[122] but "out of the abundance of the heart his mouth speaks" (6:45) appropriately prefaces the rebuke in 6:46 of those who vainly say, "Lord, Lord." Moreover, both 6:43–45 and 6:46–49 call for examination of one's deeds. Third, 6:39–42, 43–45, and 46–49 all draw the line not between insiders and outsiders (cf. 6:27–38) but between good disciples and bad. In theological terms, 6:39–49 raises the possibility of sin within the Christian community itself. Thus 6:41–42 instructs disciples to worry about their own faults before attempting to address the faults of others. Q 6:39 similarly warns that one who is blind cannot lead others.[123] Q 6:43–45 invites reflection upon whether one is producing good or rotten fruit. And 6:46–49 demands sober evaluation of whether one's Christian confession of "Lord" is genuine or not. It would seem, then, that the Q editor, stimulated by the "Do not judge" of 6:37, expanded the SP by collecting traditions which together issue in a call to judge not others but oneself.

One question remains. Q 6:40 is a puzzle for any reconstruction. Here Jesus says that a disciple is not above the teacher, but everyone who is fully qualified will be like the teacher. The commentators on Q are as baffled as those on Luke, and any number of suggestions have been offered.[124] The link with the immediate context is so obscure that one might wonder whether 6:40 was joined to 6:39 before 6:41ff. was added and so had a meaning that is lost in its present context.[125] Or perhaps 6:39 and 6:40 were once joined by catchword in an Aramaic source and the catchword connection became lost in translation.

---

119. Whether the sayings 6:43–45 were already united before Q cannot be determined.

120. Against the conjecture of Schürmann, *Lukasevangelium*, vol. 1, pp. 385–86, who argues that 6:39–45 preserves an old anti-Pharisaic collection, see Kloppenborg, *Formation*, pp. 183–85.

121.  Q 3:8–9                             Q 6:43

ποιήσατε καρπόν/ποιοῦν καρπόν     ποιοῦν καρπόν (twice)
δένδρον                               δένδρον
καρπὸν καλόν                         καρπὸν καλόν

122. On the application of 6:43–45 to the community see R. A. Piper, *Wisdom*, pp. 49–51.

123. Ibid., p. 40: "The reference to 'leading' is...parallel in thought to 'judging': that is, putting oneself in a position of superiority."

124. See the review in Marshall, *Luke*, pp. 269–70.

125. This is the suggestion of Joachim Wanke, " 'Kommentarworte': Älteste Kommentierungen von Herrenworten," *BZ* 24 (1980): 213–14.

I should like, however, to raise the possibility that 6:40 was added in Q, and that its meaning may be discerned from looking at the broader context within the SP.

Commentators regularly assume, probably because of the parallels in Mt 10:24–25; Jn 13:16; and 15:20 that the "teacher" of 6:40 must be Jesus.[126] Yet because the example of Jesus appears nowhere else in the discourse, this assumption requires one to read quite a bit into the text. It may be better to look for another starting point.

Although the SP does not feature the example of Jesus, it does feature the example of God. In 6:35 the call to love enemies and to turn the other cheek is reinforced by reference to the Most High being good to the ungrateful and the wicked. In 6:36 Jesus asks his followers to be merciful even as their divine Father is merciful. Might this use of the *imitatio Dei* just a few verses before 6:40 be the key to interpretation? The notion of God as teacher was well known in Jewish tradition.[127] This notion found its way into early Christianity, as Jn 6:45; 1 Cor 2:13; 1 Thess 4:9; and *Barn.* 4:9 prove. With this in mind it is possible that Q 6:40 carries forward the theme that one must be like God, whose example is precept: if God shows mercy, then how can one condemn a brother or sister? The disciple is not above the divine teacher but rather hopes to become like that teacher.

Whether or not this is the correct interpretation of Q 6:40, the observations made about the SP herein lead to the following compositional history. Q 6:27–36, 37–38 already existed before being taken up into Q. A coherent piece exhorting disciples to love their enemy and show mercy, it (or a near relative) was evidently known to Paul, Clement, Polycarp, and a contributor to the *Didache*. Q then expanded this little discourse by (1) creating a preface with the beatitudes (6:20–23); (2) inserting a series of traditions which call those within the community to worry about making themselves rather than others better (6:39–45); and (3) constructing a conclusion, 6:46–49, which makes it plain that eschatological judgment will fall not only upon outsiders but also upon the household of God.

---

126. Cf. Kloppenborg, *Formation*, p. 185.
127. See, e.g., 2 Chr 6:27; Pss 25:12; 32:8; 71:17; 119:102, 171; Isa 54:13; Jer 32:33 (cf. 31:34); Hos 11:3; *Ps. Sol.* 17:32.

# – 3 –

# FOUR BEATITUDES, Q 6:20–23

## A Unified Composition

It has become a commonplace of scholarship that the four beatitudes in the Sermon on the Plain were not originally a literary unit.[1] The first three rather circulated on their own for a time before someone added the fourth. The reasons for this far-flung conviction have been concisely stated by John Kloppenborg: "The first three use the formula μακάριοι οἱ + substantive while the fourth uses μακάριοί ἐστε ὅταν; the first three are bipartite, consisting of a beatitude and a ὅτι clause but the fourth has a beatitude and an imperative with a motive clause; and the first three depend upon a logic of eschatological reversal, while the last uses the motif of eschatological reward. Finally, 6:20b–21 presupposes the general human conditions of poverty and suffering, while 6:22–23 is oriented toward the specific situation of persecution of the Christian community."[2]

What are we to make of these arguments, which have persuaded so many? They come down to this: the first three beatitudes differ from the fourth in having (1) a different introductory formula, (2) a different form, (3) a different content, and (4) a different setting in life. The publication of a recent Dead Sea Scroll, however, moves one to reconsider the force of these observations.

In 1991 Emile Puech published the fragments of three columns of a sapiential text.[3] Joseph Fitzmyer has translated the text as follows:

---

1. Cf. Bultmann, *History,* pp. 109–10; Catchpole, *Quest,* p. 91; Davies and Allison, *Matthew,* vol. 1, p. 435; Josef Ernst, *Das Evangelium nach Lukas,* RNT (Regensburg: Friedrich Pustet, 1977), p. 215; Guelich, *Sermon on the Mount,* p. 112; Jacobson, *First Gospel,* pp. 99–100; J. Meier, *Mentor, Message, and Miracles,* p. 322; Myung-Soo Kim, *Die Trägergruppe von Q: Sozialgeschichtliche Forschung zur Q-Überlieferung in den synoptischen Evangelien,* Wissenschaftliche Beiträge aus Europäischen Hochschulen, ser. 1, vol. 1 (Ammersbek: Lottbek/Peter Jensen, 1990), pp. 103–106; Mack, *Lost Gospel,* pp. 73, 83; Manson, *Sayings,* p. 49; Schürmann, *Lukasevangelium,* vol. 1, p. 335.

2. *Formation,* pp. 172–73.

3. "4 Q525 et les péricopes des béatitudes en Ben Sira et Matthieu," *RB* 98 (1991): 80–106. See also idem, "Un Hymne essénien en partie retrouvé et les Béatitudes. IQH V 12–VI 18 (= col. XIII–XIV 7) et 4QBéat," *RevQ* 13 (1988): 59–88.

> Blessed are those who cling to her statutes and cling not (2) to paths of iniquity. Bles[s]ed are those who rejoice in her and babble not about paths of iniquity. Blessed are those who search for her (3) with clean hands and seek not after her with a deceitful heart. Blessed is the man who has attained wisdom and walks (4) by the law of the Most High and fixes his heart on her ways, gives heed to her admonishments, delights al[wa]ys in her chastisements, (5) and forsakes her not in the stress of [his] trou[bles]; (who) in time of distress abandons her not and forgets her not [in days of] fear, (6) and in the affliction of his soul rejects [her] not. For on her he meditates, and in his anguish he ponders [on the law]; and in al]l (7) his existence [he considers] her [and puts her] before his eyes so as not to walk in the paths of [   ].[4]

These lines are instructive for a number of reasons, not the least of them being the light they shed on the question of the unity of Q 6:20–23. For three of the four arguments for dissociating Q 6:22–23 (the fourth beatitude) from Q 6:20–21 (the first three beatitudes) appear equally applicable to the newly published Qumran text. So unless one wishes to argue that the latter is composite — and it does not appear to be[5] — we evidently need to reconsider our views about the former.

To cite Kloppenborg again, "The first three [beatitudes] use the formula μακάριοι οἱ + substantive while the fourth uses μακάριοί ἐστε ὅταν." The Hebrew of 4Q525, although it uses the third person throughout, offers a comparable phenomenon. For here too the final introduction is different from the first three. The first three beatitudes in 4Q525 are prefaced by "Blessed are those," the last by "Blessed is the man."[6] At a glance:

אשרי + plural subject (תומכי)
אשרי + plural subject (הגלים)
אשרי + plural subject (דורשיה)
אשרי + singular subject (אדם)

In addition to this irregularity in 4Q525, I note that still other texts contain switches from third to second person or vice versa. Examples

---

4. Fitzmyer, "Palestinian Collection," p. 512. The first extant beatitude is preceded by "with a pure heart and slanders not with his tongue." Puech turns this into a beatitude by prefacing it with "Blessed is the one who speaks truth" (cf. Ps 15:2–3). But the text is missing, and Puech's arguments that there were eight beatitudes altogether fails to persuade. In the following investigation I shall only make use of the text that has been preserved, not of Puech's conjectures.

5. The fourth beatitude, like the previous three, concerns Wisdom and is linked by catchword to the preceding blessings (דרך appears in lines 2 and 4, לב in lines 1, 3, and 4).

6. Cf. the MT of Pss 32:2; 84:6, 84:13; Prov 8:34.

appear in Isa 63:10–14;[7] Ecclus 47:12–23,[8] 48:1–12;[9] 4Q286 10 ii 2–
13;[10] *Gos. Thom.* 68–69;[11] and *Acts of Thomas* 94.[12] Only *Gos. Thom.*
68–69 might plausibly be explained in terms of multiple sources, so we
should perhaps speak here of a rhetorical pattern, in which the alteration between second and third person is used for good effect. Perhaps
the move in Q from μακάριοι οἱ to μακάριοί ἐστε is not the sign of a
secondary joining but a way of getting our attention.

Kloppenborg's second argument for the separation of Q 6:22–23
from 6:20–21 is that the first three beatitudes have a bipartite arrangement whereas the last has a beatitude and an imperative with a motive
clause. In other words, the forms are different. But such is also the case
with 4Q525. The first three beatitudes are short antithetical couplets
which bless those who do one thing but not another:

> Blessed are those
> who cling to her statutes
> and cling not (ולא) to paths of iniquity.

> Blessed are those
> who rejoice in her
> and babble not (ולוא) about paths of iniquity.

> Blessed are those
> who search for her with clean hands
> and seek not (ולוא) after her with a deceitful heart.

But the fourth beatitude has an altogether different pattern. It is not
even clear where the beatitude ends:

> Blessed is the man who
> has attained wisdom
> and walks by the law of the Most High
> and fixes his heart on her ways,
> gives heed to her admonishments,

---

7. Here the prophet first speaks of God in the third person, then in the second person.
The rhetorical effect is to move from reminiscence to prayer.

8. This is the story of Solomon. It begins and ends with a third-person narrative —
"Solomon reigned...God gave him rest"/"Solomon rested with his father" (vv. 12–13,
23) — but in the middle it becomes an address to Solomon: "How wise you became," etc.
(vv. 14–22).

9. This is the story of Elijah; it, like that of Solomon, is an address to the prophet
himself (vv. 4–11) that is framed with a third-person account (vv. 1–2, 12).

10. This series of curses opens with lines in the third person — "Cursed be Belial,"
etc. — but then becomes more intense as it moves on to address evil spirits directly —
"Damned be you," etc.

11. Here there are three beatitudes. The first uses the second person, the next two the
third person.

12. This is a list of eleven beatitudes. The first three are in the third person, the
remainder in the second.

> delights al[wa]ys in her chastisements,
> and forsakes her not in the stress of [his] trou[bles];
> (who) in time of distress abandons her not
> and forgets her not [in days of] fear,
> and in the affliction of his soul rejects [her] not.
> For on her he meditates . . .

However one analyzes this, it is clearly not formed on the same design as the other beatitudes. Once more the parallel with Q 6:20–23 is striking.[13]

Kloppenborg also urges against the unity of Q 6:20–23 that while the first three beatitudes are about eschatological reversal, the last uses the motif of eschatological reward. This argument is not something to which 4Q525, which is thoroughly sapiential, addresses itself. But Kloppenborg can be countered on other grounds. Where is it written that an ancient author could not move from one subject to another closely related to it, here from the subject of eschatological reversal to that of eschatological reward? Indeed, might one not think the two subjects nearly one and the same? Surely one can imagine that it is precisely eschatological reversal which will bring about eschatological reward.

What about the fourth argument, that while Q 6:20b–21 addresses the general human conditions of poverty and suffering, 6:22–23 reflects the persecution of the Christian community? Here once more 4Q525 may be relevant. In the first three Qumran beatitudes the focus is upon what the blessed do and do not do — they cling to the statutes of wisdom and cling not to the paths of iniquity, and so forth. But in the final beatitude — as in the final Q beatitude — the situation is different. The man who is blessed is admonished. He suffers chastisements and trouble. He experiences fear and is afflicted in soul. And his lot is anguish. Here we have the same sort of paradoxical teaching as in Q's beatitudes: it is the unhappy and miserable who are said to be blessed. The main point, however, is that 4Q525's final beatitude, like Q's final beatitude, addresses a different set of experiences than the three beatitudes which precede it.

But there is probably more to Kloppenborg's fourth argument, and it requires further discussion. Kloppenborg probably assumes what Rudolf Bultmann explicitly stated: the blessing of those hated and excluded, reviled and defamed on account of the Son of man must be "*ex eventu* and for that reason created by the Church"; the direct reference to the person of Jesus is decisive.[14] In other words, the Christology and the situation of persecution, both of which are missing from the earlier blessings —

---

13. Cf. Benedict T. Viviano, "Beatitudes Found among Dead Sea Scrolls," *BAR* 18, no. 6 (1992): 66.

14. Bultmann, *History*, pp. 110, 128.

which Bultmann, along with just about everybody, assigns to Jesus —
are things we should credit to the community.[15] Once more, however,
there is cause for doubt.

Luke, who here probably preserves Q,[16] refers to hatred, social ostracism, reproach, and defamation. One is hard-pressed to explain why
these sorts of things could not have been reflected upon and spoken
about in a pre-Easter setting.[17] John the Baptist, with whom Jesus was
closely identified, was arrested and executed; and, unless the synoptics
cannot be trusted at all, Jesus himself engaged in verbal fisticuffs with
at least some Pharisees and scribes. Q 9:58 depicts him as a rejected
figure, with nowhere to lay his head. Certainly there is no doubt that
he ended up on a cross, a circumstance which demonstrates *somebody's*
hostility towards him. Further, Jesus and his followers engaged in a mission which must on occasion have met with an unfavorable, even hostile
reception (cf. Mk 6:1–6). This fact is attested in Q's missionary discourse — "lambs in the midst of wolves," "whenever you enter a town
and they do not welcome you," "it will be more tolerable for Sodom
than for that town" (Q 10:3, 10, 12) — as well as in the woes upon
Chorazin, Bethsaida, and Capernaum (Q 10:13–15).[18] It is in addition
overwhelmingly likely that Jesus interpreted his own time, or at least the
near future, as that of the messianic woes and that he anticipated severe
suffering for himself and his followers. Q 6:22–23 would fit such an
outlook perfectly. Did Jesus not proclaim that he lived in a period not
of peace but of the sword, in a time when, in fulfillment of the eschatological prophecy in Mic 7:6, a man would be divided against his father
and a daughter against her mother and a daughter-in-law against her
mother-in-law?[19] The argument that Q 6:22–23 reflects a later situation
beyond the ministry of the historical Jesus because it envisages hatred,
social ostracism, reproach, and defamation is not compelling.

But perhaps the problem is the supposition that Jesus could not have
spoken about persecution at the same time that he blessed the poor and
the hungry and those in mourning. Does not Q 6:22–23 envisage a
smaller group than Q 6:20–21, which is of more general application?

---

15. Cf. Luz, *Matthew 1–7*, p. 229.

16. Matthew's love of the triad probably explains why in his Gospel persecution takes
only three forms.

17. In addition to what follows see now Jerome H. Neyrey, "Loss of Wealth, Loss of
Family, and Loss of Honour: The Cultural Context of the Original Makarisms in Q," in
*Modelling Early Christianity: Social Scientific Studies of the New Testament in Its Context,*
ed. Philip F. Esler (London: Routledge, 1996), pp. 139–58. Neyrey's thesis is that "the
original four makarisms describe the composite fate of a disciple who has been ostracized
as a 'rebellious son' by his family for loyalty to Jesus" (p. 145).

18. On the authenticity of Q 10:3, 10, 12, and 13–15 see above, p. 61, n. 276.

19. For the authenticity and eschatological interpretation of Q 12:51–53 see Allison,
*End of the Ages*, pp. 118–20.

As Kloppenborg has it, Q 6:20b–21 presupposes the general human conditions of poverty and suffering, Q 6:22–23 the specific situation of persecution of the Christian community. But in truth we have not a clue as to whom Jesus originally addressed Q 6:20–21. Nothing more than supposition leads us to find here the general human conditions of poverty and suffering.[20] Certainly Jesus may very well have composed his beatitudes for a group of oppressed Galilean peasants. But he may equally have addressed Q 6:20–23 to people who had embraced his message, or no less plausibly to a small group of disciples or missionaries.[21] And in either of these last two cases there is no reason at all to find the content of Q 6:22–23 out of accord with Q 6:20–21.[22]

What then about the explicit Christology? It is not at all certain that "the Son of man" stood in the earliest version of our saying: some have thought the title here due to Q or Lukan redaction.[23] In this case we would be dealing with Matthew's less-loaded "on account of me." Further, it is just not the case that the Jesus of Q 6:20–21 has no special status. On the contrary, the explicit Christology of the fourth beatitude harmonizes with the implicit Christology of the first three beatitudes, in which the speaker lays tacit claim to be the eschatological herald of Isaiah 61.[24] If, however, one nonetheless remains convinced that the historical Jesus could not have said "on account of me" or "on account of the Son of man," then why not, instead of regarding the entirety of the fourth beatitude as secondary, entertain the possibility, with Harnack and Carsten Colpe,[25] that ἕνεκα κ.τ.λ. is a secondary insertion, as is the related expression in Mt 10:39 (diff. Lk 17:33; Jn 12:25)? Certainly many have not hesitated — here with much better reasons — to regard another portion of the fourth beatitude ("for that is what their fathers did to the prophets," Q 6:23) as a later addition.[26]

Having called into question the arguments for separating Q 6:20–21 from 6:22–23, I now wish to urge that there are on the other hand some

---

20. And this supposition is not obviously supported by the background in Isaiah 61; see below.

21. The synoptics depict Jesus' disciples and missionaries as poor (Mk 10:28–31; Lk 10:4, etc.) and potentially hungry (Lk 10:7).

22. Perhaps we should also entertain the interpretation of Marshall, *Luke*, p. 252: "If the first three beatitudes are addressed to men as they now are, and invite them to discipleship with its accompanying blessings, the fourth warns of the fate that may overtake them and calls them to be joyful despite this additional burden in this world."

23. E.g., Catchpole, *Quest*, p. 93 (Q redaction); Fitzmyer, *Luke*, vol. 1, p. 635 (Lukan redaction); Barnabas Lindars, *Jesus Son of Man* (Grand Rapids: Eerdmans, 1983), pp. 134–35 (Lukan redaction).

24. See herein, pp. 6–7.

25. Harnack, *Sayings*, pp. 52–53; Carsten Colpe, "ὁ υἱὸς τοῦ ἀνθρώπος," *TDNT*, vol. 8, pp. 443, 448–49.

26. Cf. Kloppenborg, *Formation*, p. 173: the parallels in 1 Pet 4:14 and *Gos. Thom.* 68 and 69a lack the phrase.

reasons for holding the two together. First, Q 6:20–23 in its entirety should be read against the background of Isaiah 61. It is not just the first and third beatitudes that allude to Isaiah: so seemingly does the fourth. Its theme of rejoicing is paralleled in Isa 61:3 and 61:10. This is perhaps some reason for postulating the unity of Q 6:20–23. Moreover, if Q 6:20–23 blesses the poor, those who mourn,[27] and those who are hated, excluded, reproached, and spoken evil of, in Isaiah the poor and those who mourn are oppressed, despised, forsaken, and hated (Isa 60:14–15). The correlation is probably not coincidence.

Second, the *Gospel of Thomas* contains ten beatitudes. These are scattered throughout the work (7, 18, 19, 49, 54, 58, 68–69 [a series of three], 103). Those in 7, 18, 19, 49, 58, and 103 have no close synoptic parallels, but the other four recall Matthew and Luke. "Blessed are the poor, for yours is the kingdom of heaven" (54) is a variant of Q 6:20. "Blessed are you when you are hated and persecuted and no place is found where you have been persecuted" and — "Blessed are those who have been persecuted in their heart. These are they who have known the Father in truth" — resemble Q 6:22–23. And "Blessed are the hungry, so that the belly of him who desires will be filled" (68–69) is near to Q 6:21a. What is the explanation? Perhaps the decisive fact is this: the *Gospel of Thomas* finds counterparts only in Lk 6:20–23; it does not, that is, supply variants for the beatitudes that appear only in Matthew (which are from M or Q^mt or Matthew's own hand). So it is a good guess that here the *Gospel of Thomas* reflects knowledge of Luke or of Q or of the presynoptic collection of four beatitudes behind Q 6:20–23.[28] In other words, *Thomas* offers no reason for thinking that Q 6:22–23 circulated apart from Q 6:20–21.

Finally, I wish to return to the parallel in 4Q525. Whether or not Puech is correct in thinking that the four extant beatitudes were preceded by several more, there is no disputing that the pattern in the scroll's beatitudes is precisely what we find in Q: several short, similar beatitudes followed by a dissimilar and much longer beatitude. One cannot, of course, generalize from two cases, but it may be that we have here a rhetorical convention: the concluding irregularity is a way of being emphatic. Perhaps it is only the dearth of texts that have survived which prevents us from seeing the obvious.

This conjecture is reinforced by the series of beatitudes in the *Acts of*

---

27. On the originality of Matthew's "Blessed are those who mourn, for you will be comforted" see n. 33 on p. 7.

28. 1 Peter shows knowledge of Q's last beatitude (1 Pet 4:13–14) but not the first three. 1 Pet 3:14 ("But even if you suffer for righteousness' sake, you are blessed"), however, closely resembles Mt 5:10, which is presumably redactional (see Davies and Allison, *Matthew*, vol. 1, pp. 459–60). This implies that the author of 1 Peter knew and used Matthew and so is no independent witness to the beatitudes; cf. Luz, *Matthew 1–7*, p. 93.

*Paul and Thecla* 5–6 (thirteen beatitudes) and *2 Enoch* 42:6–14 J (nine beatitudes). In both, the last beatitude is the longest,[29] and its form is, compared with what goes before, irregular.[30] Furthermore, years ago, long before the publication of 4Q525, David Daube remarked that there are several ancient texts that make the last and climactic member of a series longer than the preceding members.[31] Examples appear in the canonical Gospels themselves, in Mt 1:2–17; 10:40–42; 23:13–36; and Lk 6:37–38 (another Q text from the Sermon on the Plain), as well as in lists of woes, which are so closely related to beatitudes (Lk 6:24–26; *1 Enoch* 99:10–15).[32] To all this we can add now 4Q525. Although Daube's indisputable observation has been roundly ignored,[33] it is hard to see why. Now, with the publication of 4Q525, his contention is all the more forceful. The irregular form of the concluding Q 6:22–23 is probably to be interpreted as a literary convention.

---

29. Although admittedly not by that much in the latter.

30. In the *Acts of Paul and Thecla* 5–6 the final beatitude has two motive clauses; all the rest have one. In *2 Enoch* 42:6–14 J only the last beatitude has an elaborating motive clause.

31. David Daube, *The New Testament and Rabbinic Judaism* (London: Athlone, 1956), pp. 196–201.

32. Note also the irregular final members in the noncanonical texts discussed on pp. 84–92 herein (*1 Clem.* 13:2; Polycarp, *Ep.* 2:3; *Did.* 1:3–5). One wonders whether the blessings and curses of Deuteronomy 28 were not sometimes read as series with long final members (28:6 + 7ff., and 28:19 + 20ff. being reckoned as units).

33. For exceptions see Farmer, "Sermon on the Mount," pp. 64–65, and Neyrey, "Loss of Wealth," p. 154.

# – 4 –

# THE MISSIONARY DISCOURSE, Q 10:2–16

## Its Use by Paul

### PAUL AND THE JESUS TRADITION: GENERAL REMARKS

There are many places in Paul's epistles where scholars have postulated his dependence upon the Jesus tradition.[1] While some of the suggestions are more convincing than others, two facts suggest that at least some of the alleged parallels should be taken seriously. First, as others have observed, most of the parallels regularly cited occur in well-defined portions of the Pauline corpus, namely, Romans 12–14, Colossians 3–4, 1 Thessalonians 4–5, and throughout 1 Corinthians.[2] This raises the possibility that, at certain junctures, Paul consciously turned to the sayings of Jesus.[3]

Second, there is an equally intriguing pattern if one looks at the synoptic side of the picture. If one reviews, let us say, the Pauline-synoptic parallels common to the lists drawn up by W. D. Davies and A. M. Hunter,[4] one discovers that more than half of them are from just three synoptic blocks — the Sermon on the Plain (SP), Lk 10:1–16 par., and Mk 9:33–50 par.[5] This is an intriguing result, especially when it is added

---

1. David Wenham's *Paul* contains an optimistic examination of almost all the possibilities. For a more skeptical review of the evidence see Neirynck, "Paul and the Sayings of Jesus."

2. See, e.g., W. D. Davies, *Paul and Rabbinic Judaism: Some Rabbinic Elements in Pauline Theology*, rev. ed. (New York: Harper & Row, 1967), pp. 138–40. For Romans see now the very helpful work of Thompson, *Clothed with Christ*. C. M. Tuckett, "Synoptic Tradition in 1 Thessalonians," pp. 160–82, offers an (excessively skeptical) overview of the possibilities for 1 Thessalonians. In 1 Corinthians Paul several times quotes "the Lord," and some of the citations have parallels in the synoptic tradition: 7:10–11 = Lk 16:18 par.; 9:14 = Lk 10:7 par.; 11:23–26 = Lk 22:14–20 par.

3. Cf. the pattern in Photius, *Hom.* 15 and 16: the first sections of these Homilies are seemingly bereft of references to Scripture (15:1–9; 16:1–12); but in the closing sections the patriarch begins to allude to and cite biblical texts (15:10–13; 16:13–14).

4. Davies, *Paul and Rabbinic Judaism;* Hunter, *Paul and His Predecessors*, pp. 45–51, 126–28.

5. On the SP see chap. 2 herein, pp. 67–95. The parallels with Lk 10:1–16 par. are

104

that those three blocks have been widely thought to incorporate old collections of sayings of Jesus. If Paul knew nothing more than isolated sayings, then we would not anticipate finding any pattern at all. The evangelical texts would, given the workings of chance, be more or less evenly distributed throughout the synoptic Gospels. Yet this is not the case. Surely this is significant. The form critics taught us that the Jesus tradition in its presynoptic form circulated in small blocks. Is it not then natural to explain the parallels between the synoptics and Paul with this in mind?[6]

## Paul and the Missionary Discourse

Turning from the general to the particular, several have urged that there is enough evidence for the conclusion that Paul knew some version of Jesus' missionary discourse.[7] Let me set forth the case.

(1) The text of 1 Cor 9:14 reads as follows: "In the same way, the Lord commanded that those who proclaim the gospel should get their living by the gospel." Few doubt that this line from Paul refers to the text preserved in Lk 10:7b = Mt 10:10 (Q): "The laborer (ἐργάτης) deserves to be paid (μισθοῦ)."[8] David Wenham observes that the correspondence is "particularly strong."[9] Not only does Paul indicate that he is quoting ("the Lord commanded"), but he actually cites a text that goes against his argument, for he is trying to explain why he does not take wages for his labor. Moreover, the content of 1 Cor 9:14 matches the synoptic logion, and both ἐργ- and μισθός, the key words of the Q logion, appear several times in 1 Corinthians 9.[10]

---

the subject of this chapter. On Mk 9:33–50 par. see my article, "The Pauline Parallels and the Synoptic Gospels: The Pattern of the Parallels," *NTS* 28 (1982): 1–32.

6. See further my article in the previous footnote. Against Nikolaus Walter, "Paul and the Early Christian Jesus-Tradition," in *Paul and Jesus: Collected Essays*, ed. A. J. M. Wedderburn, JSNTSS, vol. 37 (Sheffield: JSOT, 1989), p. 52, my conclusions there represent a historian's estimate of the probabilities: they have nothing at all to do with the present writer's theology.

7. So, e.g., B. Fjärstedt, *Synoptic Traditions in 1 Corinthians: Themes and Clusters of Theme Words in 1 Corinthians 1–4 and 9* (Uppsala: Theologiska Institutionen, 1974), pp. 66–94; Heinz Schürmann, " 'Das Gesetz des Christus' (Gal 6,2): Jesu Verhalten und Wort als letztgültige sittliche Norm nach Paulus," in *Neues Testament und Kirche: Für Rudolf Schnackenburg*, ed. Joachim Gnilka (Freiburg: Herder, 1974), p. 284; D. Wenham, *Paul*, pp. 190–200. For dissenting opinions see C. M. Tuckett, "Paul and the Synoptic Mission Discourse," *ETL* 60 (1984): 376–81; Neirynck, "Paul and the Sayings of Jesus," pp. 550–52; and Fleddermann, *Mark and Q*, p. 125. Tuckett's article was a response to my article, "Pauline Parallels," and my article, "Paul and the Missionary Discourse," *ETL* 61 (1985): 369–75, was a response to Tuckett.

8. Luke has τοῦ μισθοῦ, Matthew τοῦ τροφῆς.

9. *Paul*, p. 192.

10. This last observation was stressed by Fjärstedt. See 1 Cor 9:1 (ἔργον), 9:6 (ἐργάζεσθαι), 9:13 (ἐργαζόμενοι), 9:17 (μισθόν), 9:18 (μισθός).

What follows? There are two possibilities. Either Paul knew the word of the Lord in 1 Cor 9:14 as an isolated saying or he knew it as part of a collection of sayings. In the latter case the logion could be from a missionary discourse (cf. Luke 10 par.) or from some other collection.

How is one to choose among the options — isolated saying, missionary discourse, or unknown sayings collection? Given the nature of the case one can hardly approach certainty. The best we can do is offer a hypothesis that recommends itself because it explains and encompasses more data than its competitors.

(2) "The laborer deserves to be paid" was an integral part of Q's missionary discourse. It is introduced by an explanatory γάρ and continues the theme of the preceding verses. This does not, to be sure, mean that Q 10:7b could not, at one time, have been isolated. But even if it had been, the problem of how the saying came to Paul would not thereby be settled. Surely the general consensus that Q took up an already existing missionary discourse at least raises the possibility that Paul knew Jesus' word about workers and their reward as part of a missionary discourse.

This possibility is much strengthened when one looks closer at 1 Cor 9:14. "The laborer deserves to be paid" is in and of itself an abstract generalization which could be understood either literally or figuratively and applied to different situations. Paul, however, does not know the saying as an abstract generalization but rather precisely as a statement about itinerant missionaries: "The Lord commanded that those who proclaim the gospel should get their living by the gospel." That is, 1 Cor 9:14 assumes not only that "the laborer deserves to be paid" was spoken by Jesus, but also that he uttered the words to people who, like Paul, proclaimed the gospel. Indeed, it is precisely this knowledge of the saying's traditional application that causes Paul his difficulty, for he does not get his living by the gospel. When one then asks where Paul got his knowledge of the traditional application and how he could assume it on the part of the Corinthians, is it not natural to surmise that he and they knew the saying in a larger context — such as a missionary discourse — and that this made that application manifest?

Christopher Tuckett, however, cites both *Did.* 13:1–2[11] and 1 Tim 5:18[12] in order to argue that the saying about the worker's reward circulated in isolation.[13] But that a saying is quoted by itself is very far from proof that it circulated by itself.[14] The NT frequently quotes single sentences from the Hebrew Bible. Yet, to state the obvious, this is not

---

11. "But every true prophet desiring to settle among you is worthy of his food. In like manner a true teacher is also worthy, like the workman, of his food."

12. "For the Scripture says, 'You shall not muzzle an ox when it is treading out the grain,' and, 'The laborer deserves to be paid.' "

13. "Paul and the Synoptic Mission Discourse," p. 380.

14. Tuckett himself has argued that in the *Dialogue of the Savior* 3:139.9–10 "The

cause for suggesting that those sentences were known outside of their scriptural contexts. The authors of both the *Didache* and 1 Timothy could obviously have known "the laborer deserves to be paid" as part of a missionary discourse. In short, 1 Tim 5:18 and *Did.* 13:1–2 do not settle the question of how Q 10:7b came to Paul.

There are, moreover, very sound reasons for supposing that the author of the *Didache* knew and used Matthew,[15] and indeed that this is the case in the passage at hand. While 1 Cor 9:17–18 attests to the pre-Lukan form, ἄξιος ὁ ἐργάτης τοῦ μισθοῦ αὐτοῦ, the *Didache* agrees with Matthew: the laborer is worthy of τροφῆς. Now because τροφή[16] is probably to be assigned to Matthean redaction,[17] *Did.* 13:1–2 appears to depend in this particular upon canonical Matthew.[18] One must also at least wonder, given the numerous intriguing links between the Pastorals and Luke-Acts,[19] whether 1 Tim 5:18 (which quotes our saying along with Deut 25:4 as γραφή!) does not depend upon Luke 10.[20]

(3) B. Fjärstedt compiled a long list of parallels between Luke 10 and 1 Corinthians 9.[21] As Tuckett has correctly observed, not all of them are compelling. But some of them remain more than interesting:

| 1 Corinthians 9 | Luke 10 |
|---|---|
| ἀπόστολος (v. 1), ἀπόστολος (v. 2) ἀποστολῆς (v. 2), ἀπόστολοι (v. 5) | ἀπέστειλεν (v. 1), ἀποστέλλω (v. 3) ἀποστείλαντα (v. 16) |
| ἔργον (v. 1), ἐργάζεσθα ι (v. 6) ἐργαζόμενοι (v. 13) | ἐργάται (v. 2), ἐργάτας (v. 2), ἐργάτης (v. 7) |
| φαγεῖν (v. 4), ἐσθίει (v. 7) ἐσθίουσιν (v. 13) | ἐσθίοντες (v. 7), ἐσθίετε (v. 8) |
| πεῖν (v. 4) | πίνοντες (v. 7) |
| μισθόν (v. 17), μισθός (v. 18) | μισθοῦ (v. 7) |

While Tuckett admits that the link between μισθός in Lk 10:7 and 1 Cor 9:17–18 is firm, he remarks that this "involves the one point at which Paul himself acknowledged his use of Jesus tradition (1 Cor

laborer being worthy of his food" is a quotation from Matthew; see his *Nag Hammadi and the Gospel Tradition* (Edinburgh: T. & T. Clark, 1986), pp. 129–30.

15. See esp. Köhler, *Rezeption*, pp. 19–56; also pp. 89–91 herein.

16. Mt: 4; Mk: 0; Lk: 1.

17. And is recognized as such in recent commentaries. Cf. Gnilka, *Matthäusevangelium*, vol. 1, p. 361; Luz, *Matthäus*, vol. 2, p. 95. (In a footnote Luz says it is "gut möglich" that Paul knew the saying about the laborer in its Q form.)

18. Cf. Köhler, *Rezeption*, pp. 38–39.

19. See Stephen G. Wilson, *Luke and the Pastoral Epistles* (London: SPCK, 1979).

20. Cf. ibid., pp. 98–99.

21. *Synoptic Traditions*, pp. 65–77.

9:14)."[22] The same observation might be made about the common ἐργ-words. ἐργάτης appears precisely in Lk 10:7b, so there need be no allusion to the surrounding context, that is, to a missionary discourse.

The story is different, however, with ἐσθίω and πίνω (1 Cor 9:4, 7, 13). These two words appear in Lk 10:7a, which prefaces the saying about the laborer and reward: "And in the same house remain, eating (ἐσθίοντες) and drinking (πίνοντες) such things as they give." Now the references to eating and drinking in Lk 10:7a may safely be assigned to pre-Lukan tradition. That there is no parallel in Matthew 10 or Mark 6 proves nothing. There is also no Matthean or Markan parallel to the wording of Lk 22:19–20, but 1 Cor 11:23–25 establishes the pre-Lukan origin of those two verses, and Matthew's "food" (10:10) may well owe something to Q because Mk 6:6–13 does not broach this subject. Further, Lk 10:7a does not exhibit characteristic Lukan style or vocabulary,[23] and most have failed to see Luke's hand here.[24] One could not, moreover, expect Matthew to have reproduced Q 10:7a, with its command to eat and drink whatever is provided. Given his belief in the continuing validity of the Jewish food laws,[25] he would not have wanted to leave the impression that Jewish Christians, finding themselves among the unobservant, were required to eat food forbidden by Torah. For the same reason he omitted Mk 7:19 ("Thus he declared all foods clean").

Once the pre-Lukan origin of Lk 10:7a and its place in Q are established, Paul's knowledge of a missionary discourse is strongly implied. For Q 10:7a can scarcely be imagined to have circulated by itself: the saying is firmly embedded in Q's missionary discourse and takes on meaning from the surrounding verses. Further, the key words, ἐσθίω and πίνω, appear in Q 10:7a as well as in 1 Cor 9:4, 7, and 13. And the connection between both Q and Paul is not just verbal: the ideas are the same.[26] In Q missionaries are to live off what they are given by those who support what they are doing. It is the same in 1 Corinthians 9. The apostle has the right to receive food and drink from those who have profited from his preaching (9:4). He has the right to eat the fruit from the vineyard he has planted (9:7). In other words, in both the gospel text and the epistle, the itinerant missionary has, because of Jesus' words, the

---

22. Tuckett, "Paul and the Synoptic Mission Discourse," p. 378.

23. Jeremias, *Sprache*, p. 185.

24. Cf. Heinz Schürmann, "Mt 10,5–6 und die Vorgeschichte des synoptischen Aussendungsberichtes," in *Traditionsgeschichtliche Untersuchungen zu den synoptischen Evangelien* (Düsseldorf: Patmos, 1968), pp. 137–49; Hoffmann, *Studien*, pp. 267, 272–76; Polag, *Fragmenta*, p. 44; Uro, *Sheep*, p. 80. For another opinion see Vaage, *Galilean Upstarts*, pp. 128–31. Fleddermann, *Mark and Q*, pp. 105–110, thinks Q 10:7a had only: "Eat the things set before you."

25. See 5:17–20 and the commentaries on 15:1–20.

26. Contrast Tuckett, "Paul and the Synoptic Mission Discourse," p. 372, who has claimed that the references to "eating" and "drinking" in Luke 10 and 1 Corinthians 9 are "too general to carry much significance."

right to receive food and drink from those who support the Christian mission. There is thus a secure tie between the "eating" and "drinking" of Lk 10:7a and the "eating" and "drinking" of 1 Corinthians 9.[27]

(4) The text of 1 Cor 10:27 reads: "If one of the unbelievers invites you to dinner and you are disposed to go, eat whatever is set before you (πᾶν τὸ παρατιθέμενον ὑμῖν ἐσθίετε) without raising any question on the ground of conscience." Lk 10:8 reads: "Whenever you enter a town and they receive you, eat what is set before you (ἐσθίετε τὰ παρατιθέμενα ὑμῖν)." Unfortunately, scholars do not agree on the genesis of this last verse. Some assign it to Q or Q$^{lk}$,[28] others — much less plausibly — to Lukan redaction.[29] Some would also affirm that the synoptic tradition has here been influenced by Pauline tradition.[30]

Five observations, however, should be made. First, the absence of a parallel in either Matthew or Mark does not establish a redactional origin for Lk 10:8a any more than it does for 10:7a. Second, while the possibility of Pauline influence upon Lk 10:8 cannot be excluded, it cannot be demonstrated either. The direction of borrowing is an open question — especially as other definite instances of Paul's influence upon the Jesus tradition in Luke are far from manifest. Third, Q 10:10a ("But whenever you enter a town and they do not welcome you") is the antithesis of 10:8a ("Whenever you enter a town and its people welcome you"), and the former certainly belonged to Q (cf. Mt 10:14). This argues for the inclusion of 10:8a in Q. So too does the fact that this antithesis, which sets forth two different responses to Jesus' missionaries, is reminiscent of the antithesis of Q 10:6, in which some houses are welcoming and some are not ("And if a son of peace is there... but if not..."). Luke, moreover, is unlikely to have been responsible for the creation of antithetical parallelism, for he found "this Semitic mode of speech to be unattractive."[31] Fourth, the reason given above for Matthew's omission of Q 10:7a holds equally for the omission of 10:8a: the words could have been misread to imply the abrogation of Mosaic food laws. Finally, Paul knew the saying preserved in Q 10:7b. There is also, as we have seen, sufficient reason to believe that he

---

27. Tuckett, ibid., p. 378, attempts to weaken the connection between Luke 10 and 1 Corinthians 9 by raising the possibility that Lk 10:8 (which refers to eating) owes something to Pauline tradition. This is irrelevant given the reference to "eating" and "drinking" in Lk 10:7a.

28. See Polag, *Fragmenta*, p. 46; Laufen, *Die Doppelüberlieferungen*, pp. 219–20; Uro, *Sheep*, pp. 68–69, 80–83; Schürmann, *Lukasevangelium*, vol. 2, p. 73. Even if, as some have thought, Lk 10:8 was a secondary addition to the missionary discourse, this would not exclude the possibility that it was added to the tradition before Paul came to know it.

29. So Hoffmann, *Studien*, pp. 282–83, and Vaage, *Galilean Upstarts*, pp. 128–31.

30. Tuckett, "Paul and the Synoptic Mission Discourse," p. 378, thinks this possible.

31. So Joachim Jeremias, *New Testament Theology: The Proclamation of Jesus* (New York: Charles Scribner's Sons, 1971), p. 17. See further Jeremias, *Sprache*, pp. 61–62.

knew the material behind Q 10:7a. It would not, then, be surprising
if he also knew the logion preserved in Lk 10:8a. It would, rather, fit
into a developing pattern consistent with this inference: Paul knew a
form of Jesus' missionary discourse close to what we now find in Luke
10:2–16 = Q.

(5) In 1 Thess 4:8 Paul wrote, "Therefore whoever rejects this, rejects not human authority but God, who gives his Holy Spirit to you"
(τοιγαροῦν ὁ ἀθετῶν οὐκ ἄνθρωπον ἀθετεῖ ἀλλὰ τὸν θεὸν τὸν [καὶ]
διδόντα τὸ πνεῦμα αὐτοῦ τὸ ἅγιον εἰς ὑμᾶς). This warning strongly recalls Lk 10:16, which probably concluded Q's missionary discourse:[32]
"The one who hears you hears me, and the one who rejects you rejects
me, and the one who rejects me rejects the one who sent me" (ὁ ἀκούων
ὑμῶν ἐμοῦ ἀκούει, καὶ ὁ ἀθετῶν ὑμᾶς ἐμὲ ἀθετεῖ· ὁ δὲ ἐμὲ ἀθετῶν ἀθετεῖ
τὸν ἀποστείλαντά με).[33] Although Tuckett confesses the possibility of a
link between these two verses, he goes on to affirm, "It is just as likely
that they represent independent adaptations of the shaliah principle."[34]
Is it? Both lines use ἀθετέω, and Jn 5:23 ("The one who does not honor
the Son does not honor the Father who sent him," cf. 12:48) shows us
that Q was not alone in remembering that Jesus spoke something very
close to Lk 10:16.[35] In addition, we have already found links between
certain verses in Paul's epistles and Lk 10:7a, 7b, and 8. The text of
1 Thess 4:8 supplies one more link with Luke 10. All four of the verses
from Luke 10 apparently belonged to Q's missionary discourse. Is it not
economic to infer Paul's knowledge of something like Lk 10:1–16, that
is, Q 10:2–16?

Tuckett objects, finding here an error in reasoning. "Such allusions,
even if established, are from widely different contexts in the Pauline corpus; hence they do not necessarily show that Paul derived them from
the same Synoptic context."[36] It may be said, however, that three of the
four parallels to Q 10:1–16 occur within a very narrow space (1 Cor
9:4, 14; 10:27). Beyond that, if we are seeking probabilities as opposed

---

32. So also Bultmann, *History,* p. 143, and Manson, *Sayings,* p. 78. Against Hoffmann, *Studien,* pp. 285–86, Fleddermann, *Mark and Q,* pp. 153–54, and the International
Q Project, Luke's form is not secondary as compared with Mt 10:40; see David R. Catchpole, "The Poor on Earth and the Son of Man in Heaven: A Re-appraisal of Matthew
25:31–46," *BJRL* 62 (1979): 357–97; Polag, *Fragmenta,* p. 47; and Laufen, *Die Doppelüberlieferungen,* pp. 230–33. If Jn 5:23; 12:48; and 15:23 are independent of Luke
they show us the traditional character of Luke's saying. Further, "Matthew's shorter form,
lacking a rejection statement, is probably a MattR adaptation to a context (Matt 10:40–
42) which shows the influence of Mark 9:37–41; in neither Markan nor Matthaean setting
would a rejection statement have been appropriate." So Catchpole, "Mission Charge in
Q," p. 166.
33. Contrast Mk 9:37; Mt 10:40; Jn 13:20; Justin, *1 Apol.* 16:10, 63:5.
34. Tuckett, "Paul and the Synoptic Mission Discourse," p. 380. Cf. his article,
"Synoptic Tradition in 1 Thessalonians," pp. 163–64.
35. Cf. also Mt 10:40; Mk 9:37 par.; Jn 13:20.
36. "Paul and the Synoptic Mission Discourse," p. 380.

to certainties, Tuckett's words miss the mark. Of course it cannot be *demonstrated* that 1 Thess 4:8 depends upon the Jesus tradition or that Paul knew a missionary discourse. And the parallels between Luke 10 and Paul can admittedly be explained precisely as Tuckett explains them: one is undisputed (1 Cor 9:14 = Lk 10:7b); one is doubtful (1 Cor 9:4 = Lk 10:7a); one may be genuine, but this is not really certain (1 Cor 10:27 = Lk 10:8); and one just might result from "independent adaptations of the shaliah principle" (1 Thess 4:8 = Lk 10:16). But one can also apply Occam's razor and explain everything at a stroke: Paul knew a discourse akin to Q 10:2–16. Nothing stands in the way of this conclusion. On the contrary: the Jesus tradition circulated in blocks from a very early time; some of these blocks appear to have been known by Paul; Paul indisputably knew at least one saying that appeared in Q's missionary discourse; and the apostle's letters contain several lines that echo portions of Lk 10:1–16. Are we not invited to reckon seriously with the possibility that Paul knew a form of the missionary discourse related to Q 10:2–16?

## PAUL'S ALLUSIONS TO THE JESUS TRADITION

Because it was argued in chapter 1 that Paul may have been acquainted not just with units that found their way into Q but with Q itself, we cannot decide whether he might have known a missionary discourse as an isolated unit or as a part of Q. But there remains one last issue that needs to be taken up. If Paul did in fact know something like the SP,[37] something close to Q's missionary discourse, and something approximating Q 12:35–48,[38] then, whether or not he was familiar with Q, one must still ask why he did not more often explicitly cite the Jesus tradition. Only a few times does the apostle specifically refer to words of Jesus.[39] This circumstance has led many to believe that hunting for allusions to the Jesus tradition in Paul is a vain enterprise, an example of the scholarly disease Samuel Sandmel famously called "Parallelomania."[40] Paul's

---

37. See chap. 2 herein, pp. 86–87.

38. See p. 54, n. 240.

39. 1 Cor 7:10–11 ("To the married I give charge, not I but the Lord"); 7:25 ("I have no command of the Lord"); 9:14 ("the Lord commanded,"see above); 11:23–26 ("I received from the Lord"); 14:37 ("a command of the Lord" — although here a reference to the Jesus tradition seems doubtful); 2 Cor 12:9 ("he said to me: 'My grace is sufficient for you...'" — a word of the risen Lord); 1 Thess 4:15–17 ("this we declare to you by the word of the Lord" — although whether this is a reference to the Jesus tradition or a prophetic word is debated).

40. See his article by that name in *JBL* 81 (1962): 1–13.

failure to cite words of the Lord explicitly with any frequency means he did not pay much attention to or did not know the Jesus tradition.[41]

Such skepticism, however, needs to address the circumstance that the infrequency with which Paul cites the Jesus tradition is shared by other early Christian documents. As Leonhard Goppelt observed,

> When one examines the rest of the early Christian literature out-side the Gospels with an analogous inquiry one finds that it quoted the Gospel tradition as little as Paul did, even though that lit-erature was familiar with it. Luke, e.g., did not point back to the accounts of his Gospel in any of the missionary sermons of the book of Acts; the only saying of Jesus quoted in the book of Acts (20:35) was an *agraphon!*[42] The author of I John was just as reluctant to direct attention back to the Fourth Gospel. Even II Clement, a homily written around the middle of the 2d century, made hardly any use of the Gospel tradition though its author was undoubtedly familiar with it. Paul too, therefore, could have known the Jesus tradition that was written down later in the synoptic Gospels although he did not quote it.[43]

Goppelt's words make one cautious regarding the meaning of Paul's rel-ative silence. They also make one question the proposition that Paul infrequently quoted Jesus because the tradition was in the hands of his opponents and so was something usually best left alone.[44] This thesis will hardly explain the comparable silence in Acts, whose author wrote a Gospel.

We probably come nearer the truth when we observe that Paul's let-ters are not systematic statements of belief and practice but occasional pieces addressed to specific situations — and that often the Jesus tradi-tion could have had little or nothing to say to those situations.[45] Even the synoptics, which reflect decades of Christian handling of the tradi-tion, do not instruct one about speaking in tongues or spiritual gifts in general. Nor do they contain teaching about Christian baptism or the place of women in the churches. Above all, they fail to address the issue of circumcision and have next to nothing — perhaps nothing at all — to

---

41. Cf. Ulrich Wilckens, "Jesusüberlieferung und Christuskerygma — zwei Wege urchristlicher Überlieferungsgeschichte," *Theologia Viatorum* 10 (1966): 310–39.

42. Cf. Barrett, "Sayings of Jesus," p. 708: "We *know* that Luke was deeply concerned to record and communicate the teaching of Jesus; this is proved by his gospel. But in his story of the church he gives little indication of the *use* of the teaching of Jesus.... [This] seems to lead to the conclusion that the teaching of Jesus was in some sense apart from the outward life of the church."

43. *Theology of the New Testament*, vol. 2 (Grand Rapids: Eerdmans, 1982), pp. 44–45.

44. See H.-W. Kuhn, "Der irdische Jesus bei Paulus," *ZTK* 67 (1970): 295–320.

45. On how this fact affects Romans see Leander E. Keck, " 'Jesus' in Romans," *JBL* 108 (1989): 443–60.

say about Gentiles and their place in the community of salvation.[46] The implications of this lack of correspondence between the content of the Jesus tradition and many of the matters that consumed the churches is not without consequence.

One reason that Jesus' words are alluded to with greater frequency in the paraenetical sections of Paul's epistles than in the properly theological sections is that the Jesus tradition contained more moral teaching than anything else. Put otherwise, the tradition was not so relevant to the theological sections. Paul's failure to use it in, let us say, Romans 1–11, may simply signal its failure to address the issues reviewed in those chapters. Again, although Paul probably knew some of Jesus' sayings about the kingdom of God, the apostle's communities faced problems that were just not addressed by missionary proclamation, so it is altogether natural that the kingdom is not often mentioned in his letters.[47]

One guesses further that sometimes Paul and others did not cite the Jesus tradition because they had problems with its content. If the apostle, for example, knew Q 16:17, which affirms that it is easier for heaven and earth to pass away than for a letter of law to be dropped, one has no difficulty understanding why he never cited it. Again, it is no surprise that in 1 Corinthians 8, where the topic is eating food consecrated in a pagan temple, Paul fails to cite the saying in which Jesus declares, "There is nothing [οὐδέν] outside a person that by going in can defile [κοινῶσαι]" (Mk 7:15). Although Rom 14:14 ("I know and am persuaded in the Lord Jesus that nothing is profane [οὐδὲν κοινόν] in itself") probably shows us that he knew that saying[48] and could even allude to it against his own purposes,[49] it would hardly further the argument of 1 Corinthians 8, where Paul wrote that if food caused another to stumble, he would never eat meat. The apostle did not here need to quote Jesus and so encourage further those who already knew that food did not matter. He was rather trying to get those with "knowledge" to respect the scruples of those who worried about meat sacrificed to idols.

To all this it might be countered that "in a number of places in his writings Paul fails to refer to a saying of Jesus at the very point where he might well have clinched his argument by doing so."[50] But each alleged example needs to be examined. For example, it has been observed that

---

46. On Gentiles in the synoptic tradition see pp. 182–83 below.

47. Cf. Günter Haufe, "Reich Gottes bei Paulus und in der Jesustradition," *NTS* 31 (1985): 467–72.

48. Cf. James D. G. Dunn, "Jesus Tradition in Paul," in *Studying the Historical Jesus*, ed. Bruce Chilton and Craig A. Evans (Leiden: E. J. Brill, 1994), pp. 162–63; also Thompson, *Clothed with Christ*, pp. 185–99.

49. In Romans 14 Paul is not arguing that all things are clean, but that one should regard the scruples of others.

50. So Graham Stanton, *Gospel Truth? New Light on Jesus and the Gospels* (Val-

the saying about eunuchs (Mt 19:12), interpreted as a call to chastity, would have well served the argument of the latter part of 1 Corinthians 7. The point seems forceful. As the saying appears only in Matthew, it may not have been widely known. Perhaps Paul did not know it. On the other hand, Mt 19:12 is a bit cryptic, and now and then it has been given a literal interpretation. Further, "eunuch" may have called up images and associations that would only have confused the Corinthians. So one can imagine that if Paul had in fact known the saying and thought of it when writing 1 Corinthians 7 he might not have wanted to use it: it might have been more a distraction than an aid. So any final verdict on whether Paul did or did not know Mt 19:12 is unjustified.[51]

If the Jesus tradition was often irrelevant and sometimes less than helpful for those who wrote early Christian letters, there is another point to make. Often scholars have thought it significant that Paul quotes Jesus much less than he does the OT. This argument, however, comes up against an obvious fact, although it is one I cannot recall anyone discussing: in sheer volume the Jewish Bible dwarfs whatever Jesus tradition Paul could have known. Even if Paul was familiar with Q, a passion narrative,[52] and additional collections of sayings and deeds of Jesus, in size the whole could not have amounted to anything more than a very small fragment of the Tanak's total mass. The Tanak, when compared with even a generous estimation of Paul's Jesus tradition, has so many more stories, so many more proverbs, and so many more prophecies, and it treats so many more subjects than the Jesus tradition that it is, for the purposes of supplying proof texts on all sorts of subjects, much the larger and more abundant treasure. Might this indisputable fact not partly explain why Paul cites the Jewish Bible — a large portion of which he must have known by heart from youth — so much more than he cites Jesus? When Paul wanted to quote lines about human sin the Bible enabled him to compose a whole catena (Romans 3). For this the Jesus tradition would not have sufficed.

One should in addition keep in mind that there was a rich tradition of quoting the Bible to further theological argument. The Dead Sea Scrolls often formally cite the Scriptures (and do not, incidentally, quote the Teacher of Righteousness).[53] So too the Pseudepigrapha and the Mishnah. The Jesus tradition itself quotes the Bible. As a Pharisee, Paul would have been trained to cite the First Testament when doing

---

ley Forge, Pa.: Trinity Press International, 1995), p. 131. Stanton unfortunately does not supply examples.

51. On the interesting parallels between Mt 19:12 and 1 Cor 7:7 see Christian Wolff, "Niedrigkeit und Verzicht in Wort und Weg Jesu und in der Apostolischen Existenz des Paulus," *NTS* 34 (1988): 186–88.

52. The evidence is gathered in D. Wenham, *Paul*, pp. 363–66.

53. One can only wonder whether those who read the scrolls as insiders recognized in them allusions to or quotations of sayings of the Teacher.

theological thinking. This rhetorical habit would not have left him after he came to faith in Jesus, for the Christians, living as they did within the Jewish tradition, themselves felt compelled to quote the Bible in support of their convictions. "For Saul, throughout his life, scripture remained the supreme norm of all thought and action."[54]

The crucial fact here is that in Paul's Jewish-Christian world matters were traditionally settled by appeal to biblical texts, and that, although Jesus was regarded as a divinely inspired authority, the custom of citing his words to settle theological issues appears to have become common only with time. Paul and his Galatian opponents evidently argued their respective cases by appealing to Moses and the Prophets, not to Jesus and his words. The author of Acts, who was also the author of a Gospel, could depict the apostolic leaders doing the very same thing. Rhetorical habits change slowly. Not until after the canonical Gospels came to be read in the churches do we find writers quoting the Jesus tradition with the ease and frequency with which they also quote the Jewish Bible.[55] In Paul's time, on the other hand, the Jesus tradition was not yet much used as a corpus of theological proof texts; it was rather passed on in order to furnish foundational religious narratives and to supply moral guidance. For constructing theological proofs the Bible still held pride of place.

If the rhetorical habit of formally citing Jesus to settle disputes did not become common until later times, this does not mean that the Jesus tradition was before then little known or unimportant. Any writing by nature limits the matters it touches upon and thus can leave much of importance out of account. Apart from the Gospels the NT writings do not once refer to Jesus' miracles. The correct inference is not that only the evangelists found Jesus' miracles interesting or important but that for those writing letters the miracles were not germane. One thinks of the author of 1 John, who, if he did not have a hand in composing the Fourth Gospel, surely at least knew it.

In similar fashion, although *bĕrît* rarely appears in the Mishnah, this scarcely means that its authors were uninterested in the covenant. "We are misled if we think that the Mishnah was the only religious expression of the pharisaic-rabbinic movement in the first century. The Mishnah reflects their distinctive legal contributions to Judaism, but it does not subsume all that they thought about Judaism."[56] Would one want to argue from the absence of Noah, Joshua, and Elijah from the

---

54. H. J. Schoeps, *Paul: The Theology of the Apostle in the Light of Jewish Religious Thought* (London: Lutterworth, 1961), p. 38.

55. Is *2 Clement* the first Christian document, apart from sayings collections and gospels, formally to quote Jesus more than the Jewish Bible?

56. Alan F. Segal, *The Other Judaisms of Late Antiquity* (Atlanta: Scholars Press, 1987), p. 165.

Psalms that those who composed and recited the Psalter cared little or nothing for those figures? One can no more do this than urge that the Psalter's failure to mention cultic ordinances requires that its recitation had nothing to do with such ordinances. Again, Anthony the Great was of sufficient importance to Athanasius that the latter wrote the former's biography. But with the exception of that biography the large corpus of Athanasius's works takes scant notice of the desert father.

All this is to emphasize that arguments from silence can prove too much, and more particularly that Paul's relative silence regarding the Jesus tradition likely does not tell us the whole story. My own conviction is that although, for the reasons given above, Paul did not often formally cite the Jesus tradition, that tradition was still important to him. Further, like Clement and the author of the *Didache*, he alluded to it often in paraenetical sections. This is what we might have expected. For the Jesus tradition known to Paul was as much as anything else a collection of imperatives: love your enemy, be merciful, do not judge, eat what is set before you, do not fear, do not be anxious, do not cause another to stumble.

These imperatives were naturally formative for early Christian cate-chetical and moral traditions.[57] There is every reason to believe that the Pauline texts that remind us of Jesus' imperatives also reminded Paul's first readers of the Jesus tradition, and that Paul intended this. Even in 1 Cor 7:10–11 and 9:14, where Paul used a citation formula, he did not quote the Jesus tradition verbatim but paraphrased it to his own ends. Did he not then expect his readers to know the relevant words of Jesus apart from his paraphrase?

Rom 12:14 and 1 Thess 5:4 and the other Pauline texts that in-escapably recall the Jesus tradition should probably be thought of, not as unconscious echoes, but as conscious allusions.[58] There was a tradi-tional rhetoric of allusion as well as of citation,[59] and Paul was adept at it. Not only did the apostle sometimes expect his readers to recognize a scriptural citation even when it had no introductory formula (e.g., Rom 10:13; 11:34–35; 12:20; and so forth), but his letters contain numerous allusions to Scripture.[60] Moreover, as Richard Hays has persuasively re-

---

57. On this Martin Dibelius, *From Tradition to Gospel* (New York: Charles Scribner's Sons, 1935), pp. 238ff., remains helpful.

58. For the likelihood that the Jesus tradition had a life of its own independent of Christian paraenesis, so that here we should think of two different traditions, see Allison, "Pauline Parallels," pp. 22–24.

59. The Hebrew Bible often alludes to itself; see my book, *The New Moses: A Matthean Typology* (Philadelphia: Fortress, 1993), and the literature cited there. Note also Konrad R. Schaefer, "Zechariah 14: A Study in Allusion," *CBQ* 57 (1995): 66–91.

60. See the chart in E. Earle Ellis, *Paul's Use of the Old Testament* (Edinburgh: Oliver and Boyd, 1957), pp. 153–54.

minded us, often his arguments seem to assume an audience that can pick up those allusions and draw out implicit meaning.[61]

But why allude rather than cite? James Dunn has observed that, if modern scholars are correct, Paul's wont was not to cite confessional or liturgical formulas (cf. 1 Cor 15:3–4) but rather to allude to them.[62] Such formulas belonged to "the language of community discourse," and so Paul's readers must have recognized them for what they were.[63] A religious community is bound together by, among other things, a common religious idiom. As Dunn puts it, "It is the very fact that allusions are sufficient for much effective communication which provides and strengthens the bond; recognition of the allusion/echo is what attests effective membership of the group."[64] Paul's allusions to the Jesus tradition belonged to the bonding language of "insiders."

This is an important contribution to the discussion, and when added to the observations already made above we may perhaps have discovered the confluence of causes behind Paul's failure to quote Jesus formally more than a few times. But there is yet a final relevant fact. The functions of formal citation and of allusion are different. The former typically calls attention to itself for the purpose of adding authority. This explains the pattern of scriptural quotations in the authentic Paulines. There are no formal citations at all in Philippians, Colossians, 1 Thessalonians, 2 Thessalonians, or Philemon. And whereas the Corinthian correspondence averages less than one formal citation per chapter (14 + 7 citations for 16 + 13 chapters), the six chapters of Galatians contains ten such citations, and Romans, with its sixteen chapters, has forty-eight. The explanation for these distributions is that Paul tended to quote Scripture explicitly in polemical situations in which his opponents were also citing Scripture.[65] When writing to the Romans and Galatians, the apostle needed the traditional court of appeal, the authoritative Scriptures.

The primary purpose of allusions, however, is not to add authority and so to help clinch arguments. Their general effect is instead to stim-

---

61. *Echoes of Scripture in the Letters of Paul* (New Haven: Yale University Press, 1989). Cf. my own work on Matthew, *The New Moses*. According to Schoeps, *Paul*, p. 38, "Without a detailed knowledge of the Old Testament and its exegesis whole passages of the major Pauline letters remain almost unintelligible." Assuming that Paul's readers understood what he wrote, this fact implies that they could bring such knowledge to the letters.

62. "Jesus Tradition in Paul," p. 176. Rom 1:3–4 and 3:25–26 are obvious examples.

63. Ibid., pp. 176–77.

64. Ibid., p. 177.

65. Cf. Hans Conzelmann, *An Outline of the Theology of the New Testament* (New York: Harper & Row, 1969), p. 167: "The Old Testament comes to the fore where Paul is arguing thematically with Jews and Judaizers: in Galatians and Romans. . . . It again plays a role in the controversy with the Jewish-Christian enthusiasts of II Corinthians."

ulate readers to become more active.[66] In any context the explicit soon becomes tedious. The allusion is a way of fighting tedium. Meaning is infolded not to obscure but to improve communication: allusions give the imagination more to do and so heighten attention. The implicit allows the pleasure of discovery, and readers who are invited to fill gaps appreciate the authors who respect them enough not to shout. The reader who is asked to do more work is the more appreciative.

A simple illustration of how all this works appears in the book of Wisdom. Chapter 10 summarizes the stories of great men from Adam to Moses — without once mentioning anyone's name. Adam is "the first-formed father" (10:1). Cain is "an unrighteous man" (10:3). Noah, Abraham, Lot, Jacob, and Joseph are all called "a/the righteous man" (10:4, 5, 6, 9, 13). Moses is "a servant of the Lord" (10:15). Clearly the author of Wisdom intentionally avoided naming his subjects. And just as clearly he expected his readers to do this simple thing for themselves. Why? The silence draws readers further into the book by asking them to make their own contribution. Perhaps indeed the absence of names is an enticement to turn the unnamed into types (cf. the types elsewhere in Wisdom). For this purpose allusions are just what is needed. More would be less.

Matters were, I should like to suggest, similar with Paul and the Jesus tradition. Unlike Scripture, the sayings of Jesus were seemingly not the object of much controversy between Paul and his opponents; and "in paraenesis, unlike in theological argument, one normally does not *prove* the truth of one's teaching, and so is not required to cite its sources."[67] So the apostle had little occasion to cite the Jesus tradition formally or to do exegesis upon it. But he did have occasion to allude to it when offering paraenesis — as did the authors of James, 1 Peter, *1 Clement*, and the *Didache*. In this Paul was simply following tradition: Christian paraenesis regularly sent Christian imagination to the Jesus tradition.

What then was the Romans' response to Paul's call to bless those persecuting them and to repay no one evil for evil (12:14, 17)? Like the readers of Wisdom 10, they probably filled in the implicit blanks. Hearing the apostle's suggestive phrases they would have recalled what Jesus

---

66. For what follows I have borrowed from Arthur Koestler, "Literature and the Law of Diminishing Returns," in *The Heel of Achilles: Essays, 1968–1973* (New York: Random House, 1974), pp. 119–37.

67. Seyoon Kim, "Jesus, Sayings of," in *Dictionary of Paul and His Letters*, ed. Gerald F. Hawthorne, Ralph P. Martin, and Daniel G. Reid (Downers Grove, Ill.: InterVarsity, 1993), p. 489. Cf. Thompson, *Clothed with Christ*, p. 71 (cf. his argument on p. 55 regarding Ignatius's considerable inexplicit borrowing from Paul). This is sufficient answer to the question of Albert Schweitzer, *Paul and His Interpreters* (New York: Macmillan, 1951), pp. 42–43: "If so many utterances of Jesus are hovering before Paul's mind, how comes it that he always merely paraphrases them, instead of quoting them as sayings of Jesus, and thus sheltering himself behind their authority?" The situation is the same in James and 1 Peter: the Jesus traditions used in paraenesis are not attributed to Jesus.

famously said about nonretaliation. Perhaps in fact they would have re-membered not just two sayings but the corpus to which those sayings belonged, the well-known collection which lies behind the first half of the SP.[68] However that may be, their informed imaginations could have found Paul's allusions full of potential meaning. For whereas the quota-tion makes for closure, the allusion, like the parable and the apocalyptic symbol, opens up possibilities for the informed imagination. It expands the horizon of potential understanding. It evokes.

In conclusion, the argument of the preceding pages comes far short of supporting the judgment that Paul was "steeped in the minds and words of his Lord."[69] Such a verdict goes beyond the evidence marshaled in this chapter or any other evidence that could be marshaled. It is also going too far to claim that the Jesus tradition was "central to Paul's theology"[70] — even though the theological differences between Jesus and Paul have often been greatly exaggerated.[71] On the other hand, it seems unimaginative and excessively skeptical to maintain that the teaching of the historical Jesus played "no role, or practically none, in Paul,"[72] or that in Paul "the Jesus of history is apparently dismissed."[73] This is an equally unjustified extreme. The so-called minimalists — those who find very few allusions to the Jesus tradition in Paul — are as wrong as the so-called maximalists — those who find such allusions everywhere. As so often the truth lies in between. The solid allusions to the Jesus tradition in Romans and elsewhere probably show us that, in his role as missionary and pastor, Paul regularly had occasion to turn to the Jesus tradition.

---

68. See pp. 77–92 herein.

69. Davies, *Paul and Rabbinic Judaism*, p. 140.

70. D. Wenham, *Paul*, p. 399. Contrast rightly Walter, "Paul," pp. 63–74.

71. Here there is much right about D. Wenham's *Paul*. For further discussion see also W. G. Kümmel, *The Theology of the New Testament* (Nashville: Abingdon, 1973), pp. 244–54, the essays collected in Wedderburn, *Paul and Jesus*, and John Barclay, "Jesus and Paul," in Hawthorne, Martin, and Reid, *Dictionary of Paul and His Letters*, pp. 492–503.

72. So Rudolf Bultmann, *Theology of the New Testament*, vol. 1 (New York: Charles Scribner's Sons, 1951), p. 35.

73. Günther Bornkamm, *Paul* (New York: Harper & Row, 1971), p. 110.

# – 5 –

# THE RETURNING SPIRIT, Q 11:24–26
## *Multiple Meanings*

Mt 12:43–45 and Lk 11:24–26 preserve a unit — "a strange piece of material"[1] — which, being without Markan parallel, is usually assigned to Q.[2] The Matthean version clearly functions as a parable, for (unlike the Lukan version) it ends with this: "so will it be also with this evil generation."[3] This application and the Matthean context show how the First Evangelist at least interpreted "the last state of that person is worse than the first" (12:45a = Lk 11:26b). Mt 12:43–45, which the evangelist moved to a place where it functions as a sort of summary,[4] is about Jesus' relationship to "this generation."[5] The narrative of an unclean spirit[6] that leaves or is forced to leave someone, only to return later with seven other spirits more evil than itself in order to occupy the

---

1. So O. Lamar Cope, *Matthew: A Scribe Trained for the Kingdom of Heaven*, CBQMS, vol. 5 (Washington: Catholic Biblical Association, 1976), p. 33. On p. 44 Cope refers to our text as "one of the most difficult to interpret in all of the gospels."

2. For reconstruction see John S. Kloppenborg, "Q 11:14–20 [sic]: Work Sheets for Reconstruction," in *Society of Biblical Literature 1985 Seminar Papers*, ed. Kent Harold Richards (Atlanta: Scholars Press, 1985), pp. 133–51. With the exception of Mt 12:45b (see n. 3 below), the few disagreements are minor and of no consequence for my purposes.

3. The clause is redactional. So most, including Gundry, *Matthew*, p. 247; Schulz, *Q*, p. 477; and G. Strecker, *Der Weg der Gerechtigkeit*, FRLANT, vol. 82 (Göttingen: Vandenhoeck & Ruprecht, 1962), p. 103. οὕτως ἐστίν/ἦν/ἔσται is Matthean (Mt: 13; Mk: 2; Lk: 3), and the First Evangelist elsewhere added summarizing phrases with this introduction (e.g., 13:49; 20:16). "This evil generation" is from 12:39 (cf. 12:41, 42). Kloppenborg, "Work Sheets," p. 151, remarks that "there is little reason for Luke to have omitted the phrase if it were in Q."

4. Cf. Gundry, *Matthew*, p. 246. Kloppenborg, *Formation*, p. 126 n. 108, speaks of "a general consensus that Matthew has transferred the parable (12:43–45) to a position following the Sign of Jonah so that it might serve as a summary to chap. 12." See further P. Vassiliaidis, "The Original Order of Q: Some Residual Cases," in Delobel, *Logia*, p. 384, and for a review of opinion, Kloppenborg, *Q Parallels*, p. 94.

5. Jerome, *Commentaire sur S. Matthieu*, ed. É. Bonnard, vol. 1 (Paris: Cerf, 1977), pp. 258–60 ad loc., already observed that Matthew's text disallows a spiritual application to the individual.

6. In the NT "unclean spirit" (cf. Zech 13:2; *Jub.* 10:1; 11:4; 12:20; *T. Benj.* 5:2; *T. Sim.* 4:9; 6:6) means "demon"; note that the "unclean spirits" of Mk 6:7 have become "demons" in the parallel Lk 9:1, and that the "unclean spirit" of Mk 7:25 has become "possessed by a demon" in the parallel Mt 15:22.

"empty"[7] person again, represents the national condition: the people are tragically more miserable after the Messiah's advent than before it.[8]

By this point in Matthew's story, that is, by the latter half of chapter 12, unbelief has won out. While some in Israel have embraced the Messiah,[9] Israel as a corporate entity has not.[10] So while the people have had the opportunity to see and to hear one greater than Jonah and Solomon (12:41–42), they have not taken advantage of their unprecedented opportunity but rather have turned away. Their judgment will accordingly be all the greater: to whom much is given, much will be required. Israel would have been better off in ignorance. The failure to respond rightly to "the deeds of the Messiah" (11:2) is in Matthew's eyes unequaled evil, and the last state has become worse than the first.[11]

When one turns from Matthew to Luke one leaves daylight and enters darkness: it is not at all clear how the unit of the returning demon

---

7. Matthew but not Luke has σχολάζοντα; it may or may not be redactional; see Kloppenborg, "Work Sheets," pp. 149–50.

8. Cf. J. A. Bengel, *Gnomon of the New Testament*, vol. 1 (Philadelphia: Perkinpine & Higgins, 1864), p. 182 ("that which happened to the man in his body, shall be done spiritually to this generation"); A. H. McNeile, *The Gospel according to Matthew* (London: Macmillan, 1915), p. 184; T. Zahn, *Das Evangelium des Matthäus*, 4th ed. (Leipzig: Deichert, 1922), p. 472; Luz, *Matthäus*, vol. 2, p. 282; Hagner, *Matthew 1–13*, pp. 356–58. For an attempt to find an application to the Christian community see Günther Baumbach, *Das Verständnis des Bösen in den synoptischen Evangelien* (Berlin: Evangelische Verlagsanstalt, 1963), pp. 86–89. For D. A. Carson, "Matthew," in *The Expositor's Bible Commentary*, vol. 8 (Grand Rapids: Zondervan, 1984), p. 298, the parable concerns not Israel in general but specifically people from whom Jesus has driven out demons. This seems an unlikely reading of Matthew. If the demon leaves of its own accord (so Alfred Plummer, *An Exegetical Commentary on the Gospel according to Matthew* [London: Stock, 1909], p. 185) then exorcism is not the topic. But if, as most commentators assume, the demon is cast out by an exorcist, then Carson's interpretation comes up against the observation of John Lightfoot, *A Commentary on the New Testament from the Talmud and Hebraica*, vol. 2 (Oxford: Oxford University Press, 1859), p. 211: Matthew's Gospel hardly encourages the thought that a demon cast out by Jesus could later have repossessed its victim.

9. As appears esp. from the healing stories as well as from 11:25–30 and 12:46–50.

10. See esp. 11:1–24.

11. Often commentators have wrongly tried to interpret the details of the parable. For Strecker, *Weg*, pp. 105–106, the last things became worse than the first with the resurrection of Jesus. R. Hummel, *Die Auseinandersetzung zwischen Kirche und Judentum im Matthäusevangelium*, 2d ed., BEvT, vol. 33 (Munich: Kaiser, 1966), pp. 126–28, thinks this happened with the destruction of the temple in C.E. 70; cf. Hagner, *Matthew 1–13*, p. 357. For the *Wirkungsgeschichte* see Luz, *Matthäus*, vol. 2, pp. 282–84, and Stephen L. Wailes, *Medieval Allegories of Jesus' Parables* (Berkeley: University of California Press, 1987), pp. 92–95. Many have unfortunately identified the waterless places with the Gentiles. In this interpretation, after Moses (so Hilary of Poitiers, *Sur Matthieu*, vol. 1, SC, vol. 254 [Paris: Cerf, 1978], p. 290), the exile (so Henry Alford, *The Four Gospels*, vol. 1 of *The Greek Testament*, rev. ed. [Chicago: Moody, 1958], p. 134), the prophets or John the Baptist (cf. Tertullian, *Paed.* 2:6; Plummer, *Matthew*, p. 184), or Jesus (cf. McNeile, *Matthew*, p. 184) drove the demons out of Israel, they went to the heathen, but later returned to the Jews because they found them easier prey. See Wailes, *Allegories*, pp. 92–95, and Daniel W. Lowman, *A Commentary on the Gospels and Epistles of the New Testament* (Philadelphia: Corey & Hart, 1845), p. 108.

functions in the Third Gospel. Is it a parable? Is it an exhortation to persevere in the faith? Is it a warning about non-Christian exorcists? A review of the secondary literature reveals the following interpretations:

(1) "Exorcism is not enough: the spiritual world, like the natural, abhors a vacuum."[12] The passage warns those who have benefited from Jesus' ministry of exorcism that their newfound freedom will not last unless they take the further step of accepting Jesus' ministry.[13]

(2) Given that Christian baptism has traditionally been a rite of exorcism,[14] it is no surprise that some have taken Lk 11:24–26 to be paraenetic: after the unclean spirits have been driven out by baptism and entry into the church, one must be filled with Christ or else risk the return of demons.[15] The teaching is akin to Heb 6:4–6, which warns of dire consequences for those who have "once been enlightened, and have tasted the heavenly gift, and have shared in the Holy Spirit, and have tasted the goodness of the word of God and the powers of the age to come, and then have fallen away."

(3) The story serves to admonish not those exorcised but Christian disciples or exorcists that they should not be too assured over their success in combating evil. Victory can be short-lived.[16]

(4) Lk 11:24–26 "seem[s] to illustrate the futility of the methods of the Jewish exorcists (v. 19). These seem to do the same work as Christ, but really they act against Him (v. 20); for the evil spirit whom they drive out returns, making the sufferer worse than before."[17] Compare

---

12. G. B. Caird, *The Gospel of Luke* (New York: Penguin, 1963), p. 155.

13. Cf. John Martin Creed, *The Gospel according to St. Luke* (London: Macmillan, 1930), pp. 161–62; C. F. Evans, *Saint Luke* (London: SCM, 1990), p. 494; Eduard Schweizer, *The Good News according to Luke* (Atlanta: John Knox, 1984), p. 195; Charles H. Talbert, *Reading Luke* (New York: Crossroad, 1982), p. 138. For a related interpretation see Irenaeus, *Adv. haer.* 1:16:3. John J. Kilgallen, "The Return of the Evil Spirit," *Bib* 74 (1993): 45, says this is the most common interpretation for Luke.

14. Henry Ansgar Kelly, *The Devil at Baptism* (Ithaca, N.Y.: Cornell University Press, 1985).

15. See Gregory Nazianzen, *Orat.* 40:35, who associates "waterless places" with a fear of the "divine stream" of baptism. Such an interpretation may already be presupposed by 2 Pet 2:20 and Hermas, *Mand.* 9:17:5; see Richard J. Bauckham, *Jude, 2 Peter,* WBC (Waco, Tex.: Word, 1983), pp. 277–78. (Did the occurrence of "waterless" in his source [cf. Jude 12] move the author of 2 Peter to recall the story from the Jesus tradition?) Note also *Didascalia* 26; Cyprian, *Ep.* 69:15–16; Athanasius, *Ep. Fest.* 3:3; John Calvin, *Commentary on a Harmony of the Gospels,* vol. 2 (Grand Rapids: Eerdmans, 1957), pp. 83–86; Baumbach, *Bösen,* p. 130; Ernst, *Lukas,* pp. 376–77; Alois Stöger, *The Gospel according to St. Luke,* vol. 1 (London: Burns & Oates, 1969), p. 223. The *Opus Imperfectum in Matthaeum* offers this interpretation for Matthew (*PG,* vol. 56, p. 790).

16. Cf. Fitzmyer, *Luke,* vol. 2, p. 924: the text cautions "Christian disciples about too great assurance over manifestations of the defeat of physical or psychic evil."

17. Willoughby C. Allen, *A Critical and Exegetical Commentary on the Gospel according to S. Matthew* (Edinburgh: T. & T. Clark, 1906), p. 140; I. H. Marshall, *Commentary on Luke* (Grand Rapids: Eerdmans, 1978), p. 479. Augustine Stock, *The Method and Message of Matthew* (Collegeville, Minn.: Liturgical Press, 1994), p. 205, wrongly thinks this the interpretation for Matthew.

Lk 11:23: "Whoever is not with me is against me, and whoever does not gather with me scatters."

(5) Lk 11:24–26 is "an actual description of behavior and reaction under certain conditions of varieties of evil spirits. Such knowledge is an essential part of the battle. The church must know its enemy."[18]

(6) The unit, which is followed by a passage about "an evil generation" (Lk 11:29), functions as it does in Matthew, to characterize Jesus' Jewish contemporaries.[19]

(7) Lk 11:24–26 is not about literal demons or exorcism; it is instead a parable about "false hopes engendered by a short-lived improvement in the circumstances of life." These are contrasted with "the solid and lasting achievements of the ministry of Jesus himself."[20]

(8) Lk 11:24–26 is one more argument that Jesus is not on the side of Belial: whereas demons makes things worse than before, Jesus cleanses and puts in order.[21]

Two observations are in order. First, because Luke did not alter the wording of Q 11:24–26 in any significant fashion, because he (unlike Matthew) added no editorial comment, and because he appears to have passed down the material in its Q context, one cannot be very confident in affirming what he intended to communicate. In such a case the diversity of exegetical opinions is only expected.

Second, contrary to some exegetes, Matthew's interpretation — the story is a parable about Israel — does not seem to have been Luke's interpretation. Lk 11:24–26 is naturally associated with what precedes (the Beelzebul controversy), not with 11:29–32 (about "an evil generation"; note that 11:27–28 separates the two passages). And unlike the situation in Matthew there is no explicit signal for an allegorical explication. So whatever Luke may have thought, he probably did not think what Matthew thought. Already within the New Testament itself, then, the interpretation of the unit is moving in two different directions.

If Matthew is clear and if Luke is murky, what about Q?[22] The proposals most often made regarding Q are the same made most often for Luke: Q 11:24–26 teaches that those freed from demons must accept Jesus' proclamation for themselves or risk returning to their earlier state;[23] or it alerts Christians to stay on the course they have begun

---

18. John M. Hull, *Hellenistic Magic in the Synoptic Tradition*, SBT, ser. 2, vol. 28 (London: SCM, 1974), p. 102.

19. Cf. Cyril of Alexandria, *Comm. Lk.* frag. 145 (Reuss); Theodor Zahn, *Das Evangelium des Lucas* (Leipzig: A. Deichert, 1913), pp. 465–66. Bultmann, *History*, p. 164, offers that Matthew's redactional clause at the end may preserve the original application.

20. John Nolland, *Luke 9:21–18:34*, WBC, vol. 35B (Dallas: Word, 1993), p. 646.

21. Kilgallen, "Return."

22. See the review of opinions in Laufen, *Die Doppelüberlieferungen*, pp. 140–47.

23. So Richard A. Edwards, *A Theology of Q* (Philadelphia: Fortress, 1976), p. 112; Kloppenborg, *Formation*, pp. 126–27; Schenk, *Synopse*, pp. 69–70.

because there is no tertium between God and Satan;[24] or it cautions Christian exorcists to be wary of their initial success, for things can go wrong again;[25] or it is a criticism of non-Christian (presumably Jewish) exorcists;[26] or it is a lesson for the church on demonology;[27] or it is an allegory of the Jewish nation, which failed to repent during the ministry of Jesus.[28] But whereas one has trouble deciding among these proposals when it comes to Luke, we can be more confident about the meaning in Q.

The first observation to be made about Q 11:24–26 is that it belongs to a complex of sayings about exorcism:

A. Exorcism of Jesus (Q 11:14)

B. Accusation against Jesus (Q 11:15)[29]

C. Jesus' first response: the divided kingdom (Q 11:17–18a)

D. Jesus' second response: the finger of God (Q 11:19–20)

E. Jesus' third response: the strong man (Q 11:21–22)

F. Jesus' fourth response: gathering and scattering (Q 11:23)

G. Jesus' fifth response: return of unclean spirit (Q 11:24–26)

To judge from the independent parallel in Mk 3:22–27,[30] A + B + C +

---

24. According to Heinz Schürmann, "Q$^{Lk}$ 11:14–36 Kompositionsgeschichtliche Befragt," in Van Segbroeck, *Four Gospels,* vol. 1, p. 585, Q 11:24–26 is paraenesis: it reminds community members to be faithful to their baptism. Cf. Laufen, *Die Doppelüberlieferungen,* pp. 141–47; R. A. Piper, *Wisdom,* pp. 123–24. Tuckett, *Q,* pp. 289–91, offers a related interpretation: Q opposes the neutrality of "this generation."

25. So tentatively Zeller, "Redaktionsprozesse," p. 407.

26. Cf. Gnilka, *Matthäusevangelium,* vol. 2, p. 467; Gundry, *Matthew,* p. 246 (Q 11:24–26 "follows a section in which Jewish exorcists are mentioned; and it illustrates their failure, indeed, their making matters worse"); Schulz, *Q,* pp. 478–79; J. Wellhausen, *Das Evangelium Matthaei* (Berlin: Georg Reimer, 1904), p. 65.

27. So Hull, *Hellenistic Magic,* p. 102: "In Luke it remains what it originally was in Q and no doubt the teaching of Jesus...."

28. So Ernst Käsemann, "Lukas 11:14–28," in *Exegetische Versuche und Besinnungen,* 2d ed., vol. 1 (Göttingen: Vandenhoeck & Ruprecht, 1960), p. 246. Cf. Ernst, *Lukas,* p. 377.

29. Lk 11:16, without parallel in Matthew, appears to be redactional. Perhaps it is based on Mk 8:11.

30. Despite some views to the contrary, it is unlikely that Mark used Q; see Laufen, *Die Doppelüberlieferungen,* and F. Neirynck, "The Minor Agreements and Q," pp. 55–72. On Q 11:14ff. and its Markan parallel in particular see M. Eugene Boring, "The Synoptic Problem, 'Minor' Agreements, and the Beelzebul Pericope," in Van Segbroeck, *Four Gospels,* vol. 1, pp. 587–619. Boring defends the conventional two-source theory. For Albert Fuchs, *Die Entwicklung der Beelzebulkontroverse bei den Synoptikern,* SNTU, ser. B, vol. 5 (Linz: Studien zum NT und seiner Umwelt, 1980), p. 202 n. 260, Mt 12:43–45 par. belonged to Deutero-Mark.

E was a primitive unit presumably at hand before Q.[31] So somewhere along the line D, F, and G were inserted.

Whether made by the author of Q or a predecessor, the addition of D, in which Jesus associates his own exorcisms with the coming of the kingdom, creates a question which has until relatively recent times troubled most Christian exegetes: How could Jesus have acknowledged that the "sons" of his opponents cast out demons?[32] Because (against the plain sense of the text) many Christians have not wished to acknowledge the authentic religious authority of those not allied with Jesus Christ,[33] several specious answers have been given. Chrysostom urged that by "your sons" Jesus meant "my disciples" or "the apostles." The argument then is that the disciples were already casting out demons (cf. Mt 10:8) but had not been opposed by the Pharisees, who were thereby shown to be concerned only with countering the person of Jesus, not acts of exorcism.[34] In this as in so much else Chrysostom was followed by Theophylact.[35] Jerome offered a similar interpretation.[36]

Other exegetes have satisfied themselves that while Jesus' opponents thought themselves to be successful exorcists, they in fact were not: "Our Lord does not affirm that they did [cast out demons], but only argues from the point of view of the blasphemers. He appeals to the case of their own followers to silence them, without then stopping to examine the question whether their pretended expulsions were real."[37] John Lightfoot went so far as to assert that what was performed by "your sons" was not really "so much a casting out of devils, as a delusion of the people; since Satan would not cast out Satan, but by compact with

---

31. See further A. J. Hultgren, *Jesus and his Adversaries* (Minneapolis: Augsburg, 1979), pp. 100–106, and Heinz Schürmann, "Q$^{Lk}$ 11:14–36," pp. 563–86. In what follows I assume, with most who have addressed the question, that Luke has preserved the original order of Q; see n. 4.

32. The reference to the "sons" of the listeners is a reference to their own kind. The expression is, in effect, "an Oriental circumlocution for 'you'" (Allen, *Matthew*, p. 135).

33. See the discussion in Justin, *Dial.* 85. The generalization — for an early exception see Tertullian, *Adv. Marc.* 4:26:10 — holds through the eighteenth century; after that commentators are more open to allowing that "many Jewish exorcists, by faith in the help from above, performed acts which had some resemblance to the cures effected by Jesus (Acts xix.14)." So Hermann Olshausen, *Biblical Commentary on the New Testament*, vol. 1 (New York: Sheldon, Blakeman & Co., 1857), p. 451.

34. *Hom. on Mt.* 41:2. Cf. Chrysostom, *Hom. on Acts* 5:1.

35. See *PG*, vol. 123, p. 268; English translation in *The Explanation by Blessed Theophylact of the Holy Gospel according to St. Matthew* (House Springs, Mo.: Chrysostom Press, 1993), p. 104.

36. Jerome, *Matthieu*, vol. 1, pp. 258–60.

37. So John A. Broadus, *Commentary on the Gospel of Matthew* (Philadelphia: American Baptist Publication Society, 1886), p. 269. Cf. Gundry, *Matthew*, p. 235: "The argument does not necessarily imply Jesus' acceptance of the exorcisms practiced by his antagonists' followers. (His next statement, which affirms the arrival of God's kingdom only recently, implies the opposite.)"

himself and with his company he seemed to be cast out, that he might the more deceive."[38] When faced with explaining the exorcisms of their opponents, Christians have ironically often responded just like those whom Jesus rebukes in Mt 12:24 par., that is, by saying that exorcists outside their circle must be in league with demons.[39]

I should like to suggest that already for Q or its tradition the question had been raised: What should the followers of Jesus make of the exorcisms of outsiders? Could Jesus have really acknowledged their authenticity? Could he simply set his exorcisms beside theirs? Mk 9:38–41, which has the disciples ask Jesus about an outsider casting out demons, proves that these sorts of questions were asked at an early date. The best guess[40] is that they were already being asked by the author of Q or a contributor to its tradition, and that they were raised precisely by Q 11:19 ("by whom do your sons cast them out?"). Certainly one cannot believe that the compiler of or community behind Q deemed the exorcisms of Jesus and others to be of equal religious significance. Among other things, Q 7:18–23, although it admittedly does not mention exorcisms, nonetheless construes Jesus' ministry of miracles as the unique, eschatological fulfillment of passages in Isaiah.

Unlike the composer of Mk 9:38–41, who had Jesus generously say that "whoever is not against us is for us," the contributor to Q, like the author of Acts 19:11–20 and the author of Matthew (who omitted Mk 9:38–39), was not so open-minded. The insertion of Q 11:23 — "Whoever is not with me is against me" — says almost precisely the opposite of Mk 9:40. It is surely not coincidence that the two different but related sayings about being with or against Jesus both occur in the context of exorcism, indeed precisely in contexts which mention exorcisms performed by others than Jesus.[41] Q 11:23, which was perhaps formulated in opposition to the tradition behind Mk 9:38–41,[42] is what has been called a *Kommentarwort*. It makes plain, as part of a "vigorously exclusivistic" passage,[43] that although there are exorcists outside the Christian community, they cannot be truly successful because they do not promote the cause of Jesus. For if they are not with Jesus they are

---

38. *Commentary,* vol. 2, p. 206.

39. See further Justin, *1 Apol.* 54–58, and Augustine, *Civ. Dei* 10:16, 22:10. One recalls Acts 19:11–20: itinerant Jewish exorcists, even when they used the name of Jesus, failed miserably.

40. Which is not novel; it has also been held by those named in nn. 17 (for Luke) and 26 (for Q).

41. Cf. the comments of Schürmann, "Q$^{Lk}$ 11:14–36," pp. 572–73.

42. Kloppenborg, *Formation,* p. 124, calls Q 11:23 "an exclusivist variant of Mark 9.40."

43. The words are those of Paul D. Meyer, "The Community of Q" (Ph.D. diss., University of Iowa, 1967), p. 73.

against him. "Those who fail to recognize God's activity in Jesus" must be considered "God's opponents and will lie among the defeated."[44]

Q 11:24–26 should probably be interpreted along the same lines: it is a critique of exorcists outside the faith. There is no reason to regard the unit as a parable.[45] It is rather a statement about a successful exorcism whose effect does not endure because the "house" of the person exorcised, although to outside appearances cleaned and put in order, has not been filled by anything good. The demon, therefore, along with seven even stronger demons, can return to take up residence and make things worse than ever. Following Q 11:14–22 and especially the qualification of Q 11:19a in Q 11:23, the meaning is that Jesus' exorcisms alone are truly efficacious. When others cast out demons, those demons typically return, and with a vengeance. If one does not fill the space left by a demon with faith in Jesus, then no lasting good is done. The last state will be worse than the first. In other words, non-Christian exorcists are not truly effective.[46]

One is hard-pressed to say what Q 11:24–26 meant for those who passed the text on before it found its way into Q. As the foregoing discussion has illustrated, context determines meaning. But for the period before Q we do not know whether Q 11:24–26 was recited in isolation or was joined to some other portion of the oral Jesus tradition.[47] And we can hardly do more than hazard vague surmises about the concrete *Sitz im Leben* of its transmission. Indeed, it is theoretically conceivable that, before Q, the material had no ecclesiastical setting in life, for we cannot exclude the possibility that the person who inserted Q 11:24–26 into the tradition was a hearer of Jesus and that, in composing Q 11:24–26, he or she was simply drawing upon his or her own memory. However that may be, here is a territory we cannot explore.

But if we go back a step further the darkness seems to recede, for it is possible to make an informed inference as to how Q 11:24–26 functioned for Jesus (about whom we know more than about the anonymous and faceless tradents of the pre-Q tradition). That the pericope goes back to Jesus seems more probable than not, for several reasons.[48]

---

44. Kloppenborg, *Formation,* p. 126. Kloppenborg, however, sees the object of this polemic not to be non-Christian exorcists but those who accuse Jesus of partnership with Beelzebul.

45. Cf. Luz, *Matthäus,* vol. 2, p. 281.

46. Schürmann, "Q^Lk 11:14–36," pp. 572–73, proposes that this was the function of Q 11:23 + 24–26 at an early stage of the tradition.

47. But Schürmann, in ibid., argues that Q 11:23 and 11:24–26 were joined before Q.

48. In favor of authenticity: O. Böcher, *Christus Exorcista: Dämonismus und Taufe im Neuen Testament,* BWANT, ser. 5, vol. 16 (Stuttgart: Kohlhammer, 1972), p. 17 ("höchstwahrscheinlich," cf. p. 166); Gnilka, *Matthäusevangelium,* vol. 1, p. 469 ("durchaus denkbar"); Heinz Schürmann, *Lukasevangelium,* vol. 2, p. 253. Opposed: Bultmann, *History,* p. 164; John Dominic Crossan, *The Historical Jesus: The Life of a Mediterranean Jewish Peasant* (San Francisco: HarperCollins, 1991), p. 442. Robert Funk

First, the unit must be regarded as early because it was already tradition for Q.[49] Second, as Bultmann observed, Q 11:24–26 "entirely lacks any Christian features."[50] Third, in other traditions generally regarded as authentic, Jesus speaks about exorcism and the meaning of his own exorcisms.[51] Fourth, there may be something to Nolland's assertion that the unit "is too enigmatic for it to be easily attributed to the developing church."[52] Finally, as I now wish to demonstrate, an interpretation in the pre-Easter period is plausible.

If we try to set Q 11:24–26 in the pre-Easter period, we cannot get very far until we first determine whether Jesus was speaking about his own exorcisms or, as Q seems to have it, about those of others.[53] David Wenham surmises that Jesus "may be speaking...generally of his opponents' ministry. They, like Jesus, are in favor of 'exorcising Satan,' but in rejecting God's revolution in Jesus they are leaving themselves exposed to increased Satanic attack."[54] T. W. Manson seems to have offered the same interpretation: "The expulsion of the demon and the restoration of the victim to his normal condition leaves things exactly as they were before the demon first took possession. If the demon is to be kept out something more must be done than can be done by a mere exorcist. Now Jesus claims that His ejection of demons is not mere exorcism, but a manifestation of the Kingdom of God."[55] The story, that is, implicitly contrasts the limited success of ordinary exorcists with the eschatological success of the extraordinary Jesus.

Manson's interpretation, however, must read into the text a contrast

---

et al., eds., *The Five Gospels* (New York: Macmillan, 1993), prints Mt 12:43–45 in gray (indicating Jesus did not say this), Lk 11:24–26 in pink (indicating that Jesus said something like this). The explanation is that Mt 12:45b is secondary; but surely if Lk 11:24–26 is in pink, Mt 12:43–45a should be also.

49. Otherwise one would expect a more straightforward way of expressing the seemingly polemical intent of Q 11:24–26. Note also that while Q 11:24–26 refers to an unclean spirit, the previous verses refer to demons, Satan, and Beelzebul.

50. Bultmann, *History*, p. 164 — although he goes on to speculate (without offering evidence) that "perhaps it is taken from some Jewish writing." In support he could have cited *Midr. Prov.* 24:31: "As if a king went into the steppe and found dining halls and large chambers, and went and dwelt in them. So with the evil inclination; if it does not find the words of the Law ruling (in the heart), you cannot expel it from your heart." But this is too late and too far from Q 11:24–26 to be of much use.

51. See J. Meier, *Mentor, Message, and Miracles*, pp. 404–23, 646–61; also Graham H. Twelftree, *Jesus the Exorcist*, WUNT, ser. 2, vol. 54 (Tübingen: J. C. B. Mohr [Paul Siebeck], 1991), passim.

52. *Luke 9:21–18:34*, p. 645.

53. Millar Burrows, *Jesus in the First Three Gospels* (Nashville: Abingdon, 1977), p. 116, thinks the passage to be about "evil influences" in general, not demonic possession. Is this not just modern moralizing?

54. David Wenham, *The Parables of Jesus* (Downers Grove, Ill.: InterVarsity, 1989), p. 38.

55. Manson, *Sayings*, p. 88.

with Jesus' own exorcisms, whose exorcisms are not, in his reading, explicitly referred to in Q 11:24–26. They are indeed referred to in the broader Q context, which is what makes Manson's interpretation so plausible for Q. But if we are speaking of Jesus we are forced to interpret the material in isolation. Wenham's polemical explanation, moreover, seems more characteristic of Christian apologetics than of the teaching of the historical Jesus. Where else does Jesus denigrate other exorcists? He at least had no difficulty recognizing God at work in the ministry of John the Baptist, and Mk 9:38–41 *might* — I do not say does — retain the memory of Jesus' approval of an exorcist outside his own circle.[56] Further, as Alfred Plummer long ago remarked, it seems that "the disastrous conclusion is the result, not of the imperfect methods of the exorcist, but of the misconduct of the exorcised,"[57] who fails to fill the emptiness left by the demon.

It is better to follow those who have imagined that Jesus was speaking about his own exorcistic ministry. While we do not know the concrete occasion or question which called forth Jesus' composition, we have no trouble envisioning him warning people who, although they had benefited from his ministry of healing and exorcism, had failed to embrace his teaching. Jesus surely helped or healed people who had doubts about much in his message, or who altogether rejected it.[58] How could it be otherwise with a miracle worker? From Jesus' point of view such people might benefit from his ministry (the healings and exorcisms) without embracing his message, with its manifold demands.

We may thus suggest that, in accordance with his ethical seriousness and insistence that people acknowledge his proclamation with their deeds (cf. Q 6:47–49), Jesus told a story in which, after an evil spirit leaves a "house" (that is, a body or person),[59] that house, although prepared for a guest ("swept and put in order"), remains empty,[60] with the result that a relapse is possible. The lesson is that one is not conclusively rescued when demons leave. One must not just be rid of something but also gain something else; the demons must be replaced by acceptance of

---

56. So Rudolf Pesch, *Kommentar zu Kap. 8,27–16,20*, vol. 2 of *Das Markusevangelium*, HTKNT (Freiburg: Herder, 1977), p. 109 (who finds here "einen Beleg für Jesu pragmatische Toleranz"). Contrast Joachim Gnilka, *Mk 8,27–16,20*, vol. 2 of *Das Evangelium nach Markus*, EKKNT (Zürich and Neukirchen-Vluyn: Benziger and Neukirchener, 1979), p. 61.

57. Alfred Plummer, *A Critical and Exegetical Commentary on the Gospel according to St. Luke*, 3d ed., ICC (Edinburgh: T. & T. Clark, 1900), p. 307.

58. Particularly interesting as illustration is the story of the ten lepers in Lk 17:11–19. Here beneficiaries of Jesus' healing ministry do not respond properly to him. The passage appears to be pre-Lukan, but its origin remains uncertain; see J. Meier, *Mentor, Message, and Miracles*, pp. 701–5.

59. Cf. *T. Naph.* 8:6; *b. Giṭ.* 52a.

60. Cf. Mt 12:44, σχολάζοντα.

Jesus or his proclamation.[61] For demons can return[62] and become even more infernal than before. To quote Manson again, "The expulsion of the demon and the restoration of the victim to his normal condition leaves things exactly as they were before the demon first took possession." Jesus did not believe that one could "maintain a neutral stance vis-à-vis God and Satan. To refuse to submit oneself wholeheartedly to the former after an exorcism would necessarily involve lapsing back into the control of the other."[63] What we presumably have in Q 11:24–26 is Jesus the missionary, the man with a message, seeking to prevent people from seeing in him (or using him as) only Jesus the exorcist.

This reading of Q 11:24–26 harmonizes well with much else in the Jesus tradition. Several old *chreiai*, whose essential authenticity almost everybody accepts, show Jesus demanding wholehearted commitment. This is what we find in Q 9:59–60 (on the dead burying their own dead), in Mk 10:17–31 (the rich man), and in Lk 9:61–62 (hand to the plow and not turning back).[64] There are in addition (although their authenticity is more questionable) passages in which Jesus makes religious demands of those he heals — something we must in any event assume he did, given what we otherwise know of him and his religious demands. Examples include Mk 1:40–45 (show yourself to the priest);[65] 5:19 (proclaim what the Lord has done for you); and Jn 8:11 (go and sin no more). In the light of all these passages it makes very good sense to interpret Q 11:24–26 as the record of an injunction given by Jesus, probably to a healed demoniac. It meant something like this: now that you have been delivered by my act of exorcism, you must embrace my proclamation, or the last state will be worse than the first. While it would be going too far to consider Q 11:24–26 an implicit call to discipleship,[66] it was presumably a call for adherence to the cause of Jesus, a call to accept his proclamation of the kingdom of God.

We have traveled from Matthew and Luke through Q to Jesus. If we

---

61. Cf. Jeremias, *Parables*, pp. 197–98. Jeremias argues, following H. S. Nyberg, "Zum grammatischen Verständnis von Matt. 12.44f.," *Arbeiten und Mitteilungen aus dem neutestamentlichen Seminar zu Uppsala* 4 (1936): 22–35, that Mt 12:44b "is really, in Semitic grammatical construction, a conditional sentence, and should be translated: 'If he (the demon) on his return finds the house empty, swept, and garnished, then he takes with him seven other spirits, more wicked than himself, and they enter in and dwell there....'"

62. Cf. Mk 9:25 ("never enter him again"); Josephus, *Ant.* 8:46–7; Philostratus, *VA* 4:20; *Acts Thom.* 46.

63. So J. Meier, *Mentor, Message, and Miracles*, p. 415; but on p. 462 (n. 38) he does not commit himself to the authenticity of our saying.

64. See further Hengel, *Charismatic Leader.*

65. I at least regard this text as preserving historical memory; cf. Davies and Allison, *Matthew*, vol. 2, p. 9.

66. I say this because " 'following' Jesus concretely as his μαθητής, as one called quite personally by him, and the related abandonment of family and possessions, cannot...have been the condition of participation in the approaching Kingdom of God for all." So Hengel, *Charismatic Leader*, p. 61.

have followed the right paths we cannot but be struck by a rather disconcerting fact: Matthew, Q, and probably Luke gave to the very same
words rather different meanings; and the original composition must
have meant something else again. The story is always the same, as is
the moral that the last state is worse than the first; but the application
of that story and moral is in each case different. For Jesus the point was
probably that to benefit from his ministry of exorcism without accepting
his message was to forfeit that benefit. But in Q the story of the returning spirit evidently served to interpret the exorcisms of outsiders: they
are not truly efficacious. In Matthew the moral is still different, that
the national rejection of Jesus has tragically made things worse than
they were before the Messiah's advent. How Luke interpreted the unit
remains unclear. But many have found the passage in Luke to be paraenetical, in which case we would have yet a fourth reading of the same
sentences.

This result is initially discouraging for the historian interested in
Jesus. We have here evidence that the Jesus tradition (or more precisely
one possibly representative portion of it) was "weak" in the sense that it
could be construed in several very different ways. This is an obstacle for
those concerned with the function or intent of the original composition.
For context determines meaning. But the context of a unit in Matthew
or Luke or Q cannot be equated with the setting in the life of Jesus. We
cannot know the latter as we do the former. The original setting, which
governed the original sense, can only be reconstructed with the imagination and so can never be more than provisional. This entails that the
original meaning can likewise never be more than provisional.

At the same time, Q 11:24–26 encourages us to think that while
the meaning of various Jesus traditions was anything but fixed, at least
sometimes the wording probably was. The Greek texts of Mt 12:43–
45 and Lk 11:24–26 are very close, and so both must stand close to
what was in Q. Further, the wording of Q 11:24–26 was presumably
fixed before the unit was taken into Q. The compiler or author of Q did
not make a point about non-Christian exorcists by freely composing (see
n. 49) but by juxtaposing preexisting texts in such a way as to convey
a new meaning.

How close the pre-Q wording takes us to Jesus we can never know,
just as we cannot know whether Jesus used the story of the returning spirit on one, two, or several occasions. But we can reasonably
conjecture that, soon after the original composition, the wording was
more or less set. This surmise is consistent with the presence of possible Semitisms,[67] which can be explained on the supposition that Q
11:24–26 was not freely composed in Greek but rather literally trans-

---

67. (1) ἐξέλθῃ could have passive sense: the demon has been driven out by an exorcist

lated from Aramaic. It is indeed the preservation of wording, not the preservation of sense, that allows us to reconstruct a plausible setting in the life of Jesus.

To sum up, in the case of Q 11:24–26, Jesus' intention, what he sought to communicate in his original composition, did not determine the interpretations of his followers. As contexts changed, so did the message. His contribution was not the meaning of a text but a story and a general principle which were variously construed as soon as they entered the life of the church.

---

(cf. Lk 11:14). (2) For parataxis for the conditional (BDF §471.3) see n. 61. (3) Asyndeton appears in Q 11:24. (4) ἄνθρωπος = τις in Q 11:24.

# 6

# THE EYE AS A LAMP, Q 11:34–36

## *Finding the Sense*

In his instructive article, "Matthew 6.22f. and Ancient Greek Theories of Vision," Hans Dieter Betz claims to find in the pre-Socratics, in Plato, and in Philo the clues to elucidate Q 11:34–35(36), the enigmatic logion about the eye as the lamp of the body.[1] He directs attention to the following texts in particular:

(1) Plato, *Timaeus* 45B–46A. In discussing the creation of the human body, Plato speaks of the "light-bearing eyes" (φωσφόρα ὄμματα), and he asserts that within the human eye is a type of fire — a fire which does not burn but is, as Bury translates, "mild."[2] When we see, this fire, which is both "pure" (εἰλικρινές) and "within us" (ἐντὸς ἡμῶν), flows through the eyes and out into the world, where it meets the light of day. As like is attracted to like, the light of the eyes coalesces with the light of day, forming one stream of substance. And then, to quote Plato, "This substance, having all become similar in its properties because of its similar nature, distributes the motions of every object it touches, or whereby it is touched, throughout all the body, even unto the soul, and brings about the sensation which we term seeing."[3] In fine, we see because we have within us a light which streams forth through our eyes.[4]

(2) Empedocles, frag. 84.[5] In describing the composition and structure of the eye, Empedocles recounts a parable about a man preparing to take a trip on a wintry evening. It being dark, he requires a lamp. But the winds of winter will put out the light as soon as he leaves his lodg-

---

1. In *Text and Interpretation: Studies in the New Testament Presented to Matthew Black*, ed. E. Best and R. McL. Wilson (Cambridge: Cambridge University Press, 1979), pp. 43–56. Reprinted in Betz, *Essays*, pp. 71–87.
2. Plato, *Timaeus* (Cambridge: Harvard University Press, 1929), p. 101.
3. Ibid.
4. For discussion and additional texts see J. I. Beare, *Greek Theories of Elementary Cognition from Alcmaeon to Aristotle* (Oxford: University Press, 1906), pp. 42–56, also Theophrastus, *De Sensu* 5–6, 86, 91, in G. M. Stratton, *Theophrastus and the Greek Physiological Psychology before Aristotle* (New York: Macmillan, 1917), pp. 68–71, 144–45, 148–51.
5. H. Diels and W. Kranz, *Die Fragmente der Vorsokratiker*, 6th ed., vol. 1 (Berlin: Weidmann, 1951), p. 253 (21 B 84). Cf. Aristotle, *De Sensu* 437b–38a.

ing. So what does the man do? He covers his lamp with linen screens. These keep the wind out but let the light through. Just so, says Empedocles, is it with the eye. The organ of sight contains the "elemental" or "primal" fire (ὠγύγιον πῦρ), a fire which would be extinguished if it were not protected from the water in the eye. But it is protected — by membranes and delicate tissues. These membranes and tissues let light out but at the same time keep the water of the eyes from going into the chamber of fire. In Empedocles, as in Plato, the eyes are a channel for an outward-flowing fire. Moreover — and this is especially noteworthy for our purposes — in fragment 84 the eye is explicitly likened to a lamp.[6]

(3) Theophrastus, *De Sensu* 1ff.[7] According to Theophrastus, who cataloged ancient opinions about sensation, Parmenides held the same theory as did Plato and Empedocles: we see according to the principle that like matches like. That is, we see because the light within goes forth and encounters the light without.

(4) Philo, *De Abr.* 150–57. The most famous of ancient Alexandrian Jews followed Plato in accepting an extramission theory of vision. His reflections on the eye and its marvels are preserved in *De Abr.* 150–57. Here we read, among other things, that the eyes "reach out" and "act upon objects," and that the light within us "goes forth towards the things seen."[8]

Starting with the texts just cited, Betz argues that the saying, "The eye is the lamp of the body," came into Christian tradition from the Greek world and that Mt 6:22b–23b offers a critical reinterpretation. The proverbial notion that the eye is the lamp of the body suggests that the eye itself sees, and this is rejected in favor of the notion that sight is a moral issue. What matters is not physiological explanation but inner disposition. While good sight depends upon an ὀφθαλμὸς ἁπλοῦς, bad sight is caused by an ὀφθαλμὸς πονηρός — ἁπλοῦς and πονηρός both being ethical terms. According to Betz, in Mt 6:22b–23 "the entire approach of Greek philosophical tradition is called into question," and this "from a Jewish point of view."[9]

Among Betz's major conclusions at least three merit assent. First, "the eye is the lamp of the body" should probably be considered prover-

---

6. For discussion and literature see Beare, *Greek Theories*, pp. 14–23, and D. O'Brien, "The Effect of a Simile: Empedocles' Theories of Seeing and Breathing," *Journal of Hellenic Studies* 90 (1970): 149–79. O'Brien himself argues that while Empedocles believed the eye to produce an outward-flowing fire, he did not connect this with the act of seeing. This is a distinctly minority position and conflicts with the impression left by Aristotle, *De Sensu* 437b–38a.

7. See Stratton, *Theophrastus*, pp. 66–151.

8. Translation by F. H. Colson for the Loeb Classical Library, *Philo*, vol. 6 (1959), pp. 76–77. For discussion see further H. Schmidt, *Die Anthropologie Philons von Alexandria* (Würzburg: Triltsch, 1933), pp. 75–79.

9. "Matthew 6.22f.," p. 55.

bial.[10] Second, Mt 6:22b–23 offers a critical reinterpretation of v. 22a: a traditional notion about the mechanism of physical sight is being taken up and reinterpreted to make a religious or moral point. Third, the theory of vision presupposed is indeed that found in certain Greek philosophical texts: we see because our eyes produce a light.

But beyond this agreement one must ask questions. For Betz's focus on Greek sources leaves an incomplete picture. Greek philosophers were not alone in imagining the eye to have its own light, nor was Empedocles the only person to liken the eye to a lamp. Both things can in fact be found in Jewish literature, and this is rather important for the interpretation of Q 11:34–35(36). So while Betz's contribution is both stimulating and helpful, one must turn to additional sources for the whole story.

## ANCIENT THEORIES OF VISION

The Greek philosophers propounded four different theories of vision, each of which was taken up by later thinkers.

(1) According to most modern authorities, Leucippos (the purported founder of the atomists),[11] Democritus, and Epicurus attributed visual sensation to "effluences," to thin material images continually streaming from the objects of sight.[12] When these effluences enter the eye it sees. This is known as the intromission theory of vision.[13]

(2) Alcmaeon, Parmenides, the Pythagoreans, and the Stoics held versions of the so-called extramission theory of vision, according to which the eye produces or is the channel for some sort of visual ray.[14] This

---

10. It certainly became proverbial later on; see Betz, *Sermon on the Mount*, p. 441 n. 135.

11. Leucippos is said to have held that "all the senses are a variety of touch."

12. So also later the Roman philosopher Lucretius; see his *De Rer. Nat.* 4.26–378.

13. Texts and discussion in C. Bailey, *The Greek Atomists and Epicurus* (Oxford: Clarendon, 1928), pp. 53–55, 103–105, 165–70, 184, 242–43, 406–13; Edward N. Lee, "The Sense of an Object: Epicurus on Seeing and Hearing," in *Studies in Perception*, ed. Peter K. Machamer and Robert G. Turnbull (Columbus: Ohio State University Press, 1975), pp. 27–59; K. von Fritz, "Democritus' Theory of Vision," in *Science, Medicine, and History: Essays on the Evolution of Scientific Thought and Medical Practice, Written in Honor of Charles Singer*, ed. E. A. Underwood, vol. 1 (Oxford: Oxford University Press, 1953), pp. 83–99; and R. E. Siegel, "Did the Greek Atomists Consider a Non-corpuscular Visual Transmission? Reconsideration of Some Ancient Visual Doctrines," *Archives internationales d'histoire de sciences* 22 (1969): 3–16. For the argument that both Leucippos and Democritus have been misinterpreted see Walter Burkert, "Air-Imprints or Eidola: Democritus' Aetiology of Vision," *Illinois Classical Studies* 2 (1977): 97–109. He makes a strong case for thinking that Democritus believed in the emission of some sort of sight ray. See also W. van Hoorn, *As Images Unwind: Ancient and Modern Theories of Visual Perception* (Amsterdam: University Press, 1972), pp. 49–57, 70–71.

14. On Alcmaeon see Theophrastus, *De Sensu* 26, available in Diels and Kranz, *Fragmente*, vol. 1, p. 132 (14 A 5). Discussion in Beare, *Greek Theories*, pp. 11–13. On the Stoics see S. Sambursky, *Physics of the Stoics* (London: Routledge and Keagan Paul, 1959),

ray reaches out and comes into contact with objects in the world. The analogy with the hands is close.

(3) In Plato, not only does an intraocular fire issue forth into the world but, at the same time, perceived objects produce emanations or effluences. Vision occurs when the light of the eye, after coalescing with the light of day, encounters an emanation or effluence from an external object. This has been labeled the intromission-extramission theory. According to most who have studied the question, a similar idea can already be found in Empedocles.

(4) In Aristotle's psychological works, the accounts of Plato, the Stoics, and the atomists are all rejected and another put in their place.[15] There is, so Aristotle claims, always of necessity a diaphanous or transparent medium between objects and observers, a medium that is moved by color. When we see, this medium (air, for example) is continuous between our eyes and the things seen, and once its transparency has been actualized, it in turn acts upon the eye. The sensory organ, the eye, is thus a passive receptor, the object seen a passive sender. The active mechanism is the medium between the two.[16]

Of the four theories just introduced, Aristotle's had little following in antiquity. It in fact had to wait until the great Islamic natural philosopher Avicenna before receiving notable defense.[17] Further, the idea of effluences was largely confined to the atomists. The dominant conception seems to have been either that of the Pythagoreans and Stoics, that is, the extramission hypothesis, or some version of Plato's intromission-extramission theory.[18] Why this should have been the case is a problem which shall be addressed shortly. For the moment all that needs to be stressed is that belief in an intraocular fire or light was, to judge from the extant evidence, taken for granted by the populace at large. In other words, the conviction was not just a philosophical doctrine but part of the common wisdom. In Aeschylus, *Prom.* 356, Prometheus says of Ty-

---

pp. 27–29, 126–27, and Heinrich von Staden, "The Stoic Theory of Perception and Its 'Platonic' Critics," in Machamer and Turnbull, *Studies in Perception*, pp. 96–136. On Pythagoras, who is said to have called the eye the "gates of the sun," see Aetius 4.14.3.

15. Discussion in Beare, *Greek Theories*, pp. 56–92.

16. Aristotle's accounts in *De Sensu* and *De Anima* seem to reflect his mature opinion. Another, presumably earlier account of vision, more strongly under the influence Plato, appears in *Meteorologica*. See the helpful note in D. C. Lindberg, *Theories of Vision from Al-kindi to Kepler* (Chicago: University of Chicago Press, 1976), p. 217 n. 39, and David E. Hahm, "Early Hellenistic Theories of Vision and the Perception of Color," in Machamer and Turnbull, *Studies in Perception*, p. 63.

17. See D. C. Lindberg, "The Intromission-Extramission Controversy in Islamic Visual Theory," in Machamer and Turnbull, *Studies in Perception*, pp. 141–52.

18. Cf. V. Ronchi, *The Nature of Light: An Historical Survey* (Cambridge: Harvard University Press, 1970), pp. 36, 57–58. Note the endorsement of Theophrastus, *De Sensu* 27–32, and the comments of Stratton, *Theophrastus*, pp. 30–31.

phon, ἐξ ὀμμάτων δ' ἤστραπτε γοργωπὸν σέλας.[19] In Theocritus, *Idylls* 24.18–19, we read of the snakes approaching the infant Hercules: ἀπ' ὀφθαλμῶν δὲ κακὸν πῦρ ἐρχομένοις λάμπεσκε.[20] In Sophocles, *Ajax* 70, Athena says, ἐγὼ γὰρ ὀμμάτων ἀποστρόφους αὐγὰς ἀπείρξω.[21] And in Euripides, *Andr.* 1180, the wretched Peleus asks, δὴ φίλον αὐγὰς βάλλων τέρψομαι.[22] One assumes that the giant statue of Helios at Rhodes had his right hand raised to his eyes not in order to shade them[23] but to direct their light beams throughout the world. However that may be, Zeus was for the Greeks "sun-eyed";[24] and in the words of Macrobius, "Antiquity calls the sun the eye of Zeus."[25] The moon was also the eye of Zeus.[26] The Greeks moreover imagined lightning to be a flash from the heavenly eye of one of the gods, including Zeus.[27] Finally, one should note that, according to Aristotle's generalization in *De Sensu* 437a, "everyone" (πάντες) believes the organ of sight to consist of fire.[28] The notion that the eyes contain a fire or light was, obviously, not confined to the philosophers.[29]

To this important fact, which Betz's contribution overlooks, must be added another: an extramission understanding of vision was held by people outside Greece. Egyptian sources, for instance, not only tell us that after Seth threw away Horus's eye its parts were used to assemble the moon,[30] but they generally call the sun a divine eye — the eye of the High God, the winged *'iret'*.[31] Clearly presupposed is the similarity of eyes and heavenly bodies: these things give off light. Further, heaven

---

19. "From his eyes flashed a shining glare."

20. "An evil fire flashed from their eyes."

21. "For I divert the beam proceeding from his eyes."

22. "What loved one shall I have the joy of casting rays upon?" Cf. Euripides, *Phoen.* 1564.

23. Against Herbert Maryon, "The Colossus of Rhodes," *Journal of Hellenic Studies* 76 (1956): 72.

24. Euripides, frag. (p. 531), quoted in Arthur Bernard Cook, *Zeus: A Study in Ancient Religion*, vol. 1 (Cambridge: Cambridge University Press, 1914), p. 196. Cf. Homer, *Il.* 13.3, 7; 14.236; 16.645. In all four places Zeus has "bright eyes" (ὄσσε φαεινώ). For others with "bright eyes" see *Il.* 13.435; 17.679; 21.415. Note that the Cyclops has an eye like the sun in Ovid, *Met.* 13.851–53.

25. Macrobius, *Sat.* 1.21.12 (314).

26. See Cook, *Zeus*, vol. 1, pp. 197–98.

27. Texts in Cook, *Zeus*, vol. 2, pp. 501–5. The belief is common in world folklore. Cf. Silius Italicus, *Punica* 12.724, where fire flashes forth from the eye of the Thunder-god.

28. His explanation for this fact is, unfortunately, obscure: "When the eye is pressed and moved, fire appears to flash from it. This naturally takes place in darkness, or when the eyelids are closed...." For discussion of these disputed words see O'Brien, ibid., 161–62.

29. Cf. O'Brien, ibid., pp. 144–45.

30. W. J. Verdenius, *Studia varia Carolo Guilielmo Vollgraff a discipulius oblata* (Amsterdam: University Press, 1948), pp. 155–64.

31. On the symbolism of the eye in ancient Egypt see A. T. Rundle, *Myth and Symbol in Ancient Egypt* (London: Thames and Hudson, 1959), pp. 218–30. Gary A. Rendsburg, "Targum Onqelos to Exod 10:5, 10:15, Numb 22:5, 22:11," *Henoch* 12 (1990): 15–17,

was pictured as a face with two eyes, and the Egyptians could use the same word for the eye and the sun.[32] This last fact especially leaves little doubt as to how they thought the eye worked.

Matters were the same in ancient India. The sun was the eye of Mitra and Varuna, and according to the *Nyāya Sūtras* of Gotama (3d cent. B.C.E.), "Certain rays emanate from the eye and go to the object [seen, and] . . . sense contact is thereby produced. . . . "[33] Of Ramanuja (b. 11th cent. C.E.), the great Indian philosopher, S. Dasgupta has written: "The case of the appearance of a conch-shell as yellow to a person with jaundiced eyes is explained by him as due to the fact that yellow color emanates from the bile of the eyes, and is carried to the conch-shell through *the rays of the eyes* which turn the shell yellow."[34]

At this point I shall shorten the discussion by passing over other civilizations[35] and instead refer to three recurring themes in world literature and mythology, namely, (1) the harmful or even deadly glance or stare — the evil eye, *fascinum*, (2) the destructive fire that issues from the eyes

---

argues that the Pentateuch shows Jewish awareness that the sun-god Ra was known as "the eye of the land."

32. Cf. E. A. Wallis Budge, *The Gods of the Egyptians*, vol. 1 (London: Methuen, 1904), p. 467. Similar beliefs have been held elsewhere. See, e.g., R. B. Dixon, *Oceanic*, vol. 9 of *The Mythology of All Races* (Boston: Marshall Jones, 1916), p. 37 (the South Seas), and H. B. Alexander, *North America*, vol. 10 of the same series (1916), p. 257 (Native Americans).

33. S. Dasgupta, *A History of Indian Philosophy*, vol. 4 (Cambridge: Cambridge University Press, 1955), p. 342.

34. Ibid., vol. 3 (1952), p. 182 (italics mine).

35. The indefatigable Joseph Needham, in his magnum opus, *Science and Civilization in China*, confesses that "so far as we can find, the theory of visual ray emission was quite foreign to ancient Chinese thought" (vol. 4, *Physics, Physical Technology*, pt. 1, *Physics* [Cambridge: Cambridge University Press, 1962], p. 86). Yet he does note that a passage in the *Kungsun Lung Tzu* can be read so as "to conform with the idea that light radiated from the eye" (ibid., note j); and Needham himself, in another section of his history, reproduces a text from the old *Thai I Chin Hua Tsung Chih* in which the eye is likened to the sun, and in which we read, "Man's heart belongs to the elemental Fire, and the light of [the] fire presses upwards into the two eyes. When they are looking at worldly things this may be called natural-current vision. Now if one closes the eyes and reverses the gaze, directs it inward to contemplate the 'primordial cavity,' that may be called the 'counter-current' method" (ibid., vol. 5, pt. 5, p. 249). The continuation of this text, which contrasts the emission of semen with the value of its retention, shows plainly enough that the eye is here thought of as an organ which can either throw its light into the world or cast it into the self's inward parts. Needham has also, as far as I can tell, not considered the pertinent fourth century C.E. text by Ko Hung, *Nei P'ien* 15.10a.4. Here it is affirmed "since they knew how to draw bright sheen from the Three Cookers [esophagus, lining of the stomach, and urethra] in the body, muster the great fire from the south, and wash their eyes with mica, soothe them with sunlight, and burn *ping-ting* (fire) and *tung-shih* (profound vision) amulets with wine, the Ancients used to write in the dark" (translation by J. W. Ware, *Alchemy, Medicine, Religion in the China of A.D. 320: The Nei P'ien of Ko Hung (Pao-p'u tzu)* [Cambridge: Cambridge University Press, 1966], p. 257). In other words, the wise ones of old knew the secret of proper eye care, with the result that they could see without external light; and the explanation of this is that their eyes were able to absorb light (from both external and internal sources) and then emit it.

of gods and monsters, such as the flame from Shiva's eye that burned up Kama,[36] and (3) the comparison between the eye and stars or moon or sun.[37] Because of our own understanding of sight we are inclined to think of these themes, especially the third, as having little or nothing to do with how the ancients thought about visual perception. But this is to make the mistake of reading ancient texts with modern preconceptions. Only in comparatively recent times, since perhaps about 1500 in the West, did an intromission theory of vision become generally accepted,[38] and the list of those who thought of the eye as a producer of or a channel for some sort of ray, light, fire, or visual fluid is most impressive. It includes, beyond the Pythagoreans, Stoics, and Peripatetics[39] in general, the following:[40]

Alcmaeon (6th cent. B.C.E.)

Parmenides (5th cent. B.C.E.)

Empedocles (5th cent. B.C.E.)

Plato (5th–4th cent. B.C.E.)

Archytas of Tarentum (4th cent. B.C.E.)

The early Aristotle (4th cent. B.C.E.; see n. 16)

Theophrastus (4th–3d cent. B.C.E.)

Euclid (3d cent. B.C.E.)

Hipparchus (2d cent. B.C.E.)

Seneca (1st cent. C.E.)

---

36. Cf. also the monster in Chrysostom, *Hom. on Mt.* 28:5 — "fire darted from his eyes" — and the demon in the *Martyrdom of the Apostle Bartholomew* (ANF, vol. 8, p. 557).

37. Jacquetta Hawkes, *Man and the Sun* (London: Cresset, 1962), p. 72, writes that "the interplay between eye and sun, sun and eye is one of the unbroken threads in solar myth and imagery." See further Miranda Green, *The Sun-Gods of Ancient Europe* (London: B. T. Batsford, 1991), pp. 38–39. Mata Hari took her name from a Malay expression for the sun which literally means "eye of the day." Plato said the eye is ἡλιοειδέστατον (*Rep.* 508B). Pindar wrote: the sun is "the mother of the eyes" (*Paean* 9.2). According to Plotinus, *Enn.* 1.6.9, no one has ever seen the sun without being sunlike. For Ephraem, *De Dom. nos.* 27, eye and sun are "of kindred nature." The likening of eye to sun has much to do with the principle of "the knowledge of like by like." Cf. Goethe's words in n. 54 and see W. J. Verdenius, *Parmenides: Some Comments on his Poem* (Amsterdam: Adolf M. Hakkert, 1964), pp. 72–73.

38. According to van Hoorn, *Images*, p. 105, the notion of the eye-emitted ray had its defenders even in the early nineteenth century, until Gruithuisen's demonstration in 1812 that the light issued by a cat's eye in darkness is always reflective.

39. On the Peripatetics see Calcidius, *In Tim.* 238.

40. Discussion of many of the following thinkers can be found in van Hoorn, *Images;* in Ronchi, *Nature of Light;* or in Lindberg, *Vision* — although I have added most of the patristic references. See also D. C. Lindberg, "The Science of Optics," in *Science in the Middle Ages*, ed. D. C. Lindberg (Chicago: University of Chicago Press, 1978), pp. 338–68. To the list should be added the author of Ps.-Aristotle, *Prob.* 11.58; 15.6, 7, 12; 25.9; 31.8, 15, 16, 19–21, 25, and the author of *Ps.-Clem. Hom.* 17:7 (God's brilliance implies that God can see on every side). This text incidentally refers to "the visual spirit [less brilliant than God's] which is in us."

Philo of Alexandria (1st cent. C.E.)[41]
Pliny the Elder (1st cent. C.E.)
The author of the Heraclitian epistles (1st cent. C.E.)[42]
Hero of Alexandria (1st cent. C.E.)
Galen (2d cent. C.E.)
Claudius Ptolemy (2d cent. C.E.)
Origen (3d cent. C.E.)[43]
Calcidius (4th cent. C.E.)
Ephrem the Syrian (4th cent. C.E.)[44]
Basil the Great (4th cent. C.E.)[45]
Gregory of Nazianzen (4th cent. C.E.)[46]
Gregory of Nyssa (4th cent. C.E.)[47]
Augustine of Hippo (4th–5th cent. C.E.)[48]
Macrobius Theodosius (4th–5th cent. C.E.)
Theon of Alexandria (5th cent. C.E.)
Philoxenus (5th cent. C.E.)[49]
Boethius (5th–6th cent. C.E.)[50]
John of Damascus (7th–8th cent. C.E.)[51]
Photius (9th cent. C.E.)[52]
al-Kindi (9th cent. C.E.)
Hunain ibn Kshan (9th cent. C.E.)
al Farabi (Alpharabius, 10th cent. C.E.)
William of Conches (11th–12th cent. C.E.)

---

41. In addition to the texts cited above see *De Cherub.* 96–97.

42. *Ep.* 9:7.

43. Note that in *Comm. Mt.* 11:2, Origen refers to the rays of Jesus' eyes (ταῖς ἀκτῖσι τῶν ὀφθαλμῶν).

44. On the eye in Ephrem see Sebastin Brock, *The Luminous Eye: The Spiritual World of Ephrem the Syrian* (Kalamazoo, Mich.: Cistercian, 1992), pp. 71–79. Note also *Serm. Dom. Nost.* 27 (the eyes and sun are of kindred nature) and 31–32 (on the shining eyes of Moses, Paul, and Christians); see CSCO 270 = SS 116, pp. 24, 28–31.

45. See *Hex.* 2:7; 6:9.

46. Nicodemus of the Holy Mountain, *Symvoulevtikon Encheiridion* 3, quotes Gregory the Theologian: "The lamps of the eyes touch the untouchable."

47. See *Infant.*, in PG 46.173D: "For just as the eye enjoys the light by virtue of having light within itself to seize its kindred light, and neither the finger nor any other member of the body can effect the act of vision because none of this natural light is organized in any of them..."; also *Orat. cat. mag.* 5 ("the eye, by virtue of the bright ray which is by nature wrapped up in it, is in fellowship with the light, and by its innate capacity draws to itself that which is akin to it").

48. See, e.g., *Ep.* 211; *De Trin.* 9.3.3; *De Quant. Anim.* 23:43.

49. See below, p. 155.

50. See, e.g., *De Cons.* 5.4; cf. 1.1–2.

51. Note *Phil. Chapts*, the Dictionum Solutio: "An iris is a majestic reflection of the sun in a hollow moist cloud" (PG 94 673D).

52. See *Hom.* 17:5 (Mango, p. 294), where Photius defends the power of icons: the "outpouring and effluence of the optical rays" touches and encompasses objects and sends the essence of things to the mind.

> Adelard of Barth (12th cent. C.E.)
> Robert Grosseteste (12th–13th cent. C.E.)
> Jalāl al-Dīn Rūmī (13th cent. C.E.)[53]
> Salah al-Dib ibn Yusuf (13th cent. C.E.)
> Roger Bacon (13th cent. C.E.)
> John Pecham (13th cent. C.E.)
> Nasīr al-Dīn al Tunsī (13th cent. C.E.)
> Leonardo da Vinci (15th–16th cent. C.E.)
> Galileo (16th–17th cent. C.E.)
> Thomas Willis (17th cent. C.E.)
> Goethe (18th–19th cent. C.E.)[54]

Given the belief of so many in literal ocular rays of one sort or another one can hardly dismiss ancient comparisons of eye to sun and sun to eye as mere poetry.[55] There was a real point of analogy: both gave off light. This explains why in Siberian mythology Adam's eyes are created from the sun;[56] why in India it is traditionally believed that while breath goes back to the wind, eyes go back to the sun; why Maidu Indian myth tells of how Toyeskӧm, a small bird with a red eye, cooks food simply by staring at it;[57] why in Apuleius, *Met.* 2:28, a temporary restoration of light to a dead man's eyes is spoken of as a borrowing

---

53. See R. C. DeLamotte, *Jalaluddin Rumi: Songbird of Sufism* (Lanham, Md.: University Press of America, 1980), pp. 129–30.

54. Goethe wrote in the introduction to his *Farbenlehre:*

The eye may be said to owe its existence to light, which calls forth, as it were, a sense that is akin to itself; the eye, in short, is formed with reference to light, to be fit for the action of light; the light it contains corresponding with the light without. We are here reminded of a significant adage in constant use with the ancient Ionian school — "Like is only known by like"; and again, of the words of an old mystic writer, which may be thus rendered, "If the eye were not sunny, how could we perceive light? If God's own strength lived not in us, how could we delight in divine things?" [cf. Manilius, *Astron.* 2.115–16]. This immediate affinity between light and the eye will be denied by none; to consider them as identical in substance is less easy to comprehend. It will be more intelligible to assert that a dormant light resides in the eye, and that it may be excited by the slightest cause from within or from without. In darkness we can, by an effort of imagination, call up the brightest images; in dreams objects appear to us as in broad daylight; awake, the slightest external action of light is perception, and if the organ suffers an actual shock, light and colors spring forth (*Goethe's Theory of Colors*, trans. C. H. Eastlake [London: John Murray, 1840], p. xxxix).

55. Cf. Waldemar Deonna, *Le symbolisme de l'oeil* (Paris: E. de Boccard, 1965), pp. 251–70. The assertion of Hagner, *Matthew 1–13*, that "when ancient writers said that the eye itself contained fire or light...it is doubtful that they meant this literally or meant to imply anything about their theory of sight" is so demonstrably wrong as to be baffling.

56. See U. Holmberg, *Finno-Ugric, Siberian,* vol. 4 of *The Mythology of All Races* (1927), p. 371.

57. See R. B. Dixon, "Maidu Myths," *Bulletin of the American Museum of Natural History* 17 (1902): 65.

from the sun;[58] and why in art the world over, eyes, like the sun, have
frequently been drawn with sight rays. (One recalls the all-seeing eye
of the Freemasons and the picture on the obverse of the American one-
dollar bill.) All presumption, moreover, is in favor of supposing that the
evil eye was modeled on the normal eye, both being senders of rays.[59]
Plutarch in fact clearly says this in one place. In defending the reality
and great power of the evil eye, he observes:

> Odor, voice, and breathing are all emanations of some kind,
> streams of particles from living bodies. . . . In all probability the
> most active stream of such emanations is that which passes
> through the eye. For vision, being of an enormous swiftness and
> carried by an essence that gives off a flame-like brilliance, diffuses
> a wonderful influence. In consequence, a man both experiences
> and produces many effects through his eyes. . . . Vision provides
> access to the first impulse to love, that most powerful and vio-
> lent experience of the soul, and causes the lover to melt and be
> dissolved when he looks at those who are beautiful, as if he were
> pouring forth his whole being towards them. . . . The answering
> glances of the young and the beautiful and the stream of influence
> from their eyes, whether it be light or a current of particles, melts
> the lovers and destroys them. . . . Neither by touch nor by hearing
> do they suffer so deep a wound as by seeing and being seen. Such
> are the diffusion of effluences and the kindling of passion through
> the eyesight that only those unacquainted with love itself could,
> in my judgment, be astonished at the natural phenomenon that
> takes place when Median naphtha catches fire at a distance from a
> flame.[60]

Comment is needless.

Before proceeding further mention should perhaps be made of those
reasons that have encouraged so many to accept the belief under review.
There is first of all the fact that the cornea reflects light and so appears to

---

58. *Da brevem solis usuram et in aeternum conditis oculis modicam lucem infunde.*

59. On the evil eye see F. T. Elworthy, *The Evil Eye* (New York: Crown, 1958);
Clarence Maloney, ed., *The Evil Eye* (New York: Columbia University Press, 1976); and
Tobin Siebers, *The Mirror of Medusa* (Berkeley: University of California Press, 1983). On
the evil eye in the biblical tradition see esp. John H. Elliott, "The Fear of the Leer: The Evil
Eye from the Bible to Li'l Abner," *Forum* 4, no. 4 (1988): 42–71. On p. 57 he makes what
is for us an important point: "The eye was considered a channel to and from the heart,
the locus of thought and intention. Rays emanating from the eye powerfully conveyed the
dispositions of the heart. A good eye signalled an honorable and benevolent individual.
An Evil Eye and its possessor, on the other hand, were judged malicious, spiteful, and
dangerous."

60. Plutarch, *Moralia*, trans. P. A. Clement and H. B. Hoffleit, vol. 8, Loeb Classical
Library (1919), pp. 420–23 (5.7.681).

have a sort of glow.[61] When to this one adds the phenomenon of animal eye-shine — who has not seen the fiery glow produced by a cat's eyes in the night? — one not already persuaded otherwise would have impressive evidence for thinking the eye to have its own light.[62] There are reported instances of human eye-shine under exceptional circumstances: the retina and choroid can act like a mirror and reflect a visible light to others.[63]

Then there is the widespread but persistent belief that some animals, which get on so well at night, even when the moon is not visible, must be able to see in the dark. This has surely stimulated people to imagine that animals produce their own light.[64] Our ability to see things with our eyes closed — our dreams are filled with lights and colors — would only reinforce the point.

Another consideration has probably been the circumstance that we all see lightning before hearing the thunder (cf. Aristotle, *De Mundo* 395a). Why? According to Heraclides of Pontus, while our sight goes out to the lightning, we have to wait for sound to come to us.[65] Surely others made the same inference.

Finally, there is the psychological question. We see when we look, when we direct our gaze where we will. This would seem to imply that it is the eye, not something in the external world, that is the active agent in the process of visual perception. At least al-Kindi so argued, and it must have been natural for others to think the same thing.[66]

---

61. Cf. J. M. Heaton, *The Eye* (Philadelphia: J. B. Lippincott, 1948), p. 76.

62. Cf. Theophrastus, *De Sensu* 26, and Democritus, in Diels and Kranz, *Fragmente*, vol. 2, p. 52 (55 A 157), according to which owls see at night by the fire in their eyes. According to Pliny, *N.H.* 11.55, "The eyes of night-roaming animals like cats shine and flash in the dark so that one cannot look at them, and those of the wild goat and the wolf gleam and shoot out light."

63. See the articles reviewed in William R. Corliss, *Biological Anomalies: Humans I* (Glen Arm, Md.: Sourcebook Project, 1992), pp. 47–48, 84–85.

64. Cf. Aristotle, *GA* 780a; Democritus in Diels and Kranz, *Fragmente*, vol. 2, p. 127 (68 A 157); Theophrastus, *De Sensu* 18; John Pecham, *Perspectiva communis*, prop. I.46(49); Nicole Oresme, *The Marvels of Nature*, vol. 4, pp. 338–39 (Hansen edition, p. 300). According to Pliny, *N.H.* 11.54, the emperor Tiberius could see in the dark, at least upon first getting up.

65. See Burkert, "Air-Imprints or Eidola," p. 99.

66. See Lindberg, *Theories of Vision*, p. 22. Some have also found support for belief in a visual ray in physiology. The ears, which receive sounds, and the nose, which receives smells, bulge inward; they are orifices. Eyes, in contrast, bulge outward. Heliodorus of Larissa, Theon of Alexandria, and al-Kindi thought the difference in shape to indicate a difference in mechanism. See Ronchi, *Nature of Light*, pp. 24–25, and Lindberg, *Theories of Vision*, p. 22. One also wonders about the effects of cataracts. The world, to those suffering from cataracts, seems to grow dimmer and dimmer. The cause is an ever thickening cover. But that cover is not always highly visible, especially at first, and without knowledge of it one might imagine the eyes to be losing light, for obviously the cause is not in the external world.

## JEWISH SOURCES

Because the extramission theory of vision was not confined to the Greeks but was the common property of so many, one must ask whether Jews of the biblical era might not also have thought of the eye as a source of light. The relevant considerations are these:

(1) The Bible nowhere explains how the human eye works. This is not surprising. The Scriptures also fail to say how the ear hears, how the nose smells, or how the tongue tastes — for the good and simple reason that religious issues preoccupied those who wrote the Scriptures, and the mechanisms of elementary cognition are not religious issues. There are, nonetheless, a number of pertinent biblical texts.

(*a*) Several verses mention "the light of the [or: my] eyes." The Hebrew is אור עיני(ם), which the LXX renders as τὸ φῶς τῶν ὀφθαλμῶν.[67] This expression could well assume that the eye has its own light. Most commentators do not say this. For in our modern novels and short stories, men and women, consumed by anger and passion, often have eyes that sparkle or flicker or glow; and, when we read of such experiences, we are not put in mind of flashlights.[68] For us, the light of the eyes is poetry. Beyond this, a metaphorical meaning cannot be excluded for Ps 38:11 and Prov 15:10 (where the light of the eyes may mean health, vitality[69]), and it is demanded for Tob 10:5 and 11:13 (S) ("my child...you who are the light of my eyes"). So may we not infer that the ancients were no more literal about the expression than we are?

(*b*) There is, however, more to be said. In several places eyes become dimmed or darkened.[70] Because in some of these texts literal loss of eyesight is the subject,[71] surely the most natural inference is that Jews, like Egyptians and others, conceived the eye to be like the sun.[72] Just as the heavenly source of light could become darkened, so too could the body's source of light become dim, usually as a result of old age. The author of Bar 2:18 wrote of his "eyes suffering eclipse" (οἱ ὀφθαλμοὶ οἱ ἐκλείποντες), and the Sibyl in *Sib. Or.* 3:420 prophesied Homer's blindness with the words, "the light will go out in his eyes."

---

67. See Ps 38:11; Prov 15:30; Tob 10:5, 11:13 (S); Bar 3:14. Cf. Prov 19:13.

68. Cf. perhaps already Homer, *Il.* 12:466: Hector's eyes "blazed with fire." Does this have metaphorical meaning?

69. The equation is natural given the correlation between old age and loss of eyesight.

70. Gen 27:1; 48:10; Deut 34:7; 1 Sam 3:2; Job 17:7; Ps 69:23; Lam 5:17; Zech 11:17; Ecclus 18:18. Cf. Rom 11:10; *T. Benj.* 4:2; *Ahiqar* 67 (Lindenberger); Athanasius, *Vit. Ant.* 93; *b. Ḥag.* 16a.

71. Gen 27:1; 48:10; Deut 34:7; 1 Sam 3:2; Athanasius, *Vit. Ant.* 93; *b. Ḥag.* 16a.

72. Cf. *Hist. Rech.* 5:4; *Sepher ha-Razim* 3:5 (cf. 2:45, 108; 7:5); *Lev. Rab.* 31:9. The sun sees in 2 Sam 2:11; *3 Bar.* 8.204; *Sib. Orac.* 3:385, 8:204. *Tg. Onq.* on Exod 10:5 and 15 turns "the eye of the (whole) land (of Egypt)" into "the eye of the sun of the (whole) land (of Egypt)." See Bernard Grossfeld, *The Targum Onkelos to Exodus* (Edinburgh: T. & T. Clark, 1988), p. 27.

(*c*) In Ezra 9:8; 19:9; Ecclus 34:17; and Bar 1:12 we read of God "enlightening" or "brightening" the eyes.[73] Later this expression came to be used sometimes in a purely figurative manner, as in Eph 1:18 ("having the eyes of your hearts enlightened"). Yet given the ancient belief that rays "shine through the eyes and touch whatever they see,"[74] one naturally presumes that the metaphorical meaning was a derivative one, that a literal meaning lay in the background,[75] that it was also possible to talk about enlightenment with reference to the physical eyes and the internal light which, so it was thought, made vision possible.[76] One thinks of our own use of "to open the eyes." This expression can have either a literal or figurative sense.[77]

(*d*) In Ecclus 23:19 a fornicator's "fear is confined to the eyes of others, and he does not realize that the eyes of the Lord are ten thousand times brighter than the sun; they look upon all the ways of human beings and perceive even the hidden places." This simile assumes that eyes see because they are self-luminous, so God's eyes must be very bright.[78]

(*e*) Wis 11:18 records the notion that, just as monsters can spew "blasts of fiery breath," so too can their eyes shoot "terrible sparks."[79]

(2) Passing from canonical to noncanonical sources there is first (*a*) the so-called *Paraleipomena Jeremiou* (= 4 Baruch), a Jewish pseudepigraphon perhaps composed near Jerusalem in the first half of the second century C.E. In chapter 7 Baruch holds a conversation with an eagle who is supposed to go to Babylon to deliver a message to Jeremiah. The scribe's words include the following: "You who speak are chosen from among all the birds of heaven, for this is evident ἐκ τῆς αὐγῆς of your eyes" (v. 3). Now αὐγή can mean "light," "ray," or "beam" (LSJ, s.v.), so the eagle's eyes are shining. The parallel with Sophocles, *Ajax*

---

73. Hiphal of אור + עיני/φωτίζω + ὀφθαλμός. Cf. *T. Gad* 5:7; *Od. Sol.* 11:14; *b. Yeb.* 63a; *b. Meg.* 12b; *Num. Rab.* 11:6; *Frag. Tg.* Gen 38:25. Note also Heraclitus, *Ep.* 9:7: ἀλλὰ θεὸς μὲν οὐκ ἐφθόνησεν ἐπίσης ἅπασιν ὀφθαλμοὺς ἅψαι.

74. So Augustine, *de Trin.* 9.3.3.

75. Cf. "the light of the blind" (as in *T. Job* 53:1); this metaphorical phrase presupposes a physical fact.

76. Cf. Ephraem, *Nat.* 17: "Let him who is without eyeballs come to Him who will make clay and transform it, who will make flesh, who will enlighten eyes." Here "enlighten eyes" is part of a sequence in which literal sight and physical acts are in view. Cf. *De Dom. nos.* 32, where Ephraem refers to "*bodily* eyes full of light."

77. According to the story in 1 Sam 14:24–31 (MT), Jonathan's eyes "became bright" after he ate honey, in unwitting disobedience of his father's oath. I am unsure of the meaning of this — the commentaries say it is just an idiom for regaining strength — as I also am of *Apoc. Sed.* 11:13, where eyes are like φωταγογοί.

78. For the possibility that some thought the lights of the menorah to represent the eyes of God, see Frey, *CIJ* 696 (this depicts a menorah with the inscription: [ε]ἰκ[ὼ] ἐνορῶ[ντος] θεοῦ = "image of the God who sees"), and the comments of E. R. Goodenough, *Jewish Symbols in the Greco-Roman Period*, vol. 2, Bollingen Series (New York: Pantheon, 1954), pp. 60–61; vol. 4, pp. 72, 79–81.

79. δεινοὺς ἀπ' ὀμμάτων σπινθῆρας ἀστράπτοντας.

70, and Euripides, *Andr.* 1180 (both quoted above), should be noted. Also comparable are 4Q186 ii 2 ("his eyes are black and glowing," DJD, vol. 5, p. 91) and *Jos. Asen.* 14:9 ("eyes like sunshine").

(*b*) A second noncanonical text of interest is *1 Enoch* 106. Here, when Noah comes into the world, his parents' house becomes lit up. The motif is widespread, and can be found in *LAE* 21:3 (Cain), *Prot. Jas.* 19:2 (Jesus), *b. Meg.* 14a (Moses), and *Sepher ha-Yasar* (Abraham), as well as in legends about Zoroaster, Hercules, and Mohammed. What is noteworthy about *1 Enoch* 106, however, is the mention of Noah's eyes: "When he opened his eyes he lighted up the whole house like the sun, and the whole house was very bright" (v. 2); "and his eyes are as the rays of the sun, and his countenance is glorious" (v. 5); "and his eyes are like the rays of the sun, and he opened his eyes and thereupon lighted up the whole house" (v. 10). According to these lines Noah's eyes produced visible light rays.

(*c*) Closely related to *1 Enoch* 106 are those Jewish legends in which fire comes forth from human or divine eyes — a motif common, as already remarked, in world mythology and literature. In *b. B. Meṣ.* 59b, for example, after Eleazar ben Hyrcanus suffers excommunication by his fellow rabbis, everything he looks upon is burned up. The same power is attributed to R. Simeon ben Yoḥai and his son in *b. Šabb.* 33b: whatever they cast their eyes upon was immediately consumed by fire. In *Sepher ha-Razim* 2:45 fire issues from angelic eyes. In *2 Enoch* 1:5 the two angels who appear to Enoch in his sleep have eyes "like a burning light."[80] Similar statements are made about Michael and Jesus in Dan 10:16; Rev 1:14; 2:18; and 19:12.[81]

(*d*) Perhaps attention should also be called to *3 Enoch*, although this book was apparently composed for the most part in the fifth or sixth century C.E. In *3 Enoch* 1:7–8 the Seraphim fix their eyes upon Enoch; he is then bemused by "the radiant image of their eyes" and God must tell them to cover their eyes so that Enoch will not tremble or shudder. Then in *3 Enoch* 9:4 we read about God fixing on Metatron 365 eyes, and that each is "as the great luminary" (cf. 26:6). According to 18:25, the hosts of heaven have eyes like the sun, and in 25:2–3 the Ophannim are described as having two eyes from which lightnings flash forth, and from which firebrands are burning (cf. 48 C 6). These same creatures are

---

80. Translation of Charles of Slavonic version A; for version B the translation is "like burning candles."

81. According to a marginal note in a manuscript of Peter of Riga's *Aurora*, in one of the gospels read by the Nazarenes the following appeared: "Rays went forth from his [Jesus'] eyes, by which they were frightened and fled." See E. Hennecke, *New Testament Apocrypha*, ed. W. Schneemelcher and R. McL. Wilson, vol. 1 (Philadelphia: Westminster, 1963), p. 150. Note also M. R. James, *Latin Infancy Gospels* (Cambridge: Cambridge University Press, 1927), p. 70 (Arundel ms.: there came from Jesus' infant eyes *lux magna…tanquam choruscus magnus*; cf. the Hereford text on p. 71).

elsewhere said to be full of eyes and full of brightness, their eyes having a "shining appearance" (25:6–7).

What do we make of all these texts? Do they not presuppose that the normal eye produces a subtle ray or light, and that under the right conditions or with exceptional individuals or supernatural beings such as angels, this light or ray can become intense and visible, even destructive?[82] The parallel with the phenomenon of fire issuing forth from the mouths of gods and mythological monsters is in this regard instructive and encourages one to return a positive answer. For the fire that spews forth from the mouths of dragons and divinities is simply a fabulous exaggeration of the warm mist that can be seen to stream out of our own mouths on cold mornings. In like fashion, we should regard the rays or destructive fire from eyes, human and divine, as an exaggerated version of the common human eye light.

(3) In Jn 11:9–10 Jesus says, "Are there not twelve hours in the day? Those who walk during the day do not stumble, because they see the light of this world. But those who walk at night stumble, because the light is not in them." There is nothing exceptional about the first two sentences. Light belongs to the day, and therefore in the day one can see to walk. The conclusion, however, is peculiar: "But those who walk at night stumble, because the light is not in them."[83] This does not make sense in any modern understanding of vision, for we know that sight depends upon external sources of light. But if some sort of extramission theory of vision is presupposed, Jn 11:10 becomes intelligible, as both Rudolf Schnackenburg and C. K. Barrett have observed. According to the latter, "Ancient thought did not clearly grasp the fact that vision takes place through the entry of light into the eye, and [in Jn 11:10] a new point is accordingly introduced; absence of light without is matched by absence of light within."[84] If this is correct then Jn 11:9–10 is more evidence that ancient Jews accepted the common premodern

---

82. Recall the Greeks' Medusa. The eyes of the Antichrist were often described as bright and shining like the sun — e.g., in Codex Trevirensis 36 fol. 113 and Arabic versions of the Tiburtine Sibyl; see M. E. Stone and J. Strugnell, *The Books of Enoch Parts 1–2* (Missoula, Mont.: Scholars Press, 1979), pp. 30–36. For other references see J.-M. Rosenstiehl, "Le portrait de l'Antichrist," in *Pseudépigraphes de l'ancien Testament et Manuscrits de la Mer Morte* (Paris: Universitaires de France, 1967), pp. 47, 48, 50, 56–57. Suetonius, *Aug.* 79, reports that the emperor "had clear, bright eyes, in which he liked to have it thought that there was a kind of divine power, and it greatly pleased him, whenever he looked keenly at anyone, if he let his eye fall as if before the radiance of the sun."

83. Cf. *T. Jud.* 18:6: "He is a slave to two contrary passions, and cannot obey God, for they have blinded his soul, and he walks in the day as in the night."

84. *The Gospel according to St. John*, 2d ed. (Philadelphia: Westminster, 1978), p. 392; cf. R. Schnackenburg, *The Gospel according to St. John*, vol. 2 (New York: Seabury, 1980), p. 325.

understanding of vision: sight is an active process involving the body's own light.[85]

## THE EYE AS A LAMP

Having shown that old Jewish sources seemingly take for granted the pre-modern notion that the human eye is a source of light, it remains to consider more precisely the background of the metaphor in Q 11:34–36: the eye is the lamp of the body. The comparison appears in Empedocles. What of Jewish sources?

Two passages from the Jewish Bible are relevant. In the first, LXX Dan 10:2–9, Daniel the seer has a vision of a glorious man. He describes him in v. 6 as follows: "His body was like beryl, his face like the appearance of lightning, his eyes like flaming torches, his arms and legs like the gleam of burnished bronze, and the sound of his voice was like the noise of a multitude." The clause to be underlined is the third: οἱ ὀφθαλμοὶ αὐτοῦ ὡσεὶ λαμπάδες πυρός, "his eyes like flaming torches."[86] The significance of this is evident. The difference between "torch" and "lamp" is not very great, and in fact λαμπάς can mean either (BAGD, s.v.).

The second text worth notice is Zech 4:1–4. Here Zechariah tells of a vision in which he saw a lampstand all of gold with a bowl on its top, and seven lamps (נרתיה/λύχνοι) on it (v. 2). The record of this vision (vv. 2–3) is followed by a conversation with an angelic interpreter (vv. 4–14). V. 10 concludes thus: "These seven [lamps] are the eyes of the Lord which range throughout the whole earth."[87] The import of this sentence is all the greater since λύχνος is the very word used in Q 11:34. We have, then, in Daniel 10 and especially Zechariah 4 passages that bring us rather close to the Q saying. And despite all that has been said of late about the interpenetration of Hellenism and Judaism this fact seems much more directly relevant for the understanding of a saying in Q than a parable from Empedocles.

Two additional Jewish texts containing the eye/lamp comparison are, unfortunately, of late or uncertain date, and one must be cautious in cit-

---

85. The rabbis, significantly enough, used the same words, נהור and נהורא for both "light" and "eye-sight" (see Jastrow, s.v.); and סני נהורא = "full of light" means "blind" (Jastrow, ibid). According to J. Abelson, *The Immanence of God in Rabbinic Literature* (London: Macmillan, 1912), pp. 215–17, in some rabbinic sources the Holy Spirit, conceived of as a material light, is "somehow associated with some kind of visual sensation" and, at least in *Gen. Rab.* 91.6 (where Joseph's sight goes bad after the Holy Spirit leaves him), "materialised as the inner light in man's eye...."

86. MT: ועיניו כלפידי אש, "and eyes as flames of fire." Cf. *3 Enoch* 35:2.

87. Vv. 6–10a are probably secondary; if so, originally v. 10b immediately followed v. 5: "Then the angel who talked with me answered me, 'Do you not know what these are?' I said, 'No, my Lord.' 'These are the eyes of the Lord which range throughout the whole earth.'" See the commentaries.

ing them as background for Q 11:34–36. Nevertheless they should not be passed over. The first is *b. Šabb.* 151b: "Our rabbis taught: He who closes the eyes of a dying man is a murderer. This may be compared to a lamp (נר) that is going out. If a man places his finger upon it, it is immediately extinguished." The other late text is *2 Enoch* 42:1 (A): "And I saw the guardians of the keys of hell, standing by the very large doors, their faces like those of very large snakes, their eyes like extinguished lamps...."

A last pertinent text for the background of Q 11:34 may appear in the *Testament of Job*. At one point in this pseudepigraphon, as he is within his house, watching it being ransacked by his fellow countrymen, Job, according to manuscript S and the Slavic, says this: "My eyes saw those who make lamps at my tables and couches" (18:4). In context this makes very little if any sense. What do makers of lamps have to do with anything? Manuscripts P and V understandably omit the clause. But Robert Kraft has made the reasonable conjecture that the Greek behind manuscript S and the Slavic must have been οἱ ἐμοὶ ὀφθαλμοὶ τοὺς λύχνους ποιοῦντες ἔβλεπον. He then translates: "My eyes, acting as lamps, looked about."[88] The conjecture commends itself because the emendation is minor (α→ε) and because it brings good sense to a line which is otherwise most peculiar. The reading in P and V can then be explained as secondary over against S and the Slavic: confronted by an unintelligible sentence, someone resorted to excision. In other words, ποιοῦντες (original) became through error ποιοῦντας (Sslav) which in turn was omitted (PV).

If Kraft is correct then *T. Job* 18:4 is of double importance for this study. We would have here in the first place a clear statement of the extramission theory of vision. In the second place, Job's eyes are likened to lamps (λύχνους, the word used in Q). So here again is the simile used in Daniel 10, Zechariah 4, *b. Šabb.* 151b, and *2 Enoch* 42:1 (A) — and precisely with reference to the act of seeing.

My conclusion is that the Jewish sources discourage one from following Betz's proposal that Greek philosophical texts hold pride of place for the exegesis of Q 11:34. What he finds in Greek philosophy can also be found in popular Greek thought, in popular thought worldwide, and in the Jewish tradition in particular. Indeed, if Betz can find one philosophical text which likens the eye to a lamp, Jewish sources offer four or five examples of this simile.[89] With this in mind we may finally turn to Q.[90]

---

88. See *The Testament of Job* (Missoula, Mont.: Scholars Press, 1974), pp. 11, 40.

89. Prov 21:5 might also be thought to link eye and lamp; but the text is difficult, may be corrupt, and has laid itself open to various interpretations; see the commentaries.

90. It may also be relevant that some antique Jewish lamps have eyes on their sides; see Goodenough, *Jewish Symbols*, vol. 1, p. 163; vol. 2, p. 240.

Betz, *Sermon on the Mount*, p. 442, urges that our saying is "a good example" of "the great confrontation between Judaism and Hellenism." He cites *Gk. Apoc. of Ezra* 6:3–

## THE RECONSTRUCTION OF Q[91]

The opening line requires little attention. Both Matthew and Luke have ὁ λύχνος τοῦ σώματός ἐστιν ὁ ὀφθαλμός. The only difference is the presence in Luke of σου after ὀφθαλμός. Was the pronoun in Q? Word statistics do not prove decisive. Matthew uses σου about 120 times, as does Luke, and there is no tendency in the triple tradition for either evangelist to add or drop it from Markan material. It also does not help that σου occurs after ὀφθαλμός in Mt 6:22b = Lk 11:34b and three more times in Mt 6:22c–23 = Lk 11:34c–36. All this proves is that σου occurred in the equivalent of Mt 6:22b–23 = Lk 11:34b–36. It does not eliminate the possibility of σου being a redactional addition in Lk 11:34a, or the possibility that Matthew dropped the pronoun in order to obtain a more general statement.

The differences between Mt 6:22b = Lk 11:34b are more important. The conditional in Matthew is expressed by introductory ἐὰν οὖν ᾖ, in Luke by ὅταν... ᾖ. Luke is probably original. Matthew shows a greater preference for ἐάν than the other synoptic evangelists[92] while at the same time he has sometimes dropped ὅταν.[93] In addition, the construction, ἐὰν οὖν, is unique in the synoptics to Matthew,[94] and ἐὰν ᾖ may be redactional in Mt 24:28 diff. Lk 17:37b. So the placement of the verb at the end of the line (so Luke) is presumably original, as it is in Mt 6:23a = Lk 11:34d.

In Mt 6:22c = Lk 11:34c there are two differences. A καί introduces the apodosis in Luke, and Luke has the present, ἐστίν, while Matthew has the future, ἔσται. Certainty on these two minor points is elusive. But ἔσται is a favorite of Matthew,[95] and he may have dropped καί as unnecessary. Luke surely is less likely to have added the Semitic conjunction[96] here and again at v. 34e.

---

7:4 and *Apoc. Sed.* 9–10 as additional examples of Jewish responses to Greek theories of sense perception. But even if these two texts and those he cites from the *Testaments of the Twelve Patriarchs* (e.g., *T. Benj.* 4:2; 5:3; *T. Levi* 14:4) show an awareness of Greek philosophy (a matter for debate), Q 11:34–36 is probably not in any conscious way in dialogue with Hellenistic philosophy. For even if one were to suppose that the notions of an inner light and of the eye as a lamp first entered Judaism via Hellenism (additional matters for debate), the two ideas had, by the first century of our era, been thoroughly domesticated; that is, they had become part of Jewish tradition.

91. There is no need for the conjecture of Betz, *Sermon on the Mount*, p. 440, that Mt 6:22–23 is from a different version of Q than Lk 11:34–36.

92. Mt: 56; Mk: 26; Lk: 29.

93. As in 13:19–20 = Mk 4:15–16; 13:32 = Mk 4:32; 17:9 = Mk 9:9; and 22:30 = Mk 12:25.

94. 5:19, 23; 6:22; 24:26; cf. 28:3.

95. He has added it to parallel material seventeen times.

96. BDF §442.7: in the NT "the use of καί to introduce an apodosis is... due primarily to Hebrew." See further Elliott C. Maloney, *Semitic Interference in Marcan Syntax,*

With regard to Mt 6:23a = Lk 11:34d, Matthew, in accordance with his love of parallelism, has probably inserted ὁ ὀφθαλμός σου to bring the line closer to v. 22b. His ἐάν is also probably secondary, for the same reason: it reinforces the parallel with v. 22b (where, as argued above, ἐάν is probably redactional). Luke's ἐπάν lays higher claim to originality, occurring as it does only three times in the New Testament (including probably another Q — in my reconstruction another $Q^3$ — text).[97]

Next, Mt 6:23b differs from Lk 11:34e in not having an opening καί and in using the verb, ἔσται. The same differences were encountered in 6:22c = Lk 11:34c, and for the reasons given there, Luke is probably closer to Q. Also, Matthew has probably affixed ὅλον to enhance the parallelism with 6:22c.

Compared with the differences so far considered, those between Mt 6:23c and Lk 11:35 are considerable. Both verses do contain the phrase, τὸ φῶς τὸ ἐν σοὶ σκότος ἐστίν. But whereas Matthew has an exclamation (εἰ οὖν... τὸ σκότος πόσον), Luke has an admonition (σκόπει οὖν μή...). Luke we may think preserves Q, for two reasons.[98] First, Lk 11:34, as already seen, brings one close to Q. Luke has at the most added the σου to 11:34a, and even this is uncertain. Matthew, on the other hand, has introduced a number of changes. These betray his concern to reformulate the saying about the eye as lamp and so cause us to anticipate Matthean redactional touches in 6:23c. Second, the Matthean phrase, εἰ οὖν... τὸ σκότος πόσον, should be assigned to Matthew on the basis of two considerations: Matthew uses εἰ (or ἐάν) + οὖν more than Mark or Luke,[99] and he inserts πόσον[100] into 10:25 and 12:12. So Lk 11:35 is probably closer to Q than is Mt 6:23c.[101]

The only issue left concerning the formulation of Mt 6:22–23 = Lk 11:34–36 in Q is the source of Lk 11:36, which has no parallel in Matthew. Q, as so far reconstructed, ran as follows:

ὁ λύχνος τοῦ σώματός ἐστιν ὁ ὀφθαλμός (σου)
ὅταν ὁ ὀφθαλμός σου ἁπλοῦς ᾖ καὶ ὅλον τὸ σῶμα σου
   φωτεινόν ἐστιν

---

SBLDS, vol. 51 (Chico, Calif.: Scholars Press, 1981), pp. 72–73. Maloney observes that *waw* of the apodosis exists in middle Aramaic as well as Hebrew, and also that Matthew and Luke omit the καί's that introduce the apodosis in Mk 7:11–12 (variant reading); 8:38; and 14:9.

97. Mt 2:8; Lk 11:22 (Q?), 34.

98. Contrast E. Sjöberg, "Das Licht in dir. Zur Deutung von Matth. 6.22ff. Par.," *ST* 5 (1951): 89, who affirms that Luke's line is a paraenetical reformulation.

99. Mt: 7; Mk: 0; Lk: 3.

100. Mt: 8; Mk: 6; Lk: 6.

101. Was Matthew's εἰ οὖν here stimulated by knowledge of Q 11:36, which also begins with εἰ οὖν?

ἐπὰν δὲ πονηρὸς ᾖ καὶ τὸ σῶμά σου σκοτεινόν
σκόπει οὖν μὴ τὸ φῶς τὸ ἐν σοὶ σκότος ἐστίν

As it stands this parable is complete in itself. It consists of a thesis statement followed by two parallel observations followed by a neat paraenetical conclusion.[102] It is difficult to see that anything is missing. And in fact the addition of the line from Luke seems anticlimactic. So one guesses that Lk 11:36 is a *Kommentarwort*; it is someone's attempt to add a second edifying conclusion, an attempt "eine neue Anwendung des Bildwortes zu finden."[103] But at what stage in the tradition was the sentence added?

Lk 11:36 could be redactional.[104] Or it could be from Q^lk, which at this point had no parallel in Q^mt. Or it could be that the line was present in both Q^lk and Q^mt but that Matthew chose to omit it.[105] Against the first option, Lk 11:36 does not, apart from the adjectival τι,[106] contain distinctly Lukan diction,[107] nor are distinctly Lukan themes present. Against the second option, the difficulty of wringing sense out of Lk 11:36 — a difficulty only too well reflected by the commentaries[108] — could easily have led Matthew to pass it over, so its absence in the First Gospel is explicable even assuming the presence of the verse in Q^mt. The argument is all the more forceful as D, seven old Latin manuscripts, and the Curetonian Syriac have all omitted Lk 11:36 — no doubt because they could make nothing of it. So we are left, it appears, with the third option: Lk 11:36 comes from Q but was nonetheless not an original part of the composition taken up into Q 11:34–35.[109]

---

102. Cf. Q 16:13 and Mt 5:14–16.
103. Sjöberg, "Das Licht in dir," p. 89. Cf. Betz, *Sermon on the Mount*, p. 440 (an "ancient gloss").
104. So Schulz, *Q*, pp. 468–69.
105. So Manson, *Sayings*, pp. 93–94, and Schürmann, *Lukasevangelium*, vol. 2, pp. 300–302.
106. Adjectival τις: Mt: 1; Mk: 2; Lk: 105.
107. Ferdinand Hahn, "Die Worte vom Licht Lk 11,33–36," in *Orientierung an Jesus*, ed. Paul Hoffmann (Freiburg: Herder, 1973), p. 133, observes that φωτίζω is a Lukan *hapax legomenon*, and that ἀστραπή is elsewhere from Luke's tradition (10:18; 17:24). On the non-Lukan character of εἰ οὖν see Jeremias, *Sprache*, p. 205. But μέρος τι does appear again in Acts 5:2. Although offered by Schulz as evidence for a redactional origin, the statistics on λύχνος — Mt: 2; Mk: 1; Lk: 5 — are misleading; for two occurrences of the word are from the very passage under discussion; one (Lk 8:16) is from Mk 4:21; and the uses in 12:35 and 15:8 are presumably from Luke's tradition.
108. See Marshall, *Luke*, pp. 489–90; also below, p. 162.
109. J. Wanke, "*Bezugs- und Kommentarworte" in den synoptischen Evangelien*, ETS, vol. 44 (Leipzig: St. Benno, 1981), p. 62, speculates that at one time the saying about the eye as a lamp ended with something close to the following: "When the light in you is dark (cf. Mt 6:23), your whole body will be dark. But when the light in you is brilliant, your whole body will also be light (cf. Lk 11:36)." Cf. Hahn, "Worte vom Licht," pp. 114–17.

## INTERPRETATION

(1) "The eye is the lamp of the body." This line has a proverbial ring. One suspects that Jesus was not the first to utter it — especially in view of Dan 10:6; Zechariah 4; *b. Šabb.* 151b; *2 Enoch* 42:1 (A); and *T. Job* 18:4. The sentence in any event hardly sets forth a new thesis. If such were the case what follows, that is, Q 11:34b–35, would *explain* that new thesis. But as the history of exegesis shows so well, Q 11:34b—35 does not make plain the import of Q 11:34a. On the contrary, one's understanding of the opening line determines the meaning of what follows. So the first question is, What would a first-century Jew have thought upon hearing, "The eye is the lamp of the body"?

The material already gathered returns the likely answer. Jewish tradition was familiar with the likening of the eye to a lamp; and ancient Jews, like other premodern peoples, tended to think, when they thought of the matter, of the eye as a source of light. So would Q 11:34a not have moved first-century hearers to think of the well-known idea that the eye sends light into the world?[110]

Most modern commentators have not thought so. They have instead thought that the eye is a lamp in that it illumines the body by letting light in.[111] This is the natural reading for those of us who do not believe that eye sends light into the world. And it fits well with the rest of the saying: if the eye is good the body will have light; if the eye is bad the body will be dark.

Such an interpretation already appears in Jerome. In his *Dialogue against the Luciferians*, Jerome, in a context which cites Mt 6:22–23, has his opponent ask, "How will the light enter into me when my eye is blind?"[112] One guesses that the church father, so well educated in the Latin classics, held the common philosophical view that the eyes send light into the world as well as into the body (cf. Plato).[113] With such a view one could construe Q 11:34 either as a statement about the eye

---

110. So also Betz, "Matthew 6.22f."; George Wesley Buchanan, *The Gospel according to Matthew* (Lewiston, N.Y.: Mellen, 1996), pp. 322–23; Evans, *Luke*, p. 500; David E. Garland, *Reading Matthew* (New York: Crossroad, 1993), p. 82; Robert H. Gundry, *SŌMA in Biblical Theology*, SNTSMS, vol. 29 (Cambridge: Cambridge University Press, 1976), p. 25 (our saying "rests on the ancient notion that the eye radiates brightness from within the body..."; Gundry cites Robert H. Smith, "The Household Lamps of Palestine in New Testament Times," *BA* 19 [1966]: 10); Douglas R. A. Hare, *Matthew* (Louisville: John Knox, 1993), p. 72; and Dan O. Via, "Matthew's Dark Light and the Human Condition," in *The New Literary Criticism and the New Testament*, ed. Edgar V. McKnight and Elizabeth Struthers Malbon (Valley Forge, Pa.: Trinity Press International, 1994), pp. 355–57.

111. See, e.g., H. A. W. Meyer, *The Gospel of Matthew*, vol. 1 (Edinburgh: T. & T. Clark, 1877), pp. 216–17, and Marshall, *Luke*, p. 488.

112. *Alt. Lucif. 5.*

113. Cf. *Adv. Jov.* 2:8, where the eye is a "window."

letting light in or as a statement about the eye letting light out: and Jerome chose the former. Chrysostom and Theophylact also appear to have taken our saying to mean that the eye lets light into the body.[114]

But the interpretation of Jerome, Chrysostom, and Theophylact should probably be rejected. For, to begin with, what exactly is a lamp? It is not a medium through which light from an outside source is channeled to an otherwise dark place. A lamp is rather a radiating light whose source is itself (cf. Q 11:33). From this alone it follows that the comparison of eye to lamp would be more natural for one holding an extramission understanding of vision than it would for one holding an intromission understanding.[115] In line with this, in the other Jewish sources in which the eye is likened to a lamp, the image is never of the eye conveying light to the inward parts.[116] On the contrary, in each instance — in Dan 10:6, in Zechariah 4, in *T. Job* 18:4, in *b. Šabb.* 151b, and in 2 *Enoch* 42:1 (A) — the picture is of an eye or eyes emitting light. Should this not be the starting point for the exegesis of Q 11:34?

There is patristic support for this conclusion. For although most of the fathers equate the eye and lamp with the νοῦς[117] and so typically neglect the possible physiological interpretation of Mt 6:22–23 and Lk 11:34–35, some, in contrast to Jerome, Chrysostom, and Theophylact, did explicitly associate the synoptic saying with the notion that the physical eye emits light. Clement of Alexandria, *Paed.* 3.11.70, for example, speaks of lust going out through the eyes (ἀκροβολιζομένης τῆς ἐπιθυμίας δι᾽ αὐτῶν), then says the lamp of the body is the eye, and then adds that through it (δι᾽ οὗ) appear (καταφαίνεται) the interior things (τὰ ἔνδον) that are illuminated (καταυγαζόμενα) by the shining light (φωτὶ τῷ φαινομένῳ). Here the eye is a lamp that reveals the inner state — a

---

114. Chrysostom, *Hom. on Mt.* 20:5 ("when the eyes are blinded most of the energy of the other members is gone, their light being quenched"); Theophylact, *Comm. on Mt.* ad loc. ("the eye that is sound [ἁπλοῦς] or healthy [ὑγιής] brings light to the body").

115. Sjöberg, "Das Licht in dir," p. 94: "Eine sehr merkwürdige Lampe, die als Empfänger des eindringenden Lichtes fungiert! Nein, die Lampe ist selbst Licht — sie is Lichtquelle, nicht Lichtempfänger." One holding an intromission theory would more naturally liken the eye to a window or glass.

116. I do not recall running across any ancient Jewish text that speaks of the eyes lighting up the body. The text closest to this idea appears to be Prov 15:30: "The light of the eyes rejoices the heart."

117. See, e.g., Origen, *Comm. Lk.* frags. 121, 186, 187 (Klostermann) (although even in this last he speaks of "rays" [τὰς αὐγάς]); Jerome, *Comm. Mt.* ad loc.; Chrysostom, *Hom. on Mt.* 20:5; Isho'dad of Merv, *Comm. Mt.* ad loc.; also Nag Hammadi's *Dialogue of the Savior* 125.18. Here the fathers have been influenced by Philo (see, e.g., *De Op. Mundi* 17 and W. Michaelis, *TDNT*, vol. 5, p. 376) and the Greek philosophical tradition in general, which used the eye as a metaphor for the soul and mind; cf. Hugo Grotius, *Annotationes in Novum Testamentum*, vol. 1 (Gronigen: W. Zuidema, 1826), pp. 240–41. Particularly interesting is Plutarch, *Quaest. Rom.* 72 (281B): "The lantern is like the body which encompasses the soul. The soul within is a light and the part of it that comprehends and thinks should be ever one and clear-sighted and should never be closed or remain unseen."

Hellenistic variant of the old folk belief that the eye is the doorway of the soul.[118] In other words, and as we would expect from one so influenced by Plato, the eyes carry the inner light to the outside world.[119] Clement makes the point while citing Mt 6:22–23.

Clement was not the only one to interpret Jesus' saying in this fashion. The sixth-century Syrian monk Martyrius in his *Book of Perfection* 8 §§55–56 refers to Mt 6:22 in a context which plainly sets forth the extramission theory of vision.[120] Similarly, Philoxenus, when recounting in detail the Platonic theory of vision, alludes to Mt 6:23 = Lk 11:35 with the phrase, "the light that is within us."[121] And then there is the author of Pseudo-Macarius, *Hom.* 1:4 (in *PG* 34.453B–C). He explicitly quotes Mt 6:22–23 and then goes on to argue that the apostles are the eyes and light of the world (cf. Mt 5:14–16); that is, they illuminate the body of the world by giving their light to others. Pseudo-Macarius seems to assume here that the eye is self-luminous.

There is yet another good reason for doubting the common interpretation of Q 11:34 and for supposing instead that the saying would have prodded premodern Jews to envisage the eye sending out light. *Gos. Thom.* 24 preserves this saying: "There is light within a man of light and he lights (*r ouoein*) the whole world. When he does not shine (*r̄ ouoein*) there is darkness." Whether or not this logion depends upon the synoptics, and whether or not it is "gnostic,"[122] it is evidently a variant of Q 11:34–35. The point for us is that the logion is unambiguous about the direction the light is moving: "[H]e lights the whole world." In this rewritten edition of the Q saying the light goes out, not in.

To sum up the argument so far: "The eye is the lamp of the body" probably means not that the eye conveys light to the body but that the eye is the body's light in the sense that it is the bodily organ that sends light into the world. The genitive is "subjective," not "objective."

(2) Following the opening thesis we read, "When your eye is ἁπλοῦς, your whole body is full of light." To what class of conditional sentences does this belong? Most commentators assume, apparently without reflection, that Matthew's ἐάν and Luke's ὅταν introduce conditional

---

118. See Deonna, *Symbolisme*, pp. 28–52.

119. Note also *Strom.* 7.99, where Clement says that just as a disordered (τεταραγμένος) eye cannot see light, so the soul darkened by false doctrines cannot see the light of truth.

120. A. de Halleux, *Martyrius (Sahdona), Œuvres Spirituelles III*, in CSCO 252, Scriptores Syri 110 (Louvain, 1965), p. 18. After alluding to Mt 6:22 (note the use of פשיטא, the word used for ἁπλοῦς in the Syriac versions of Mt 6:22 and Lk 11:34), Martyrius goes on to say that "when the vision of the eye of the body is clear and its light is mixed with the shining rays of the sun it can see with the sun's light."

121. נוהרא דבך; see Antoine Tanghe, "Memra de Philoxène de Mabboug sur l'inhabitation du Saint-Esprit," *Le Museon* 73 (1960): 51 (f. 23 r°). Cf. Mt 6:23 sy[c.p.h] = Lk 11:35 sy[s.c.p]: נוהרא דבך.

122. So Betz, *Sermon on the Mount*, p. 440.

sentences in which the realization of the protasis (A) would entail the realization of the apodosis (B). In other words, an ὀφθαλμός ἁπλοῦς makes the body full of light. Is this correct?

The proposed reading harmonizes with the common understanding of Q 11:34–35, according to which the eye is a channel for and so, in a sense, a source of, the light that enters the body: the eye is like a window. But this interpretation is, we have argued, unlikely to capture the original sense. So what is the alternative?

There is a common type of conditional sentence in which the causal condition is found not in the protasis but in the apodosis, and in which the protasis names the effect.[123] One example of this sentence type is the saying attributed to Jesus in Q 11:20 (which appears only a few lines before Q 11:34–35): "But if I by the finger of God cast out demons, then the kingdom of God has come upon you." It is, obviously, not Jesus' exorcisms that have caused the arrival of the kingdom of God. On the contrary, the arrival of the kingdom explains the striking success of Jesus' battle against the demonic hordes. The exorcisms are a sign, a pointer. The meaning is: "But if I by the finger of God cast out demons, then this is because the kingdom of God has come upon you." Instead of "this is because" one could also insert, "it shows that." The protasis states not a true condition but an effect that depends upon and hence implies or shows to be true what the apodosis expresses.

Q 11:20 is hardly the only example of such a sentence. Consider the following texts (to which I have added bracketed material in order to make the point clearer):

Num 16:29: "If these people die the death common to all people, or if they share the fate of all [it will show that] the Lord has not sent me."

1 Kgs 22:28: "If you return in peace [it will show that] the Lord has not spoken to me."

Prov 10:19: "When words are many [this shows that] transgression is not lacking."

Prov 24:10 (MT): "If you faint in the day of adversity [it shows that] your strength is small."

Mt 12:26: "And if Satan casts out Satan [this proves that] he is divided against himself."[124]

---

123. Cf. A. T. Robertson, *A Grammar of the Greek New Testament in the Light of Historical Research*, 2d ed. (New York: Hodder & Stoughton, 1914), p. 1008.

124. Cf. ibid.: "He *was* already divided against himself, in that case, before he casts himself out."

Mt 19:10: "If such is the case of a man with his wife [this shows that] it is better not to marry."

Jn 19:12: "If you release this man [this will prove that] you are no friend of Caesar's."

Rom 7:20: "But if I do not do what I will [this shows that] it is no longer I who do it but sin dwelling in me."

Rom 8:9: "If anyone has not the Spirit of Christ [this shows that] he is none of him."[125]

Rom 14:15: "For if your brother is being injured because of food [this shows that] no longer do you act according to love."

Gal 5:18: "If you are led by the Spirit [this shows that] you are not under law."

In each of these sentences, as in the saying about casting out demons and the coming of the kingdom, the form is A → B, but in terms of causation, B explains A,[126] or B and A explain each other.

Q 11:34–35, like other sentences that feature ἐάν or ὅταν plus the subjunctive,[127] apparently offers one more instance of this type of sentence.[128] "When your eye is ἁπλοῦς, your whole body is full of light" does not, read as a statement about the physical facts, mean that a good eye illuminates the body's interior. Rather, it could be paraphrased, "When your eye is ἁπλοῦς, this shows that your whole body is full of light." In other words, "By this you know that your whole body is full of light, when your eye is ἁπλοῦς." A good eye is the proof of inner light, for the condition of the former is the existence of the latter. As in Q 11:20, so also in Q 11:34–36: the state signaled by the apodosis accounts for the state signaled by the protasis. The thought then is similar to that expressed by Ephraem the Syrian in one place: "Because the

---

125. In this passage the apodosis and the protasis mutually imply each other. The form may be, If A, (then) B, but B implies A every bit as much as A implies B: to be Christ's is to have the Spirit, and to have the Spirit is to be Christ's.

126. That is, the protasis is more properly evidence for, rather than the cause of, the fact or condition of the apodosis: A implies B because the explanation of A is B.

127. E.g., Euripides, *Ion* 744 ("Also [καί] this [my staff] is blind when [ὅταν] I am short-sighted"); Lk 21:31 ("When you see these things taking place, know that the kingdom of God is near"); Jn 5:31 ("If [ἐάν] I witness concerning myself, my witness is not true"); Jn 8:44 ("When he speaks he lies according to his own nature"); Jn 13:35 ("By this everyone will know that you are my disciples, if you have love for one another"); Rom 2:14 ("For when [ὅταν] Gentiles without the law do by nature what the law requires, they, although they do not have the law, are a law to themselves"); 1 Cor 3:4 ("When one says, 'I belong to Paul,' and another, 'I belong to Apollos,' are you not merely human?"); 1 Cor 12:10 ("For when [ὅταν] I am weak, then I am strong"); and 1 Jn 5:2 ("By this we know that we love the children of God, when we love God and obey his commandments").

128. Cf. now also Simon Chow, *The Sign of Jonah Reconsidered*, CB, vol. 27 (Stockholm: Almqvist & Wiksell, 1995), p. 121.

inward eyes of Moses shone clear his outward eyes were also made to shine clearly."[129] That is, his inner light made his eyes shine.

But what is the meaning of ἁπλοῦς? The word can mean several things. For our purposes these fall into two categories, the ethical and the physical. If ἁπλοῦς is an ethical term, as in Job 1:1 Aq.; *Barn.* 19:2; *T. Iss.* 3:4; 4:6; and *Ps.-Phoc.* 50, then it could mean either "single," that is, "single-minded," "sincere," "undivided"[130] or — and this is much more probable, as ὀφθαλμὸς ἁπλοῦς is the antithesis of ὀφθαλμὸς πονηρός, a fixed expression for a grudging or selfish spirit — it could mean "generous,"[131] and the Jewish notion of a "good eye" probably lies in the background.[132] If, on the other hand, ἁπλοῦς is taken to refer to a physical state, as in Damascius, *Vi. Isis* 6, and perhaps Prov 11:25 (LXX), ὀφθαλμὸς ἁπλοῦς must signify an eye that functions properly or is in good health (so BAGD, s.v. ἁπλοῦς).[133] Are we compelled, however, to choose between an ethical and a physical signification?

The question is not resolved by supposing that a hypothetical Semitic original must have been less ambiguous. Erik Sjöberg proposed the following Aramaic retranslation of Q 11:34b: אי עינך שלימה כל גופך נהיר.[134] On this reconstruction, ἁπλοῦς = שלים.[135] Now שלימ was used of unblemished animals, of animals without defect, of animals ready for sacrifice; the dictionaries include as one of its meanings "uninjured," "healthy." But the same word was also employed to describe a virtuous or sincere person, as in *b. Meg.* 23a.[136] So עינך שלימה might equally have referred to a healthy eye or, as the antithesis of "bad eye," to a

---

129. *De Dom. nos.* 32.

130. This understanding may lie behind *Gos. Thom.* 61: "When he is the same [lit., deserted] he will be filled with light, but if he is divided he will be filled with darkness."

131. See esp. H. J. Cadbury, "The Single Eye," *HTR* 47 (1954): 69–74. On p. 70 he remarks, "The characteristic Hellenistic Greek words for generousness in giving are the adverb ἁπλοῦς, or the noun ἁπλότης." And on p. 73 he observes that the phrasing, ὀφθαλμὸς ἁπλοῦς, "is due to the exigencies of a parable, which, using the word eye with the adjective evil in the familiar sense of niggardliness, must retain for contrast the word eye and add a Greek adjective which while not the usual opposite of evil is its opposite in this connotation."

132. See Prov 22:9; Ecclus 32:8, 10; *T. Iss.* 3:4; *m. 'Abot* 2:13; *m. Ter.* 4:3; *b. Soṭa* 38b. For additional texts and discussion see R. Ulmer, *The Evil Eye in the Bible and in Rabbinic Literature* (Hoboken, N.J.: KTAV, 1994), esp. pp. 33–61. Prov 22:9 (MT) — "the one that has a good eye" — becomes in the LXX "the one that pities the poor." This and the contexts of the other occurrences of "good eye" show that the primary meaning is generous giving.

133. Note that Ps.-Macarius, *Hom.* 1.4 (*PG* 453B-C), in his paraphrase of our line, refers to eyes that are ὑγιεῖς, "healthy." Cf. Theophylact, *Comm. on Mt.* ad loc.

134. "Das Licht in dir," p. 97.

135. Cf. SB, vol. 1, p. 431, and Conny Edlund, *Das Auge der Einfalt*, ASNU, vol. 19 (Lund: Gleerup, 1952), pp. 19ff.

136. See further BDB, s.v.; Levy, s.v.; Jastrow, s.v. Cf. the ambiguity of the expression "beautiful eye." While this could be taken literally, עין יפה (cf. *Tg. Onq.* on Num 24:3: שפיר חזי for MT שתם העין) means "generous" in *b. Šabb.* 74a and other texts (SB, vol. 1, p. 834).

generous, upright disposition.[137] The ambiguity remains — as it would if one were to propose an original עינך טובה (see below).

"The eye is the lamp of the body" makes good sense as a picturesque way of expressing a premodern theory of vision, and we have also been able to make sense of the second clause ("when your eye is ἁπλοῦς, your whole body is full of light") as a statement about the physical eye. But Q 11:34–35 undoubtedly has a moral thrust, as the conclusion proves: "So watch lest the light within you be darkness." Surely ὀφθαλμὸς πονηρός comes from the ethical vocabulary of Judaism. So Q 11:34–35 appears to be a saying that can be read on two different levels.[138] One first hears a statement that is taken to refer to the physical eye; but by the time one reaches the conclusion one realizes that the text treats higher matters. So the listener is led to backtrack, to rethink the whole of what has been said. "The eye is the lamp of the body" now becomes more than a physical truth. It becomes also a spiritual truth. One's moral disposition correlates with an inner darkness or light within. "When your eye is ἁπλοῦς, your whole body is full of light" means that the source of generosity is inner light.

To understand exactly what is meant by φωτεινόν (as well as by σκοτεινόν in Q 11:36) it is unnecessary to suppose a well-developed and carefully considered dualism such as that found in Zoroastrianism or 1QS 3:13–4:26.[139] Nor need one look to Greek philosophy for an explanation.[140] Already the Hebrew Bible says that God dwells in light,[141] has light for countenance,[142] and gives light to people.[143] And although light is sometimes an eschatological hope,[144] God's children are even now illuminated by the light of life (Ps 56:13), and they pos-

---

137. This is how Matthew obviously understands the expression, for he places 6:22–23 between a saying about treasure (6:19–21) and another about mammon (6:24); cf. Cadbury, "Single Eye."

138. So also F. Zimmermann, *The Aramaic Origin of the Four Gospels* (New York: KTAV, 1979), p. 36: "The passage is skillfully contrived. It can be read on a physical and spiritual level." Cf. Betz, "Matt. 6.22f.," pp. 54–55: "Naturally, the reader will think first of the physiological facts, but will then be moved to the ethical level of meaning." Already Gregory Nazianzen, *Ep.* 41, observes there is both a bodily and a spiritual sense. Cf. Theophylact, *Comm. on Mt.* ad loc.

139. But Marc Philonenko, "La parabole sur la lampe (Luc 11 33–36) et les horoscopes qoumrâniens," *ZNW* 79 (1988): 145–51, contends that at least Q 11:36 has direct reference to Qumran doctrine. The Qumran texts are indeed useful for interpreting our saying, but the Q saying does not directly depend upon the Scrolls.

140. For Betz, *Sermon on the Mount*, p. 443, Mt 6:22–23 presupposes a dualism of body and soul. If so the dualism is of the sort that already appears in the Old Testament; see Gundry, *SŌMA.*

141. Ps 104:2; Dan 2:22; Hab 3:3–4; cf. *1 Enoch* 38:4; *Par. Jer.* 6:12; *Jos. Asen.* 6:3.

142. Pss 31:16; 44:3; 67:1; 89:15; 90:8; cf. Hab 3:4.

143. Job 29:2–3; Pss 4:6; 18:28; 43:3; cf. 1QS 11:3; 4QAmram^c 9–14; 2 Cor 4:6; *2 Bar.* 38:1.

144. Isa 60:20; cf. Rev 21:23; 22:5.

sess wisdom, which is light.[145] Indeed, the righteous are sometimes even called light[146] — and it is light which determines the direction of all their activities. They "walk in the light of the Lord."[147]

So it was natural enough for ancient Jews to speak occasionally of an inner light. Already Prov 20:27 says that "the human spirit is the lamp of the Lord, searching every innermost part."[148] Among the Dead Sea Scrolls are horoscopes in which individuals are made up of various parts of light.[149] And 1QS 4:2 refers the "giving of light (להאיר) to the heart of man." In 2 Cor 4:6 Paul says that God "has shone in our hearts to give the light of the knowledge of the glory of God in the face of Christ." The author of Eph 1:18 can speak of God enlightening (πεφωτισμένους) the eyes of believers' hearts. And according to 2 Bar. 38.1 God gives light to the understanding. Our saying belongs with these texts, in which those who have within themselves the divine light share the divine life and know salvation (Ps 27:1).

(3) The third clause of Q 11:34–35 says that "when your eye is bad, your (whole) body is full of darkness." According to the extramission theory of vision this observation is true because when there is darkness within, there can be no sight. A "sick eye,"[150] that is, can be the result of inner darkness. But there is much more here than this. ὀφθαλμὸς πονηρός is a moral term. Jewish texts often refer to the "beguiling eye," the "impudent eye," or the "evil eye."[151] In such texts the eye is the location of an emotion or intention.[152] The three expressions envisage the antithesis of generosity — selfishness, covetousness, an evil and envious disposition, hatred of others.[153] As Mt 20:15 has it, "Am I not allowed to do what I choose with what belongs to me? Or is your eye evil because I am good?" This last means, as the NRSV translates, "Or are you envious because I am generous?" Q 11:34 accordingly says that

---

145. Wis 7:10, 26. Cf. *T. Levi* 4:3 ("the light of knowledge").

146. Isa 42:6; 49:6; cf. Mt 5:14; *1 Enoch* 104:2; *T. Levi* 14:3; *T. Job* 31:5; 53:3.

147. Isa 2:5; cf. *T. Naph.* 2:10; *Apoc. Zeph.* 2:7.

148. For rabbinic uses of this verse see SB 1, pp. 432–33.

149. 4QHoroscope (4Q186).

150. For πονηρός used of a sick eye, BAGD, s.v., cites Plato, *Hipp. Min.* 374D. For the meaning "ill" see Plato, *Prot.* 313A, and Justin, *1 Apol.* 22.

151. Deut 15:9; Prov 22:9; 23:6; 28:22; Tob 2:10; 3:12; 4:7, 17; 5:20; 6:8; 10:5; 11:7, 11–13; Ecclus 14:8, 10; 26:9, 11; 32:8, 10; 34(31):13; *T. Iss.* 4:6; *m. 'Abot* 2:9, 11; 5:13; *b. Ber.* 60b; etc. See further Ulmer, *Evil Eye.* Cf. the interchange in Greek sources between "jealous eye" and "evil eye."

152. Cf. Cadbury, "Single Eye," p. 69: the bad eye "belongs to that nomenclature of what I may call physiological psychology that is so conspicuous, especially in the Old Testament. Functions are located in different parts of the anatomy — pity in the bowels, anger in the nostrils, and so forth." Note the expression for integrity in *Jub.* 41:28: "in the innocence of his eyes." Gregory the Great, *Mor.* 10:41; 13:29; and 28:30, equates the eye of our saying with intention.

153. For πονηρός meaning "grudging" see Edwin Hatch, *Essays in Biblical Greek* (Oxford: Clarendon, 1889), pp. 79–82.

just as a "good eye," a proper disposition towards others, is an effect of the light within, so similarly is a bad eye, that is, a selfish, ungenerous, miserly spirit, the companion of inner darkness. To be in darkness is to be separated from God — which is why first Hades and then later on hell (despite its fire) are dark places.[154] As it says in Job, "Surely the light of the wicked is put out, and the flame of their fire does not shine. The light is dark in their tent, and the lamp above them is put out."[155] Inner light leads to loving one's neighbor, inner darkness to illiberality and selfishness. 1QS 4:9–11 naturally enough associates a greedy mind with blindness of eye.

(4) Q 11:34–35 concludes by passing from the theoretical to the personal: "So watch, lest the light within you be darkness!" With this exhortation, whose warning about light being darkness reminds one not of Greek philosophical texts but of Jewish laments or prophecies of judgment,[156] the listener is called to self-examination. Am I filled with light or with darkness? Has my spirit become darkened? And how do I know one way or the other? Is my eye good, or is it bad? These questions, raised by the paraenetic conclusion of Q 11:35, reveal that our passage belongs to that class of synoptic logia that move one to ponder the relation between outward acts and inward states.[157] The proof of right religion resides in deeds, for that which is within is the source of that without. This is why the healthy eye and inner light[158] are found together and why the bad eye and inner darkness entail one another. Darkness and light are contrary powers with opposite effects. Light without unselfish good deeds is darkness. So one can discern whether within the self there is darkness or light by looking at the character of one's deeds.

## A PARALLEL IN *Testament of Benjamin* 4:2

*T. Benj.* 4:2 reads, "See, then, children, the end of the good person. Imitate him in his goodness because of his compassion, so that you also may wear crowns of glory. The good person has not a dark eye (σκοτεινὸν ὀφθαλμόν), for he shows mercy to all, even though they be sinners."

---

154. Job 10:21–22; 1QS 2:8; *1 Enoch* 103:7; Mt 8:12; 22:13; etc.

155. Cf. Job 18:5–6; cf. 38:15; *T. Job* 43:3–4; *T. Sol.* 25:7.

156. E.g., Job 3:4 ("let that day be darkness"); 10:24 (in the land of death "light is like darkness"); Zeph 1:15 ("a day of darkness and gloom"); 1QH 5:32 ("the light of my countenance is darkened to deep darkness"); *T. Job* 43:6 ("his lamp, extinguished, obliterated its light; and the splendor of his lantern will depart from him").

157. See, e.g., Q 6:43–44, 45; Mk 7:15–23; Mt 12:33, 34; 23:27.

158. Against Luz, *Matthew 1–7*, p. 398, and Via, "Matthew's Dark Light," "the light in you" is not identical with the lamp of the body that is the eye. Our saying is rather about the relationship between these two distinct things.

This is an intriguing text. Although the mechanism of physical vision is not being considered, the expression, "dark eye," could have as its background the extramission theory of vision: an eye becomes dark and fails to function when no light flows from it, when the inner light is darkness. Further, a "dark eye" belongs to one who is unmerciful and without compassion — much like the ὀφθαλμὸς πονηρός of Q.[159] That is, the eye of the wicked, ungenerous individual contains or sends forth no light. This is very close to saying that "when your eye is bad, also your whole body is full of darkness." In addition, the mention of a "dark eye" in *T. Benj.* 4:2 perhaps implies the existence of a corresponding "eye of light," an eye that would presumably belong to the good man, to the man who shows mercy and compassion. At least the potential for such a conceptual corollary is implicit. So *T. Benj.* 4:2 brings one close to Q 11:34–35. The composer of the Q saying may not have been the first to associate the physical light of the eyes with the good and evil eyes of Jewish tradition.

## LUKE 11:36 AGAIN

Lk 11:36, probably an early addition to the saying about the eye as a lamp, has been called "vapid,"[160] "very obscure,"[161] "senseless Greek,"[162] "hopelessly platitudinous,"[163] and "flat and tautologous."[164] One indeed has great difficulty seeing the point. Several — including Blass, Westcott and Hort, and Wellhausen[165] — have thought the text corrupt. More recently Gottfried Nebe has urged that Luke's future ἔσται is actually an imperative.[166] But C. C. Torrey made sense of the

---

159. Cf. also Ecclus 18:18, where one giving with envy (δόσις βασκάνου) makes his eyes "melt away" (ἐκτήκει).

160. Goulder, *Luke — A New Paradigm*, p. 514.

161. Creed, *Luke*, p. 164.

162. Manson, *Sayings*, p. 94.

163. Caird, *Luke*, p. 156.

164. Evans, *Luke*, p. 500. Cf. Sjöberg, "Das Licht in dir," p. 89: "das dunkle, tautologisch klingende Wort." But for an interesting attempt to make sense of the saying in the broader Lukan context see Susan R. Garrett, " 'Lest the Light in You Be Darkness': Luke 11:33–36 and the Question of Commitment," *JBL* 110 (1991): 93–105. She follows Hahn, "Worte vom Licht," pp. 129–31, in holding that the future of 11:36 is eschatological.

165. J. Wellhausen, *Das Evangelium Lucae* (Berlin: Georg Reimer, 1904), p. 59: "Den Vers 36 in der meist bezeugten Fassung nennt Blass mit Recht übel verdebt und unverständlich. Die Syra S. liest hin anders ["your body also, therefore, when there is in it no lamp that shines, becomes darkened; so while your light is shining, it gives light to you"], aber nicht besser. D lässt ihn aus, ebenso de Syra C. und die meisten Latinae; indessen wie eine Interpolation sieht er nicht aus."

166. "Das ἔσται in Lk 11,36 — ein neuer Deutungsvorschlag," *ZNW* 83 (1992): 108–14. Luke does elsewhere use the future as an imperative (e.g., 19:31; 22:11, etc.).

words by arguing for an Aramaic original that was imperfectly translated into Greek. According to him the meaning originally was, "If however your whole body is lighted up with no part dark, then all about you will be light, just as the lamp lights you with its brightness."[167] The key to this reconstruction is the supposition that φωτεινὸν ὅλον mistranslates נהיר כלא. According to Torrey, כלא, "rendered correctly as the adjective in the first clause of the verse, is here unquestionably the noun, 'the whole, everything.' The man who is full of light lights the world about him."[168]

It is of course hardly possible to show that Torrey — who was followed by T. W. Manson[169] — was right. Two things, however, may be said. First, the reconstruction produces a sentence whose image of an individual lighting up the world has parallels in Mt 5:14–16 and *Gos. Thom.* 24. Second, "If however your whole body is lighted up with no part dark, then all about you will be light..." means that when individuals have light within themselves all about them is light. They are like lamps that spread light. This makes Lk 11:36 an extension of the eye as lamp metaphor.[170] Just as the healthy, good eye sends light into the world, so too do the righteous, filled with the light of God, dispel the darkness around them. The picture is not of light coming in but of light going out. So Torrey's conjecture turns Lk 11:36 into evidence that the earliest interpreter of Q 11:34–35 was thinking about the eye as a source of light. Perhaps Torrey was right.[171]

## THE ORIGIN OF Q 11:34–35

The vast majority of commentators seem to suppose that Jesus composed Q 11:34–35. Their instincts are probably correct. The saying is indeed early if Lk 11:36 preserves commentary originally composed in Aramaic. However that may be, Q 11:34–35 contains nothing distinctively Christian. There is no Christology, either explicit or implicit. On the other hand the stress on the correlation between inner disposition and outward acts must be regarded as characteristic of Jesus.[172] Also

---

167. C. C. Torrey, *The Four Gospels* (London: Hodder and Stoughton, n.d.), pp. 309–10; cf. idem, *Our Translated Gospels* (New York: Harper and Brothers, 1936), pp. 33–34.

168. *Four Gospels*, p. 309.

169. *Sayings*, pp. 93–94.

170. It is also possible that the connection of Q 11:33 with Q 11:34–36 was felt appropriate because the latter, like the former, was thought to be about a light seen publicly.

171. Cf. Fitzmyer, *Luke*, vol. 2, p. 941: Torrey's conjecture "is not impossible, if the theory of mistranslation is admissible."

172. According to Cadbury, "Single Eye," pp. 73–74, the saying falls "into that commonest of synoptic areas of Jesus' teaching — ethics, and has that characteristic negative emphasis on freedom from self-seeking."

characteristic is the taking up of traditional materials for some novel end — here the use of the eye as lamp image to make a moral or religious statement.[173] Q 11:34–35, which might be considered a riddle,[174] offers more of the same: it undoes expectations generated by a traditional statement.

Another reason for crediting the composition of Q 11:34–35 to Jesus is that the saying has exactly the same structure as Q 16:13. Both Q sayings are quatrains which consist of a thesis statement followed by two expository sentences in antithetical parallelism followed by the conclusion or application.[175] If one thinks Q 16:13 dominical,[176] one is encouraged to think the same for Q 11:34–35.

The arguments just made scarcely put the dominical origin of the parable of the eye as a lamp beyond doubt. They do, however, make it plausible. That is, it is a reasonable judgment that Q 11:34–35, which presupposes an extramission theory of vision and which plays upon the twin concepts of the עין טובה and the עין רעה, was probably composed by Jesus himself.[177] He likely authored the clever parable which explains

---

173. The parable of the rich man and Lazarus (Lk 16:19–31), for example, offers a new twist to a tale which is otherwise known both from Egyptian and rabbinic sources. See K. Grobel, "…Whose Name Was Neves," *NTS* 10 (1964): 373–82. Likewise the parable of the wedding guests (Q 14:16–24) follows an old story line only to offer a surprising ending (see Jeremias, *Parables*, pp. 178–80), and the parable of the barren fig tree (Lk 13:6–9) almost certainly gained its force by turning an old motif on its head. Cf. *Ahiqar* 8:30 (Arabic); Q 3:9; and perhaps *ARN* A 16.

174. On riddles in the Jesus tradition see Jeremias, *Theology*, pp. 30–31.

175. I cannot follow Ian H. Henderson, "Gnomic Quatrains in the Synoptics: An Experiment in Genre Definition," *NTS* 37 (1991): 481–98, who classifies Q 11:34–35 and 16:13 together with Q 12:2–3; Mt 7:6; 10:24–25; Mk 2:21–22b; and Lk 16:10–12 as "gnomic quatrains." I also see little profit in Betz's attempt in *The Sermon on the Mount*, p. 441, to compare the structure of Q 11:34–35 with the entirety of Theophrastus's *De Sensu* and Epictetus, *Diss.* 3.3.20–22.

176. Q 16:13 coheres well with the proclamation of Jesus (cf. Q 12:13–21), and signs of a Semitic original are present: μαμωνᾶς (= ממונא/ממין); εἷς…ἕτερος (see Black, *Aramaic Approach*, p. 108). Instead of ἀντέχω and καταφρονέω *Gos. Thom.* 47 has τιμᾶν and ὑβρίζειν; these might be translation variants. On the unity of 16:13 see Guelich, *Sermon on the Mount*, p. 333.

177. Retranslation into Aramaic, although necessarily conjectural, presents no difficulty:

שרנא דגשמא עינא
הן  עינך  טובה  וגשמך כלה נהיר
והן (עינך)  באישה וגשמך   חשוך
זהיר  כן דלמא נהורא דבך חשוכא

Following Cadbury, I presume that ἁπλοῦς represents a free translation which attempts to emphasize the moral dimension (a translation perhaps stimulated by a traditional contrast between ἁπλοῦς and πονηρός; cf. *T. Iss.* 4:6). Cf. the translation of עין רע by βάσκανος (cf. Lat. *fascinum, fascinatio*) in Prov 23:6 (LXX); 28:22; and Ecclus 14:3, and of עין טוב by ἱλαρός in Prov 22:9 (LXX). ἁπλοῦς could also be a more literal translation of שלימה (cf. Sjöberg) or תמימא (cf. Philonenko). But as F. C. Fensham, "The Good and Evil Eye in the Sermon on the Mount," *Neotestamentica* 1 (1967): 55–56, observes, these two words do not appear with "eye" in the Tanak or any other ancient Jewish text.

the root causes of generous goodwill on the one hand and of selfish ill will on the other, and that exhorts hearers to take care, lest the light within them become darkness.

## 11:34–36 AND Q

One last question remains. What was the function of 11:34–36 in Q? The question cannot be answered without also asking about the function of Q 11:33 (the word about the lamp on a lampstand), for the sayings about light stood side by side in Q.[178]

One possibility is that in Q 11:33–36 the light stands first for Jesus and/or his proclamation. In the words of Goulder, commenting on Luke: "The light symbolizes the preaching of the greater than Jonah, the light to lighten the Gentiles...."[179] Similar is Marshall:

> Jesus (or his message of the kingdom) is like a light which illuminates those who enter a house. There is nothing hidden about this light. Any lack of illumination is due to the recipient.... Let Jesus' hearers, then, beware lest the light they think they have within them is really darkness. But if they are truly possessed by the light now, they will receive the illumination of the heavenly light Jesus at the final judgment.[180]

Although it is indeed likely that the light of 11:33 should be linked with Jesus' mission, there is a difficulty in Marshall's interpretation, or at least where his interpretation places its emphasis. The materials on either side of Q 11:33–36 are thoroughly polemical. In fact the entirety of Q 11:14–52, Q's third major section, features polemic. There is the debate about Jesus' exorcisms, the story of the return of the unclean spirit,[181] this generation's request for a sign, Jesus' woes against the Pharisees, and his woes against the lawyers. So if 11:33–36 is not polemic aimed at outsiders it seems out of place.

---

178. We do not know whether 11:34–36 was joined to 11:33 before Q, although this seems likely enough. For the reconstruction of a complex tradition-history see Schürmann, "Q^{Lk} 11,14–36." D. Wenham, *Rediscovery*, p. 88, raises the possibility that Matthew's sequence, in which the saying about the eye as a lamp (Mt 6:22–23/Lk 11:34–36) directly follows the saying about treasure (Mt 6:19–21/Lk 12:33–34), is more primitive than Luke's sequence (which is usually thought to reproduce Q). But this (1) destroys the catchword connection between Q = Lk 12:33–34 and Lk 12:35–40 (see p. 29), (2) overlooks that the use of πονηρός in Lk 12:34–36 = Q weds the unit to the surrounding material (see below), and (3) neglects Matthew's habit of linking materials according to theme (the subject of Mt 6:19ff. is what to do with worldly goods).

179. *Luke — A New Paradigm*, vol. 2, p. 513.

180. *Luke*, p. 487.

181. On the polemical meaning of this unit see pp. 16–17 herein.

But it is not out of place. Q 11:33–36 is where it is because of the key word, πονηρός. Q 11:24–26 is about an unclean spirit who recruits seven spirits more evil (πονηρότερα) than itself. Q 11:29–33 relates the request of an evil (πονηρά) generation. Q 11:37–41 tells the Pharisees that they are full of evil (πονηρίας).[182] And in the middle of this is Q 11:33–36, which warns of the darkness created by an evil (πονηρός) eye.

The verbal link cannot be dismissed as simply a formal connection. For nowhere else does the compiler of Q³ join units by simple catchword. Q³ is rather characterized by large thematic sections.[183] This fact moves one to suppose that the repeated use of πονηρός is an important signal for interpretation.

If one highlights πονηρός and takes into account the polemical context, then Q 11:33–36 would appear to be where it is because it helps explain the state of Jesus' opponents. They are self-centered and unable to treat Jesus in a generous fashion because they are filled with darkness (11:35)—even though a great light has come to them (11:33). This light gives them no excuse, so that their unbelief is their own fault. Their fault is that their eye is evil.

Interestingly enough, exegetical history shows that just such an understanding of our text has suggested itself to more than a few interpreters. B. W. Bacon imagined that Q 11:34–35 originally had a polemical intent: Jesus was rebuking Jewish leaders.[184] Joachim Jeremias cited Lk 11:34–36 in illustrating Jesus' conviction that his contemporaries were blind and hardened.[185] Erik Sjöberg thought that in Luke our unit is a warning to and judgment against Jesus' opponents, those who think they have light: these do not recognize that they belong to the world of darkness.[186] C. F. Evans has contended that the sentences in Lk 11:34–36 "locate the condemnation of this generation in its blindness." "The connecting link . . . is failure to recognize the truth when present."[187] Susan Garrett similarly has maintained that in their present context the verses in Lk 11:33–36 are about the absence of a good eye; the verses are "the climax of Jesus' warning to those who test his works."[188] More recently Richard Horsley has urged that Q 11:34–36 explains why the

---

182. See n. 86 on p. 20.
183. See above, pp. 8–11, 16–21.
184. "The 'Single' Eye," *AJT* 7 (1914): 275–88.
185. *Theology*, p. 142. Cf. Jeremias, *Parables*, p. 163.
186. "Das Licht in dir," p. 105. Cf. Edlund, *Auge*, pp. 113–17.
187. *Luke*, p. 499.
188. "Luke 11:33–36," p. 103 (italics deleted). She continues: "The ensuing material, Jesus' denunciation of the Pharisees, then serves as a counterexample to the behavior that Jesus promotes in the saying about the single eye: the Pharisees' duplicity and internal corruption are the antithesis of integrity, of single-minded commitment to the will of God."

Pharisees are "full of darkness."[189] Kloppenborg has offered a similar interpretation.[190]

If Q 11:33–36 was indeed polemic in Q, then we have here the same phenomenon that appeared in chapter 5 in the discussion of Q 11:24– 26. As argued there, the story of the return of the unclean spirit was, when Jesus composed it, probably a warning to people who had been helped by his ministry of exorcism, a warning that they needed also to heed his proclamation. But in Q the text became a way of dismissing exorcisms performed by other groups. It became argument directed at the exorcisms of outsiders.

The same transition from exhortation to polemic seems to explain the history Q 11:33–36. The addition of Q 11:36 to Q 11:34–35 in the pre-Q tradition clearly furthered the paraenetical goal of the original composition: one must seek to be filled with light. But when Q 11:34–36, which may already have been linked to 11:33 at an early time, was inserted between the passage about the sign of Jonah and the woes against the Pharisees, it was made a sort of rationalization, a means of clarifying opposition to Jesus. Like the units on either side it became polemic addressed to outsiders, which helped insiders to understand unbelief. A self filled with darkness cannot come to the light. The explanation is the same as that offered by Jn 3:19: "[P]eople loved darkness rather than light because their deeds were evil."

---

189. "Q and Jesus," p. 192.
190. *Formation*, pp. 138–39. Cf. also Talbert, *Reading Luke*, p. 139.

# 7

# THE HAIRS OF YOUR HEAD
# ARE NUMBERED, Q 12:7a

## Evil and Ignorance

### INTERPRETATION

In the Q saying, Mt 10:30 = Lk 12:7a, Jesus tells disciples that "the hairs of your head are all counted."[1] Most commentators, whether discussing the meaning for Q, Matthew, or Luke, take the assertion to be about "the watchfulness of the Father's care."[2] In John Meier's words, God "knows and cares for the small details of their [the disciples'] lives, down to the number of their hairs, something they themselves do not know or care about."[3] This is also Joachim Gnilka's judgment. Citing 1 Sam 14:45, 2 Sam 14:11, and *b. B. Bat.* 16a,[4] he observes that this last is part of a commentary on Job 38, in which the theme is God's care for his creation.[5]

On first reading the standard interpretation seems to commend itself.[6] It appears appropriate to the context, which is an attempt to comfort persecuted missionaries or disciples by referring them to God's providential care: "Are not five sparrows sold for two pennies? Yet not one of them is forgotten in God's sight. Fear not; you are of more value than

---

1. The differences here between Matthew and Luke are insignificant and do not affect interpretation of the saying.

2. McNeile, *Matthew*, p. 146. Cf. Luz, *Matthäus*, vol. 2, p. 126. So already Novatian, *De trin.* 8:6. For an exception see Garland, *Reading Matthew*, pp. 117–18, who has accepted the argument of the article upon which this chapter is based.

3. J. Meier, *Matthew*, p. 112. For similar statements see Manson, *Sayings*, p. 108; Marshall, *Luke*, p. 514.

4. "I have created many hairs in humankind, and for every hair I have created a separate groove, so that two should not suck from the same groove, for if two were to suck from the same groove they would impair the sight of a person. I do not confuse one groove with another."

5. *Matthäusevangelium*, vol. 1, pp. 388–89.

6. What follows concerns the interpretation of the saying and its functions in Q. But there is no reason why my conclusions should not also be accepted for both Matthew and Luke in their canonical form–as well as for the historical Jesus, if he composed Q 12:7a.

many sparrows." Furthermore, that God could take care of human hairs was a proverbial notion, as the following texts demonstrate:

> 1 Sam 14:45: "As the Lord lives, not one hair of his head shall fall to the ground; for he has worked with God today."

> 2 Sam 14:11: "As the Lord lives, not one hair of your son shall fall to the ground."

> 1 Kgs 1:52: "If he proves to be a worthy man, not one of his hairs shall fall to the ground; but if wickedness is found in him, he shall die."

> Luke 21:18: "But not a hair of your head will perish."

> Acts 27:34: "None of you will lose a hair from your heads."[7]

Upon further reflection, however, the conventional explication of Mt 10:30 = Lk 12:7a proves to be unsatisfying.

The passages just cited reproduce a proverb. It is characterized by two elements–mention of "a" hair or "one" hair and falling to the ground or perishing. Neither element appears in Q 12:7a.[8] The Q saying is not about one hair but about all the hairs (plural) of one's head, and nothing is said about those hairs falling or perishing. Rather, what is asserted is that they are numbered. As if that were not enough to raise questions about the appropriateness of citing 1 Sam 14:45 and its parallels, the Old Testament texts promise deliverance from physical evil. But it is manifest, even to the commentators who cite 1 Sam 14:45 par., that our saying can mean nothing of the kind.[9] In neither Matthew nor Luke do disciples escape danger. Instead they are to be comforted by the thought that while the body may be killed, the one with true power is God, who can destroy both soul and body in Gehenna. Certainly the point about the sparrow is not that it will not fall to the ground[10] but rather that

---

7. Cf. also Dan 3:27 ("the hair of their heads was not singed"); 3 Macc 6:6 ("delivered unharmed to the very hair of their head"); *Andreas Salos Apoc.* 864C ("could not even touch [= harm] a hair of my head").

8. Schweizer, *Luke*, p. 205, is simply wrong when he states that Lk 12:7a "is repeated in [Lk] 21:18."

9. Cf. R. T. France, *Matthew*, Tyndale New Testament Commentaries (Grand Rapids: Eerdmans, 1985), p. 187 (although he does not indicate how he understands Mt 10:30). On the problem created by the juxtaposition of Lk 21:18 (not a hair will perish) with 21:16 (some will be put to death) see Marshall, *Luke*, pp. 769–70. Verse 16 may envisage a smaller circle than v. 18, or perhaps we have here "another instance of Luke's lack of concern about ironing out things he puts together from various sources" (Fitzmyer, *Luke*, vol. 2, p. 1341). Perhaps most modern commentators, however, have tried rather to give a spiritual interpretation to 21:18 (cf. Ambrose, *De Spiritu Sancto* 2, intro. 14–16, where hairs are equated with spiritual virtues).

10. Only Matthew refers to falling to the earth; but in this he is probably closer to Q; see Davies and Allison, *Matthew*, vol. 2, p. 208 (conjecturing as original: "and one of them will not fall without God"); Jeremias, *Sprache*, pp. 212–13.

when it does the event will somehow be within God's will. One wonders how Q 12:7a can have the same import as a proverb that promises rescue from trouble.

If 1 Sam 14:45 and similar passages are of questionable value for understanding Q 12:7a, what is the alternative? The key lies in the idea of numbering. The Q text is not about a hair falling or perishing but about hairs being counted. This recalls not the proverb in 1 Sam 14:45 and so forth, but Ps 40:12: "Evils have encompassed me without number; my iniquities have overtaken me, until I cannot see; they are more than the hairs of my head, and my heart fails me." Here the number of hairs on the head is, as also in Ps 69:4 and Irenaeus, *Adv. haer.* 2.28.9,[11] an expression of innumerableness. The human being cannot count hairs, for they are too small and too many. Like the sands of the sea,[12] the hairs of a head represent a number beyond our ability to count.[13]

How does this bear upon Q 12:7a? "Are all counted" is, as has always been recognized, a divine passive: the hairs are numbered by God.[14] This means that the key to Q 12:7a is not in the texts so often cited for comparison but in those old Jewish and Christian texts in which God can count what human beings cannot. Both wisdom and apocalyptic literature supply numerous passages in which God's omniscience is contrasted with human ignorance through the mention of things only God can count. The following are typical:

Job 38:37: "Who has the wisdom to number the clouds?"

Ecclus 1:2: "The sand of the sea, the drops of rain, and the days of eternity–who can count them?"

4 Ezra 4:7: "How many dwellings are in the heart of the sea, or how many streams are at the source of the deep, or how many streams above the firmament?"

1 *Enoch* 93:14: "Is there anyone who could discern the length of heaven…and how great is the number of the stars?"

Gk. *Apoc. Ezra* 2:32–3:2: "Count the stars and the sand of the sea and if you will be able to count this, you will also be able to argue the case with me…I bear human flesh. And how can I count the stars of heaven and the sand of the sea?"

---

11. Here Irenaeus says, let "Valentinus or Ptolemaeus or Basilides or any other of those who maintain that they have searched out the deep things of God" first demonstrate that he has knowledge about this easier-to-understand world, including "the number of hairs on his own head." Note also Gregory of Nyssa, *Infant., ad init.*

12. Cf. Gen 32:12; 41:49; 1 Kgs 4:20, 29; Jer 33:22; Hos 1:10; Rev 20:8.

13. The latest *Encyclopaedia Britannica*, however, tells us that the average human head has about 150,000 hairs.

14. Cf. *Ps.-Clem. Hom.* 12:31; Origen, *C. Cels.* 8:70; Augustine, *De civ. dei.* 12:18.

*Apoc. Sed.* 8:7: "Since heaven and earth were created how many trees have been made in the world, and how many shall fall and how many shall be made, and how many leaves do they have?"

*Apoc. Sed.* 8:8: "Since I [God] made the sea how many waves have billowed, and how many have rolled slightly, and how many will arise, and how many winds blow near the shore of the sea?"

*Apoc. Sed.* 8:9: "Since the creation of the world...how many drops have fallen upon the world and how many shall fall?"

*b. Sanh.* 39a: "Some say the Emperor spoke thus to him [Rabban Gamaliel]: 'The number of the stars is known to me.' Thereupon Rabban Gamaliel asked him, 'How many molars and (other) teeth have you?' Putting his hand in his mouth, he began to count them. Said he to him: 'You know not what is in your mouth and yet wouldst know what is in heaven!' "

These texts do not function to proclaim God's providential care for his own. They rather serve to underline human ignorance and underscore divine omniscience. The questions these and other[15] passages raise have one answer: only God knows. God alone knows the number of the clouds, of the sand of the sea, and of the stars of heaven. God "determines the number of the stars, he gives to all of them their names" (Ps 147:4). "Lift up your eyes on high and see: who creates these? He who brings out their host by number" (Isa 40:26). God alone has "searched out the constellations and numbered the stars and regulated the rain," and God alone knows "the number of all generations before they are born" (*LAB* 21:2). Only God "causes the rain to fall on earth with a specific number of raindrops" (2 *Bar.* 21:8).

For our purposes it is crucial to observe that the notices of God's ability to number what human beings cannot are found more than once in passages concerned with the problem of evil, including Job 38:37; 4 Ezra 4:7; and *Apoc. Sed.* 8:7, 9. This is altogether natural. The stumbling block set by innocent suffering and unmerited physical (or natural) evil has no rational solution. It is accordingly natural to construe the creation as an argument against God's goodness, power, or even existence. But the authors of Job, *4 Ezra*, and the *Apocalypse of Sedrach* refused the seemingly logical inference. They believed that human understanding has definite limits and that God and the creation are truly mysterious. On the face of it, a God of love and justice does not seem to be in control of the universe. But as the angel of 4 Ezra 4:10–11 declares, "You cannot understand the things with which you have grown up; how then

---

15. See also Gen 15:5; Job 36:26; 39:2–3; 4 Ezra 5:36; *Apoc. Abr.* 20:1–5; *Gk. Apoc. Ezra* 2:32, 4:2–4.

can your mind comprehend the way of the Most High?" Human ignorance and the mystery of God make evil endurable and prevent one
from making rash and uninformed inferences. "My thoughts are not
your thoughts" (Isa 55:8).

Returning to Q 12:7a, could it not be, in the light of the foregoing
passages, not a promise of some kind of protection or care (as the persistent scholarly citation of 1 Sam 14:45 and like passages suggests),
but instead an attempt to offer intellectual consolation for the problem
of evil? That is, might not the saying be where it is in order to remind
readers that, while they cannot understand the trying events that befall
believers and how they can be permitted by the divine will, comfort may
nonetheless be found in the thought that God knows what human beings do not? If one does not even know the number of concrete hairs on
one's own mundane head, how can one presume to judge the Creator,
who knows the number of hairs on every human head? In this interpretation the point is not God's care but God's supreme knowledge — God
knows and understands all things — and its corollary, human ignorance.
If there is much which passes our understanding, nothing about us or
our world falls outside God's knowledge. God even knows the numbers
of hairs on our head. Things that make no sense to us may make sense
to the supreme being.

This reading of Q 12:7a finds a striking parallel in the *Apocalypse
of Sedrach*. This work, although Christian in its present form, almost
certainly rests upon a Jewish original, one whose date has been placed as
early as the second century C.E.[16] In its eighth chapter the seer, Sedrach,
ponders perceived injustices and asks God for an explanation. In v. 6
God responds with this: "Since I created everything, how many people
have been born, and how many have died and how many shall die and
how many hairs do they have?" Here God knows what Sedrach does
not, namely, among other things, the number of hairs on people's heads.
The meaning is not that God, through divine providence, takes care of
God's own. The verse rather functions to rid human reason of hubris.
God is not to be judged because none is capable of judging such a one.
How does one argue with the one who can count hairs? It is wisdom to
recognize one's place.

## THE COMPOSITION OF Q 12:4–7

Q 12:7a does not function as an isolated proverb but rather belongs
with Q 12:4–7. These verses, which are part of a larger section offering

---

16. See S. Agourides, in Charlesworth, *Apocalyptic Literature*, pp. 605–7.

consolation and encouragement for wandering missionaries,[17] appear to have been brought together by an editor of Q (my Q[1]). Q 12:7a seems to interrupt the connection between Q 12:6 and 7b,[18] and Q 12:4–5 (with its parallel in 4 Macc 13:14–15[19]) was an originally isolated saying which may be independently attested in *2 Clem.* 5:4.[20] Evidently someone placed Q 12:4–5 before 6 + 7b and then inserted 7a.[21]

In putting together Q 12:4–7 this contributor to Q evidently used Q 11:9–13 as a model. As observed in chapter 1, both Q 11:9–13 and 12:4–7 are formally related:

Identification of speaker and audience:
  "I say to you" (11:9)
  "I say to you" (12:4)

Opening imperative:
  "Ask . . . seek . . . knock" (11:9)
  "Do not fear those" (Q 12:4)

Supporting statement (introduced with preposition):
  "For (γάρ) everyone who asks receives . . . " (Q 11:10)
  "But (δέ) I will warn you whom to fear" (Q 12:5)

First illustration:
  "And which of you that is a father . . . ?" (11:11)
  "Are not five sparrows sold . . . ?" (Q 12:6)

Second illustration:
  "Or if he shall ask for an egg" (Q 11:12)
  "Even the hairs of your head" (Q 12:7a)

Conclusion (with *inclusio*):
  "If you know how . . . them who ask him?" (Q 11:13)
  "Fear not; you are of more value" (Q 12:7b)

Given that Q 12:4–7 is a collection of once-independent sayings whereas Q 11:9–13 appears on the contrary to resist decomposition, it seems more than a good guess that the former was composed in

---

17. See above, pp. 21–25.

18. Cf. Sato, *Q und Prophetie*, p. 174.

19. "Let us have no fear of him who thinks he kills. Great is the ordeal and peril of the soul that lies in wait in eternal torment for those who transgress the commandment of God."

20. "Jesus said to Peter: Let not the lambs fear the wolves after they are dead; and you also, fear not those who kill you and are unable to do anything to you. But fear him who after you are dead has power over soul and body, to cast them in to the gehenna of fire." Karl Paul Donfried, *The Setting of Second Clement in Early Christianity*, NovTSup, vol. 38 (Leiden: E. J. Brill, 1974), pp. 68–71, argues that this is independent of the synoptics. For a different view see Crossan, *Fragments*, pp. 271–72. Cf. also Justin, *1 Apol.* 19:6–7.

21. Cf. Gnilka, *Matthäusevangelium*, vol. 1, p. 390.

order to resemble the latter. Both serve to encourage missionaries who lead hard lives, both argue from the lesser to the greater, and, in my compositional theory of Q, both were at one time adjacent units.[22]

Q 12:4–7 functions within its larger context as a sort of theodicy. Q 12:4 foresees the possibility of death for the faithful missionary, and Q 12:11 prophesies being brought before synagogues and rulers and authorities. The entirety of Q 12:2–12 depicts the present as a time of conflict, when the consequences of confessing the Son of man in public (Q 12:8–9) may lead to affliction. So this section of Q raises the problem of evil: how can all this be if our God is sovereign? Q 12:4–7 offers three answers.

The first answer appears in Q 12:4–5. Although death is naturally frightening, the disciples should not fear those who can kill only the body. For what matters is not one's fate in this world but one's destiny in the world to come: "Fear him who, after he has killed, has the power to cast into hell."[23] In other words, here the problem of evil is answered by eschatology. Justice may not be done in this world, but it will be done in the world to come. So Jesus, instead of promising deliverance from physical death, persuades his followers to face death with courage in the knowledge of what lies on the other side.

Yet lest the faithful wrongly think that God's will is done only in the future, Q 12:6 and 7b, through the illustration of the sparrow and an argument *a fortiori*, assert that God is sovereign even now.[24] So whatever happens must, despite appearances, somehow be within the divine will. Even a sparrow does not fall to the ground without God's knowledge or permission.[25] Providence rules.

This, however, poses the unanswerable enigma. How can God be the sovereign Lord of this world when it is full of ills and wrongs? The question seems to have been asked by a contributor to Q. Q 12:7a, which interrupts the line about the sparrow, is what Joachim Wanke has called a *Kommentarwort*. Perhaps proverbial, with the meaning that God's knowledge admits no rival, it was inserted not only in order to fashion Q 12:4–7 into the structural twin of Q 11:9–13 but also to make a theological point: the eschatological solution to the problem of

---

22. On Q 11:14–52 as an interpolation see pp. 30–36.

23. Cf. the discussion of whom one should rightly fear in *1 Enoch* 101:4–9. The object of fear is not the devil (as some have thought) but God; see Harry S. Pappas, "The 'Exhortation to Fearless Confession'–Mt. 10.26–33," *Greek Orthodox Theological Review* 25 (1980): 242–43.

24. Cf. Chrysostom, *Hom. on Mt.* 34:2: "Lest they should think, when killed and butchered, that as those forsaken they suffered this, he introduces again the argument of God's providence."

25. Cf. Theophylact, *Comm. Mt.* ad Mt 10:29–31 (in *PG*, vol. 123, p. 244). J. G. Cook, "The Sparrow's Fall in Mt 10:29b," *ZNW* 79 (1988): 138–44, even argues that God causes the sparrow to fall: "without your father" means "without your father's will."

evil (Q 12:4–5) and the affirmation of God's sovereignty (Q 12:6, 7b) still leave us with questions to which we have no good answers. Some things just do not make sense. So the faithful must, in the end, join with Job and confess human inability to fathom the depths. God is a mystery, and God knows what the creatures do not. If much is hid from us, "nothing that is done is hid from him."[26] In that is solace: "But even the hairs of your head are all counted."

---

26. Chrysostom, *Hom. on Mt.* 34:2 (on 10:29–30).

# – 8 –

# FROM EAST AND WEST, Q 13:28–29

## Salvation for the Diaspora

In his influential study, *Jesus' Promise to the Nations*,[1] Joachim Jeremias drew two major conclusions. He claimed first that Jesus limited his own preaching to Israel and forbade his disciples to preach to non-Jews and, second, that Jesus promised Gentiles a share in salvation because he looked forward to their eschatological pilgrimage to Zion. In making this second and crucial point, Jeremias placed great weight upon the Q text, Mt 8:11–12, which reads: "I tell you, many will come from east and west and will eat with Abraham and Isaac and Jacob in the kingdom of heaven, while the sons of the kingdom will be thrown into the outer darkness, where there will be weeping and gnashing of teeth."[2] These words, according to Jeremias, were composed by Jesus and envisage God's rejection of the Jews ("the sons of the kingdom") on the one hand and God's acceptance of the Gentiles (the "many from east and west") on the other.[3]

Jeremias's interpretation of Mt 8:11–12 and its Lukan parallel has become a commonplace of contemporary scholarship. Whether exegetes are discussing Jesus or Q or Matthew or Luke they almost always identify those coming from east and west as Gentiles and "the sons of the kingdom" as the Jewish people.[4] These equations, however, are neither

---

1. Philadelphia: Fortress, 1982.

2. Cf. Lk 13:28–29: "There will be weeping and gnashing of teeth when you see Abraham and Isaac and Jacob and all the prophets in the kingdom of God, and you yourselves thrown out. Then people will come from east and west, from north and south, and will eat in the kingdom of God."

3. *Promise*, pp. 55–63.

4. See, e.g., Hagner, *Matthew 1–13*, pp. 205–6; Luz, *Matthäus*, vol. 2, pp. 13–16; J. Meier, *Mentor, Message, and Miracles*, p. 315; Tuckett, *Q*, p. 194. In church history the passage has usually been understood in either one of two ways. Most have thought the prophecy to symbolize the evangelization of the Gentiles, that is, the building up of the church throughout the world; so, e.g., *Ps.-Clem. Hom.* 8:4; *Ps. Clem. Rec.* 4:4; Cyprian, *De dom. orat.* 13; idem, *Ad Quirinum* 1:23; Jerome, *Comm. Mt.* ad loc.; Augustine, *Serm.* 12:6; Bernard of Clairvaux, *Serm. super Cant. cant.* 77:7; Calvin, ad loc. But others have maintained an eschatological and more literal interpretation; see Justin, *Dial.* 140; Ambrose, *De bono mort.* 12:53–54; Patrick, *Ep.* 18; Isaac of Nineveh, *Asc. Hom.* 6:12; Broadus, *Matthew*, p. 179. Both interpretations equate the "many" with Gentiles.

necessary nor obvious, and some have had other ideas. A. H. McNeile, in his commentary on the First Gospel, contended that "in the Lord's mouth the words [sons of the kingdom] can mean 'all Jews who trust in their Judaism,' in contrast not necessarily with Gentiles, as Mt. understands it... but with Jews whose character truly fitted them for the Kingdom...."[5] More recently, N. Q. King has argued that, in its Lukan context, Lk 13:28–29 has to do with saved and unsaved Jews;[6] and E. P. Sanders has acknowledged the possibility that, on Jesus' lips, Q 13:28–29 was about the ingathering of the Jewish Diaspora, not the pilgrimage of the Gentiles.[7]

Given the importance of Q 13:28–29 for evaluating the place of the Gentiles both in Q and the thought of Jesus, it is rather disconcerting to learn that neither Jeremias nor anyone else has established that the "many" are really non-Jews. For Jeremias this conclusion follows from the contrast with "the sons of the kingdom" and from biblical prophecies about Gentiles.[8] But neither alleged reason holds up to scrutiny. Furthermore, there are a number of signs which point in precisely the opposite direction. My own conclusion is that, whether one is thinking of Q or the historical Jesus, Q 13:38–39 has nothing to do with Gentiles. It proclaims rather God's judgment upon unfaithful Jews in the land of Israel and the eschatological ingathering of Jews from the Diaspora.

## Q 13:28–29 as an Isolated Saying

Q 13:28–29 belongs to a small Q complex which combines four originally independent units — Q 13:24 (the narrow door), Q 13:25–27 (the parable of the closed door),[9] Q 13:28–29 (a prophetic oracle of doom and salvation), and Q 13:30 (the last will be first, the first last). A contributor to Q — in my compositional theory the compiler of $Q^2$ —

---

5. *Matthew*, p. 105. Dissatisfaction with the common reading also appears in Blaine Charette, *The Theme of Recompense in Matthew's Gospel*, JSNTSS, vol. 79 (Sheffield: JSOT, 1992), pp. 69–71, and Amy-Jill Levine, *The Social and Ethnic Dimensions of Matthean Salvation History* (Lewiston, N.Y.: Edwin Mellen Press, 1988), pp. 124–30.

6. "The 'Universalism' of the Third Gospel," in *Studia Evangelica*, ed. K. Aland, vol. 1, TU, vol. 73 (Berlin: Akademie Verlag, 1959), pp. 202–3.

7. *Jesus and Judaism* (Philadelphia: Fortress, 1985), pp. 119–120. Cf. George Wesley Buchanan, *Jesus: The King and His Kingdom* (Macon, Ga.: Mercer University Press, 1984), pp. 34–35. Note also now Richard Horsley, "Social Conflict in the Synoptic Sayings Source Q," in Kloppenborg, *Conflict and Invention*, p. 38, and the doubts of Theissen, *Gospels in Context*, pp. 45–46. The latter wonders whether both Gentiles and Diaspora Jews might not have originally been in view.

8. *Promise*, p. 56 n. 3, pp. 62–63.

9. Lk 13:25 has no Matthean parallel. There is no agreement as to whether it stood in Q or was inserted by Luke; see Kloppenborg, *Q Parallels*, p. 154.

presumably gathered the materials for hortatory ends. The sayings are warnings to the faithful. They are not addressed to unfaithful Israel, and nothing in the immediate context of Q 13:28–29 suggests teaching about Gentiles.

The Q context, then, does not invite us to follow Jeremias's interpretation, and it also needs to be stressed that our text, in both its Matthean and Lukan forms, does not explicitly mention either Jews or Gentiles. In Matthew neither the "many" nor "the sons of the kingdom" are identified in the saying itself. The same is true of the subjects — "they" and "you" — in Luke.

That most nonetheless have thought in terms of a contrast between Jews and Gentiles is undoubtedly due to the Matthean setting. As it stands, Mt 8:11–12 belongs to the story of the healing of a centurion's servant or son (Mt 8:5–13), and the saying immediately follows Jesus' remark that he has not found in Israel such faith as the centurion exhibits. Most readers have understood Mt 8:11–12 par. in the light of this statement about faith, or rather the lack of it, in Israel and so have surmised that those who will come from east and west to sit with Abraham, Isaac, and Jacob at the messianic banquet are people like the centurion, who is assumed to be a Gentile. But Lk 7:1–10, which is Luke's version of the story in Mt 8:5–13, contains no counterpart to Mt 8:11–12, and, further, the Lukan parallel to the latter, as already observed, appears in Lk 13:24–30, a short collection of originally independent sayings. So Mt 8:11–12 = Lk 13:28–29 should be assigned to Q and the Matthean context regarded as secondary.[10] This means that the Matthean context should not dictate our interpretation of Q 13:28–29. We must approach the saying as an isolated unit.[11]

## EAST AND WEST AND NORTH AND SOUTH

There are some pronounced differences between Mt 8:11–12 and Lk 13:28–29. Most of these are fortunately not significant for our purposes. One difference, however, cannot be ignored. Matthew refers to many coming "from east and west," Luke to people coming "from east and west and north and south." Whose wording is original? Here the re-

---

10. Cf. U. Wegner, *Der Hauptmann von Kafarnaum*, WUNT, ser. 2, vol. 14 (Tübingen: J. C. B. Mohr [Paul Siebeck], 1985), pp. 3–5.

11. Although some have found in Q 13:28–29 two originally independent sayings (so, e.g., Jacques Schlosser, *Le Règne de Dieu dans les dits de Jésus*, vol. 2, Ebib [Paris: J. Gabalda, 1980], p. 614), this appears quite unlikely; see Kloppenborg, *Formation*, pp. 226–27.

constructions of Q differ, and there is no room for certainty.[12] Whereas Luke, or a transmitter of Q[lk], might have added "and north and south" in order to highlight the theme of universalism[13] or to gain an allusion to Ps 107:3, Matthew, in accordance with the divine habit of abbreviating, might have omitted the words as superfluous.

Because the status of Luke's "and north and south" remains in doubt it is necessary to investigate the background of both Matthew's phrase and Luke's fuller expression. To take the former first — how should we interpret "from east and west"? The two directions occur in Jewish texts in connection with the return of Jews to the land promised to Abraham. Consider the following:

> Zech 8:7–8: "Thus says the Lord of hosts: I will save my people from the east country and from the west country; and I will bring them to Jerusalem."

> Bar 4:4: "Behold, your sons are coming, whom you sent away; they are coming, gathered from east and west, at the word of the Holy One, rejoicing in the glory of God."

> Bar 5:5: "Arise, O Jerusalem, stand upon the height and look toward the east, and see your children gathered from west and east, at the word of the Holy One, rejoicing that God has remembered them."

> *Ps. Sol.* 11:2: "Stand on a high place, O Jerusalem, and look at your children, from the east and west assembled together by the Lord."

> 1 *Enoch* 57:1: "And it happened afterward that I had another vision of a whole array of chariots loaded with people; and they were advancing upon the air from the east and from the west until midday."

Also worth quoting is Deut 30:4 (LXX): "Even though your diaspora be from one border of the heaven to the other, from thence the Lord your God shall deliver you."

Although "east and west" is common in prophetic texts about the restoration of Jews to their land, my research has not turned up a single text in which the expression refers to an eschatological ingathering

---

12. For a review of the various proposals see M. Eugene Boring, "A Proposed Reconstruction of Q 13:28–29," in Lull, *1989 Seminar Papers*, pp. 1–22. See also J. Meier, *Mentor, Message, and Miracles*, pp. 309–14.

13. Cf. Acts 2:9–11. So J. Meier, *Mentor, Message, and Miracles*, p. 313. When all the world is in mind, "north and south and east and west" is more common than just "east and west." Recall the play upon Adam's name in *Sib. Or.* 3:24–26 and 2 *Enoch* 30:13 (in Greek the four letters of Adam's name are taken to represent the four cardinal directions). Note also Gen 28:14; 1 Kgs 7:25; Isa 43:5–6; *b. Šabb.* 118b.

of Gentiles. Schlosser, although he recognizes that, in the Jewish Bible, "from the east and to the west" is used principally of the return of dispersed Israel, also asserts that the phrase appears in lines about the universal recognition of Israel's God. He cites Pss 50:1; 113:3; Isa 25:6; 59:19; and Mal 1:11. But Schlosser's words conceal that the phrase is never used of Gentiles coming to the holy land; and of the five texts just cited only one uses both "east" and "west" (Isa 59:19).[14]

In Jewish tradition "east and west" first calls to mind not the Gentile world but the Jewish Diaspora. This is because, from a Palestinian perspective, Assyria and Babylon, where there was concentration of exiled Jews, were to the east[15] while Egypt, which was also a center of the Diaspora, was in the other direction.[16]

Confirmation of the point I am making can be found in passages in which the exiles return not from "east and west" but from "Assyria and Egypt." In Isa 27:12–13 there is this: "On that day the Lord will thresh from the channel of the Euphrates to the Wadi of Egypt, and you will be gathered one by one, O people of Israel. And on that day a great trumpet will be blown, and those who were lost in the land of Assyria and those who were driven out to the land of Egypt will come and worship the Lord on the holy mountain of Jerusalem." Comparable are Hos 11:11 ("they shall come trembling like birds from Egypt, and like doves from the land of Assyria") and Zech 10:10 ("I will bring them home from the land of Egypt and gather them from Assyria"). It is plain that, in connection with the hope for dispersed Jews, "east and west" and "Assyria and Egypt" were interchangeable expressions. The implications for Mt 8:11–12 are obvious.[17]

But what of Luke's longer expression, "from east and west and north and south"? If it stood in Q was it intended, as so many commentators have thought, to allude to Ps 107:2–3? This last includes a phrase

---

14. Ps 50:1, which refers not to "east" (מזרח) and "west"(מערב), but to the rising of the sun (מזרח-שמש) and its setting (מבוא), seems to be about a noneschatological theophany. Similar is Ps 113:3: "From the rising of the sun (מזרח-שמש) to its setting (מבואו) the name of the Lord is to be praised." Isa 25:6 speaks of a feast "for all peoples," but nothing is said about their geographical origin. Isa 59:19, which uses מערב and מזרח-שמש, says nothing of Gentiles coming to the holy land. Finally, Mal 1:11 is about the greatness of God's name among the nations, "from the rising of the sun (מזרח-שמש) to its setting (מבואו)."

15. Cf. Isa 46:11; Jer 49:28; *Sib. Or.* 5:113; *As. Mos.* 3:1, 13–14.

16. In 1 Kgs 4:30 and *Sib. Or.* 5:112–13 "Egypt" and "east" are counterparts. In the Babylonian Talmud "west" is used for Palestine (e.g., *b. Yeb.* 117a); but that is a late development and obviously represents a non-Palestinian perspective.

17. France, *Matthew*, p. 156, writes: "In describing their coming *from east and west*, he [Jesus] uses words which in the Old Testament relate to the world-wide gathering of *Israel....*" This rightly recognizes the scriptural background; but an ironic interpretation is only suggested by the common understanding of Matthew's version. If Q 13:28–29 is interpreted in isolation, there is no reason at all to take the scriptural language as ironic; one naturally thinks simply of "the world-wide gathering of Israel."

which reads in the NRSV: "from the east and from the west, from the
north and from the south." Unhappily there is some doubt as to whether
this is a correct translation. The Hebrew and the LXX both have "from
the east and from the west, from the north and from overseas" (ומים; καὶ
θαλάσσα). The NRSV translators, it seems, inferred that the MT is corrupt. Their English presupposes a Hebrew text with ומימין ("and from
the right," that is, "the south"). Are they to be followed? Although one
always hesitates to emend without manuscript authority, the ומים of the
Masoretic text seems redundant; for "from the sea" is naturally understood to signify "from the west" (from the Mediterranean) and "from
the west" has already been used. It is accordingly possible that, through
corruption, ומימין became ומים, and that Ps 107:3 originally had "from
the east and from the west, from the north and from the south." Indeed, perhaps a Hebrew or Greek text with this reading was known to
Luke or to his tradition. Another possibility is that ומים is original but
referred not to the Mediterranean but to "the southern seas" (cf. the
targum), that is, the Gulf of Aqabah (cf. 2 Chr 8:17).[18] In any event the
link between Lk 13:28–29 and Ps 107:3 remains possible.

What happens when Lk 13:28–29 is set against the background of Ps
107:3? Here are the first three verses of the psalm:

> O give thanks to the Lord, for he is good; for his steadfast love
> endures forever. Let the redeemed of the Lord say so, those he re-
> deemed from trouble and gathered in from the east and from the
> west, from the north and from the south [or: overseas].

These words introduce a psalm of thanksgiving. Whether or not, as
some have supposed, vv. 2–3 are a secondary interpolation, the psalm
as it stands refers to Jewish pilgrims or immigrants coming to Palestine:
those gathered from the four points of the compass are God's scattered
people. Gentiles are not in the picture at all. What follows? Whoever
catches an allusion in Lk 13:28–29 to Ps 107:3 will immediately think
of Jewish exiles returning to their land.[19]

Further, even if we miss a specific allusion to Ps 107:3 we might still
think of an ingathering of the Diaspora. This is because Ps 107:3 is not
the only text to envisage the return of scattered Jews as a coming from
the four points of the compass. Isa 43:5–6 offers another example:

> Do not fear, for I am with you; I will bring your offspring from the
> east, and from the west I will gather you; I will say to the north,
> "Give them up," and to the south, "Do not withhold; bring my
> sons from far away and my daughters from the end of the earth."

18. So M. Dahood, *Psalms III, 101–150*, AB, vol. 17A (Garden City, N.Y.: Doubleday,
1970), p. 81.

19. The *Midrash* on the Psalms offers an eschatological interpretation for Ps 107:3 (Isa
11:11–12 is cited).

Then there is this in *Ps. Sol.* 11:2–3:

> Stand on a high place, Jerusalem, and see your children, from the east and the west gathered together by the Lord. From the north they come in the joy of their God; from far distant islands God has gathered them.

Similarly, Zech 2:10 (LXX) prophesies that God will gather exiles "from the four winds of heaven." All these texts prophesy the eschatological ingathering of the diaspora. Does Lk 13:28–29 not belong with them?

## THE GENTILES

If the picture of people coming from "east and west (and north and south)" is characteristic not of the eschatological pilgrimage of the Gentiles but rather of the restoration of scattered Jews to their land, there are additional reasons for doubting that Q 13:28–29 concerns non-Jews. Not once in the Tanak is the coming of the nations conceived as a judgment upon Israel or those in the land. On the contrary, the coming of the Gentiles always serves, as D. Zeller has seen, to exalt Zion.[20] So the common interpretation of Q 13:28–29 requires that the saying turn a traditional motif on its head and employ the pilgrimage of Gentiles in order to deny Jewish hopes rather than confirm them. But how likely is that? It is true that parts of the Jesus tradition sometime refer to Gentiles in order to humble Israel. Q 10:12 says that Sodom will fare better at the judgment than the city that rejects Jesus, Q 10:13–14 that Tyre and Sidon would have repented if they had heard Jesus' messengers, and Q 11:29–32 that the queen of the south and the citizens of Nineveh will condemn "this generation." But all this is not enough to tip the scales, for (1) Q 13:28–29 (unlike the texts just cited) does not explicitly mention Gentiles, (2) both Jesus himself and Q looked forward to the fulfillment of God's promises to Israel,[21] and (3) there is little evidence that either Jesus or the earliest Jesus tradition said much if anything about the eschatological pilgrimage of the Gentiles.

Concerning this last point Jeremias has indeed argued to the contrary that "the conception of the pilgrimage of the Gentiles is not confined to Matt. 8.11 in the gospels, but finds frequent expression in the sayings

---

20. "Das Logion Mt 8,11f./Lk 13,28f. und das Motiv der 'Völkerwallfahrt,' " *BZ* 15 (1971): 222–37; 16 (1972): 84–93.

21. For Jesus himself see Sanders, *Jesus and Judaism*, pp. 77–119, 222–41. Regarding Q, Q 22:28–20 is decisive, for "judging the twelve tribes of Israel" refers not to a one-time judgment but to the exercise of authority over time. In other words, as the twelve phylarchs once directed the twelve tribes under Moses, and as Israel was once ruled by judges, so shall it be at the end: Jesus' disciples will rule the ingathered tribes. See further Davies and Allison, *Matthew*, vol. 3, pp. 55–56.

of Jesus."[22] Upon examination, however, his evidence evaporates. The gathering of "all the nations" in Mt 25:31–46 is probably a redactional feature[23] and in any case has as its background not the expectation of Gentiles streaming to Zion but of all humanity standing before God's throne for judgment. The reference to sheep of another fold in Jn 10:16 (cf. Jer 23:3) is scarcely from Jesus and may very well be editorial. Mk 11:17 ("My house shall be called a house of prayer for all the nations"), which draws upon Isa 56:7 and Jer 7:11, is probably a Markan insertion[24] and need have nothing to do with the eschatological trek of the Gentiles to the holy land. The city set on a hill in Mt 5:14 is only doubtfully to be linked with the new Jerusalem,[25] and even if it were otherwise, there is no talk of Gentiles coming to Zion. Jn 7:37–38 speaks of living water, and Jeremias associates this with Rev 22:2, where the river of the water of life is associated with healing for the nations; but the association is made only in Revelation, and surely we are not here dealing with speech of the historical Jesus or early tradition. Jeremias's suggestion that Mk 13:10 and 14:9 be interpreted in terms of an eschatological angelic summons to the nations (cf. Mk 13:27; Rev 14:6–7)[26] has not won much acceptance. Mt 5:15 is also scarcely good evidence for Jeremias's case: one can hardly infer anything about eschatological expectation from the simple use of "the city of the great king."

The one place where Jeremias may be right is in a Q text, Q 13:18–19 (par. Mk 4:30–32), the dominical parable of the mustard seed. It is possible that the birds who nest in the shade of the tree are Gentiles. Ezek 17:23 (which has been taken to refer to the nations as birds); *1 Enoch* 90:30 ("I saw all the sheep that had survived as well as all the animals upon the earth and the birds of heaven, falling down and worshiping those sheep"); and *Jos. Asen.* 15:7 ("under your wings many peoples trusting in the Lord God will be sheltered") certainly suggest this conclusion. On the other hand, the image of a large tree with birds resting in it or under it does not always have to do with Gentiles,[27] so even here caution is in order.

Even if one declines to find the pilgrimage in the parable of the mustard seed, it need not be denied that Jesus and those who paid heed to Q looked forward to the eschatological gathering of the nations. For this

---

22. *Promise*, p. 63. Cf. now Eckhard J. Schnabel, "Jesus and the Beginnings of the Mission to the Gentiles," in *Jesus of Nazareth: Lord and Christ*, ed. Joel B. Green and Max Turner (Grand Rapids: Eerdmans, 1994), pp. 37–58.

23. So rightly J. Friedrich, *Gott im Bruder?* CTM, vol. 7 (Stuttgart: Calwer, 1977), pp. 249–57.

24. Cf. Gnilka, *Markus*, vol. 2, p. 127.

25. See Davies and Allison, *Matthew*, vol. 1, p. 475.

26. See *Promise*, pp. 22–23.

27. Cf. Ezek 31:5–6; Dan 4:10–12, 14, 20–21.

ingathering is foretold in some biblical texts, and the Jesus tradition contains no indication that Jesus or his post-Easter followers expected the eschatological destruction of non-Jews. But Jeremias's assertion about "frequent expression" holds neither for properly dominical materials nor for Q nor for the Gospels as they stand. This fact stands in the way of the common interpretation of Q 13:28–29.

Similarly problematic, at least if we are thinking of Jesus himself, is the issue of whether, without clear and explicit prodding, his Jewish hearers would ever have understood a prophecy foretelling the coming of people from east and west, and their banqueting with the patriarchs, to be about redeemed Gentiles. If Jesus frequently addressed himself to this topic and made his own opinion plain then we could think this. But the evidence, as already indicated, is very much against supposing that he did so. What in Jesus' message would have encouraged anyone to construe Q 13:28–29 as having to do with non-Jews? Jesus could not even have taken for granted that his audience would believe in the eschatological salvation of the nations. In Ezekiel, Ecclesiasticus 36, the Qumran War Scroll, 1QSa, *Jubilees* 20, 4 Ezra 13, and *Mek.* on Exod 21:30 (R. Ishmael) the nations are destroyed or lost (cf. Zeph 3:8). In *1 Enoch* 90:30 only some repent. There was no one Jewish opinion on the ultimate fate of non-Jews.

Despite all this, the "many," according to Jeremias, must be Gentiles because they are set over against the "sons of the kingdom."[28] The argument does not compel. Neither the "many" nor the "sons of the kingdom" appears in Luke's version of our logion, and they may not have belonged to the original. Even if (as seems more likely) they did appear, "many" cannot be reckoned a fixed expression with fixed meaning. Certainly in the LXX πολλοί can be used of Gentiles (e.g., Isa 2:3), but there are also texts that stress that "many" Jews are in the Diaspora and that "many" will return to the land.[29] Josephus, *Ant.* 11:133, even refers to the ten tribes beyond the Euphrates as "countless myriads whose number cannot be ascertained."

No less important, how credible is it that either Jesus or a contributor to Q intended Q 13:28–29 to refer to the Jews as a whole and thus, at least hyperbolically, to consign all Israel to hell? Jesus' disciples were Jews. He directed his mission to Jews (as Mt 10:5–6 and 15:24, whatever their origin, rightly assume; cf. Rom 15:8). And Q contained eschatological sayings that take for granted the presence of Jews in the

---

28. Cf. already Cecil John Cadoux, *The Historic Mission of Jesus* (New York: Harper & Brothers, n.d.), p. 155: "Those (in Mt. 'many') who come from east and west, etc., are clearly Gentiles: they cannot be Jews of the Dispersion, since these, as Jews, are already included among 'the sons of the kingdom,' some at least of whom are to be expelled." The same reasoning also appears in J. Meier, *Mentor, Message, and Miracles*, p. 315.

29. E.g., Zech 10:8–12; *1 Enoch* 57:1; 4 Ezra 13:39; *2 Baruch* 77–87.

eschatological kingdom of God (e.g., Q 6:20 — the poor in Israel; Q 13:28–29 — the patriarchs; Q 22:28–30 — the restored tribes[30]). It is indeed more than likely that Jesus, like Paul after him (Rom 11:26), and in accordance with biblical prophecies, hoped for Israel's redemption (which is not to say the salvation of every single Jew; cf. *m. Sanh.* 10:1). However that may be, Q 13:28–29 just cannot be about the damnation of all Jews. Such an interpretation could only be correct if Q 13:28–29 were composed by one who had already given up on the mission to Israel. But how likely is this given that both Q materials as well as sayings we can trace with assurance to Jesus (1) assume a positive response to Jesus on the part of some in Israel (cf. Q 10:6–7, 21), and (2) nowhere clearly reflect a mission to Gentiles?

## The Eschatological Ingathering of the Dispersion

Many first-century Jews undoubtedly looked forward to the final salvation of what Paul called "all Israel" (Rom. 11:26); and, as already indicated, the ingathering of scattered Israel, including the ten lost tribes (cf. 2 Kings 15–17), was a common hope. I have already cited Deut 30:4 (LXX); Isa 27:12–13; 43:5–6; Hos 11:11; Zech 2:6 (LXX); 8:7; 10:10; Bar 4:37; 5:5; *Ps. Sol.* 11:2–3; and *1 En.* 57:1. While one might wish to refer some of these texts to the return of exiles after the Babylonian captivity, and while some first-century Jews just might have thought the same thing, most of them were undoubtedly believed to pertain to the future.[31]

This is without question true of the great number of texts that unambiguously proclaim or assume that the ten lost tribes will someday return to Palestine. Examples include Ecclus 36:11 ("gather all the tribes of Jacob, and give them their inheritance as at the beginning"); 48:10 ("to restore the tribes of Jacob"); 1QM 2:1–3 (the restoration of the twelve tribes seems to be assumed); 4QpIsa[d] line 7 ("the interpretation of it concerns the heads of the tribes of Israel at the end"); 11QTemple 57:5–6 ("and he shall select for himself a thousand of them from each tribe, so that there are twelve thousand men of war with him"); *4 Ezra* 13:32–50 ("as for your seeing him gather to himself another multitude that was peaceable, these are the ten tribes"); *2 Bar.* 78:1–7 (Baruch writes to the "nine and a half tribes" that they have suffered in order to be found worthy, and that God will "with much mercy assemble all those again who were dispersed"); *Sib. Or.* 2:170–73 ("a people of ten tribes will

---

30. On this last see n. 21.
31. Cf. 2 Macc 1:27–28; 2:18; Tob 13:13; *Ps. Sol.* 8:28; Philo, *De praem.* 117, 165–72.

come from the east"); *T. Jos.* 19:3–8 (Arm.) ("the nine stags were gathered to him, and they all became like twelve sheep"); and *m. Sanh.* 10:3 ("R. Eliezer says: Like as the day grows dark and then grows light, so also after darkness is fallen upon the ten tribes shall light hereafter shine upon them").[32] Further, there is some reason to believe that near the turn of the era there was a Jewish apocalypse describing the life of the hidden lost tribes and foretelling their coming to the land of Judah.[33] Clearly the hope for a renewed Israel was a very real feature of Jewish expectation.[34]

The widespread expectation also appears in Q (see n. 21), which in this regard is likely to be in line with Jesus. It is surely suggestive that Jesus associated himself with a special group of twelve disciples. Did he not thereby indicate his belief in the eschatological restoration of the twelve tribes? And, if so, are we not invited to read Q 13:28–29 in these terms?

G. R. Beasley-Murray has observed that "many passages in the OT ...speak of the nations making their way to Zion at the end of the age to pay homage to Yahweh and to Israel (e.g., Isa 2:1ff), but in not one of these is mention made of the nations sharing in the feast of the kingdom of God. On the other hand, Isa 25:6ff., which provides the classic description of the feast for the nations given by God, makes no mention of the peoples streaming from all parts of the world to Zion...."[35] Although Beasley-Murray does not remark on the fact, it is also true that in Psalm 107 God satisfies the thirsty and hungry Diaspora Jews who come to Jerusalem; and in Ezekiel 39 the feast upon the remains of Gog (vv. 17–20) is followed by the eschatological union of divided Israel (vv. 25–29). Which is to say: while the gentile pilgrimage and the eschatological feast are not linked in the Tanak, the ingathering of scattered Israel and feasting are. So once again Q 13:28–29 stands in line with the traditions about the eschatological return of Israel, not the eschatological coming of Gentiles. And once more the usual interpretation of Q 13:28–29 is not what comes to mind to one steeped in the Bible. The festal imagery rather points to the theme of Israel's restoration.

## Q 13:28–29 AND JESUS

Jesus, in all probability, intended to draw a stark contrast not between unbelieving Jews and believing Gentiles but between saved and unsaved

---

32. See also *T. Naph.* 6:1–10.
33. The evidence is collected in M. R. James, *The Lost Apocrypha of the Old Testament* (London: SPCK, 1920), pp. 103–6.
34. Cf. Davies, *Paul and Rabbinic Judaism*, pp. 78–82.
35. *Jesus and the Kingdom of God* (Grand Rapids: Eerdmans, 1986), p. 170.

Jews.[36] Jesus believed that those who rejected him and his message would suffer judgment on the last day.[37] In particular, he delivered warnings to some of the Jewish leaders, including the Pharisees. When to this one adds that he evidently thought of such people as being wise and pious in their own eyes, might he not have ironically labeled them "sons of the kingdom" (if the phrase is original) and warned them of judgment? If Q 13:28–29 was originally addressed to the Pharisees, or to the Jerusalem establishment, or to some other group of religious Palestinian Jews that Jesus perceived to be opposed to him, the text can be understood as yet one more example of his conviction that the first would be last, the last first. The "sons of the kingdom" had not responded to Jesus and his preaching. They had remained complacent, with tragic result. Those from east and west, that is, Jews who had not had the benefit of encountering Jesus or the bearers of his message, will find eschatological salvation while those who have heard Jesus or his messengers will not. The privileged will have their places taken by the underprivileged.

Such an understanding of Q 13:28–29 is consistent with other materials in the Jesus tradition. For example, if the logion is really about the eschatological ingathering of Jewish exiles, it harmonizes well with Jesus' attitude towards the land. W. D. Davies has shown that, as far as we can gather, Jesus apparently did not emphasize the land in his teaching.[38] Now although Q 13:28–29 does assume that the land of Israel will be the geographical center of the eschatological scenario, it simultaneously negates any advantages that might accrue from dwelling in Palestine. We have here the rejection of the sort of thinking found in *2 Bar.* 29:2; 71:1; 4 Ezra 9:7–8; and *b. Ketub.* 111a. In these and other texts it is prophesied that, in the latter days, the land will protect its own from eschatological dangers. In Jesus' proclamation, however, inhabi-

---

36. This interpretation eliminates the reason most often given for denying that our saying originated with Jesus, namely, that it reflects a definitive rejection of the Christian mission to Jews. Cf. Joseph Klausner, *Jesus: His Life, Times, and Teaching* (New York: Macmillan, 1925), p. 367. In favor of authenticity are Gnilka, *Matthäusevangelium*, vol. 1, p. 305; Luz, *Matthäus*, vol. 2, p. 14; and Helmut Merkel, "Die Gottesherrschaft in der Verkündigung Jesu," in *Königsherrschaft Gottes und himmlischer Kult im Judentum, Urchristentum und in der hellenistischen Welt*, ed. Martin Hengel and Anna Maria Schwemer, WUNT, vol. 55 (Tübingen: J. C. B. Mohr [Paul Siebeck], 1991), p. 142. Bruce Chilton, *God in Strength: Jesus' Announcement of the Kingdom*, SNTU, ser. B, vol. 1 (Freistadt: F. Plöchl, 1979), pp. 179–201, upholds the authenticity of Mt 8:11 alone. Cf. Perrin, *Rediscovering*, pp. 161–64. The Jesus Seminar's *The Four Gospels* prints Mt 8:11–12 and Lk 13:28–29 in black (meaning Jesus did not say this) and explains: "The Fellows of the Seminar do not think such wholesale condemnations are typical of Jesus" (p. 348). In view of the abundant evidence to the contrary one is at a loss to understand this verdict. If Jesus did not warn his contemporaries of eschatological judgment then the Jesus tradition is so unreliable as to make our quest for him impossible.

37. See my article, "Jesus and the Covenant: A Response to E. P. Sanders," *JSNT* 29 (1987): 57–78.

38. *The Gospel and the Land* (Berkeley: University of California Press, 1974).

tants of the land will be cast out. Their living in Palestine will not, any more than their descent from Abraham (cf. Q 3:8), bring them merit. Quite the contrary. It is precisely those inside the borders of Israel, those who have been blessed with the presence of God's eschatological herald, who will face the more dire consequences. To whom much is given will much be required.

It is easy to imagine Jesus drawing an ironic contrast between the dismal fate of certain prestigious Palestinian opponents and the good fortune of unknown multitudes outside the land, who were perhaps thought by many to be inferior Jews.[39] In Q 14:16–24, the parable of the great banquet, those first invited turn down the invitations, after which the poor, the maimed, the blind, the lame, and the invalids come. Here those who should participate in the messianic feast lose their places to unlikely characters. This eschatological reversal, this overturning of the expected, runs throughout the Jesus tradition. It would hardly surprise to learn that Jesus, with the exaggerated rhetoric of prophetic antithesis, and in the disappointment of a failed mission to Palestinian Jews, foretold a bright future for those in the Diaspora, including the hidden lost tribes, but warned of the doom coming upon those in the land who were confident that they would be the focus of God's end-time blessings.

Such a reading of Q 13:28–29 finds some interesting and close parallels in the Tanak's prophetic literature.[40] Jer 24:1–10 contains Jeremiah's famous vision of the two baskets of figs, one very good, like first-ripe figs, the other very bad, so bad they could not be eaten. The good figs are identified with the exiles from Judah, whom God will return to the land and make his own. The bad figs are identified with Zedekiah, his princes, the remnant of Jerusalem in the land, and those in Egypt: "I will send sword, famine, and pestilence upon them, until they are utterly destroyed from the land that I gave to them and their ancestors" (v. 10). Here the exiles are saved while those in the land are condemned. The same idea appears in Jer 29:10–32.

Ezekiel 11 likewise promises return to Palestine for those in exile but foretells terrible punishment for those who have remained in the land. Those in the Diaspora have had divine protection (v. 16) and God will give them a new heart and assemble them in the land of Israel (v. 17). "But as for those whose heart goes after their detestable things and their abominations, I will requite their deeds upon their own hands, says the Lord God" (v. 21).

---

39. There are, on the other hand, texts that depict the lost tribes as particularly pious; cf. 4 Ezra 13:42.

40. For what follows I am indebted to Theodore A. Bergren, "The 'People Coming from the East' in 5 Ezra 1:38," *JBL* 108 (1989): 675–83.

## THE LITERARY INTERPRETATIONS

All the evidence indicates that, against Jeremias and so many others, Q 13:28–29 originally had nothing to say about Gentiles. It was rather composed to say something similar to what is said in Jeremiah 24 and Ezekiel 11. It took up the stock theme of the eschatological ingathering of dispersed Jews in order to threaten certain Jews in the land with judgment.

There is further no reason to suppose that Q or Luke saw matters very differently. Q/Lk 13:28–29 is paraenesis. To judge from the context, it is a warning to the self-assured that many who want to enter the narrow door will be unable to do so (cf. Q/Lk 13:23), that many who think the master knows them will be surprised at the end to find that he does not (Q/Lk 13:25–27), that many who believe themselves first will on the contrary be among the last (Q/Lk 13:30).[41] The subject is neither God's rejection of Israel nor his acceptance of Gentiles but the demands God makes upon the faithful. Q/Lk 13:28–29 reinforces Jesus' moral demand by uprooting complacency.[42]

But what does the saying mean in Matthew? Most interpreters take Mt 8:11–12 to foretell the salvation of Gentiles and the doom of Jews. This is thought to follow from the identification of the centurion with a Gentile and the contrast in 8:10: "Truly I tell you, among none in Israel have I found such faith." Yet the inference is very uncertain. The ethnic status of the soldier is — as both Chrysostom, *Hom. on Mt.* 26:3, and Philoxenus, ad loc., recognized — not explicitly made out.[43] Some commentators have thought him a Jew.[44] Matthew's "not even in Israel have I found such faith" (8:10) hardly implies the centurion's Gentile status, for in 9:33 the similar "never was anything like this seen in Israel" has to do with the ministry of Jesus the Jew. Mt 8:10 may just mean that in no other Israelite has Jesus found such faith. If so, "in Israel" should probably be given geographical sense: it refers to the land (cf. Mt 2:20, 21; 9:33; 10:23).[45] The point then would lie not in the salvation of Gen-

---

41. Given the use of catchwords in the latter part of Q (see pp. 29–30 herein) and the appearance of "many" in Q 13:34 and 14:16 (and perhaps Q 13:30; cf. Mt 19:30), Matthew's use of "many" is likely original (see p. 29, n. 129).

42. Cf. the homiletical interpretation of Mt 8:11–12 in Garland, *Reading Matthew*, p. 96.

43. This is also true for Luke and Q.

44. See, e.g., Buchanan, *Matthew*, p. 382. David R. Catchpole, "The Centurion's Faith and its Function in Q," in Van Segbroeck, *Four Gospels*, vol. 1, pp. 517–40, makes a good case that, at least in Q, the centurion was not a Gentile (cf. Catchpole, *Quest*, pp. 280–308; but contrast Tuckett, *Q*, pp. 395–97). See further Henry Innes MacAdam, "Gethsemane, Gabbatha, Golgotha: The Arrest, Trials, and Execution of Jesus of Nazareth," *IBS* 17 (1995): 156–57. Herod's army, like the Roman army, had "centurions."

45. Israel is certainly not here a personal name — although a scholion to the Greek

tiles as opposed to Jews but in the unfortunate lot of those in the land, those who have been privileged to encounter the Messiah and yet have not accepted his proclamation. On this reading, the many from east and west serve primarily as a foil, and Matthew could readily have thought of them as Diaspora Jews. Their happy future fate will be altogether different than the judgment that will fall upon those in the land who have heard and yet rejected God's messianic herald.

There is, however, also another possibility to be reckoned with. Given his immersion in the Bible and Jewish tradition, it seems unlikely that the First Evangelist would fail to recognize that Q 13:28–29 uses language associated with the eschatological ingathering of scattered Israel. But this does not require that he interpreted the saying in a literal sense. Although commentators (including myself) have neglected the fact when interpreting Mt 8:11–12, there was evidently a well-established habit of speaking of early Christians as though they were the Jewish Diaspora. Consider the following examples:

> Jn 11:51–52: "[H]e prophesied that Jesus was about to die for the nation, and not for the nation only, but to gather into one the dispersed children of God."

> Jas 1:1: "James, a servant of God and of the Lord Jesus Christ, to the twelve tribes in the dispersion..."[46]

> 1 Pet 1:1: "Peter, an apostle of Jesus Christ, to the exiles of the dispersion in Pontus, Galatia, Cappadocia, Asia, and Bithynia..."

> 1 Pet 1:17: "[L]ive in reverent fear during the time of your exile..."

> 1 Pet 2:11: "I urge you as aliens and exiles to abstain from the desires of the flesh that wage war against your soul."

Also pertinent are (1) the use of πάροικος, παροικία, and παροικεῖν in still other texts,[47] (2) *5 Ezra's* reinterpretation of the expectation of the eschatological gathering of Diaspora Jews as fulfilled in the church,[48] and (3) the identification of the 144,000 out of every tribe of the people of Israel (Revelation 7) with the church.[49]

---

text of Theophylact's commentary on Matthew construes it as such: while the patriarch at Bethel thought God was in a particular place, the Gentile centurion understood that God is everywhere and by his word can do all things. Cf. Gregory of Nyssa, *Hom. Cant.* 10, in *PG*, vol. 44, p. 981.

46. Some accept a literal meaning for this verse; but for the metaphorical sense see Martin Dibelius, *James*, Hermeneia (Philadelphia: Fortress, 1976), pp. 66–67, and Sophie Laws, *A Commentary on the Epistle of James* (San Francisco: Harper & Row, 1980), pp. 47–49.

47. E.g., *1 Clem.* inscription; *2 Clem.* 5:1, 5; *M. Polyc.* inscription; Diogenes, *Ep.* 5:5.

48. See Bergren, "5 Ezra 1:38."

49. See R. H. Charles, *A Critical and Exegetical Commentary on the Revelation of St. John*, vol. 1, ICC (Edinburgh: T. & T. Clark, 1920), pp. 199–201.

In the light of all this it *may* be that Matthew interpreted 8:11–12 not as a yet-to-be-fulfilled prophecy of salvation for those in the Jewish Diaspora but rather as an already realized or partially realized prediction of the arrival of the Christian church, made up of Jews as well as Gentiles. Such a reading is certainly consistent with 21:43, in which the church is the new people of God. It also coheres with Matthew's eschatology. Throughout the First Gospel, Jewish eschatological expectations are recast as having been fulfilled or partly fulfilled in the Messiah's first advent.[50] Perhaps Mt 8:11–12 offers one more example of this sort of "realized eschatology." The expectation of the ingathering of the dispersed children of God has begun to come to pass in the spread of the Christian community.

---

50. Allison, *End of the Ages*, pp. 40–50; John P. Meier, *Law and History in Matthew's Gospel*, AnBib, vol. 71 (Rome: Biblical Institute, 1976), pp. 27–40.

# THE FORSAKEN HOUSE, Q 13:34–35

## *Jerusalem's Repentance*

### TWO DIFFERENT INTERPRETATIONS

Q 13:35b reads as follows: "And I tell you, you will not see me until the time comes when you say, 'Blessed is the one who comes in the name of the Lord.' "[1] Whether with reference to Matthew (cf. 23:39) or Luke, to Jesus or Q, interpretations of this verse have generally followed one of two paths. Either it has been construed as a declaration of unqualified judgment, or commentators have thought the verse to hold forth the hope that Israel might one day accept her Messiah, Jesus. The two readings agree in assuming that the eschatological redemption is in view.[2] John Calvin, representing the first alternative, wrote that Jesus "will not come to them [the Jews] until they cry out in fear — too late — at the sight of His Majesty, 'truly He is Son of God.' "[3] T. W. Manson paraphrased to similar effect: "The time will come when you will be ready to say to me, 'Blessed is he that cometh in the name of the Lord'; but then it will be too late."[4] And J. C. Fenton has affirmed that, according to Mt 23:39, "Jesus will not be seen by Jerusalem again before he comes in judgement, and they will greet him, but with mourning."[5]

---

1. Luke does not have Matthew's "from now on" (ἀπ' ἄρτι), which must be regarded as redactional (cf. Mt 26:29, 64). Matthew does not have Luke's "the time comes when" (ἥξει ὅτε), which may have stood in Q; but there is much uncertainty here. ἥξει ὅτε has weak textual support (D lat sy^s.c). Simple ἕως is read by P^75 B L R 892. ἕως ἄν is found in P^45 ℵ N Θ f^13. Nestle^26 has ἥξει ὅτε but in brackets, indicating doubtful authenticity.

2. For the reasons see Manson, *Sayings*, pp. 127–28. Luke, however, may have seen the saying's fulfillment in the triumphal entry; see Lk 19:38. This interpretation is supported by Cyril of Alexandria, *Hom. on Lk.* 100, and Luke Timothy Johnson, *The Gospel of Luke*, Sacra Pagina, vol. 3 (Collegeville, Minn.: Michael Glazier, 1991), p. 219. In Matthew, where the verse is placed after Jesus' arrival in Jerusalem, this possibility is excluded.

3. *A Harmony of the Gospels Matthew, Mark, and Luke*, vol. 3 (Edinburgh: Saint Andrew, 1972), p. 71.

4. *Sayings*, p. 128.

5. *Saint Matthew* (Baltimore: Penguin, 1963), p. 377. Cf. Schulz, *Q*, p. 358 (for Q); Gnilka, *Matthäusevangelium*, vol. 2, p. 305 (for Matthew); Garland, *Intention*, pp. 204–9; J. Meier, *Matthew*, p. 275 (for Matthew); Sato, *Q und Prophetie*, pp. 157–60.

But against Calvin, Manson, and Fenton, εὐλογημένος is not an expression of fear and trembling, nor is it typically voiced by the ignorant, the condemned, or those in mourning. In the LXX — including, notably Ps 117:26, which is cited in our text — and in the NT, εὐλογεῖν and εὐλογημένος (like the Hebrew ברך) are often expressions of joy, and they consistently have a very positive connotation: "to praise," "to extol," "to bless," "to greet."[6] For this reason alone it is not easy to envisage the words of Ps 118[117]:26 as coming, begrudgingly or otherwise, from the lips of those for whom the messianic advent must mean only damnation. Further, what precedent is there in ancient Jewish or Christian literature for the notion that unbelievers and the wicked will utter a blessing when the Lord or the Messiah comes to the earth? When the Son of man comes on the clouds of heaven with power and great glory, the faithless tribes of the earth will not bless him and God; rather will they weep and wail.[7] As it says in Q 13:28, when those who are not destined to enter the kingdom of God see its arrival, there will be weeping and gnashing of teeth.

Over against the interpretation just criticized, Q 13:35b can be understood to mean that, when the Messiah comes, Jerusalem will know salvation. That is, the recitation of Ps 118[117]:26 will be offered freely and with joy. The Messiah will come to his people and they will welcome him and say, "Blessed is he who comes in the name of the Lord." This interpretation, which has as much scholarly support as its opposite,[8] is more in accord with the spirit of Ps 118[117]; and it is

---

6. See H. van der Kwaak, "Die Klage über Jerusalem (Matth. 23:37–39)," *NovT* 8 (1966): 165–66; W. Beyer, "εὐλογέω κ.τ.λ.," *TDNT*, vol. 2, pp. 754–65; and J. Scharbert, "ברך," *TDOT*, vol. 2, pp. 279–308.

7. Mt 24:30; Rev 1:7; *Apoc. Pet.* E 6. Note however *1 Enoch* 62:6, 9–10, and 63:1–12, where condemned sinners bless God in an attempt to alter their fate. According to E. Schweizer, *The Good News according to Matthew* (Atlanta: John Knox, 1975), p. 445, Mt 21:9 shows "that one can rejoice while still in ignorance, without realizing what one is doing." This, however, hardly applies to Q 13:35, where the eschatological vindication of Jesus is in view: that vindication can only be realized in public revelation, so people will not be left in ignorance.

8. Cf. Bengel, *Gnomon*, ad loc.; Alford, *Four Gospels*, p. 234; F. Godet, *A Commentary on the Gospel of St. Luke*, 5th ed., vol. 2 (Edinburgh: T. & T. Clark, 1957), pp. 131–32; Adolf Schlatter, *Der Evangelist Matthäus* (Stuttgart: Calwer, 1948), p. 691; W. G. Kümmel, *Promise and Fulfilment*, 2d ed., SBT, vol. 23 (London: SCM, 1961), p. 81 (for Jesus); Joachim Jeremias, *The Eucharistic Words of Jesus* (London: SCM, 1966), pp. 259–60 (for Jesus: "even in the blind and obdurate city God will arouse a remnant which will greet the coming one"); Goulder, *Midrash and Lection*, pp. 429–30 (for Matthew); Ernst, *Lukas*, p. 434; Gundry, *Matthew*, p. 474 (for Matthew); D. Patte, *The Gospel according to Matthew* (Philadelphia: Fortress, 1987), pp. 329–30 (for Matthew); Uro, *Sheep*, pp. 235–40 (for Q); G. N. Stanton, "Aspects of Early Christian-Jewish Polemic and Apologetic," *NTS* 31 (1985): 377–92 (reprinted in his *Gospel*, pp. 232–55); G. R. Beasley-Murray, *Jesus*, p. 306 (for Jesus); David R. Catchpole, "Temple Traditions in Q," in *Templum Amicitiae*, ed. William Horbury, JSNTSS, vol. 48 (Sheffield: JSOT, 1991), pp. 319–20, 323 (cf. idem, *Quest*, pp. 271, 274); Tuckett, "Les Logia et le Judaïsme," pp. 86–88 (for Q; cf. idem, *Q*, pp. 204–207); Garland, *Reading Matthew*, pp. 232–33

interesting that, in *b. Pesaḥ.* 117a, Rab Judah says in Samuel's name that God's people will sing the Hallel (Psalms 113–18) at the eschatological redemption.

Many have rejected the positive interpretation of Q 13:35b because the half verse can hardly be read in isolation; rather it is bound up with Q 13:35a, which is a pronouncement of judgment. But if the sequel to Q 13:35a is nothing but a straightforward declaration of salvation in the offing, is not the result the coupling of discontiguous sentiments? One naturally expects a harsher note to conclude the preceding lines.[9] As David Garland has observed, "Verse 39 is very difficult to interpret because 'Blessed is he who comes in the name of the Lord' has a joyous content in Psalm 118:26 and when uttered by the crowds at Jesus' entry to the city (Mt. 21:9); but interpreting it in this manner renders discordant the mood of harsh judgment" in the immediate context.[10] If one regards 13:35b as a promise of salvation, then one might wonder whether the line is an infelicitous secondary addition.[11]

Such surgery, however, is not an attractive option. Not only should one prefer, if possible, to make sense of a text as it stands, but Q 13:35b is more firmly wedded to its immediate context than has been recognized. Ps 118[117]:26a is the Scripture quoted in Q 13:35, and the OT verse is followed by this: "We bless you from the house (בית/οἴκου) of the Lord" (Ps 118[117]:26b). Is it just coincidence that the prophecy of Q 13:35b is also joined to a statement about the "house" (οἶκος) of the Lord: "Behold, your house is forsaken" (Q 13:35a)?[12] Ps 118[117] tells not only of worshipers blessing the one who comes in the name of the Lord; it also speaks of a blessing that comes from the house of the Lord, from the temple. This fact best explains why Q's assertion about the forsaken house — which embraces both Jerusalem and the temple[13] —

---

(for Matthew; this represents a change of opinion; see n. 5); Darrell L. Bock, *Luke* (Leicester: IVP, 1994), p. 248 (for Luke). Schweizer, *Matthew*, p. 445, and Hill, *Matthew*, p. 316, think this a possibility but come to no final decision on the matter. Plummer, *Matthew*, p. 325, offers that our text means that the "opportunity for conversion will always remain open."

9. Cf. van der Kwaak, "Klage," p. 165.

10. Garland, *Intention*, p. 204.

11. Cf. Bultmann, *History*, p. 115; Ernst Haenchen, "Matthäus 23," *ZTK* 48 (1951): 57; Schweizer, *Matthew*, p. 437; and see further the review of opinion in Garland, *Intention*, p. 204 n. 129.

12. Matthew adds ἔρημος. (Its omission in B L ff² sy^s sa bo^pt is probably assimilation to Luke. But many — including Westcott and Hort — have thought the word a later interpolation.)

13. Scholars have debated whether "your house" — the pronoun itself implies that the house has already been abandoned — refers to the temple (cf. 1 Kgs 9:1–10; Isa 64:11; Jer 7:10–14; 26:6; *Jub.* 49:19; Mt 12:4; 21:13; Lk 6:4; 11:51; 2 *Bar.* 8:2–4), to Jerusalem (cf. Jer 22:1–6; *1 Enoch* 89:50–51, 56, 67; *T. Levi* 10:5), or to "the house of Israel" (cf. Jer 12:7; Lk 1:27, 33, 69; Acts 2:36; SB, vol. 1, pp. 943–44). But Jewish texts — such as Ezra and 2 *Baruch* — do not always distinguish between the temple and the capital,

is accompanied by another which concerns the coming redemption. Q 13:35a implies that Jerusalem and its temple have fallen into sin and so are headed for disaster.[14] It follows that the temple in the capital cannot be, as it is in Ps 118[117]:26, the source of any proper blessing. That is, those in the temple do not now bless God's spokesman, Jesus, he who will someday come as Messiah. But this means that the words of Ps 118[117]:26, if they be understood (as Q understands them) as prophetic,[15] must refer to some time yet ahead. And this is precisely what one finds in our synoptic text: the time for the blessing of the one who comes in the name of the Lord is moved into the future. So it appears that Q 13:35 reflects a consistent interpretation of Ps 118[117]:26. "Your house is forsaken" is the reason why there is presently no fulfillment of the prophetic Psalm, why the exclamation, "Blessed is he who comes in the name of the Lord," is thought of as outstanding. The lines from Q are accordingly best regarded as a unit, which puts a question mark over any interpretation or tradition-history that requires us to divide them.[16]

Although Q 13:35b should not be sundered from 13:35a, that is no reason to give up the interpretation of the former which finds in it the salvation of Jerusalem. For Jewish sources sometimes juxtapose, in what seems to us a jarring fashion, harsh declarations of judgment with consoling promises of salvation.[17] Furthermore, Q 13:35b is more than a straightforward declaration of Jerusalem's salvation. It is, as I shall now seek to show, an implicit call to repentance. In other words, the text foresees deliverance — but this deliverance does not come without Jerusalem's repentance.

---

both of which represent the nation. Quite often temple implies city and city implies people so that one may almost speak of their identification. See Davies, *Gospel and the Land*, pp. 144–45, 150–54.

14. Cf. Mk 11:17; 13:2; 14:58; Lk 23:27–31.

15. In the early church Ps 118 was viewed as containing messianic prophecies; it was an important source of *testimonia*. Note Acts 2:33; 4:11; Mk 11:9–10; 12:10; and 1 Pet 2:7. See B. Lindars, *New Testament Apologetic* (London: SCM, 1961), pp. 43–44, 111–12, 169–74, 179–80, 184–86. There is also some evidence to suggest that Ps 118 was given eschatological or messianic meaning in first-century Judaism; see E. Werner, " 'Hosanna' in the Gospels," *JBL* 65 (1946): 97–122, and Jeremias, *Eucharistic Words*, pp. 256–60.

16. One might also argue for the unity of Q 13:34–35 by observing that v. 35 quotes Ps 118:26 and that v. 34 probably alludes to Isa 31:5 ("like birds hovering overhead, so the Lord of hosts will protect Jerusalem"; see below), and further that the two OT texts are linked by catchword (Isa 31:5: הַצִּיל; Ps 118:26: הַצְלִיחָה; the link is maintained in the LXX with σῶσον [Psalm 117] and σώσει [Isaiah]). In other words, Q 13:34–35 may reflect the exegetical joining of two scriptural passages. (Verse 34 also has parallels in Deut 32:11; Ruth 2:12; Pss 17:8; 36:7; 57:1; 61:4; 63:7; 91:4; 2 Bar. 41:4; and 2 Esdr. 1:30. But only in Isa 31:5 is Jerusalem the explicit subject of the protecting wings.)

17. I owe this observation to Stanton, *Gospel for a New People*, p. 250. *T. Levi* 16:5 is particularly instructive in this regard.

## Q 13:35b as a Conditional Sentence

"Until you say" (ἕως ἂν εἴπητε or ἕως ἥξει ὅτε[18]) can be understood to signal a conditional sentence.[19] Q 13:35b then means not, when the Messiah comes, his people will bless him, but rather, when his people bless him, the Messiah will come.[20] In other words, the redemption will come when Israel accepts the person and work of Jesus. Four considerations encourage one to accept this understanding of Q 13:35b.

First, belief that the date of the final salvation is not fixed[21] but rather waits upon a particular circumstance to come to pass is well attested in old Jewish sources. The following are from rabbinic literature: (1) R. Eliezer b. Hyrcanus is purported to have said that if Israel does not repent she will not be delivered; but if she does repent she will be delivered (*b. Sanh.* 97b).[22] (2) According to *b. Šabb.* 118b, R. Simeon b. Yoḥai is supposed to have said that if the nation were to keep only two Sabbaths the Lord would immediately bring redemption. (3) In *b. Sanh.* 98a we read that Ze'iri declared in the name of R. Ḥanina b. Ḥama that the Son of David will not come until no conceited people remain in Israel. (4) *Sipre Deut.* 41 (79b) announces that if Israel were to keep Torah, God would therewith send Elijah. Similar sentiments are assigned to various sages in, among other places, *b. B. Bat.* 10a (R. Judah:

---

18. See n. 1 above.

19. Cf. Daniel J. Harrington, *The Gospel of Matthew,* Sacra Pagina (Collegeville, Minn.: Michael Glazier, 1991), p. 330 (the verse "appears to delay the Son of Man's coming and make it conditional"); van der Kwaak, "Klage," pp. 165–70; also Marcus Borg, *Conflict, Holiness, and Politics in the Teaching of Jesus* (New York: Edwin Mellen, 1984), pp. 182–84.

20. The messianic event itself is not contingent but only its timing. See further n. 45.

21. That God, out of grace, will hasten the coming of salvation, either by cutting days short or altering the prescribed measure, appears first in Isa 60:22 (MT) and is thereafter attested in Ecclus 36:8 ("Hasten the day, and remember the appointed time"); 4Q385 frag. 3 ("The days will hasten quickly, until [all the children of] men will say: Are not the days hastening on in order that the children of Israel may inherit [the land]? . . . I will shorten the days and the year[s]"); *Ps. Sol.* 17:45(51) ("May the Lord hasten his mercy upon Israel"); Mk 13:20; *LAB* 19:13 ("I will command the years and order the times and they will be shortened"); *2 Bar.* 20:1–2; 54:1; 83:1; 2 Esdr 2:13 ("pray that your days may be few, that they may be shortened"); *Barn.* 4:3 ("the Master has cut the seasons and the days short, that his beloved might hasten and come"); *Apoc. Abr.* 29:13 ("the curtailing of the age of impiety"); *m. 'Abot* 2:15 ("The day is short and the task is great and the labourers are lazy and the wage is abundant and the master of the house is urgent"; on this see L. H. Silberman, "From Apocalyptic Proclamation to Moral Prescription," *JJS* 40 (1989): 53–60); *y. Ta'an.* 1:1 (R. Eliezer: repentance will hasten the end); and *Trimorphic Prot.* 44:16 ("the times are cut short and the days have been shortened").

22. R. Eliezer's statement occurs in a debate with R. Joshua, who takes the other side: the redemption will come even before Israel repents. For discussion see E. E. Urbach, "Redemption and Repentance in Talmudic Judaism," in *Types of Redemption,* ed. R. J. Zwi Werblowsky and C. J. Bleeker (Leiden: E. J. Brill, 1970), pp. 191–206, and L. Landman, "Introduction," in *Messianism in the Talmudic Era,* ed. L. Landman (New York: KTAV, 1979), pp. xix–xxiii.

charity brings the redemption nearer) and *b. Yoma* 86b (R. Jonathan: repentance will bring the redemption).

Although the dating of rabbinic materials is notoriously difficult, some OT texts can be read to say that Israel's repentance will herald the latter days;[23] and Acts 3:19–21 — which probably contains pre-Lukan tradition — supplies firm evidence that some in the first century believed penitence would usher in the end.[24] Here Peter tells his audience that were they to repent God would send Messiah Jesus. In a number of places in the Pseudepigrapha, moreover, repentance and the consummation are held together, and in some of these it seems likely that repentance is assumed to be the trigger for the coming redemption.[25] Possibilities include *T. Dan* 6:4;[26] *T. Sim.* 6:2–7;[27] *T. Zeb.* 9:7–9;[28] *T. Jud.* 23:5;[29] *As. Mos.* 1:18;[30] *2 Bar.* 78:7;[31] and *Apoc. Abr.* 29.[32] One should also take into account 4 Ezra, which rebuts the thought that the kingdom of God has been delayed on account of the sins of those who dwell on the earth,[33] and thereby discounts the claim, presumably made by someone known to the author, that righteousness might hasten the

---

23. E.g., Deut 4:30–31 and Hos 3:4–5.

24. On the pre-Lukan character and interpretation of Acts 3:19–21 see esp. R. F. Zehnle, *Peter's Pentecost Discourse*, SBLMS, vol. 15 (Nashville: Abingdon, 1971), pp. 45–60, 71–75; also F. Hahn, "Das Problem alter christologischer Überlieferungen in der Apostelgeschichte unter besonderer Berücksichtigung von Act 3,19–21," in *Les Actes des Apôtres: Traditions, rédaction, théologie,* ed. J. Kremer, BETL, vol. 48 (Leuven: Leuven University Press, 1979), pp. 129–54.

25. The juxtaposition in some intertestamental literature of apocalyptic determinism and contingent eschatology is simply one more illustration of what R. Otto, *The Kingdom of God and the Son of Man,* new and rev. ed. (London: Lutterworth, 1943), pp. 59–63, called the "essential irrationality" of eschatological thinking.

26. On the day Israel repents the kingdom of the enemy will come to an end.

27. Here the eschatological promises are introduced with "if you remove your envy and every hardness of heart."

28. After Israel remembers the Lord and repents God will show compassion, after which every captive of the sons of Beliar will be liberated, and every spirit of error trampled.

29. See n. 43.

30. This refers to the "day of repentance (or: recompense)" at "the consummation of the end of days" when the Lord will "regard" the people.

31. God will "remember" the people when they act rightly.

32. In this there is a vision in which (at least in Box's translation) righteous individuals seemingly "hasten" the consummation: "And then shall righteous men of thy seed be left in the number which is kept secret by me, hastening to the glory of My Name to the place prepared beforehand for them.... " Cf. 2 Pet 3:12. This tradition has its converse: repentance can delay the end. See *Sib. Or.* 4:162–78; 5:357–60; *Gk. Apoc. Ezra* 3; Tertullian, *Apol.* 39. When the end is conceived primarily in terms of judgment, hope for its delay arises. Cf. *Mek.* on Exod 15:5–6, where God gives "an extension of time" to wicked people. Note that *b. Ketub.* 111a speaks of Israel not delaying (יְרַחֲקוּ) the end, but a variant text refers to not forcing (by excessive prayer — יְדַחֲקוּ) the end.

33. 4:39: "It is perhaps on account of us that the time of threshing is delayed for the righteous — on account of the sins of those who dwell on earth." The seer goes on to rebut this notion; see 4:40–43.

climax of the eschatological drama.[34] Such an idea may be attested not only in the texts just cited but also 11QTemple. For Ben Zion Wacholder has argued that in 59:7–13[35] and other passages in 11QTemple "the ultimate acceptance" of the document's Torah will "redeem Israel unto eternity."[36]

Second, ἕως can function, especially after a negation, to express contingency in Greek sentences: the state depicted in the first half of the sentence lasts only until the state depicted in the second half is realized.[37] In such cases the meaning of ἕως is often not simply temporal ("until")[38] but properly conditional, and thus close to "unless." Consider the following texts, one of which (Mt 5:26 = Lk 12:59) is from Q:

> Plato, *Phaed.* 101D: "You would let him be and would not answer until (ἕως) you have examined the consequences."

> Xenophon, *Cyr.* 5.5.37: "These must always make trouble until (ἕως) they are put in order."

> Mt 5:26 = Lk 12:59: "[Y]ou will not get out until (ἕως) you have paid the last penny."

> Mt 10:23: "[Y]ou will not have gone through the cities of Israel until (ἕως) the Son of man comes."

> Mt 17:9: "Tell no one about the vision until (ἕως) the Son of man has been raised from the dead."

> Lk 22:18: "I will not drink of the fruit of the vine until (ἕως) the kingdom of God comes" (cf. v. 16).

---

34. In the *Assumption of Moses* it is the death of Taxo and his sons — a death that is actively sought — which "forces" the end; see J. Licht, "Taxo, or the Apocalyptic Doctrine of Vengeance," *JJS* 12 (1961): 95–103, and D. C. Carlson, "Vengeance and Angelic Mediation in *Testament of Moses* 9 and 10," *JBL* 101 (1982): 85–95. Further, *Ps. Sol.* 17 places the promises of redemption within a context of moral exhortation, which led S. Mowinckel, *He That Cometh* (Oxford: Basil Blackwell, 1956), p. 297, to suppose that here national penitence can hasten the divine intervention.

35. Here we read, "Afterwards they will turn to me with all their heart and with all their soul, according to all the words of this Torah and I shall save them from the hand of their enemies and redeem them from the hand of those who hate them, and bring them into the land of their fathers. I shall redeem them and increase them and rejoice over them. I shall be their God, and they shall be my people."

36. *The Dawn of Qumran: The Sectarian Torah and the Teacher of Righteousness* (Cincinnati: Hebrew Union College, 1983), p. 21. Cf. p. 13.

37. Cf. W. W. Goodwin, *Syntax of the Moods and Tenses of the Greek Verb* (New York: St. Martin's, 1965), pp. 235–37.

38. In some instances ἕως, like the Hebrew and Aramaic עַד, loses altogether the idea of termination and expresses "a limit which is not absolute (terminating the preceding action), but only relative, beyond which the action or state described in the principal clause still continues" (E. Kautzsch and A. E. Cowley, *Gesenius' Hebrew Grammar*, 2d ed. (Oxford: Clarendon, 1919), p. 503). Cf. Gen 26:13; Mk 13:19.

Acts 23:12: "The Jews joined in a conspiracy and bound themselves by an oath neither to eat nor drink until (ἕως) they had killed Paul" (cf. vv. 14, 21).

2 Thess 2:7: "[O]nly he who now restrains (will do so) until (ἕως) he is out of the way."

*Did.* 14:2: "Everyone having a dispute with a fellow should not be allowed to assemble with you, until (ἕως) they have reconciled."

Similarly, the Hebrew or Aramaic עד — which so often translates ἕως in the LXX[39] and probably stands behind the ἕως of Q 13:35[40] — sometimes signifies more than the inevitable passing of a temporal span: it can also be used when an envisioned state is contingent upon some act that may or may not be performed. Illustrations of this are abundant and include the following:

Gen 19:22: "I can do nothing until (עד; LXX: ἕως) you arrive there."

Gen 29:8: "We cannot water the sheep until (עד; LXX: ἕως) all the flocks are gathered and the stone is rolled away from the mouth of the well."

Deut 22:2: "It shall be with you until (עד; LXX: ἕως) your brother seeks it" (cf. 11QTemple 64:15).

Ezra 4:21: "Make a decree . . . that this city not be built again until (עד) a decree is made by me."

*Ahiqar* 130–31 (saying 43, Lindenberger): "Rest for your soul do not take until (עד) you have paid back the loan."

Cowley 2:17: "Ours you have a right to seize until (עד) you are indemnified in full."

1QS 8:19: "No member of the covenant who blatantly takes away a word from all that is commanded shall touch the sacred meal . . . until (עד) his deeds are cleansed from all error."

*m. Ber.* 7:5: "The blessing over wine may not be said until (עד) water be added to it."

In most of these texts "unless" would be no less adequate a translation than "until."

Third, the structure of Q 13:35b argues for the conditional interpretation. At least in later times there appears to have been a standard way

---

39. See below and Gen 3:19; 6:7; 7:23; 10:19; etc.
40. Cf. the עדמה of the Syriac versions.

of expressing one's belief as to what condition(s) would immediately precede the eschatological redemption. Consider the following passages:

> *b. Sanh.* 98a: Ze'iri said in R. Ḥanina's name: "The Son of David will not come until (עד) there are no conceited men in Israel."

> *b. Sanh.* 98a: R. Ḥama b. Ḥanina said: "The Son of David will not come until (עד) even the pettiest kingdom ceases to hold power over Israel."

> *b. Sanh.* 98a: R. Simlai said in the name of R. Eleazar b. Simeon: "The Son of David will not come until (עד) all judges and officers are gone from Israel."

> *b. Sanh.* 98a: R. Ḥanina said: "The Son of David will not come until (עד) a fish is sought for an invalid and cannot be procured."

> *b. 'Abod. Zar.* 5a: R. Jose said: "The Son of David will not come until (עד) all the souls destined for bodies are exhausted."

> *b. Sanh.* 98b: Rab said: "The Son of David will not come until (עד) the [Roman] power enfolds Israel for nine months."

Each of these texts has the same structure, which can be set forth thus:

(a) statement about the messianic advent with adverbial particle of negation attached ("The Son of David will not come");

(b) conditional particle (עד);

(c) condition to be met (in Israel) for fulfillment of the messianic advent (e.g., "no conceited men in Israel").

It is striking that Q 13:35b can be analyzed as having precisely the same structure:

(a) statement about the messianic advent with adverbial particle of negation attached ("You will not see me," "me" being the messianic figure Jesus);

(b) conditional particle (ἕως);

(c) condition to be met (in Israel) for fulfillment of the messianic advent (the people bless Jesus and so acknowledge his person and work).

The Q text appears to set forth, in a traditional fashion, a circumstance that will precede the great redemption.

Fourth, and as already argued, whereas Q 13:35b is not likely on the one hand to be a statement of utter rejection, it is equally unlikely on the other hand, following Q 13:35a, to be nothing more than an unqualified announcement of salvation. The conditional interpretation commends itself by finding a middle ground that avoids the pitfalls of the alternatives. The thought of judgment is present because, for now, Israel has not received God's messenger; the people have refused to accept the one sent to them, and so the redemption has not come. And yet, despite this element of judgment, the thought of salvation is also present. For Jesus affirms that Jerusalem will be forsaken[41] only until[42] the time when the people bless in the name of the Lord the one who will come, an act which will lead to deliverance.[43] We have here, in effect, a call to repentance.[44] When the holy city recognizes its error and accepts the Messiah, he will come.[45]

## THE LOCATION AND FUNCTION OF Q 13:35b IN Q

There is no consensus as to where Q 13:34–35 stood in Q. Many have surmised that Matthew may have arranged things to make the lament culminate the polemic of chapter 23 and prepare for chapter 24.[46] In favor of this view, which implies that only Luke's order can reproduce the sequence of Q, are two points: (1) Luke is, as a general rule, closer to Q's order, and (2) Q 13:34–35 does not follow naturally upon Q 11:49–51

---

41. "Is forsaken" is for Q presumably a divine passive, perhaps referring to the Shekinah (cf. Ezek 10:1–22; 11:22–25; Josephus, *Bell.* 6.300). Cf. Theissen, *Gospels in Context*, p. 220–21 (who finds here reason to suppose Q was composed before 70 C.E.: after that date one would expect a clear reference to the destruction). Contrast Matthew, where the subject may be Jesus himself (cf. Mt 24:1). Is it relevant to observe that the speaker of Ps 118:26 says a bit earlier that God has punished him severely (v. 18)? Perhaps the transition in Q 13:35 from punishment to thanksgiving and salvation reflects the sequence of the psalm it quotes.

42. Cf. the eschatological ἕως of *T. Levi* 16:5: "You will be a curse and a dispersion among the nations until (ἕως) he [God] will again have regard for you and take you back in compassion." Also comparable is *T. Zeb.* 9:9: "You will be rejected until (ἕως) the time of the end." Here ἕως must, in view of 9:7–8, refer to a state which is undone at the consummation.

43. Cf. the juxtaposition of repentance and salvation in *T. Jud.* 23:5: Israel will suffer judgment until the people return to the Lord in integrity of heart.

44. Cf. Bengel, *Gnomon*, ad loc. ("with this verse their repentance will begin"); Alford, *Four Gospels*, p. 234 ("until that day, the subject of all prophecy, when your repentant people shall turn"); Godet, *Luke*, pp. 131–32; van der Kwaak, "Klage."

45. The text does not say whether God moves the people to repentance (cf. Ezekiel 36; Zech 12:10–14); but given the apparent certainty of the prophecy such a notion might be assumed. France, *Matthew*, pp. 332–33, contends that while Mt 23:39 "expresses the condition on which Israel may again see its Messiah," it "makes no promise that this condition will be fulfilled." This is a view I once held. But it does not harmonize with the Q texts which look forward to Israel's restoration; and there is no good reason to imagine that the Jewish tradents of Q had abandoned or given a figurative meaning to the Bible's eschatological promises for Jerusalem (e.g., Zech 14:8–11). Further, does Q 13:34 not lose its rhetorical impact if those to whom it is addressed never in fact bless the speaker?

46. So Garland, *Intention*, pp. 187–97; Jacobson, *First Gospel*, pp. 209–10; Schulz, *Q*, p. 349.

because, whereas the latter is prophetic ("I will send," "they will kill"), the former is retrospective ("how often would I have gathered").[47]

These arguments are, however, outweighed by those which suggest that Luke positioned the piece after Jesus' remark that a prophet should not perish away from Jerusalem (Lk 13:33).[48] (1) Luke could have moved the unit in order to bring together texts about Jerusalem. Lk 13:22–30 (with its redactional introduction naming Jerusalem) is followed by 13:31–33 ("it is impossible for a prophet to be killed outside of Jerusalem"), which is followed by 13:34–35 ("Jerusalem, Jerusalem, the city that kills the prophets"). Do we not have here an editorial scheme? (2) The feminine imagery in Q 13:34–35 ("as a hen gathers her own brood under her wings") and ποσάκις are consistent with the proposal that the unit was in Q (as in Matthew) a continuation of the words of Wisdom (Q 11:49–51). (3) Q 13:34–35 naturally belongs with the cluster of polemical sayings in Q 11:14–26, 29–52, not with the hortatory material in Q 13:33ff. (4) As argued on pp. 29–30 herein, Q 12:34ff. is strung together largely by catchword. But Q 13:34–35 is not linked by catchwords with the Q materials on either side. It is as intrusive in its Q context as is the rest of the Lukan material between Q 13:30 and Q 14:15ff.[49]

If the best guess is that Matthew's order is the order of Q, then Q 13:34–35 belongs with the polemical discourse in Q 11:37–52. This makes it, according to my compositional history of Q, a part of Q[3] and of the large interpolation in Q 11:14–52. It would indeed be almost the very last thing added by Q[3]. What function then did it serve?

As observed elsewhere, Q 11:14–52 is, like Q 3:7–9 and 7:18–35, filled with polemical utterances. But if Q 13:35 is indeed a prophecy of salvation, albeit one which acknowledges the contingency of the date of its arrival,[50] the verse serves as a sort of modifier. It shows that divine judgment is not the final word. Q 13:35b functions as does Amos 9:11–15: it balances oracles of doom with the hope of restoration. Although "your house is forsaken," there will nonetheless come a day

---

47. But at most this establishes that Q 13:34–35 and 11:49–51 did not belong together from the beginning, not that a contributor to Q could not have joined them. Why must the noted inconcinnity be attributed to Matthew?

48. Cf. J. Hugh Michael, "The Lament over Jerusalem," *American Journal of Theology* 22 (1918): 101–13; Bultmann, *History,* pp. 114–15; Lührmann, *Redaktion,* p. 45; M. J. Suggs, *Wisdom, Christology, and Law in Matthew's Gospel* (Cambridge: Harvard University Press, 1970), pp. 64–66; Catchpole, "Temple Traditions in Q," pp. 307–308. This position allows the assertion that the lament is, like Q 11:49–51, also from a Jewish source (so Strauss, Schmiedel, Harnack, and many others after them).

49. Although Lk 14:11 is a Q saying (cf. Mt 23:12) that perhaps followed Q 13:30 as commentary.

50. Q 11:2 ("thy kingdom come") might be compared, for it has occasionally been construed to imply that God will respond to the prayers of God's people to hasten the end. Why else pray for the kingdom's coming?

when "you say, 'Blessed is he who comes in the name of the Lord.' " One is reminded of Hos 2:23: "I will say to Not my people, 'You are my people.' " One also recalls the Dead Sea Scrolls. In these most Jews continue to remain outside the covenant; but there is hope that "all the congregation of Israel" will in the end join the community and "walk according to the laws of the sons of Zadok" (1QSa 1:1–2). Q 13:34–35 similarly posits that unbelief and abandonment will finally be overcome by reconciliation.

"You will not see" recalls Q 17:22, according to which people will long to see one of the days of the Son of man but will not see it. In both places the present is marked by the Son of man's absence.[51] But that absence will become a presence when unbelief gives way to belief. The unseen will then be seen. So Q 13:34–35 tempers all that has come before. Not only does Q 13:35 hold out hope, but the image of Jesus as the mother hen conveys care and compassion and so casts an aura of sadness over the woes. Q 13:34 and 35 together make Jesus, like Jeremiah, a reluctant prophet of doom.

Q 13:35b not only keeps the Christian hopes of Q in line with those of Jewish eschatology but also helps preserve the unity of Q. For elsewhere in Q it is clear that, although many in the land will suffer eschatological damnation, Israel itself will be restored. Those in the Diaspora will stream into Eretz Israel from east and west (Q 13:29),[52] and the people of God will again be constituted by twelve tribes (Q 22:30). The Messiah will be welcomed by his own people.[53]

## CONCLUSION

Even if it does not require a *Sitz im Leben* within Judaism or the early church, we can hardly be confident that the lament over Jerusalem, in-

---

51. Jesus' absence may be interpreted as a punishment. In any case "your house is abandoned" must be so understood. This means that our text resembles others which speak of (1) Israel's sin, (2) Israel's punishment, (3) Israel's redemption; see, e.g., Deut 4:25–31; 30; *T. Levi* 16; and Justin, *Dial.* 108. Discussion in M. de Jonge, "The Future of Israel in the Testaments of the Twelve Patriarchs," *JSJ* 17 (1986): 196–211; Stanton, *Gospel for a New People*, pp. 232–55.

52. See pp. 176–91. In this, however, Palestinian Jews, or a portion of them, seem to run the risk of damnation. The apparent tension with our text may be due to a different origin for the two sayings (maybe Jesus authored Q 13:28–29 [from my Q²] but not Q 13:35 [from my Q³]; see n. 54), or maybe we simply have here again the "essential irrationality" of apocalyptic.

53. According to Jacobson, "Literary Unity of Q," *JBL*, pp. 384–85, Q exhibits six out of the seven elements Steck identified as characteristic of the Deuteronomistic tradition in its later form; the one element lacking is, "If Israel repents, Yahweh will restore her, gathering those scattered among the nations." But if 13:28–29 and 13:34–35 are interpreted as I have interpreted them herein, all seven elements would be present.

cluding Q 13:35b, was spoken by Jesus.[54] But whatever one decides concerning the genesis of Q 13:34–35, its conclusion, Q 13:35b, was evidently formulated and added to Q to give expression to the conviction that, when Jerusalem repents, the end will come. The verse should be compared with Acts 3:19–21 and the other passages in early Christianity which associate the kingdom's coming with the repentance of God's people.[55]

---

54. Concerning a possible origin with Jesus, I remain undecided. Q 13:34–35, even though joined to Q 11:49–51 in Q, was originally isolated and must be treated independently. Note the different points of view (in Q 13:34–35 the prophets have been sent, whereas in Q 11:49–51 ["I will send"] they are yet to be sent) and different tones (in Q 13:34–35 there is a feeling of sorrow, in Q 11:49–51 only accusation). A dominical origin has had its defenders. See David E. Aune, *Prophecy in Early Christianity and the Ancient Mediterranean World* (Grand Rapids: Eerdmans, 1983), pp. 175–76; Catchpole, "Temple Traditions in Q," pp. 327–28; Gnilka, *Matthäusevangelium*, vol. 2, p. 307 (minus v. 35b); Horsley, *Jesus and the Spiral of Violence*, pp. 300–304; Kümmel, *Promise and Fulfilment*, pp. 79–81; Otto, *Kingdom of God*, p. 172 (suggesting a noneschatological interpretation: after ministering in Jerusalem for the Feast of Tabernacles Jesus declared he would stay away from the city until the Passover, when pilgrims recite Ps 118:26). Jeremias, *Theology*, p. 284, suggested that Jesus may have expected stoning for himself, and F. C. Burney, *The Poetry of Our Lord* (Oxford: Clarendon, 1925), p. 146, arranged vv. 34–35 par. in *Kina* metre. Q 13:34–35 coheres with Jesus' prophetic consciousness and his prediction of the temple's destruction. Further, no explicit claim to messiahship is made — the status of the speaker is only indirectly indicated; and there are synoptic texts which, if authentic, show us that Jesus did not think of the time of the end as unalterably fixed; see, e.g., Lk 13:6–9; 18:1–8; and Mk 13:20. Many, however, now assign the saying to a Jewish source or to the Christian community. See, e.g., Suggs, *Wisdom*, p. 66; Sato, *Q und Prophetie*, pp. 159–60; and Dieter Zeller, "Entrückung zur Ankunft als Menschensohn (Lk 13,34f.; 11,29f.)," in *A cause de L'Évangile: Études sur les Synoptiques et les Actes*, LD, vol. 123 (Paris: Cerf, 1985), p. 519. R. J. Miller, "The Rejection of the Prophets in Q," *JBL* 107 (1988): 225–40, claims to show that Q 13:34–35 can only be understood as a word of the risen Jesus. Against authenticity, Jesus here speaks as a suprahistorical figure ("How often would I have gathered your children"). Cf. Bultmann, *History*, pp. 114–15 ("the whole verse has to be understood in the light of divine Wisdom"). Wisdom texts for comparison include Prov 8:4–5, 17 (Wisdom's call); Ecclus 24:7–12 (Wisdom dwelling in Jerusalem); *1 Enoch* 42:1–3 (Wisdom's descent and ascent); 4 Ezra 5:9–10 (Wisdom's withdrawal). 1 Esdr 1:28ff., which is largely a rewriting of our oracle, is spoken by God, not Jesus. There is also the tension between Q 13:34–35 and the authentic Q 13:29; see n. 52.

55. See, e.g., 2 Pet 3:11–12 and *2 Clem.* 12:6.

# MODERN WORKS CITED

Abelson, J. *The Immanence of God in Rabbinic Literature.* London: Macmillan, 1912.

Alexander, H. B. *North America.* Vol. 10 of *The Mythology of All Races.* Boston: Marshall Jones, 1916.

Alford, Henry. *The Four Gospels.* Vol. 1 of *The Greek Testament.* Rev. ed. Chicago: Moody, 1958.

Allen, Willoughby C. *A Critical and Exegetical Commentary on the Gospel according to S. Matthew.* Edinburgh: T. & T. Clark, 1906.

Allison, Dale C., Jr. "Anticipating the Passion: The Literary Reach of Matthew 26:47–27:56." *CBQ* 56 (1994): 701–14.

———. "Behind the Temptations of Jesus." In *Authenticating the Deeds of Jesus,* by B. Chilton and C. A. Evans. Leiden: E. J. Brill, forthcoming.

———. *The End of the Ages Has Come.* Philadelphia: Fortress, 1985.

———. "Jesus and the Covenant: A Response to E. P. Sanders." *JSNT* 29 (1987): 57–78.

———. "A New Approach to the Sermon on the Mount." *ETL* 54 (1988): 205–14.

———. *The New Moses: A Matthean Typology.* Philadelphia: Fortress, 1993.

———. "Paul and the Missionary Discourse." *ETL* 61 (1985): 369–75.

———. "The Pauline Parallels and the Synoptic Gospels: The Pattern of the Parallels." *NTS* 28 (1982): 1–32.

———. "A Plea for Thoroughgoing Eschatology." *JBL* 113 (1994): 651–68.

———. "The Structure of the Sermon on the Mount." *JBL* 106 (1987): 423–45.

Attridge, Harold W. "Reflections on Research into Q." In *Early Christianity, Q, and Jesus,* edited by John S. Kloppenborg and Leif E. Vaage, pp. 223–34. Atlanta: Scholars Press; *Semeia* 55 (1992).

Aune, David E. *Prophecy in Early Christianity and the Ancient Mediterranean World.* Grand Rapids: Eerdmans, 1983.

Bacon, B. W. "The 'Single' Eye." *AJT* 7 (1914): 275–88.

Bailey, C. *The Greek Atomists and Epicurus.* Oxford: Clarendon, 1928.

Balz, Horst Robert. *Methodische Probleme der neutestamentlichen Christologie.* WMANT, vol. 25. Neukirchen-Vluyn: Neukirchener, 1967.

Bammel, Ernst. "Das Ende von Q." In *Verborum Veritas: Festschrift für Gustav Stählin zum 70. Geburtstag,* edited by O. Böcher and K. Haacker, pp. 39–50. Wuppertal: Rolf Brockhaus, 1970.

Barclay, John. "Jesus and Paul." In *Dictionary of Paul and His Letters,* edited by Gerald F. Hawthorne, Ralph P. Martin, and Daniel G. Reid, pp. 492–503. Downers Grove, Ill.: InterVarsity, 1993.

Barrett, C. K. *The Gospel according to St. John.* 2d ed. Philadelphia: Westminster, 1978.

———. "Sayings of Jesus in the Acts of the Apostles." In *A cause de l'Évangile. Études sur les Synoptiques et les Actes offertes au P. Jacques Dupont,* pp. 681–708. LD, vol. 123. Paris: Cerf, 1985.

Bauckham, Richard. *Jude, 2 Peter.* WBC. Waco, Tex.: Word, 1983.

———. "Synoptic Parousia Parables and the Apocalypse." *NTS* 23 (1977): 162–76.

———. "Synoptic Parousia Parables Again." *NTS* 29 (1983): 129–34.

Baumbach, Günther. *Das Verständnis des Bösen in den synoptischen Evangelien.* Berlin: Evangelische Verlagsanstalt, 1963.

Beare, J. I. *Greek Theories of Elementary Cognition from Alcmaeon to Aristotle.* Oxford: Oxford University Press, 1906.

Beasley-Murray, G. R. *Jesus and the Kingdom of God.* Grand Rapids: Eerdmans, 1986.

Bengel, J. A. *Gnomon of the New Testament*. Vol. 1. Philadelphia: Perkinpine & Higgins, 1864.

Bergemann, Thomas. *Q auf dem Prüfstand: Die Zuordnung des Mt/Lk-Stoffes zu Q am Beispiel der Bergpredigt*. FRLANT, vol. 158. Göttingen: Vandenhoeck & Ruprecht, 1993.

Bergren, Theodore A. "The 'People Coming from the East' in 5 Ezra 1:38." *JBL* 108 (1989): 675–83.

Best, Ernest. "Mark's Preservation of the Tradition." In *L'Évangile de Marc: Tradition et redaction*, edited by M. Sabbe, pp. 21–34. BETL, vol. 34. Leuven: Leuven University Press, 1974.

———. "1 Peter and the Gospel Tradition." *NTS* 16 (1969): 95–113.

Betz, Hans Dieter. *Essays on the Sermon on the Mount*. Philadelphia: Fortress, 1985. Also published as *Studien zur Bergpredigt*. Tübingen: J. C. B. Mohr (Paul Siebeck), 1985.

———. "Matthew 6.22f. and Ancient Greek Theories of Vision." In *Text and Interpretation: Studies in the New Testament Presented to Matthew Black*, edited by E. Best and R. McL. Wilson, pp. 43–56. Cambridge: Cambridge University Press, 1979.

———. *The Sermon on the Mount: A Commentary on the Sermon on the Mount, Including the Sermon on the Plain (Matthew 5:3–7:27 and Luke 6:20–49)*. Hermeneia. Minneapolis: Fortress, 1995.

———. "The Sermon on the Mount and Q." In *Gospel Origins and Christian Beginnings*, edited by James E. Goehring et al., pp. 19–34. Sonoma, Calif.: Polebridge, 1990.

Beyer, W. "εὐλογέω κ.τ.λ." *TDNT* 2 (1964), pp. 754–65.

Black, Matthew. *An Aramaic Approach to the Gospels and Acts*. 3d ed. Oxford: Clarendon, 1967.

———. "The Aramaic Dimension in Q with Notes on Luke 17:22 and Matthew 24:26 (Luke 17:23)." *JSNT* 40 (1990): 33–41.

———. "The Use of Rhetorical Terminology in Papias on Mark and Matthew." *JSNT* 37 (1989): 31–41.

Böcher, O. *Christus Exorcista: Dämonismus und Taufe im Neuen Testament*. BWANT, ser. 5, vol. 16. Stuttgart: Kohlhammer, 1972.

Bock, Darrell L. *Luke*. Leicester: IVP, 1994.

Boling, Robert G. *Judges*. AB, vol. 6A. Garden City, N.Y.: Doubleday, 1975.

Borg, Marcus. *Conflict, Holiness, and Politics in the Teaching of Jesus*. New York: Edwin Mellen, 1984.

Boring, M. Eugene. "A Proposed Reconstruction of Q 13:28–29." In *Society of Biblical Literature 1989 Seminar Papers*, edited by David J. Lull, pp. 1–22. Atlanta: Scholars Press, 1995.

———. "The Synoptic Problem, 'Minor' Agreements, and the Beelzebul Pericope." In *The Four Gospels 1992: Festschrift Frans Neirynck*, edited by F. Van Segbroeck et al., pp. 587–619. Vol. 1. BETL, vol. 100. Leuven: Leuven University Press, 1992.

Bornkamm, Günther. *Paul*. New York: Harper & Row, 1971.

Broadus, John A. *Commentary on the Gospel of Matthew*. Philadelphia: American Baptist Publication Society, 1886.

Brock, Sebastin. *The Luminous Eye: The Spiritual World of Ephrem the Syrian*. Kalamazoo, Mich.: Cistercian, 1992.

Brooks, Stephenson H. *Matthew's Community: The Evidence of the Special Sayings Material*. JSNTSS, vol. 16. Sheffield: JSOT, 1987.

Buchanan, George Wesley. *The Gospel according to Matthew*. Lewiston, N.Y.: Mellen, 1996.

———. *Jesus: The King and his Kingdom*. Macon, Ga.: Mercer University Press, 1984.

Budge, E. A. Wallis. *The Gods of the Egyptians*. Vol. 1. London: Methuen, 1904.

Bultmann, Rudolf. *History of the Synoptic Tradition*. New York: Harper & Row, 1963.

———. *Theology of the New Testament*. Vol. 1. New York: Charles Scribner's Sons, 1951.

Burkert, Walter. "Air-Imprints or Eidola: Democritus' Aetiology of Vision." *Illinois Classical Studies* 2 (1977): 97–109.

Burney, C. F. *The Poetry of Our Lord*. Oxford: Clarendon, 1925.

Burrows, Millar. *Jesus in the First Three Gospels*. Nashville: Abingdon, 1977.

Cadbury, H. J. "The Single Eye." *HTR* 47 (1954): 69–74.

Cadoux, Cecil John. *The Historic Mission of Jesus*. New York: Harper & Brothers, n.d.

Caird, G. B. *The Gospel of Luke*. New York: Penguin, 1963.

Cameron, Ron. *Sayings Traditions in the Apocryphon of James*. Philadelphia: Fortress, 1984.

———. " 'What Have You Come Out to See?' Characterizations of John and Jesus in the Gospels." In *The Apocryphal Jesus and Christian Origins*, edited by Ron Cameron, pp. 35–69. Atlanta: Scholars Press; *Semeia* 49 (1990).

Carlson, D. C. "Vengeance and Angelic Mediation in *Testament of Moses* 9 and 10." *JBL* 101 (1982): 85–95.

Carlston, Charles E. "Betz on the Sermon on the Mount: A Critique" *CBQ* 50 (1988): 47–57.

———. "Wisdom and Eschatology in Q." In *Logia: Les Paroles de Jésus — The Sayings of Jesus*, edited by J. Delobel, pp. 101–19. BETL, vol. 59. Leuven: Leuven University Press, 1982.

Carlston, Charles E., and D. Norlin. "Once More — Statistics and Q." *HTR* 64 (1971): 59–78.

Carson, D. A. "Matthew." In *The Expositor's Bible Commentary*, pp. 1–599. Vol. 8. Grand Rapids: Zondervan, 1984.

———. "Matthew 11:19b/Luke 7:35: A Test Case for the Bearing of Q Christology on the Synoptic Problem." In *Jesus of Nazareth: Lord and Christ*, edited by Joel B. Green and Max Turner, pp. 128–46. Grand Rapids: Eerdmans, 1994.

Catchpole, David R. "The Anointed One in Nazareth." In *From Jesus to John: Essays on Jesus and New Testament Christology in Honour of Marinus de Jonge*, edited by Martinus C. de Boer, pp. 230–51. JSNTSS, vol. 84. Sheffield: JSOT, 1993.

———. "The Centurion's Faith and its Function in Q." In *The Four Gospels 1992: Festschrift Frans Neirynck*, edited by F. Van Segbroeck et al., pp. 517–40. Vol. 1. BETL, vol. 100. Leuven: Leuven University Press, 1992.

———. "The Mission Charge in Q." In *Early Christianity, Q, and Jesus*, edited by John S. Kloppenborg and Leif E. Vaage, pp. 147–74. Atlanta: Scholars Press; *Semeia* 55 (1992).

———. "The Poor on Earth and the Son of Man in Heaven: A Re-appraisal of Matthew 25.31–46," *BJRL* 62 (1979): 357–97.

———. *The Quest for Q*. Edinburgh: T. & T. Clark, 1993.

———. "The Question of Q." *Sewanee Theological Review* 36 (1992): 3–44.

———. "Temple Traditions in Q." In *Templum Amicitiae*, edited by William Horbury, pp. 305–29. JSNTSS, vol. 48. Sheffield: JSOT, 1991.

Charette, Blaine. *The Theme of Recompense in Matthew's Gospel*. JSNTSS, vol. 79. Sheffield: JSOT, 1992.

Charles, R. H. *A Critical and Exegetical Commentary on The Revelation of St. John*. ICC. Edinburgh: T. & T. Clark, 1920.

———, ed. *Pseudepigrapha*. Vol. 2 of *The Apocrypha and Pseudepigrapha of the Old Testament in English*. Oxford: Clarendon, 1913.

Charlesworth, James H., ed. *Apocalyptic Literature and Testaments*. Vol. 1 of *The Old Testament Pseudepigrapha*. Garden City, N.Y.: Doubleday, 1983.

Childs, Brevard S. *Introduction to the Old Testament as Scripture*. Philadelphia: Fortress, 1979.

Chilton, Bruce. *God in Strength: Jesus' Announcement of the Kingdom*. SNTU, ser. B, vol. 1. Freistadt: F. Plöchl, 1979.

Chow, Simon. *The Sign of Jonah Reconsidered*. CB, vol. 27. Stockholm: Almqvist & Wiksell, 1995.

Collins, J. J. "Cosmos and Salvation: Jewish Wisdom and Apocalyptic in the Hellenistic Age." *HR* 17 (1977): 121–42.

————. "The Court Tales of Daniel and the Development of Apocalyptic." *JBL* 95 (1975): 218–34.

————. "Wisdom, Apocalypticism, and Generic Compatibility." In *In Search of Wisdom: Essays in Memory of John G. Gammie,* edited by L. G. Perdue, B. B. Scott, and W. J. Wiseman, pp. 165–86. Louisville: Westminster/John Knox, 1993.

Collins, Marilyn F. "The Hidden Vessels in Samaritan Tradition." *JJS* 3 (1972): 97–116.

Colpe, Carsten. "ὁ υἱὸς τοῦ ἀνθρώπου," *TDNT* 8, pp. 400–77.

Conzelmann, Hans. *An Outline of the Theology of the New Testament.* New York: Harper & Row, 1969.

Cook, Arthur Bernard. *Zeus: A Study in Ancient Religion.* 2 vols. (Cambridge: Cambridge University Press, 1914–25).

Cook, J. G. "The Sparrow's Fall in Mt 10:29b." *ZNW* 79 (1988): 138–44.

Cope, O. Lamar. *Matthew: A Scribe Trained for the Kingdom of Heaven.* CBQMS, vol. 5. Washington: Catholic Biblical Association, 1976.

Corliss, William R. *Biological Anomalies: Humans I.* Glen Arm, Md.: Sourcebook Project, 1992.

Cotter, Wendy. "Prestige, Protection, and Promise: A Proposal for the Apologetics of Q2." In *The Gospel Behind the Gospels: Current Studies in Q,* edited by R. A. Piper, pp. 117–38. NovTSup, vol. 75. Leiden: E. J. Brill, 1994.

Creed, John Martin. *The Gospel according to St. Luke.* London: Macmillan, 1930.

Crossan, John Dominic. *In Fragments: The Aphorisms of Jesus.* San Francisco: Harper & Row, 1983.

————. *The Historical Jesus: The Life of a Mediterranean Jewish Peasant.* San Francisco: Harper Collins, 1991.

Dahood, M. *Psalms III, 101–150.* AB, vol. 17C. Garden City, N.Y.: Doubleday, 1970.

Dasgupta, S. *A History of Indian Philosophy.* Vols. 3 and 4. Cambridge: Cambridge University Press, 1952–55.

Daube, David. *The New Testament and Rabbinic Judaism.* London: Athlone, 1956.

Davids, Peter H. "James and Jesus." In *The Jesus Tradition Outside the Gospel.* Vol. 5 of *Gospel Perspectives,* edited by David Wenham, pp. 63–84. Sheffield: JSOT, 1985.

Davies, W. D. *The Gospel and the Land.* Berkeley: University of California Press, 1974.

————. *Paul and Rabbinic Judaism: Some Rabbinic Elements in Pauline Theology.* Rev. ed. New York: Harper & Row, 1967.

————. *The Setting of the Sermon on the Mount.* Cambridge: Cambridge University Press, 1963.

Davies, W. D., and Dale C. Allison, Jr. *A Critical and Exegetical Commentary on the Gospel according to St. Matthew.* 3 vols. ICC. Edinburgh: T. & T. Clark, 1988–97.

DeLamotte, R. C. *Jalaluddin Rumi: Songbird of Sufism.* Lanham, Md.: University Press of America, 1980.

Delobel, J. "La rédaction de Lc. IV.14–16a et le 'Bericht vom Anfang.' " In *L'Évangile de Luc,* edited by Frans Neirynck, pp. 113–33, 306–12. 2d ed. BETL, vol. 32. Leuven: Leuven University Press, 1989.

Delobel, J., ed. *Logia: Les Paroles de Jésus — The Sayings of Jesus.* BETL, vol. 59. Leuven: Leuven University Press, 1982.

Denaux, Adelbert. "Criteria for Identifying Q-Passages: A Critical Review of a Recent Work by T. Bergemann." *NovT* 37 (1995): 105–29.

Deonna, Waldemar. *Le symbolisme de l'oeil.* Paris: E. de Boccard, 1965.

Dibelius, Martin. *From Tradition to Gospel.* New York: Charles Scribner's Sons, 1935.

————. *James.* Hermeneia. Philadelphia: Fortress, 1976.

————. *Sermon on the Mount.* New York: Charles Scribner's Sons, 1940.

Diels, H., and W. Kranz. *Die Fragmente der Vorsokratiker.* 6th ed. Berlin: Weidmann, 1951–52.

Dillon, R. J. "Ravens, Lilies, and the Kingdom of God (Matthew 6:25–33/Luke 12:22–31)." *CBQ* 53 (1991): 605–27.

Dixon, R. B. "Maidu Myths." *Bulletin of the American Museum of Natural History* 17 (1902): 48–81.

———. *Oceanic*. Vol. 9 of *The Mythology of All Races*. Boston: Marshall Jones, 1916.

Donfried, Karl P. "Paul and Judaism: 1 Thess 2:13–16 as a Test Case." *Int* 38 (1984): 242–53.

———. *The Setting of Second Clement in Early Christianity*. NovTSup, vol. 38. Leiden: E. J. Brill, 1974.

Doty, William G. *Letters in Primitive Christianity*. Philadelphia: Fortress, 1972.

Dunderberg, Ismo. "Q and the Beginning of Mark." *NTS* 41 (1995): 501–11.

Dungan, David L. *The Sayings of Jesus in the Churches of Paul*. Philadelphia: Fortress, 1971.

Dunn, James D. G. "Jesus Tradition in Paul." In *Studying the Historical Jesus*, edited by Bruce Chilton and Craig A. Evans, pp. 155–78. Leiden: E. J. Brill, 1994.

———. *Romans 1–8*. WBC, vol. 38. Dallas: Word, 1988.

Eddy, Paul Rhodes. "Jesus as Diogenes? Reflections on the Cynic Jesus Thesis." *JBL* 115 (1996): 449–69.

Edlund, Conny. *Das Auge der Einfalt*. ASNU, vol. 19. Lund: Gleerup, 1952.

Edwards, Richard A. *A Theology of Q*. Philadelphia: Fortress, 1976.

Eissfeldt, Otto. *The Old Testament: An Introduction*. New York: Harper & Row, 1965.

Elliott, John H. "The Fear of the Leer: The Evil Eye from the Bible to Li'l Abner." *Forum* 4, no. 4. (1988): 42–71.

Ellis, E. Earle. *Paul's Use of the Old Testament*. Edinburgh: Oliver and Boyd, 1957.

Elworthy, F. T. *The Evil Eye*. New York: Crown, 1958.

Ernst, Josef. *Das Evangelium nach Lukas*. RNT. Regensburg: Friedrich Pustet, 1977.

Evans, C. F. *Saint Luke*. London: SCM, 1990.

Farmer, William R. "The Sermon on the Mount: A Form-Critical and Redactional Analysis of Matt 5:1–7:29." In *Society of Biblical Literature 1986 Seminar Papers*, edited by Kent Harold Richards, pp. 56–98. Atlanta: Scholars Press, 1986.

Fensham, F. C. "The Good and Evil Eye in the Sermon on the Mount." *Neotestamentica* 1 (1967): 51–58.

Fenton, J. C. *Saint Matthew*. Baltimore: Penguin, 1963.

Fitzmyer, Joseph A. *The Gospel according to Luke*. 2 vols. New York: Doubleday, 1981–85.

———. "A Palestinian Collection of Beatitudes." In *The Four Gospels 1992: Festschrift Frans Neirynck*, edited by F. Van Segbroeck et al., vol. 1, pp. 509–16. BETL, vol. 100. Leuven: Leuven University Press, 1992.

———. "The Priority of Mark and the 'Q' Source in Luke." In *To Advance the Gospel: New Testament Studies*, pp. 3–40. New York: Crossroad, 1981.

Fjärstedt, B. *Synoptic Traditions in 1 Corinthians: Themes and Clusters of Theme Words in 1 Corinthians 1–4 and 9*. Uppsala: Theologiska Institutionen, 1974.

Fleddermann, Harry T. "The Demands of Discipleship: Matt 8,19–22 par. Luke 9,57–62." In *The Four Gospels 1992: Festschrift Frans Neirynck*, edited by F. Van Segbroeck et al., vol. 1, pp. 541–61. BETL, vol. 100. Leuven: Leuven University Press, 1992.

———. *Mark and Q: A Study of the Overlap Texts*. BETL, vol. 122. Leuven: Leuven University Press, 1995.

———. Review of *Wisdom in the Q Tradition*, by R. A. Piper. *CBQ* 53 (1991): 715–16.

Focant, C., ed. *The Synoptic Gospels: Source Criticism and the New Literary Criticism*. BETL, vol. 110. Leuven: Leuven University Press, 1993.

France, R. T. *Matthew*. Tyndale New Testament Commentaries. Grand Rapids: Eerdmans, 1985.

Friedrich, J. *Gott im Bruder?* CTM, vol. 7. Stuttgart: Calwer, 1977.

Fuchs, Albert. *Die Entwicklung der Beelzebulkontroverse bei den Synoptikern*. SNTU, ser. B, vol. 5. Linz: Studien zum NT und seiner Umwelt, 1980.

Funk, Robert, et al., eds. *The Five Gospels*. New York: Macmillan, 1993.

Gamble, Harry Y. *Books and Readers in the Early Church: A History of Early Christian Texts.* New Haven: Yale University Press, 1995.

Garland, David E. *The Intention of Matthew 23.* NovTSup, vol. 52. Leiden: E. J. Brill, 1979.

———. *Reading Matthew.* New York: Crossroad, 1993.

Garrett, Susan R. " 'Lest the Light in You Be Darkness': Luke 11:33–36 and the Question of Commitment." *JBL* 110 (1991): 93–105.

Gnilka, Joachim. *Mk 8,27–16,20.* Vol. 2 of *Das Evangelium nach Markus.* EKKNT. Zürich and Neukirchen-Vluyn: Benziger and Neukirchener, 1979.

———. *Das Matthäusevangelium.* 2 vols. HTKNT. Freiburg: Herder, 1986–1988.

———. *Theologie des Neuen Testaments.* Freiburg: Herder, 1994.

Godet, F. *A Commentary on the Gospel of St. Luke.* 5th ed. Vol. 2. Edinburgh: T. & T. Clark, 1957.

Goethe, Johann Wolfgang. *Goethe's Theory of Colors.* Translated by C. H. Eastlake. London: John Murray, 1840.

Goldstein, Jonathan A. *II Maccabees.* AB, vol. 41A. Garden City, N.Y.: Doubleday, 1983.

Goodenough, E. R. *Jewish Symbols in the Greco-Roman Period.* 12 vols. Bollingen Series. New York: Pantheon, 1953–68.

Goodwin, W. W. *Syntax of the Moods and Tenses of the Greek Verb.* New York: St. Martin's, 1965.

Goppelt, Leonard. *Theology of the New Testament.* Vol. 2. Grand Rapids: Eerdmans, 1982.

Goulder, M. D. *Luke — A New Paradigm.* Sheffield: JSOT, 1989.

———. *Midrash and Lection in Matthew.* London: SPCK, 1974.

Green, Miranda. *The Sun-Gods of Ancient Europe.* London: B. T. Batsford, 1991.

Grobel, K. "...Whose Name Was Neves." *NTS* 10 (1964): 373–82.

Grotius, Hugo. *Annotationes in Novum Testamentum.* Vol. 1. Gronigen: W. Zuidema, 1826.

Guelich, Robert A. *The Sermon on the Mount: A Foundation for Understanding.* Waco, Tex.: Word, 1982.

Guenther, Heinz O. "The Sayings Gospel Q and the Quest for Aramaic Sources: Rethinking Christian Origins." In *Early Christianity, Q, and Jesus,* edited by John S. Kloppenborg and Leif E. Vaage, pp. 41–76. Atlanta: Scholars Press; *Semeia* 55 (1992).

Gundry, Robert H. "Matthean Foreign Bodies in Agreements of Luke with Matthew against Mark: Evidence that Luke used Matthew." In *The Four Gospels 1992: Festschrift Frans Neirynck,* edited by F. Van Segbroeck et al., vol. 1, pp. 1467–95. BETL, vol. 100. Leuven: Leuven University Press, 1992.

———. *Matthew: A Commentary on His Literary and Theological Art.* Grand Rapids: Eerdmans, 1982.

———. "A Rejoinder on Matthean Foreign Bodies in Luke 10,25–28." *ETL* 71 (1995): 139–50.

———. *SŌMA in Biblical Theology.* SNTSMS, vol. 29. Cambridge: Cambridge University Press, 1976.

Haenchen, Ernst. "Matthäus 23." *ZTK* 48 (1951): 38–63.

Hagner, Donald A. *Matthew 1–13.* WBC, vol. 33A. Dallas: Word, 1993.

———. *The Use of the Old and New Testaments in Clement of Rome.* NovTSup, vol. 34. Leiden: E. J. Brill, 1975.

Hahm, David E. "Early Hellenistic Theories of Vision and the Perception of Color." In *Studies in Perception,* edited by Peter K. Machamer and Robert G. Turnbull. Columbus: Ohio State University Press, 1975.

Hahn, Ferdinand. "Das Problem alter christologischer Überlieferungen in der Apostelgeschichte unter besonderer Berücksichtigung von Act 3,19–21." In *Les Actes des Apôtres: Traditions, rédaction, théologie,* edited by J. Kremer, pp. 129–54. BETL, vol. 48. Leuven: Leuven University Press, 1979.

————. "Die Worte vom Licht Lk 11,33–36." In *Orientierung an Jesus*, edited by Paul Hoffmann, pp. 107–38. Freiburg: Herder, 1973.

Hare, Douglas R. A. *Matthew*. Louisville: John Knox, 1993.

Harnack, Adolf. *The Sayings of Jesus*. London: Williams and Norgate, 1908.

Harrington, Daniel J. *The Gospel of Matthew*. Sacra Pagina. Collegeville, Minn.: Michael Glazier, 1991.

Hartin, P. J. *James and the Sayings of Q*. JSNTSS, vol. 47. Sheffield: JSOT, 1991.

————. "The Wisdom and Apocalyptic Layers of the Sayings Gospel Q." *Hervormde Teologiese Studies* 50 (1994): 556–82.

Hatch, Edwin. *Essays in Biblical Greek*. Oxford: Clarendon, 1889.

Haufe, Günter. "Reich Gottes bei Paulus und in der Jesustradition." *NTS* 31 (1985): 467–72.

Havener, I. *Q: The Sayings of Jesus*. Wilmington, Del.: Michael Glazier, 1987.

Hawkes, Jacquetta. *Man and the Sun*. London: Cresset, 1962.

Hays, Richard B. *Echoes of Scripture in the Letters of Paul*. New Haven: Yale University Press, 1989.

Heaton, J. M. *The Eye*. Philadelphia: J. B. Lippincott, 1948.

Henderson, Ian H. "Gnomic Quatrains in the Synoptics: An Experiment in Genre Definition." *NTS* 37 (1991): 481–98.

Hengel, Martin. "Aufgaben der neutestamentlich Wissenschaft." *NTS* 40 (1994): 321–57.

————. *The Charismatic Leader and His Followers*. New York: Crossroad, 1981.

————. "Kerygma oder Geschichte? Zur Problematik einer falschen Alternative in der Synoptikerforschung aufgezeigt an Hand einiger neuer Monographien." *ThQ* 101 (1971): 323–36.

Hill, David. *The Gospel of Matthew*. New Century Bible. London: Oliphants, 1977.

Hoffmann, Paul. "Auslegung der Bergpredigt." *Bibel und Leben* 10 (1969): 57–65.

————. "The Redaction of Q and the Son of Man." In *The Gospel Behind the Gospels: Current Studies in Q*, edited by R. A. Piper, pp. 159–98. NovTSup, vol. 75. Leiden: E. J. Brill, 1994.

————. *Studien zur Theologie der Logienquelle*. 3d ed. NTAbh, vol. 8. Münster: Aschendorff, 1982.

————. *Tradition und Situation: Studien zur Jesusüberlieferung in der Logienquelle und den synoptischen Evangelien*. Münster: Aschendorff, 1995.

Holmberg, U. *Finno-Ugric, Siberian*. Vol. 4 of *The Mythology of All Races*. Boston: Marshall Jones, 1927.

Horgan, Maurya P. *Pesharim: Qumran Interpretations of Biblical Books*. CBQMS, vol. 8. Washington: Catholic Biblical Association of America, 1979.

Horsley, Richard. *Jesus and the Spiral of Violence: Popular Jewish Resistance in Roman Palestine*. San Francisco: Harper & Row, 1987.

————. "Jesus, Itinerant Cynic or Israelite Prophet?" In *Images of Jesus Today*, edited by James H. Charlesworth and Walter P. Weaver, pp. 68–97. Valley Forge, Pa.: Trinity Press International, 1994.

————. "Q and Jesus: Assumptions, Approaches, and Analyses." In *Early Christianity, Q, and Jesus*, edited by John S. Kloppenborg and Leif E. Vaage, pp. 175–209. Atlanta: Scholars Press; *Semeia* 55 (1992).

————. "The Q People: Renovation, not Radicalism." *Continuum* 1, no. 3 (1991): 49–63.

————. "Questions about Redactional Strata and the Social Relations Reflected in Q." In *Society of Biblical Literature 1989 Seminar Papers*, edited by David J. Lull, pp. 186–203. Atlanta: Scholars Press, 1989.

————. "Social Conflict in the Synoptic Sayings Source Q." In *Conflict and Invention: Literary, Rhetorical, and Social Studies on the Sayings Gospel Q*, edited by John S. Kloppenborg, pp. 37–52. Valley Forge, Pa.: Trinity Press International, 1995.

————. *Sociology and the Jesus Movement*. 2d ed. New York: Continuum, 1994.

———. "Wisdom Justified by All Her Children: Examining Allegedly Disparate Traditions in Q." In *Society of Biblical Literature 1994 Seminar Papers*, edited by Eugene H. Lovering, Jr., pp. 733–51. Atlanta: Scholars Press, 1994.

Huggins, R. V. "Matthean Posteriority: A Preliminary Proposal." *NovT* 34 (1992): 1–22.

Hull, John M. *Hellenistic Magic in the Synoptic Tradition.* SBT, ser. 2, vol. 28. London: SCM, 1974.

Hultgren, Arland J. *Jesus and His Adversaries.* Minneapolis: Augsburg, 1979.

———. *The Rise of Normative Christianity.* Philadelphia: Fortress, 1994.

Hummel, R. *Die Auseinandersetzung zwischen Kirche und Judentum im Matthäus-evangelium.* 2d ed. BEvT, vol. 33. Munich: Kaiser, 1966.

Humphrey, Hugh M. "Temptation and Authority: Sapiential Narratives in Q." *BTB* 21 (1991): 43–50.

Hunter, A. M. *Paul and His Predecessors.* 2d ed. London: SCM, 1961.

Jacobson, Arland D. *The First Gospel: An Introduction to Q.* Sonoma, Calif.: Polebridge, 1992.

———. "The History of the Composition of the Synoptic Sayings Source, Q." In *Society of Biblical Literature 1987 Seminar Papers*, edited by Kent Harold Richards, pp. 285–94. Atlanta: Scholars Press, 1987.

———. "The Literary Unity of Q." *JBL* 101 (1982): 365–89.

———. "The Literary Unity of Q: Lc 10,2–16 and Parallels as a Test Case." In *Logia: Les Paroles de Jésus — The Sayings of Jesus*, edited by J. Delobel, pp. 419–23. BETL, vol. 59. Leuven: Leuven University Press, 1982.

James, M. R. *The Lost Apocrypha of the Old Testament.* London: SPCK, 1920.

Jefford, Clayton N. *The Sayings of Jesus in the Teaching of the Twelve Apostles.* Leiden: E. J. Brill, 1989.

Jeremias, Joachim. *The Eucharistic Words of Jesus.* London: SCM, 1966.

———. *Jesus' Promise to the Nations.* Philadelphia: Fortress, 1982.

———. *New Testament Theology: The Proclamation of Jesus.* New York: Charles Scribner's Sons, 1971.

———. *The Parables of Jesus.* 2d rev. ed. New York: Charles Scribner's Sons, 1972.

———. *Die Sprache des Lukasevangeliums.* MeyerK. Göttingen: Vandenhoeck & Ruprecht, 1980.

Johnson, E. Elizabeth. *The Function of Apocalyptic and Wisdom Traditions in Romans 9–11.* SBLDS, vol. 109. Atlanta: Scholars Press, 1989.

Johnson, Luke Timothy. *The Gospel of Luke.* Sacra Pagina 3. Collegeville, Minn.: Michael Glazier, 1991.

Jonge, M. de. "The Future of Israel in the Testaments of the Twelve Patriarchs." *JSJ* 17 (1986): 196–211.

Käsemann, Ernst. *Exegetische Versuche und Besinnungen.* 2d ed. Göttingen: Vandenhoeck & Ruprecht, 1960.

———. *New Testament Questions of Today.* Philadelphia: Fortress, 1969.

Kasting, H. *Die Anfänge der urchristlichen Mission.* BEvT, vol. 55. Munich: Kaiser, 1969.

Keck, Leander, E. " 'Jesus' in Romans," *JBL* 108 (1989): 443–60.

———. "Toward the Renewal of New Testament Christology." *NTS* 32 (1986): 362–77.

Kelly, Henry Ansgar. *The Devil at Baptism.* Ithaca, N.Y.: Cornell University Press, 1985.

Kilgallen, John J. "The Return of the Evil Spirit." *Bib* 74 (1993): 45–59.

Kim, Myung-Soo. *Die Trägergruppe von Q: Sozialgeschichtliche Forschung zur Q-Überlieferung in den synoptischen Evangelien.* Wissenschaftliche Beiträge aus Europäischen Hochschulen, ser. 1, vol. 1. Ammersbek: Lottbek/Peter Jensen, 1990.

Kim, Seyoon. "Jesus, Sayings of." In *Dictionary of Paul and His Letters*, edited by Gerald F. Hawthorne, Ralph P. Martin, and Daniel G. Reid, pp. 474–92. Downers Grove, Ill.: InterVarsity, 1993.

King, N. Q. "The 'Universalism' of the Third Gospel." In *Studia Evangelica*, edited by K. Aland et al., pp. 199–205. Vol. 1. TU, vol. 73. Berlin: Akademie Verlag, 1959.

Klausner, Joseph. *Jesus: His Life, Times, and Teaching.* New York: Macmillan, 1925.

Kloppenborg, John S. " 'Easter Faith' and the Sayings Gospel Q." In *The Apocryphal Jesus and Christian Origins,* edited by Ron Cameron, pp. 71–99. Atlanta: Scholars Press; *Semeia* 49 (1990).

———. "The Formation of Q and Antique Instructional Genres." *JBL* 105 (1986): 443–62.

———. *The Formation of Q: Trajectories in Ancient Christian Wisdom Collections.* Studies in Antiquity and Christianity. Philadelphia: Fortress, 1987.

———. "Introduction." In *The Shape of Q: Signal Essays on the Sayings Gospel,* edited by John S. Kloppenborg, pp. 1–21. Minneapolis: Fortress, 1995.

———. "Literary Convention, Self-Evidence, and the Social History of the Q People." In *Early Christianity, Q, and Jesus,* edited by John S. Kloppenborg and Leif E. Vaage, pp. 77–102. Atlanta: Scholars Press; *Semeia* 55 (1992).

———. "Q 11:14–20 [*sic*]: Work Sheets for Reconstruction." In *Society of Biblical Literature 1985 Seminar Papers,* edited by Kent Harold Richards, pp. 133–51. Atlanta: Scholars Press, 1985.

———. *Q Parallels.* Sonoma, Calif.: Polebridge, 1988.

———. "The Sayings Gospel Q: Recent Opinion on the People behind the Document." *Currents in Research: Biblical Studies* 1 (1993): 9–34.

———. "Tradition and Redaction in the Synoptic Sayings Source." *CBQ* 46 (1984): 36–45.

———, ed. *Conflict and Invention: Literary, Rhetorical, and Social Studies on the Sayings Gospel Q.* Valley Forge, Pa.: Trinity Press International, 1995.

Knoch, Otto. "Kenntnis und Verwendung des Matthäus-Evangeliums bei den Apostolischen Vätern." In *Studien zum Matthäusevangeliums: Festschrift für Wilhelm Pesch,* edited by Ludger Schenke, pp. 159–77. SBS. Stuttgart: Katholisches Bibelwerk, 1988.

Koester, Helmut. *Ancient Christian Gospels: Their History and Development.* Philadelphia: Trinity Press International, 1990.

———. "Apocryphal and Canonical Gospels." *HTR* 73 (1980): 105–30.

———. "Q and Its Relatives." In *Gospel Origins and Christian Beginnings,* edited by J. E. Goehring et al., pp. 49–63. Sonoma, Calif.: Polebridge, 1990.

Koestler, Arthur. "Literature and the Law of Diminishing Returns." In *The Heel of Achilles: Essays, 1968–1973,* pp. 119–37. New York: Random House, 1974.

Köhler, Wolf-Dietrich. *Die Rezeption des Matthäusevangeliums in der Zeit vor Irenäus.* WUNT, ser. 2, vol. 24. Tübingen: J. C. B. Mohr (Paul Siebeck), 1987.

Kollmann, B. "Lk 12.35–38 — ein Gleichnis der Logienquelle." *ZNW* 81 (1990): 254–61.

Körtner, U. H. J. *Papias von Hierapolis: Ein Beitrag zur Geschichte des frühen Christentums.* FRLANT, vol. 133. Göttingen: Vandenhoeck & Ruprecht, 1983.

Kuhn, Heinz-Wolfgang. "Der irdische Jesus bei Paulus." *ZTK* 67 (1970): 295–320.

———. "Das Liebesgebot Jesu als Tora und als Evangelium." In *Vom Urchristentum zu Jesus: Für Joachim Gnilka,* edited by Hubert Frankemölle and Karl Kertelge, pp. 194–230. Freiburg: Herder, 1989.

Kümmel, Werner Georg. *Introduction to the New Testament.* Rev. ed. Nashville: Abingdon, 1975.

———. *Promise and Fulfilment.* 2d ed. SBT, vol. 23. London: SCM, 1961.

———. *The Theology of the New Testament.* Nashville: Abingdon, 1973.

Kürzinger, J. *Papias von Hierapolis und die Evangelien des Neuen Testaments.* Regensburg: F. Pustet, 1983.

LaCocque, André. *Daniel in His Time.* Columbia: University of South Carolina Press, 1988.

Landman, L. "Introduction." In *Messianism in the Talmudic Era,* edited by L. Landman, pp. xi–xxxv. New York: KTAV, 1979.

Laufen, Rudolf. *Die Doppelüberlieferungen der Logienquelle und des Markusevangeliums.* BBB, vol. 54. Königstein: Peter Hanstein, 1980.

Laws, Sophie. *A Commentary on the Epistle of James.* San Francisco: Harper & Row, 1980.

Lee, Edward N. "The Sense of an Object: Epicurus on Seeing and Hearing." In *Studies in Perception*, edited by Peter K. Machamer and Robert G. Turnbull, pp. 27–59. Columbus: Ohio State University Press, 1975.

Levine, Amy-Jill. *The Social and Ethnic Dimensions of Matthean Salvation History*. Lewiston, N.Y.: Edwin Mellen, 1988.

Licht, J. "Taxo, or the Apocalyptic Doctrine of Vengeance." *JJS* 12 (1961): 95–103.

Lightfoot, J. B. *The Apostolic Fathers*. Rev. ed. Vol. 1, pt. 1, *S. Clement of Rome*. London: Macmillan, 1890.

Lightfoot, John. *A Commentary on the New Testament from the Talmud and Hebraica*. Vol. 2. Oxford: Oxford University Press, 1859.

Lindars, Barnabas. *Jesus Son of Man*. Grand Rapids: Eerdmans, 1983.

———. *New Testament Apologetic*. London: SCM, 1961.

Lindberg, David C. "The Intromission-Extramission Controversy in Islamic Visual Theory." In *Studies in Perception*, edited by Peter K. Machamer and Robert G. Turnbull, pp. 141–52. Columbus: Ohio State University Press, 1975.

———. "The Science of Optics." In *Science in the Middle Ages*, edited by David C. Lindberg, pp. 338–68. Chicago: University of Chicago Press, 1978.

———. *Theories of Vision from Al-kindi to Kepler*. Chicago: University of Chicago Press, 1976.

Löning, Karl. "Die Füchse, die Vögel und der Menschensohn (Mt 8,19f par Lk 9,57f)." In *Vom Urchristentum zu Jesus: Für Joachim Gnilka*, edited by Hubert Frankemölle and Karl Kertelge, pp. 82–102. Freiburg: Herder, 1989.

Lowman, Daniel Whitby. *A Commentary on the Gospels and Epistles of the New Testament*. Philadelphia: Corey & Hart, 1845.

Lührmann, Dieter. "The Gospel of Mark and the Sayings Collection Q." *JBL* 108 (1989): 51–71.

———. "Liebet eure Feinde (Lk 6:27–36/Mt 5:39–48)." *ZTK* 69 (1972): 427–36.

———. *Die Redaktion der Logienquelle*. WMANT, vol. 33. Neukirchen-Vluyn: Neukirchener, 1969.

Luz, Ulrich. *Das Evangelium nach Matthäus*. 2 vols. EKKNT. Zürich and Neukirchen-Vluyn: Benziger and Neukirchener, 1985–89. English translation of vol. 1 appeared as *Matthew 1–7: A Commentary*. Minneapolis: Augsburg, 1989.

———. *Matthew in History: Interpretation, Influence, and Effects*. Minneapolis: Fortress, 1994.

———. "Sermon on the Mount/Plain: Reconstruction of $Q^{Mt}$ and $Q^{Lk}$." In *Society of Biblical Literature 1983 Seminar Papers*, edited by Kent Harold Richards, pp. 473–79. Chico, Calif.: Scholars Press, 1983.

———. "Die wiederentdeckte Logienquelle." *EvT* 33 (1973): 527–33.

MacAdam, Henry Innes. "Gethsemane, Gabbatha, Golgotha: The Arrest, Trials, and Execution of Jesus of Nazareth." *IBS* 17 (1995): 156–57.

Machamer, Peter K., and Robert G. Turnbull, eds. *Studies in Perception*. Columbus: Ohio State University Press, 1975.

Mack, Burton. *The Lost Gospel: The Book of Q and Christian Origins*. San Francisco: Harper, 1993.

McNeile, A. H. *The Gospel according to Matthew*. London: Macmillan, 1915.

Maloney, Clarence, ed. *The Evil Eye*. New York: Columbia University Press, 1976.

Maloney, Elliott C. *Semitic Interference in Marcan Syntax*. SBLDS, vol. 51. Chico, Calif.: Scholars Press, 1981.

Manson, T. W. "The Gospel of Matthew." In *Studies in the Gospels and Epistles*, edited by Matthew Black, pp. 68–104. Edinburgh: T. & T. Clark, 1962.

———. *The Sayings of Jesus*. London: SCM, 1949.

———. *The Teaching of Jesus*. Cambridge: Cambridge University Press, 1935.

Marcus, Joel. "The Jewish War and the *Sitz im Leben* of Mark." *JBL* 113 (1992): 441–62.

Marshall, I. H. *Commentary on Luke*. Grand Rapids: Eerdmans, 1978.

Martin, Raymond A. *Syntactical Evidence of Semitic Sources in Greek Documents.* Cambridge, Mass.: Society of Biblical Literature, 1974.

———. *Syntax Criticism of the Johannine Literature, the Catholic Epistles, and the Gospel Passion Accounts.* Lewiston, N.Y.: Edwin Mellen, 1989.

———. *Syntax Criticism of the Synoptic Gospels.* Lewiston, N.Y.: Edwin Mellen, 1987.

Maryon, Herbert. "The Colossus of Rhodes." *Journal of Hellenic Studies* 76 (1956): 68–86.

März, Claus-Peter. "Das Gleichnis vom Dieb. Überlegungen zur Verbindung von Lk 12,39 par Mt 24,43 und 1 Thess 5,2.4." In *The Four Gospels 1992: Festschrift Frans Neirynck,* edited by F. Van Segbroeck et al., vol. 1, pp. 633–48. BETL, vol. 100. Leuven: Leuven University Press, 1992.

———. "*. . . lasst eure Lampen brennen!*" *Studien zur Q-Vorlage von Lk 12,35–14,24.* ETS, vol. 20. Leipzig: St. Benno, 1991.

———. "Zur Q-Rezeption in Lk 12,35–13,35 (14,1–24)." In *The Synoptic Gospels: Source Criticism and the New Literary Criticism,* edited by Camille Focant, pp. 177–208. BETL, vol. 110. Leuven: Leuven University Press, 1993.

Massaux, Édouard. *The Influence of the Gospel of Saint Matthew on Christian Literature before Saint Irenaeus.* Bk. 1, *The First Ecclesiastical Writers.* Bk. 2, *The Later Christian Writings.* Edited by Arthur J. Bellinzoni. Macon, Ga.: Mercer University Press, 1990.

Meadors, Edward P. *Jesus the Messianic Herald of Salvation.* WUNT, ser. 2, vol. 72. Tübingen: J. C. B. Mohr (Paul Siebeck), 1995.

———. "The Orthodoxy of the 'Q' Sayings of Jesus." *TynBull* 43 (1992): 233–57.

Meier, John P. *Law and History in Matthew's Gospel.* AnBib, vol. 71. Rome: Biblical Institute, 1976.

———. *Matthew.* Wilmington, Del.: Michael Glazier, 1980.

———. *Mentor, Message, and Miracles.* Vol. 2 of *A Marginal Jew: Rethinking the Historical Jesus.* ABRL. New York: Doubleday, 1994.

Meier, Paul D. "The Community of Q." Ph.D. diss., University of Iowa, 1967.

Merkel, Helmut. "Die Gottesherrschaft in der Verkündigung Jesu." In *Königsherrschaft Gottes und himmlischer Kult im Judentum, Urchristentum und in der hellenistischen Welt,* edited by Martin Hengel and Anna Maria Schwemer, pp. 119–61. WUNT, vol. 55. Tübingen: J. C. B. Mohr (Paul Siebeck), 1991.

Metzner, Rainer. *Die Rezeption des Matthäusevangeliums im 1.Petrusbrief.* WUNT, ser. 2, vol. 74. Tübingen: J. C. B. Mohr (Paul Siebeck), 1995.

Meyer, H. A. W. *The Gospel of Matthew.* Vol. 1. Edinburgh: T. & T. Clark, 1877.

Meyer, Paul D. "The Gentile Mission in Q." *JBL* 89 (1970), pp. 405–17.

Michael, J. Hugh. "The Lament over Jerusalem." *American Journal of Theology* 22 (1918): 101–13.

Miller, R. J. "The Rejection of the Prophets in Q." *JBL* 107 (1988): 225–40.

Moffatt, James. *The Historical New Testament.* Edinburgh: T. & T. Clark, 1901.

Mowinckel, S. *He That Cometh.* Oxford: Basil Blackwell, 1956.

Murphy, Roland E. *Wisdom Literature: Job, Proverbs, Ruth, Lamentations, Ecclesiastes, and Esther.* Grand Rapids: Eerdmans, 1981.

Murphy-O'Connor, Jerome. "La Genèse littéraire de la règle de la communauté." *RB* 76 (1969): 528–49.

Nebe, Gottfried. "Das ἔσται in Lk 11,36 — ein neuer Deutungsvorschlag." *ZNW* 83 (1992): 108–14.

Needham, Joseph. *Science and Civilization in China.* 8 vols. Cambridge: Cambridge University Press, 1954–.

Neirynck, Frans. "Assessment." In *Mark and Q: A Study of the Overlap Texts,* by Harry T. Fleddermann, pp. 263–303. BETL, vol. 122. Leuven: Leuven University Press, 1995.

———. "Literary Criticism: Old and New." In *The Synoptic Gospels: Source Criticism and the New Literary Criticism*, edited by C. Focant, pp. 11–38. BETL, vol. 110. Leuven: Leuven University Press, 1993.

———. "Luke 10:25–28: A Foreign Body in Luke?" In *Crossing the Boundaries: Essays in Biblical Interpretation in Honour of Michael D. Goulder*, edited by S. E. Porter, P. Joyce, and D. E. Orton, pp. 149–65. Leiden: E. J. Brill, 1994.

———. "The Minor Agreements and Lk 10,25–28." *ETL* 71 (1995): 151–60.

———. "The Minor Agreements and Q." In *The Gospel Behind the Gospels: Current Studies in Q*, edited by R. A. Piper, pp. 49–72. NovTSup, vol. 75. Leiden: E. J. Brill, 1994.

———. "Paul and the Sayings of Jesus." In *Evangelica II: 1982–1991*, pp. 511–67. BETL, vol. 99. Leuven: Leuven University Press, 1991.

———. "Recent Developments in the Study of Q." In *Logia: Les Paroles de Jésus — The Sayings of Jesus*, edited by J. Delobel, pp. 29–75. BETL, vol. 59. Leuven: Leuven University Press, 1982.

Neyrey, Jerome H. "Loss of Wealth, Loss of Family, and Loss of Honour: The Cultural Context of the Original Makarisms in Q." In *Modelling Early Christianity: Social-Scientific Studies of the New Testament in its Context*, edited by Philip F. Esler, pp. 139–58. London: Routledge, 1996.

Nickelsburg, George W. E. "Wisdom and Apocalypticism in Early Judaism: Some Points for Discussion." In *Society of Biblical Literature 1994 Seminar Papers*, edited by Eugene H. Lovering, Jr., pp. 715–32. Atlanta: Scholars Press, 1994.

Niederwimmer, Kurt. *Die Didache*. Göttingen: Vandenhoeck & Ruprecht, 1989.

Nolland, John. *Luke 9:21–18:34*. WBC, vol. 35B. Dallas: Word, 1993.

Nyberg, H. S. "Zum grammatischen Verständnis von Matt. 12.44f." *Arbeiten und Mitteilungen aus dem neutestamentlichen Seminar zu Uppsala* 4 (1936): 22–35.

O'Brien, D. "The Effect of a Simile: Empedocles' Theories of Seeing and Breathing." *Journal of Hellenic Studies* 90 (1970): 149–79.

Olshausen, Hermann. *Biblical Commentary on the New Testament*. Vol. 1. New York: Sheldon, Blakeman & Co., 1857.

Orchard, J. B. "Thessalonians and the Synoptic Gospels." *Bib* 19 (1938): 19–42.

Otto, R. *The Kingdom of God and the Son of Man*. New and rev. ed. London: Lutterworth, 1943.

Pappas, Harry S. "The 'Exhortation to Fearless Confession' — Mt. 10.26–33." *Greek Orthodox Theological Review* 25 (1980): 239–48.

Patte, D. *The Gospel according to Matthew*. Philadelphia: Fortress, 1987.

Patterson, Stephen J. "Wisdom and Q and Thomas." In *In Search of Wisdom: Essays in Memory of John G. Gammie*, edited by Leo Perdue, Bernard Brandon Scott, and William Johnston Wiseman, pp. 187–222. Louisville: Westminster, 1993.

Pearson, Birger. "1 Thess 2.13–16: A Deutero-Pauline Interpolation." *HTR* 64 (1971): 79–94.

Perrin, Norman. *Rediscovering the Teaching of Jesus*. New York: Harper & Row, 1976.

Pesch, Rudolf. *Das Markusevangelium*. Pt. 2, *Kommentar zu Kap. 8,27–16,20*. HTKNT, ser. 2, vol. 2. Freiburg: Herder, 1977.

Pesch, W. "Zur Exegese von Mt 6,19–21 und Lk 12,33–34." *Bib* 40 (1960): 356–78.

Petzke, G. *Die Traditionen über Apollonius von Tyana und das Neue Testament*. Leiden: E. J. Brill, 1970.

Philonenko, Marc. "La parabole sur la lampe (Luc 11 33–36) et les horoscopes qoumrâniens." *ZNW* 79 (1988): 145–51.

Piper, John. *"Love Your Enemies:" Jesus' Love Command*. SNTSMS, vol. 38. Cambridge: Cambridge University Press, 1979.

Piper, R. A. *Wisdom in the Q Tradition: The Aphoristic Teaching of Jesus*. SNTSMS, vol. 61. Cambridge: Cambridge University Press, 1989.

———, ed. *The Gospel Behind the Gospels: Current Studies in Q*. NovTSup, vol. 75. Leiden: E. J. Brill, 1994.

Plummer, Alfred. *A Critical and Exegetical Commentary on the Gospel according to St. Luke.* 3d ed. ICC. Edinburgh: T. & T. Clark, 1900.

———. *An Exegetical Commentary on the Gospel according to Matthew.* London: Stock, 1909.

Polag, Athanasius. *Die Christologie der Logienquelle.* WMANT, vol. 45. Neukirchen-Vluyn: Neukirchener, 1977.

———. *Fragmenta Q: Textheft zur Logienquelle.* Neukirchen-Vluyn: Neukirchener, 1979.

Puech, E. "Un Hymne essénien en partie retrouvé et les Béatitudes: IQH V 12–VI 18 (= col. XIII–XIV 7) et 4QBéat." *RevQ* 13 (1988): 59–88.

———. "4 Q525 et les péricopes des béatitudes en Ben Sira et Matthieu." *RB* 98 (1991): 80–106.

Reed, Jonathan L. "The Social Map of Q." In *Conflict and Invention: Literary, Rhetorical, and Social Studies on the Sayings Gospel Q,* edited by John S. Kloppenborg, pp. 17–36. Valley Forge, Pa.: Trinity Press International, 1995.

Rendsburg, Gary A. "Targum Onqelos to Exod 10:5, 10:15, Numb 22:5, 22:11." *Henoch* 12 (1990): 15–17.

Richardson, Peter. "The Thunderbolt in Q and the Wise Man in Corinth." In *From Jesus to Paul: Studies in Honor of F. W. Beare,* edited by Peter Richardson and J. C. Hurd, pp. 91–111. Waterloo: Wilfred Laurier, 1984.

Rigaux, B. *Les Épîtres aux Thessaloniciens.* Paris: J. Gabalda, 1956.

Robertson, A. T. *A Grammar of the Greek New Testament in the Light of Historical Research.* 2d ed. New York: Hodder & Stoughton, 1914.

Robinson, James M. "The History-of-Religions Taxonomy of Q: The Cynic Hypothesis." In *Gnosisforschung und Religionsgeschichte,* edited by Holger Preissler and Hubert Seiwert, pp. 247–65. Marburg: Diagonal, 1994.

———. "The *Incipit* of the Sayings Gospel Q." *RHPR* 75 (1995): 9–33.

———. "Kerygma and History." In *Trajectories through Early Christianity,* edited by James M. Robinson and Helmut Koester, pp. 20–70. Philadelphia: Fortress, 1971.

———. "Die Logienquelle: Weisheit oder Prophetie? Anfragen an Migaku Sato, *Q und Prophetie.*" *EvT* 53 (1993): 367–89.

———. *The Nag Hammadi Library.* New York: Harper & Row, 1977.

———. "The Q Trajectory: Between John and Matthew via Jesus." In *The Future of Early Christianity: Essays in Honor of Helmut Koester,* edited by B. A. Pearson et al., pp. 173–94. Minneapolis: Fortress, 1991.

———. "The Sayings Gospel Q." In *The Four Gospels 1992: Festschrift Frans Neirynck,* edited by F. Van Segbroeck et al., vol. 1, pp. 361–88. BETL, vol. 100. Leuven: Leuven University Press, 1992.

Ronchi, V. *The Nature of Light: An Historical Survey.* Cambridge: Harvard University Press, 1970.

Rordorf, Willy. "Does the Didache Contain Jesus Tradition Independently of the Synoptic Gospels?" In *Jesus and the Oral Gospel Tradition,* edited by Henry Wansbrough, pp. 394–423. JSNTSS, vol. 64. Sheffield: JSOT, 1991.

Rosenstiehl, J.-M. "Le portrait de l'Antichrist." In *Pseudépigraphes de l'ancien Testament et Manuscripts de la Mer Morte.* Paris: Universitaires de France, 1967.

Rundle, A. T. *Myth and Symbol in Ancient Egypt.* London: Thames and Hudson, 1959.

Sambursky, S. *Physics of the Stoics.* London: Routledge and Keagan Paul, 1959.

Sand, Alexander. *Das Evangelium nach Matthäus.* RNT. Regensburg: Friedrich Pustet, 1984.

Sanders, E. P. *Jesus and Judaism.* Philadelphia: Fortress, 1985.

———. *The Tendencies of the Synoptic Tradition.* SNTSMS. Cambridge: Cambridge University Press, 1969.

Sandmel, Samuel. "Parallelomania." *JBL* 81 (1962): 1–13.

Sato, Migaku. *Q und Prophetie: Studien zur Gattungs- und Traditionsgeschichte der Quelle Q.* WUNT, ser. 2, vol. 29. Tübingen: J. C. B. Mohr (Paul Siebeck), 1988.

————. "Wisdom Statements in the Sphere of Prophecy." In *The Gospel Behind the Gospels: Current Studies in Q*, edited by R. A. Piper, pp. 139–58. NovTSup, vol. 75. Leiden: E. J. Brill, 1995.

Sauer, J. "Traditionsgeschichtliche Erwägungen zu den synoptischen und paulinischen Aussagen über Feindesliebe und Wiedervergeltungsverzicht." *ZNW* 76 (1985): 1–28.

Schaefer, Konrad R. "Zechariah 14: A Study in Allusion." *CBQ* 57 (1995): 66–91.

Schenk, Wolfgang. *Synopse zur Redenquelle der Evangelien*. Düsseldorf: Patmos, 1981.

————. "Die Verwünschung der Küstenorte Q 10,13–15: Zur Funktion der konkreten Ortsangaben und zur Lokalisierung von Q." In *The Synoptic Gospels: Source Criticism and the New Literary Criticism*, edited by C. Focant, pp. 477–90. BETL, vol. 110. Leuven: Leuven University Press, 1993.

Schippers, R. "The Pre-synoptic Tradition in 1 Thessalonians 2:13–16." *NovT* 9 (1967): 223–34.

Schlatter, Adolf. *Der Evangelist Matthäus*. Stuttgart: Calwer, 1948.

Schlosser, Jacques. "Le Logion de Mt 10,28 par. Lc 12,4–5." In *The Four Gospels 1992: Festschrift Frans Neirynck*, edited by F. Van Segbroeck et al., vol. 1, pp. 621–31. BETL, vol. 100. Leuven: Leuven University Press, 1992.

————. *Le Règne de Dieu dans les dits de Jésus*. Vol. 2. Ebib. Paris: J. Gabalda, 1980.

Schlueter, Carol J. *Filling Up the Measure: Polemical Hyperbole and 1 Thessalonians 2.14–16*. JSNTSS, vol. 98. Sheffield: JSOT, 1994.

Schmeller, Thomas. *Brechungen: Urchristliche Wandercharismatiker im Prisma soziologisch orientierter Exegese*. SBS, vol. 136. Stuttgart: Katholisches Bibelwerk, 1989.

Schmidt, Daryl. "1 Thess. 2:13–16: Linguistic Evidence for an Interpolation." *JBL* 102 (1983): 269–79.

Schmidt, H. *Die Anthropologie Philons von Alexandria*. Würzburg: Triltsch, 1933.

Schmidt, Thomas E. *Hostility to Wealth in the Synoptic Gospels*. JSNTSS, vol. 15. Sheffield: JSOT, 1987.

Schmithals, Walter. *Einleitung in die drei ersten Evangelien*. Berlin: Walter de Gruyter, 1985.

Schnabel, Eckhard J. "Jesus and the Beginnings of the Mission to the Gentiles." In *Jesus of Nazareth: Lord and Christ*, edited by Joel B. Green and Max Turner, pp. 37–58. Grand Rapids: Eerdmans, 1994.

Schnackenburg, Rudolf. "Der eschatologische Abschnitt Lk 17, 20–37." In *Mélanges Bibliques en hommage au R. P. Béda Rigaux*, edited by A. Descamps and R. P. André de Halleux, pp. 213–34. Gembloux: Duculot, 1970.

————. *The Gospel according to St. John*. Vol. 2. New York: Seabury, 1980.

————. *The Moral Teaching of the New Testament*. New York: Seabury, 1979.

Schoeps, H. J. *Paul: The Theology of the Apostle in the Light of Jewish Religious Thought*. London: Lutterworth, 1961.

Schottroff, Luise, and Wolfgang Stegemann. *Jesus and the Hope of the Poor*. Maryknoll, N.Y.: Orbis, 1986.

Schüling, Joachim. *Studien zum Verhältnis von Logienquelle und Markusevangelium*. FB, vol. 65. Würzburg: Echter, 1991.

Schulz, Siegfried. *Q: Spruchquelle der Evangelisten*. Zürich: Theologischer Verlag, 1972.

Schürmann, Heinz. " 'Das Gesetz des Christus' (Gal 6,2): Jesu Verhalten und Wort als letztgültige sittliche Norm nach Paulus." In *Neues Testament und Kirche: Für Rudolf Schnackenburg*, edited by Joachim Gnilka, pp. 282–300. Freiburg: Herder, 1974.

————. *Das Lukasevangelium*. 2 vols. HTKNT. Freiburg: Herder, 1969–94.

————. "Mt 10,5–6 und die Vorgeschichte des synoptischen Aussendungsberichtes." In *Traditionsgeschichtliche Untersuchungen zu den synoptischen Evangelien*, pp. 137–49. Düsseldorf: Patmos, 1968.

————. "Q$^{Lk}$ 11:14–36 Kompositionsgeschichtliche Befragt." In *The Four Gospels 1992: Festschrift Frans Neirynck*, edited by F. Van Segbroeck et al., pp. 562–86. Vol. 1. BETL, vol. 100 Leuven: Leuven University Press, 1992.

————. "Das Zeugnis der Redenquelle für die Basileia-Verkündigung Jesu." In *Logia: Les Paroles de Jésus — The Sayings of Jesus*, edited by J. Delobel, pp. 121–200. BETL, vol. 59. Leuven: Leuven University Press, 1982.

Schweitzer, Albert. *Paul and His Interpreters*. New York: Macmillan, 1951.

Schweizer, Eduard. *The Good News according to Luke*. Atlanta: John Knox, 1984.

————. *The Good News according to Matthew*. Atlanta: John Knox, 1975.

Segal, Alan F. *The Other Judaisms of Late Antiquity*. Atlanta: Scholars Press, 1987.

Sellew, P. "Reconstruction of Q 12:33–59." In *Society of Biblical Literature 1987 Seminar Papers*, edited by Kent Harold Richards, pp. 617–68. Atlanta: Scholars Press, 1987.

Sevenich-Bax, Elisabeth. *Israels Konfrontation mit den letzten Boten der Weisheit: Form, Funktion und Interdependenz der Weisheitselemente in der Logienquelle*. Münsteraner Theologische Abhandlungen, vol. 21. Altenberge: Oros, 1993.

Siebers, Tobin. *The Mirror of Medusa*. Berkeley: University of California Press, 1983.

Siegel, R. E. "Did the Greek Atomists Consider a Non-corpuscular Visual Transmission? Reconsideration of Some Ancient Visual Doctrines." *Archives internationales d'histoire de sciences* 22 (1969): 3–16.

Silberman, L. H. "From Apocalyptic Proclamation to Moral Prescription." *JJS* 40 (1989): 53–60.

Sjöberg, Erik. "Das Licht in dir. Zur Deutung von Matth. 6.22ff. Par." *ST* 5 (1951): 89–105.

Smith, Jonathan Z. "Wisdom and Apocalyptic." In *Religious Syncretism in Antiquity*, edited by B. A. Pearson, pp. 131–70. Missoula, Mont.: Scholars Press, 1975.

Smith, M. H. "No Place for a Son of Man." *Forum* 4, no. 4 (1988): 83–107.

Sparks, H. F. D., ed. *The Apocryphal Old Testament*. Oxford: Clarendon, 1984.

Stanton, Graham N. "Aspects of Early Christian-Jewish Polemic and Apologetic." *NTS* 31 (1985): 377–92.

————. *A Gospel for a New People: Studies in Matthew*. Edinburgh: T. & T. Clark, 1992.

————. *Gospel Truth? New Light on Jesus and the Gospels*. Valley Forge, Pa.: Trinity Press International, 1995.

Steck, O. H. *Israel und das gewaltsame Geschick der Propheten*. WMANT, vol. 23. Neukirchen-Vluyn: Neukirchener, 1967.

Steinhauser, Michael G. "The Sayings on Anxieties." *Forum* 6, no. 1 (1990): 67–79.

Stock, Augustine. *The Method and Message of Matthew*. Collegeville, Minn.: Liturgical Press, 1994.

Stöger, Alois. *The Gospel according to St. Luke*. Vol. 1. London: Burns & Oates, 1969.

Stone, Michael. "Lists of Revealed Things in the Apocalyptic Literature." In *Magnalia Dei: The Mighty Acts of God*, edited by Frank Moore Cross, Werner E. Lemke, and Patrick D. Miller, Jr., pp. 414–52. Garden City, N.Y.: Doubleday, 1976.

Stone, M. E., and J. Strugnell. *The Books of Enoch Parts 1–2*. Missoula, Mont.: Scholars Press, 1979.

Stratton, G. M. *Theophrastus and the Greek Physiological Psychology before Aristotle*. New York: Macmillan, 1917.

Strecker, G. *Der Weg der Gerechtigkeit*. FRLANT, vol. 82. Göttingen: Vandenhoeck & Ruprecht, 1962.

Streeter, B. H. *The Four Gospels*. London: Macmillan, 1936.

Suggs, M. J. *Wisdom, Christology, and Law in Matthew's Gospel*. Cambridge: Harvard University Press, 1970.

Syreeni, Kari. *The Making of the Sermon on the Mount: A Procedural Analysis of Matthew's Redactional Activity*. Pt. 1, *Methodology and Compositional Analysis*. Annales Academiae Scientiarum Fennicae Dissertationes Humanarum Litterarum, vol. 44. Helsinki: Suomalainen tiedeakatemia, 1987.

Talbert, Charles H. *Reading Luke*. New York: Crossroad, 1982.

Tanghe, Antoine. "Memra de Philoxène de Mabboug sur l'inhabitation du Saint-Esprit." *Le Museon* 73 (1960): 39–71.

Taussig, Hal. "The Lord's Prayer." *Forum* 4, no. 4 (1988): 25–42.

Taylor, N. H. "Palestinian Christianity and the Caligula Crisis: Part 1, Social and Historical Reconstruction." *JSNT* 61 (1996): 101–24.

Taylor, Vincent. *The Formation of the Gospel Tradition.* London: Macmillan, 1968.

Theissen, Gerd. *The Gospels in Context: Social and Political History in the Synoptic Tradition.* Minneapolis: Fortress, 1991.

———. *Sociology of Early Palestinian Christianity.* Philadelphia: Fortress, 1978.

Thompson, M. *Clothed with Christ: The Example and Teaching of Jesus in Romans 12:1–15:13.* JSNTSS, vol. 59. Sheffield: JSOT, 1991.

Torrey, C. C. *The Four Gospels.* London: Hodder and Stoughton, n.d.

———. *Our Translated Gospels.* New York: Harper and Brothers, 1936.

Tuckett, Christopher M. "A Cynic Q?" *Biblica* 70 (1989): 349–76.

———. "The Existence of Q." In *The Gospel Behind the Gospels*, edited by R. A. Piper, pp. 19–47. NovTSup, vol. 75. Leiden: E. J. Brill, 1995.

———. "1 Corinthians and Q." *JBL* 102 (1983): 607–19.

———. "Les Logia et le Judaïsme." *Foi et Vie* 92, no. 5 (1993): 67–88.

———. "Luke 4:16–30 and Q." In *Logia: Les Paroles de Jésus — The Sayings of Jesus*, edited by J. Delobel, pp. 343–54. BETL, vol. 59. Leuven: Leuven University Press, 1982.

———. "Mark and Q." In *The Synoptic Gospels: Source Criticism and the New Literary Criticism*, edited by C. Focant, pp. 149–75. BETL, vol. 110. Leuven: Leuven University Press, 1993.

———. *Nag Hammadi and the Gospel Tradition.* Edinburgh: T. & T. Clark, 1986.

———. "Paul and the Synoptic Mission Discourse." *ETL* 60 (1984): 376–81.

———. *Q and the History of Early Christianity: Studies on Q.* Edinburgh: T. & T. Clark, 1996.

———. "Q and Thomas: Evidence of a Primitive 'Wisdom Gospel'? A Response to H. Koester." *ETL* 67 (1991): 346–60.

———. "Synoptic Tradition in 1 Thessalonians." In *The Thessalonian Correspondence*, edited by R. F. Collins, pp. 160–82. BETL, vol. 87. Leuven: Leuven University Press, 1990.

———. "Synoptic Tradition in the Didache." In *The New Testament in Early Christianity*, edited by J.-M. Servin, pp. 197–230. Louvain: Louvain University Press, 1989.

———. "The Temptation Narrative in Q." In *The Four Gospels 1992: Festschrift Frans Neirynck*, edited by F. Van Segbroeck et al., vol. 1, pp. 479–507. BETL, vol. 100. Leuven: Leuven University Press, 1992.

Tuilier, André. "La Didachè et le problème synoptique." In *The Didache in Context: Essays on Its Text, History, and Transmission*, edited by Clayton N. Jefford, pp. 110–30. NovTSup, vol. 77. Leiden: E. J. Brill, 1995.

Turner, Nigel. "Q in Recent Thought." *ExpT* 80 (1969): 324–28.

Twelftree, Graham H. *Jesus the Exorcist.* WUNT, ser. 2, vol. 54. Tübingen: J. C. B. Mohr (Paul Siebeck), 1991.

Ulmer, R. *The Evil Eye in the Bible and in Rabbinic Literature.* Hoboken, N.J.: KTAV, 1994.

Urbach, E. E. "Redemption and Repentance in Talmudic Judaism." In *Types of Redemption*, edited by R. J. Zwi Werblowsky and C. J. Bleeker, pp. 191–206. Leiden: E. J. Brill, 1970.

Uro, R. *Sheep among the Wolves: A Study of the Mission Instructions of Q.* Helsinki: Suomalainen tiedeakatemia, 1987.

Vaage, Leif E. *Galilean Upstarts: Jesus' First Followers according to Q.* Valley Forge, Pa.: Trinity Press International, 1994.

———. "Q and Cynicism: On Comparison and Social Identity." In *The Gospel Behind the Gospels: Current Studies in Q*, edited by R. A. Piper, pp. 198–229. NovTSup, vol. 75. Leiden: E. J. Brill, 1994.

————. "Composite Texts and Oral Myths: The Case of the 'Sermon' (6:20b–49)." In *Society of Biblical Literature 1989 Seminar Papers*, edited by David J. Lull, pp. 428–32. Atlanta: Scholars Press, 1989.

Vaage, Leif E., and John S. Kloppenborg. "Early Christianity, Q, and Jesus: The Sayings Gospel and Method in the Study of Christian Origins." In *Early Christianity, Q, and Jesus*, edited by John S. Kloppenborg and Leif E. Vaage, pp. 1–14. Atlanta: Scholars Press; *Semeia* 55 (1992).

van der Kwaak, H. "Die Klage über Jerusalem (Matth. 23:37–39)." *NovT* 8 (1966): 156–70.

van Hoorn, W. *As Images Unwind: Ancient and Modern Theories of Visual Perception.* Amsterdam: University Press, 1972.

Van Segbroeck, F., et al., eds. *The Four Gospels 1992: Festschrift Frans Neirynck.* 3 vols. BETL, vol. 100. Leuven: Leuven University Press, 1992.

Vassiliaidis, P. "The Original Order of Q: Some Residual Cases." In *Logia: Les Paroles de Jésus — The Sayings of Jesus*, edited by J. Delobel. BETL, vol. 59. Leuven: Leuven University Press, 1982.

Verdenius, W. J. *Parmenides: Some Comments on His Poem.* Amsterdam: Adolf M. Hakkert, 1964.

————. *Studia varia Carolo Guilielmo Vollgraff a discipulius oblata.* Amsterdam: University Press, 1948.

Via, Dan O. "Matthew's Dark Light and the Human Condition." In *The New Literary Criticism and the New Testament*, edited by Edgar V. McKnight and Elizabeth Struthers Malbon, pp. 348–66. Valley Forge, Pa.: Trinity Press International, 1994.

Vielhauer, Philipp. *Geschichte der urchristlichen Literatur: Einleitung in das Neue Testament, die Apokryphen und die Apostolischen Väter.* Berlin: de Gruyter, 1975.

Viviano, Benedict T. "Beatitudes Found among Dead Sea Scrolls." *BAR* 18, no. 6 (1992): 53–55, 66.

von Fritz, K. "Democritus' Theory of Vision." In *Science, Medicine, and History: Essays on the Evolution of Scientific Thought and Medical Practice, Written in Honor of Charles Singer*, edited by E. A. Underwood, pp. 83–99. Vol. 1. Oxford: Oxford University Press, 1953.

von Staden, Heinrich. "The Stoic Theory of Perception and Its 'Platonic' Critics." In *Studies in Perception*, edited by Peter K. Machamer and Robert G. Turnbull, pp. 96–136. Columbus: Ohio State University Press, 1975.

Wacholder, Ben Zion. *The Dawn of Qumran: The Sectarian Torah and the Teacher of Righteousness.* Cincinnati: Hebrew Union College Press, 1983.

Wailes, Stephen L. *Medieval Allegories of Jesus' Parables.* Berkeley: University of California Press, 1987.

Walter, Nikolaus. "Paul and the Early Christian Jesus-Tradition." In *Paul and Jesus: Collected Essays*, edited by A. J. M. Wedderburn, pp. 51–80. JSNTSS, vol. 37. Sheffield: JSOT, 1989.

Wanke, Joachim. *"Bezugs- und Kommentarworte" in den synoptischen Evangelien.* ETS, vol. 44. Leipzig: St. Benno, 1981.

————. "'Kommentarworte': Älteste Kommentierungen von Herrenworten." *BZ* 24 (1980): 208–33.

Ware, J. W. *Alchemy, Medicine, Religion in the China of A.D. 320: The Nei P'ien of Ko Hung (Pao-p'u tzu).* Cambridge: Cambridge University Press, 1966.

Weatherly, Jon A. "The Authenticity of 1 Thessalonians 2.13–16: Additional Evidence." *JSNT* 42 (1991): 79–98.

Wedderburn, A. J. M., ed. *Paul and Jesus: Collected Essays.* JSNTSS, vol. 37. Sheffield: JSOT, 1989.

Wegner, U. *Der Hauptmann von Kafarnaum.* WUNT, ser. 2, vol. 14. Tübingen: J. C. B. Mohr (Paul Siebeck), 1985.

Weinfeld, Moshe. *Deuteronomy 1–11.* AB, vol. 5. New York: Doubleday, 1991.

Wellhausen, J. *Einleitung in die drei ersten Evangelien.* Berlin: G. Reimer, 1905.

———. *Das Evangelium Lucae.* Berlin: Georg Reimer, 1904.

———. *Das Evangelium Matthaei.* Berlin: Georg Reimer, 1904.

Wengst, Klaus. *Tradition und Theologie des Barnabasbriefes.* Berlin: de Gruyter, 1971.

Wenham, David. *The Parables of Jesus.* Downers Grove, Ill.: InterVarsity, 1989.

———. *Paul: Follower of Jesus or Founder of Christianity?* Grand Rapids: Eerdmans, 1995.

———. "Paul's Use of the Jesus Tradition: Three Samples." In *The Jesus Tradition Outside the Gospels.* Vol. 5 of *Gospel Perspectives,* edited by David Wenham, pp. 5–37. Sheffield: JSOT Press, 1985.

———. *The Rediscovery of Jesus' Eschatological Discourse.* Sheffield: JSOT, 1984.

Wenham, Gordon J. *Genesis 1–15.* WBC, vol. 1. Waco, Tex.: Word, 1987.

Werner, E. " 'Hosanna' in the Gospels." *JBL* 65 (1946): 97–122.

Westermann, Claus. *The Roots of Wisdom: The Oldest Proverbs of Israel and Other Peoples.* Louisville: Westminster/John Knox, 1994.

Wilckens, Ulrich. "Jesusüberlieferung und Christuskerygma — zwei Wege urchristlicher Überlieferungsgeschichte." *Theologia Viatorum* 10 (1966): 310–39.

Williams, James G. "Neither Here Nor There: Between Wisdom and Apocalyptic in Jesus' Kingdom Sayings." *Forum* 5, no. 2 (1989): 7–30.

Williamson, H. G. M. *The Book Called Isaiah: Deutero-Isaiah's Role in Composition and Redaction.* Oxford: Clarendon, 1994.

Wilson, Stephen G. *Luke and the Pastoral Epistles.* London: SPCK, 1979.

Wischmeyer, Odar. "Matthäus 6,25–34 par. Die Spruchreihe vom Sorgen." *ZNW* 85 (1994): 1–20.

Witherington, Ben, III. *Jesus the Sage: The Pilgrimage of Wisdom.* Minneapolis: Fortress, 1994.

Wolff, Christian. "Niedrigkeit und Verzicht in Wort und Weg Jesu und in der apostolischen Existenz des Paulus." *NTS* 34 (1988): 183–96.

Worder, Ronald D. "Redaction Criticism of Q: A Survey." *JBL* 94 (1975): 532–46.

Yarbrough, R. W. "The Date of Papias: A Reassessment." *JETS* 26 (1983): 181–91.

Zahn, Theodor. *Das Evangelium des Lucas.* Leipzig: Deichert, 1913.

———. *Das Evangelium des Matthäus.* 4th ed. Leipzig: Deichert, 1922.

Zehnle, R. F. *Peter's Pentecost Discourse.* SBLMS, vol. 15. Nashville: Abingdon, 1971.

Zeller, Dieter. "Entrückung zur Ankunft als Menschensohn (Lk 13,34f.; 11,29f.)." In *A cause de L'Évangile: Études sur les Synoptiques et les Actes,* pp. 513–30. LD, vol. 123. Paris: Cerf, 1985.

———. "Das Logion Mt 8,11f./Lk 13,28f. und das Motiv der 'Völkerwallfahrt.' " *BZ* 15 (1971): 222–37; 16 (1972): 84–93.

———. "Redaktionsprozesse und wechselnder 'Sitz im Leben' beim Q-Material." In *Logia: Les Paroles de Jésus — The Sayings of Jesus,* edited by J. Delobel, pp. 395–409. BETL, vol. 59. Leuven: Leuven University Press, 1982.

———. "Eine Weisheitliche Grundschrift in der Logienquelle?" In *The Four Gospels 1992: Festschrift Frans Neirynck,* edited by F. Van Segbroeck et al., vol. 1, pp. 389–401. BETL, vol. 100. Leuven: Leuven University Press, 1992.

———. *Die weisheitlichen Mahnsprüche bei den Synoptikern.* FB, vol. 17. Würzburg: Echter, 1977.

Zimmermann, F. *The Aramaic Origin of the Four Gospels.* New York: KTAV, 1979.

# Index of Scriptural References

# INDEX OF MODERN AUTHORS

# INDEX OF SUBJECTS